The Politics of Consumption

Leisure, Consumption and Culture

General Editor: Rudy Koshar, *University of Wisconsin-Madison*

Leisure regimes in Europe (and North America) in the last two centuries have brought about far-reaching changes in consumption patterns and consumer cultures. The past twenty years have seen the evolution of scholarship on consumption from a wide range of disciplines but historical research on the subject is unevenly developed for late modern Europe, just as the historiography of leisure practices is limited to certain periods and places. This series encourages scholarship on how leisure and consumer culture evolved with respect to an array of identities. It relates leisure and consumption to the symbolic systems with which tourists, shoppers, fans, spectators, and hobbyists have created meaning, and to the structures of power that have shaped such consumer behaviour. It treats consumption in general and leisure practices in particular as complex processes involving knowledge, negotiation, and the active formation of individual and collective selves.

Editorial Board

Leora Auslander, *University of Chicago, USA*
John Brewer, *University of Chicago, USA*
Alon Confino, *University of Virginia, USA*
Martin Daunton, *University of Cambridge, UK*
Stephen Gundle, *University of London, UK*
Heinz-Gerhard Haupt, *University of Bielefeld, Germany*
Michael Kater, *York University, Canada*
John Pemble, *University of Bristol, UK*
Daniel Roche, *CNRS, France*
Adelheid von Saldern, *University of Hannover, Germany*
Dominique Veillon, *IHTP-CNRS, France*

The Politics of Consumption

Material Culture and Citizenship in Europe and America

Edited by
Martin Daunton and Matthew Hilton

Oxford • New York

First published in 2001 by
Berg
Editorial offices:
150 Cowley Road, Oxford, OX4 1JJ, UK
838 Broadway, Third Floor, New York, NY 10003-4812, USA

Berg is an imprint of Oxford International Publishers Ltd.

Library of Congress Cataloging-in-Publication Data
A catalogue record for this book is available from the Library of Congress.

British Library Cataloguing-in-Publication Data
A catalogue record for this book is available from the British Library.

ISBN   1 85973 466 9 (Cloth)
1 85973 471 5 (Paper)

Typeset by JS Typesetting, Wellingborough, Northamptonshire
Printed in the United Kingdom by Biddles Ltd, Guildford and King's Lynn

Contents

Contents

Acknowledgements

The Politics of Consumption arises from a colloquium on 'Material politics: states, consumers and political cultures' held at Churchill College, Cambridge on 3–5 September 1999. Discussions were lively, stimulating, provocative and entertaining – not least because the participants created a relaxed and friendly environment for critical and constructive engagement with the papers. The editors would particularly like to thank the commentators and chairs whose remarks on each panel helped us to define the major themes of this book. Unfortunately, reasons of space mean that we are not able to include their comments nor all of the papers given at the colloquium, but their ideas and insights will be found throughout the volume. In particular we would like to thank Tony Badger, Chris Bonnell, Geoff Crossick, Ben Fine, Peter Gurney, James Obelkevich, Manuel Schramm, John Styles, Nick Tiratsoo, Jim Tomlinson, James Vernon and John Walton.

The colloquium was made possible as a result of a generous grant from the George Macaulay Trevelyan Fund of the Faculty of History, University of Cambridge, and assistance from Churchill College. The appearance of the book owes much to the enthusiasm and support of Maike Bohn who attended the colloquium and helped to shape the agenda of the publication. Kathryn Earle at Berg took over the project and saw the book through to publication.

Martin Daunton
Matthew Hilton

Notes on Contributors

Leora Auslander teaches modern European history at the University of Chicago. She has recently written articles on Bavarian crucifixes and French headscarves, on women's suffrage and concepts of citizenship in France and Germany, and on race and racism in iconography in Paris. She is currently working on the intersections of material culture, state form and citizenship law in France and Germany.

Hartmut Berghoff is Professor of Economic and Social History at the University of Göttingen. He has written books on the social history of British businessmen 1870 to 1914, and on the harmonica. He has edited a collection of essays on *Konsumpolitik: Die Regulierung des privaten Verbrauchs im 20. Jahrhundert*, and is currently working on the history of consumption in twentieth-century Germany.

Lizabeth Cohen is the Howard Mumford Jones Professor of American Studies in the history department of Harvard University. She is finishing a book on *A Consumers' Republic: The Politics of Mass Consumption in Postwar America.*

Gary Cross is Professor of History at the Pennsylvania State University. He is the author of *An All-Consuming Century: Why Commercialism Won in Modern America* and *Kids' Stuff: Toys and the Changing World of American Childhood.* He is working now on an Anglo-American study of childhood innocence and the modern commercialized family.

Martin Daunton is Professor of Economic History in the University of Cambridge and Fellow of Churchill College. His most recent research has been on the politics of taxation in Britain since 1799, and he is currently completing an economic history of Britain, 1850–1950.

Margot C. Finn is a Warwick Research Fellow and Lecturer in the Department of History, University of Warwick. She is the author of *After Chartism: Class and Nation in English Radical Politics, 1848-1874* (Cambridge, 1993), and she is completing a book manuscript on 'The Character of Credit: Social, Legal and Cultural Constructions of Debt in England, c. 1740–1914'.

Philipp Heldmann is a doctoral student at the University of Tübingen, working on consumption in the GDR.

Matthew Hilton is Lecturer in Social History at the University of Birmingham. He is the author of *Smoking in British Popular Culture, 1800–2000* (Manchester University Press, 2000). He is currently working on a history of fair trade and the politics of consumption in Britain.

Meg Jacobs is assistant professor of history at the Massachusetts Institute of Technology.

Rebecca L. Spang is a Lecturer in the Department of History at University College London and is the author of *The Invention of the Restaurant: Paris and Modern Gastronomic Culture*. She is now working on the cultural history of the weather.

Noel Thompson is Professor of History at University of Wales, Swansea. His most recent book is *The Real Rights of Man: Political Economies for the Working Class, 1775–1850* (Pluto, 1998). He is currently completing a book on *Left in the Wilderness: A History of British Democratic Socialist Economics, 1979–2001* (to be published by Acumen/Michigan University Press).

Frank Trentmann has been Assistant Professor at Princeton University, Visiting Professor at the Universität Bielefeld, and Visiting Professor at the British Academy. He now teaches modern history at Birkbeck College in the University of London. Most recently, he has edited *Paradoxes of Civil Society: New Perspectives on Modern German and British History* (Oxford and New York: Berghahn Books, 2000), and is the author of *Food and Freedom: Consumption, Commerce, and Civil Society in Britain, 1890s–1930s* (forthcoming).

Gunnar Trumbull is a post-doctoral fellow at the Center on the United States and France at The Brookings Institute. His research focuses on recent challenges and successes of the French political economy.

Material Politics: An Introduction

Matthew Hilton and *Martin Daunton*

Today, it is relatively easy for shoppers to extend their economic purchasing decisions into political acts or moral statements. Across western Europe and America, we as consumers have a range of options available to us. Rational, value-for-money consumers can buy specialist magazines and join various movements which seek to inform the purchaser about different brands of a type of product. As empowered, information-laden consumers they can try to behave independently of marketing and sales techniques, judging for themselves the quality of a commodity, the fairness of its price, its fitness for the purpose for which it was sold, its safety of use and even the quality of its design aesthetics. They might also support these consumer organizations to lobby governments to enact further consumer protection legislation, to introduce more effective competition policy and to establish more powerful institutions concerned with consumer represent-ation. All such measures will set precedents in, re-conceptualize and re-theorize the relationship between the state, the commodity and the collective mass of consumers. Alternatively, the politics of consumption might be based on moral or ethical forms of individual or organized protest. In opposition to mass production, globalization, the industrialization of agriculture and to the potential health and environmental consequences of genetically-modified (GM) crops, such consumers might choose to purchase organic produce, possibly even direct from a local producer co-operative rather than through the nearest outer-city supermarket. They might choose to buy their coffee, tea, wine, cereal and fruit from companies which promote 'fair trade', ensuring a better deal in terms of wages and employment conditions for the workers of the developing world. And their heightened consumer consciousness might persuade them to boycott certain goods or companies. In recent years, some of the more prominent organized protest boycotts have been against Nike (for its employment conditions in East Asia), Nestlé (for its marketing of breast-milk substitutes), Shell (for its activities in the Ogoni region in Nigeria), Proctor and Gamble (for its use of animal testing) and McDonalds for a whole range of ethical and environmental issues.[1]

1. *Ethical Consumer Magazine*, April/May 2000, p. 28.

None of these politics of consumption, of course, represents a coherent ideological movement mobilizing a unified consumer interest in the same sense that socialism or communism was perceived to act as the potential mobilizing force of a labour interest. For instance, while one consumer activist campaign might be motivated by concerns for animal welfare, it might fail to win the support of groups concerned with the employment policies of multinational enterprises. Both these issues might further run into direct conflict with those of consumer movements motivated by cheaper prices and better-quality produce whose aims to reduce the profits of near-monopoly traders pay little attention to trade union concerns or the ethics of animal experimentation. Indeed, many instances of direct contradiction in consumer politics seem to occur: while Levi-Strauss has been accepted as a member of the Ethical Trading Initiative, sitting alongside such ethical consumer groups as Oxfam, Traidcraft Exchange, CAFOD, Fairtrade Foundation and War on Want, at the time of writing it is also being boycotted for its 'continued failure to pay adequate compensation to workers who lost their jobs when a factory was relocated to Costa Rica'.[2] And, perhaps in starkest opposition, the largely middle-class movements campaigning for fair prices and better deals for consumers seem to share little common ground with the more radical advocates of belligerent anti-consumerism which annually come to prominence on the Friday after the American celebration of Thanksgiving, the now well-established 'Buy Nothing Day'.[3]

For many critics, this incoherence inherent to modern-day consumer politics explains the failure to create a potentially unifying consumer consciousness or even a single definition of 'the consumer interest'.[4] Yet searching for a general principle of consumer politics is to miss the point. The politics of consumption has always combined both abstract theories and practical everyday issues, the latter of which constantly give rise to new political considerations as the specificity of commodity purchasing often crystallizes other general political concerns. This was no more apparent than at the recent protests against the World Trade Organization in Seattle in 1999 and in the campaigns against GM foods which have seen united action between an enormous range of non-government organizations (NGOs) as diverse as trade unions, Greenpeace, consumers' associations, Friends of the Earth, the Fairtrade Foundation and even the Women's Institute. The alliances

---

2. *Ibid.*; the Ethical Trading Initiative list of members is available at the following website: http://www.ethicaltrade.org/_html/members/list/framesets/f_shell.shtml

3. See Adbusters' website: http://adbusters.org/home/index.html

4. On defining a consumer interest see, for example, D.A. Aaker and G.S. Day (eds), *Consumerism: Search for the Consumer Interest*, 3rd edn (Basingstoke: Macmillan, 1978); G. Smith, *The Consumer Interest* (London: John Martin, 1982); J.D. Forbes, *The Consumer Interest: Dimensions and Policy Implications* (London: Croom Helm, 1987); R.N. Katz (ed.), *Protecting the Consumer Interest: Private Initiative and Public Response* (Cambridge, Mass.: Ballinger, 1976).

may break up after the end of each single issue, but the flexibility of many of these consumer bodies and organizations concerned with consumer issues represent what many critics have conceptualized as a new type of politics arguably more appropriate to the age of the global economy. However, it is the contention of this book that the politics of consumption have always been marked by single-issue campaigns, fragile alliances and ever-changing agendas. While others might suggest that this is a cause of weakness in the creation of a general consumers' movement, the essays in this collection demonstrate that the politics of consumption obtains its strength from its very diversity. Certainly, this is the belief of many present-day anti-corporate activists and commentators. While idealistic and utopian hopes and beliefs underpin much of the new writing on globalization, a consensus is beginning to emerge on the importance of diversity in consumer protest. Most famously, the Canadian journalist Naomi Klein, while offering no grand narrative for collective action, argues forcibly that the varied direct-action campaigns against multinational enterprises mark a new and lasting stage in global politics. The link that will continue to bind these different groups, she claims, is the common realization of the economic structures behind commodity culture. The politics of consumption is no longer about shopping for identity, but about the global institutions that shape and determine the markets we are forced to operate within.[5]

The Politics of Consumption aims to draw out these issues to help re-conceptualize the relationship between material culture and citizenship. The twelve individual chapters, focusing on France, Germany, Britain and the United States over the last two centuries, are united here through their analysis of a number of key themes. First, they all discuss the particular moralities which have been relevant to any discussion of consumption. In general terms, social commentators and economists have pondered the moral, social and economic desirability of consumption: did it subvert the social order or did it integrate classes into one nation? On a more specific level, the status of individual goods has inspired particular moral critiques. Goods have been criticized for undermining control of the self such as alcohol, tobacco and other narcotics. Goods themselves may be morally acceptable, but the way in which they are produced, by non-free or sweated labour, may be the cause of moral and political complaint. And goods have been criticized when consumed by particular sections of the community, such as by children or by those who have inspired 'moral panics'. A common theme has always been the question of what constitutes the boundary between a necessity and a luxury, for

---

5. N. Klein, *No Logo* (London: Harper Collins, 2000). See also G. Monbiot, *Captive State: The Corporate Takeover of Britain* (London: Macmillan, 2000); K. Lasn, *Culture Jam: The Uncooling of America* (New York: Eagle Brook, 1999); J. Schor (ed.), *Do Americans Shop Too Much?* (New York: Beacon Press, 2000).

whom, when and in what circumstances. Questions concerning the economic and social desirability of goods and preferences for deferred or hedonistic consumption are essentially moral issues with wider economic implications, especially with regard to saving and macroeconomic policy. For example, the poor have often been encouraged to defer consumption as a moral duty, while at the same time consumption by the rich has been condoned as a means of creating a prosperous economy.

To respond to these issues, it is necessary to answer a second question: who speaks for the consumer? Indeed, are consumers self-acting subjects consciously speaking for themselves and articulating their own politics of consumption, or is the consumer merely *une classe objet* to use Bourdieu's expression, an object that only exists through the attention of others. To rework Edward Thompson's famous preface, have consumers played an active role in their own 'making', or, on the contrary, have they been defined solely according to the interests of business and capital? The argument of this collection is that the politics of consumption involves both. For instance, in the post-Second World War period consumers have organized throughout the Western world in their own campaigning groups, but as many historians have attested, market structures have been formulated ostensibly in the interests of the consumer yet actually in the interests of business – the consumer plays little role in the definition of his or her own interest. It is perhaps better, then, to understand the creation of the consumer interest as a process involving an interplay between at least three centres of meaning: active consumers, whether in unstable, highly specific movements or more institutionalized organizations; commercial and political interests seeking to define the consumer in order to legitimate their own aims and ambitions; and the discourses involved in the various sites of knowledge and expertise concerned with the category of the consumer, such as marketing, public health and law, which make up the modern nexus of government.

Thirdly, to define the consumer is to define the economic system by which goods are brought to him or her. The question is: what market structures and modes of distribution have been created to serve these different notions of the consumer? There is a circular process at work. The market structure may be defined, in part, by the interests of consumers but the structures will also influence the room for action by the consumer in expressing his or her own interests. For instance, co-operative organizations were set up by consumers in opposition to the capitalist market but as they became large-scale bureaucratic organizations the role of the consumer might have been less idealistically understood. Similarly, mutual associations were in principle owned by the consumers of their services, but the extent to which consumers directed the affairs of these concerns is not so clear. The debates over the virtues of free trade or protection, competitive or monopolistic provision, private or public ownership, individual or collective consumption, are also debates over how the consumer can best be served. Should consumers have more access to the products of the world economy, with the benefits of low prices; or should they be encouraged to buy domestic goods in order to maintain a strong national economy? Was competition between producers the best means of responding to consumers' concerns, or do the economies of scale of large corporations translate into gains for consumers as well as shareholders? Are the interests of consumers made more explicit through the regulation of private concerns or through public ownership of nationalized industries? Do consumers benefit most from individual freedom of choice in education and health care, broadcasting and housing, or should these services be provided collectively?

All these questions of consumer involvement and representation imply a fourth and final theme, that of the relationship between the consumer, citizenship and the state. Defining the consumer interest, and speaking for the consumer, establishes both the extent to which the state can intervene in issues of consumption and the extent to which the consumer is active in the political process. In different times and in different political regimes, states have enshrined through market regulation the notion of the consumer as customer: that is, a rational utility-maximizing individual. Alternatively, consumer-citizenship has been more widely defined, not as protecting individuals in the market but through encouraging a more politically involved consumer activism. In addition, states have become involved in the politics of consumption by establishing the range of consumer issues to be incorporated within the institutions of government. States have provided services to consumers, they have set up ideals of national taste and aesthetics, and they have indirectly affected the consumer through issues such as public health, child protection and macroeconomic policy. But consumers have also created their own notions of consumer citizenship, often in opposition to and beyond the state as in the initial ambitions of the co-operative movement and the activities of recent NGOs. In addition, the everyday practices of consumption give rise to forms of resistance against government and the state. In short, the relationships between states and consumers are constantly being negotiated, forever developing new notions of citizenship.

In order to provide answers to this formidable list of questions, historians need to consider the most appropriate and productive approaches to the politics of consumption. The chapters in this collection seek both to answer these questions and to suggest a methodology for examining material culture and citizenship. This introduction draws out the major themes of the book, and outlines the overall approach adopted. It begins by discussing the problems within the existing literature on consumer society. It then establishes that issues of morality and politics have always been central to matters of consumption, before setting out a definition of 'material politics', a concept which the editors see as crucial to any analysis of consumer society.

Matthew Hilton and Martin Daunton

Consumer History, Cultural Studies and the Politics of Consumption

The study of consumer society has flourished over the last decade. It may be said to have emerged both from the political emphasis placed on consumerism by the Conservative and Republican governments of the 1980s and from the earlier critiques of consumer society offered by scholars such as Guy Debord and Jean Baudrillard.[6] Intriguingly, both the political and cultural rhetorics attest to similar explanatory factors for the changes in 'late-capitalist' Western democracies: the triumph of capitalism over socialism; the replacement of the worker with the consumer in the appeals of mainstream political parties; the replacement of a politics based on individual and group identities in the sphere of production with one of individual rights in the sphere of consumption. In short, it is said the society of the factory has been eclipsed by the 'society of the spectacle'. Assuming such a change, scholars have therefore turned to the cultural lives of consumers, examining the means by which identities are established in a commodified world, whether by the conscious actions of consumers themselves, the deliberate manipulation of their desires by the marketing and sales experts, or by the interaction of people with a range of goods, the function of which is hidden beneath an enormous array of symbolic meanings and imagery.[7]

Historians of the nineteenth and twentieth centuries have played a prominent role in this scholarship. In America, the role of advertising has been one of the main concerns of the history of consumer society,[8] though liberal academics continue to discuss whether consumer society has been a change for the better or

---

6. G. Debord, *Society of the Spectacle* (Detroit: Black and Red, 1970); J. Baudrillard, *The Consumer Society: Myths and Structures* (London: Sage, 1998). For useful overviews of these debates see R. Bocock, *Consumption* (London: Routledge, 1993); M. Featherstone, *Consumer Culture and Postmodernism* (London: Sage, 1991).

7. C. Lury, *Consumer Culture* (Oxford: Polity, 1996); P. Corrigan, *The Sociology of Consumption: An Introduction* (London: Sage, 1997); D. Slater, *Consumer Culture and Modernity* (Oxford: Polity, 1997); S. Miles, *Consumerism as a Way of Life* (London: Sage, 1998); H. Mackay (ed.), *Consumption and Everyday Life* (London: Sage, 1997).

8. S. Ewen, *Captains of Consciousness: Advertising and the Social Roots of the Consumer Culture* (New York: McGraw-Hill, 1976); S. Bronner (ed.), *Consuming Visions: Accumulation and the Display of Goods in America, 1880–1920* (New York, W.W. Norton, 1989); R. Marchand, *Advertising the American Dream: Making Way for Modernity, 1920–1940* (Berkeley: University of California Press, 1985); P. Johnston, *Real Fantasies: Edward Steichen's Advertising Photography* (Berkeley: University of California Press, 1997); M. Schudson, *Advertising: The Uneasy Persuasion* (New York: Basic Books, 1985); P.W. Laird, *Advertising Progress: American Business and the Rise of Consumer Marketing* (Baltimore: Johns Hopkins University Press, 1998); T.J. Lears, 'From salvation to self-realisation: advertising and the therapeutic roots of the consumer culture, 1880–1930', in R.W. Fox and T.J. Lears (eds), *The Culture of Consumption: Critical Essays in American History, 1880–1920* (New York: Pantheon, 1983), pp. 1–38; R. Ohmann, *Selling Culture: Magazines, Markets and Class at the Turn of the Century* (London: Verso, 1996).

the worse.[9] Studies of consumer society in mainland Europe are by no means as prominent, though Rosalind Williams has provided an excellent study of France, and some edited collections have allowed useful cross-country analyses to be made.[10] Historians in Britain have engaged in the consumer studies debate more enthusiastically, though an illuminating divide has appeared in the literature between the more culturalist interpretations of advertising and the deliberately sober economic and social explanations of the mass market.[11] International dialogue on consumption has been facilitated most easily in histories of perhaps the first and most visible manifestation of the global consumer society, the department store, as it appeared in Paris, London, New York and Berlin in the second half of the nineteenth century. As well as transforming retail trading methods, the department store became a focus for much cultural and political comment, Zola's *Au Bonheur des Dames* encapsulating the fears about the implications of respectable bourgeois women entering the public thoroughfares of the modern city, as well as the sense of liberation felt by many women temporarily freed from the perceived confinements of domestic life.[12] Some of the best work on the department store has demonstrated how studies of consumption are enriched if they link up with studies of labour, class and gender, as well as the politics of urban development.[13]

9. T.J. Lears, *No Place of Grace: Antimodernism and the Transformation of American Culture, 1880–1920* (Chicago: University of Chicago Press, 1994); D. Horowitz, *The Morality of Spending: Attitudes Towards the Consumer Society in America, 1875–1940* (Baltimore: Johns Hopkins University Press, 1985).

10. R.H. Williams, *Dream Worlds: Mass Consumption in Late Nineteenth Century France* (Berkeley: University of California Press, 1982); H. Siegrist, H. Kaelble and J. Kocka (Hg.), *Europäische Konsumgeschichte: Zur Gesellschafts- und Kulturgeschichte des Konsums (18. bis 20. Jahrhundert)* (Frankfurt am Main: Campus, 1997).

11. L.A. Loeb, *Consuming Angels: Advertising and Victorian Women* (Oxford: Oxford University Press, 1994); T. Richards, *The Commodity Culture of Victorian England: Advertising and Spectacle, 1851–1914* (London: Verso, 1991); W.H. Fraser, *The Coming of the Mass Market, 1850–1914* (Basingstoke: Macmillan, 1981); J. Benson, *The Rise of Consumer Society in Britain, 1880–1980* (London: Longman, 1994).

12. É. Zola, *The Ladies' Paradise [Au Bonheur des Dames]* (trans. B. Nelson; Oxford: Oxford University Press, 1998).

13. B. Lancaster, *The Department Store: A Social History* (London: Leicester University Press, 1995); M.B. Miller, *The Bon Marché: Bourgeois Culture and the Department Store, 1869-1920* (Princeton: Princeton University Press, 1981); S.P. Benson, *Counter Cultures: Saleswomen, Managers and Customers in American Department Stores, 1890–1940* (Urbana: University of Illinois Press, 1986); G. Reekie, *Temptations: Sex, Selling and the Department Store* (Sydney: Allen & Unwin, 1993); J. Walkowitz, *City of Dreadful Delight: Narratives of Sexual Danger in Late-Victorian England* (London: Virago, 1992); G. Crossick and S. Jaumain (eds), *Cathedrals of Consumption: The European Department Store, 1850–1939* (Aldershot: Ashgate, 1999); E. Rappaport, *Shopping for Pleasure* (Princeton: Princeton University Press, 2000); W. Leach, *Land of Desire: Merchants, Power, and the Rise of a New American Culture* (New York: Pantheon, 1993).

One criticism offered of this literature is that the emphasis on liberation, the freedom to construct identities and the ability of consumers to empower themselves through the deliberate orchestration of commodity meanings is perhaps merely an 'ersatz' freedom, a liberation of identity which still falls within the confines of the manufacturer's pre-arranged limits.[14] A recent trend, then, has been for historians to seek out the wider political identities of consumers, to test the extent to which consumption has become, as the anthropologist Daniel Miller has put it, the 'vanguard of history'.[15] Much of this work is still in the making, but a number of edited collections have appeared which are clearly and deliberately taking the history of consumption in new directions. In *The Sex of Things*, Victoria de Grazia has called for historians to turn away from a study of 'identity politics' – that is, the politics of style, of goods as cultural communicators about the nature of the self – and towards the 'collective and political identities' to which individual acquisitiveness can give rise.[16] Still more recently, *Getting and Spending*, by Susan Strasser, Charles McGovern and Matthias Judt, explores the interconnected nature of consumer and producer ethics and introduces the state as a crucial agent in the development of consumer society. The editors insist that consumption ought not to be regarded as a separate field, but as 'a prism through which many aspects of social and political life may be viewed'.[17] The essays, covering Europe and America, stress both how consumers have fought for certain rights and how states have rooted types of consumption in notions of citizenship. Recently edited volumes of *International Labour and Working-Class History* and *Radical History Review* further build on this historiography and Lawrence Glickman's anthology of American consumption-history writing demonstrates the extent to which scholars are turning to the politics of class, gender and ethnicity and the interaction of these concepts with consumption.[18]

The Politics of Consumption builds on these works to offer a more sustained history of material culture, consumers and citizenship. It takes seriously the efforts

14. L. Tiersten, 'Redefining consuming culture: recent literature on consumption and the bourgeoisie in Western Europe', *Radical History Review*, 57 (1993), pp. 116–59.

15. D. Miller, 'Consumption as the vanguard of history: a polemic by way of an introduction', in D. Miller (ed.), *Acknowledging Consumption: a Review of New Studies* (London: Routledge, 1995), pp. 1–57. See also F. Mort, 'The politics of consumption', in S. Hall and M. Jacques (eds), *New Times: The Changing Face of Politics in the 1990s* (London: Lawrence & Wishart, 1989), pp. 160–72.

16. V. de Grazia, 'Part three: empowering women as consumers', in V. de Grazia and E. Furlough (eds), *The Sex of Things: Gender and Consumption in Historical Perspective* (Berkeley: University of California Press, 1996), p. 276.

17. S. Strasser, C. McGovern and M. Judt (eds), *Getting and Spending: European and American Consumer Societies in the Twentieth Century* (Cambridge: Cambridge University Press, 1998), p. 4.

18. *International Labour and Working-Class History*, 55 (1999); *Radical History Review* special edition, 'Markets, politics, identities: what's left?', 76 (2000); L. B. Glickman (ed.), *Consumer Society in American History: A Reader* (Ithaca: Cornell University Press, 1999).

of consumers to politicize purchasing and the ability of states and business to shape the marketplace according to particular ideologies and interests. In doing so, it focuses on what might be broadly called the modern period, that is, from the late-eighteenth century to the present, or that period which began with Adam Smith's declaration that 'consumption is the sole end and purpose of all production'.[19] It is then that models of the rational consuming individual began to shape theoretically the market and ultimately the modern liberal state, when economic citizenship became, in principle at least, tied to our abilities to act as free independent consumers and producers.

Of course, consumption has never existed outside of politics, and throughout the Middle Ages official regulation of the market existed by means of sumptuary laws, guilds and the principle of *caveat emptor*.[20] Sumptuary laws are of particular interest, John Sekora having argued that states (whether the English Parliament or the Roman Senate) utilized them in order to protect themselves from the perceived threat of luxury, a vice which involved 'the immoral and illegal lust for false wealth and station' and which 'corrupted men and nations'.[21] In England, legislation such as the Statute of Artificers of 1563 attempted to maintain the social hierarchy by setting out precise details on the type of cloth to be worn by the different social ranks.[22] The 'Assizes', regulating measurements, weights and especially the adulteration of bread, had existed since the thirteenth century and in sixteenth-century France purchasers of eggs which had turned rotten were allowed to throw them back at the vendor.[23] Religion, too, was an important element of early modern material culture and the politics of Church authority was expressed in the very vestments worn by the clergy.[24]

19. A. Smith, *The Wealth of Nations* (1776; Chicago: University of Chicago Press, 1976), vol. 2, book 4, ch. 8, p. 179; on changing attitudes to the virtues of high wages and consumption, see A.W. Coats, 'Changing attitudes to labour in the mid-eighteenth century', *Economic History Review* 2nd ser. 13 (1960–1) and on the reallocation of household resources to purchasing goods, see J. de Vries, 'Between purchasing power and the world of goods: understanding the household economy in early modern Europe', in J. Brewer and R. Porter (eds), *Consumption and the World of Goods* (Routledge: London and New York, 1993), pp. 85–132.

20. G. Borrie and A.L. Diamond, *The Consumer, Society and the Law* (Harmondsworth: Penguin edn, 1973), pp. 15–19.

21. J. Sekora, *Luxury: The Concept in Western Thought, Eden to Smollett* (Baltimore: Johns Hopkins University Press, 1977), p. 52.

22. *Ibid.*, p. 59; A. Hunt, 'The governance of consumption: sumptuary laws and shifting forms of regulation', *Economy and Society*, 25 (1996), pp. 410–27; A. Hunt, *Governance of the Consuming Passions: A History of Sumptuary Law* (Basingstoke: Macmillan Press, 1996); and on controls on wearing particular types of cloth and economic policy, see P.K. O'Brien, T. Griffiths and P. Hunt, 'Political components of the industrial revolution: parliament and the English cotton industry, 1660–1774', *Economic History Review* 2nd ser. 44 (1991).

23. Forbes, *Consumer Interest*, p. 3; S. Webb and B. Webb, 'The Assize of Bread', *The Economic Journal,* 14 (1904), pp. 196–218.

24. G. Murdock, 'Dressed to repress? Protestant clergy dress and the regulation of morality in early modern Europe', *Fashion Theory*, 4:2 (2000), pp. 179–200.

However, it was not until the eighteenth century that the modern relationship between the consumer and the state could be said to have begun. It was then that the concept of luxury and consumption gradually changed from that of a threat to the state to something which drove the economy and added to 'the wealth of nations'. The issue contested by politicians and economists was no longer the virtues of consumption, but the best means of ensuring that consumption created a prosperous, balanced economy and society, whether by preserving the home market by protection or stimulating the international economy through free trade.[25] This centrality of consumption to the expansion of the market was directly linked to political thought, tied as it was with the emergence of the bourgeois state, the 'public sphere' and notions of politeness.[26] In cafés and theatres and through a growing number of printed journals, the bourgeoisie criticized the effeminized luxurious waste of the aristocracy (while acknowledging the importance of consumption in driving the market) in order to legitimate their own political existence. In particular, the financial and political support provided through their proliferating voluntary associations enabled them to avoid the client economy of aristocratic patronage and control. Finance could be raised through independent means rather than through the credit system whereby traders were dependent on their patrician clients. As John Brewer has argued, 'Association became a way of escaping economic clientage whilst providing protection against the vicissitudes of the open market . . . The opening up of politics and of enterprise went in tandem; in the eyes of predominantly urban and bourgeois groups, the two were seen as interconnected problems whose solution was mutually reinforcing'.[27] Thus, the idea of the rational individual became the social unit at the base of both bourgeois demands for political rights and in theories of interaction between agents in economic thought.

The transitional nature of the eighteenth century has given rise to a rich literature on consumer society, in which economic, cultural, social and political analyses have been combined.[28] The same must now be done for the nineteenth and twentieth

25. A. Gambles, *Protection and Politics: Conservative Economic Discourse, 1815–1852* (Woodbridge: Boydell Press for Royal Historical Society, 1999).

26. On politeness, see L. Klein, *Shaftesbury and the Culture of Politeness: Moral Discourse and Cultural Politics in Early Eighteenth-Century England* (Cambridge: Cambridge University Press, 1994); P. Langford, *A Polite and Commercial People: England, 1727–1783* (Oxford: Clarendon, 1989).

27. J. Brewer, 'Commercialisation and politics', in N. McKendrick, J. Brewer and J.H. Plumb, *The Birth of a Consumer Society: The Commercialisation of Eighteenth-Century England* (London: Europa, 1982), pp. 200–1; see also P. Clark, *British Clubs and Societies, 1580–1800: The Origins of an Associational World* (Oxford: Clarendon, 2000).

28. C. Berry, *The Idea of Luxury: A Conceptual and Historical Investigation* (Cambridge: Cambridge University Press, 1994); Sekora, *Luxury*; M. Berg and H. Clifford, *Consumers and Luxury: Consumer Culture in Europe, 1650–1850* (Manchester: Manchester University Press, 1999), especially essays by Berg and De Marchi; Brewer and Porter, *Consumption and the World of Goods*, especially

centuries and it is tempting to look to the institutions of the state for the articulation of the politics of consumer culture. As Corrigan and Sayer have argued, states enshrine, through the bureaucracy of law and administration, categories of culture and define 'acceptable forms and images of social activity and individual and collective identity'.[29] However, consumer politics often exist deliberately in opposition to the state, the co-operative movements of Europe which followed the 'Rochdale principles' bearing testimony to this fact.[30] Similarly, the more recent boycotts of global products have been conducted by various NGOs against multi-national corporations, both of which having arguably side-stepped the nation state in the new political battlefield. And the cultural politics of style and identity, made prominent through the Birmingham School analyses, have often shown the collective or subcultural identities emerging out of class- and youth-based protest against the state.[31] Struggles of citizenship based on work, national identity, human rights and gender have been based upon the legal recognition of rights and freedoms by the state, but the history of consumer politics is not only of the struggle for citizenship within the state, but against and beyond it as well.

What is being suggested here is an expansion of our understanding of the public sphere of political debate. Jurgen Habermas omitted to consider the relevance of consumption, arguing pessimistically instead that the state's encouragement of consumerism served to weaken the genuine or idealized rational discussions of the public sphere.[32] Simon Gunn has offered a recent attempt to modify the development of the public sphere, suggesting instead that after the First World War, in Britain at least, society became based around consumption instead of production. The arguably unstable and expanding middle classes sought to establish social hierarchies through their roles as consumers and confirm their identities as

---

essays by Appleby and Burke; D. Winch, *Riches and Poverty: An Intellectual History of Political Economy in Britain, 1750–1834* (Cambridge: Cambridge University Press, 1996); A. Bermingham and J. Brewer (eds), *The Consumption of Culture 1600–1800: Image, Object, Text* (London: Routledge, 1995), especially essays by Bermingham, Lovell and Brewer; J.G.A. Pocock, *Virtue, Commerce and History: Essays on Political Thought and History, Chiefly in the Eighteenth Century* (Cambridge: Cambridge University Press, 1985).

29. P. Corrigan and D. Sayer, *The Great Arch: English State Formation as Cultural Revolution* (Oxford: Blackwell, 1985), pp. 3–4.

30. P. Gurney, *Co-operative Culture and the Politics of Consumption in England, c. 1870–1930* (Manchester: Manchester University Press, 1996); E. Furlough, *Consumer Co-operation in France: The Politics of Consumption, 1834–1930* (Ithaca: Cornell University Press, 1991); E. Furlough and C. Strikwerda (eds), *Consumers Against Capitalism? Consumer Co-operation in Europe, North America and Japan, 1840–1990* (Oxford: Rowman & Littlefield, 1999).

31. S. Hall and T. Jefferson (eds), *Resistance Through Rituals: Youth Subcultures in Post-War Britain* (London: Hutchinson, 1976); D. Hebdige, *Subculture: The Meaning of Style* (London: Routledge, 1979); P. Willis, *Common Culture: Symbolic Work at Play in the Everyday Cultures of the Young* (Milton Keynes: Open University Press, 1990).

32. J. Habermas, *The Structural Transformation of the Public Sphere: an Inquiry into a Category of Bourgeois Society* (trans. T. Burger; Oxford: Polity, 1992).

such through mainstream political debate.[33] The problem with this account is that it posits a simple linear trend from production to consumption – a trend which has been directly contradicted by other historians who point instead to a collapse of free-trade consumer Liberalism and its replacement by a concern for production in Britain between the wars.[34] The point to learn is that, as the chapters in this book demonstrate, production and consumption politics are not alternatives. Consumption has always been a part of the public sphere, and is always related to issues of production. This is true of the move to abstain from sugar in the 1790s in protest against the economics of the slave trade, right through to the current boycotts of various multinational corporations. The prominence given to consumer issues on the streets of Seattle was not so much the recognition of a new public sphere of political debate, more the confirmation that the public sphere of consumption has always existed as one of many forms of 'civil society'.[35]

How this civil society of consumption functions, though, is based on two types of consumer politics or, as it might be better termed, material politics. First, there are *the politics of material culture*, the general movements and abstract ideologies which have tried to shape the meaning of consumption and unite all consumers within a common project. Most prominent here are the theories of various liberal economists in which the consumer is understood as a rational, utility-maximizing individual. This stands in sharp contrast to the collective understanding of consumption under state socialism and to the meaning of consumer co-operation advocated by those who strove for the 'Co-operative Commonwealth'. The consumer movements of the late twentieth century also tried to construct the 'consumer interest' along universal lines, suggesting that 'consumerism' ought to be understood as the empowering of consuming individuals through the general provision of commodity information to enable informed purchasing. In contrast, a second type of consumer politics – *the material culture of politics* – must be understood as relating to specific acts of purchasing, the political meanings attached to a particular commodity and the political struggles involved in single-issue campaigns which often become focused through acts of consumption. Boycotts,

---

33. S. Gunn, 'The public sphere, modernity and consumption: new perspectives on the history of the English middle class', in A. Kidd and D. Nicholls (eds), *Gender, Civic Culture and Consumerism: Middle-Class Identity in Britain, 1800–1940* (Manchester: Manchester University Press, 1999), pp. 12–29.

34. F. Trentmann, 'The strange death of free trade: the erosion of "liberal consensus" in Great Britain, c.1903–32', in E.F. Biagini (ed.), *Citizenship and Community: Liberals, Radicals and Collective Identities in the British Isles, 1865–1931* (Cambridge: Cambridge University Press, 1996), pp. 219–50.

35. For the best discussion of the public sphere see C. Calhoun (ed.), *Habermas and the Public Sphere* (London: MIT Press, 1992), especially C. Calhoun, 'Introduction', pp. 1–48 and G. Eley, 'Nations, publics and political cultures: placing Habermas in the nineteenth century', in Calhoun (ed.), *Habermas and the Public Sphere*, pp. 289–339.

'buycotts' and the special regulations concerning the distribution of certain classified commodities all form examples in which wider political issues are brought to bear on the specific site of consumption. This latter strand of consumer politics is never stable and it demonstrates the near impossibility of constructing a unifying or universal politics of consumption as different consuming decisions can be based upon seemingly contradictory political positions. What remains constant, however, is that the everyday interactions with material culture have remained necessarily political acts, whether or not consumers are aware of this themselves. And what is also important is that these two strands of material politics – the politics of material culture and the material culture of politics – are always interconnected. Often, general theories and abstract understandings of the consumer are only crystallized through specific contexts, and specific politics of consumption create or develop into general movements. For example, abstract notions of the rational consuming individual become concrete through specific instances of competition policy and boycotts of particular manufacturers can become part of general consumer protests against the economic exploitation of the developing world.

Within the modern state, the history of consumer politics and citizenship can be better understood as the history of the rights and duties which societies and individuals attach to consumption. It is not so much a history of how consumer rights have been constructed and incorporated into state-sanctioned notions of citizenship, but a history of how rights and duties, the central pillars of liberal citizenship, have been constantly redefined in their relationship to consumption.[36] In the combined narrative of the following chapters, there is thus an avoidance of either a progressive history of an emerging consumer consciousness or a pessimistic story of the ever-expanding range of individualized consumer rights and the corresponding demise of social duties culminating, for many left-leaning academics, in Margaret Thatcher's infamous epitaph that there is 'no such thing as society, only individuals and families'. Instead, there is an assumption that there has always existed a consumer consciousness in the sense that any issue of frugality or poverty necessitated an awareness of price, distribution and one's access to consumer goods. Similarly, the essays also assume not that there has been a lessening of the social responsibility of consumers, but that these duties have adapted to new political environments. As such, there is much that links the late eighteenth-century boycott of sugar, the turn-of-the-twentieth-century American National Consumers' League's 'White Label Campaign' identifying manufacturers with good working conditions for their employees,[37] and the late twentieth-century

36. On notions of rights and duties in liberalism, see E.F. Biagini, *Liberty, Retrenchment and Reform: Popular Liberalism in the Age of Gladstone* (Cambridge: Cambridge University Press, 1992).

37. K.K. Sklar, 'The consumer's White Label Campaign of the National Consumer's League, 1898–1918', in Strasser *et al.* (eds), *Getting and Spending*, pp. 17–35.

campaigns to make consumers in the Western world aware of the conditions of the producers of the developing world.

The Morality of Consumption

Consumption has always been a moral and political as well as an economic act. Classical and neo-liberal economists have been rightly criticized for failing to theorize consumption: the assumption of the existence of the rational, consuming individual fails to accord with the lived realities of everyday purchasing decisions.[38] But if one examines the history of consumption in terms of a history of rights and duties, then there is a rich stream of moral and political posturing within liberal economic thought. From the very beginnings of political economy, both David Hume and Adam Smith recognized the economic importance of consumption, but also still regarded it as morally frivolous (hence the *Private Vices, Public Virtues* of Mandeville's subtitle to his *Fable of the Bees*). Morality played a role in Smith's conceptualization of the state and citizenship as he recognized that the 'natural laws' of the market would not always ensure that the rich man's luxury filtered down to be distributed to the rest of society. Legislators were necessary to enact laws to maintain the 'exact administration of justice' and to prevent one group within society being favoured over others.[39] Finally, because consumption was seen as both important yet frivolous, it was located in the domestic sphere where women were expected to consume to express the status of the family. That private sphere was therefore just as crucial as the public sphere as men required the former to enable them to engage in public social, economic and political activity. In the modern state, then, consumption both drove the market economy and provided the domestic base from which bourgeois males could emerge to engage in the activities of the public sphere.[40]

Throughout the nineteenth century, moral issues remained at the core of any articulation of the liberal rights and duties associated with consumption. John Stuart Mill made an important distinction between what he termed 'productive' and 'unproductive' consumption: 'whoever contributes nothing directly or indirectly to production, is an unproductive consumer'.[41] Here Mill demonstrated the primacy

38. B. Fine and E. Leopold, *The World of Consumption* (London: Routledge, 1993).

39. Winch, *Riches and Poverty*, pp. 97–8.

40. V. de Grazia, Part one, 'Changing consumption regimes', in de Grazia and Furlough (eds), *The Sex of Things*, pp. 11–24; A. Bermingham, 'Introduction. The consumption of culture: image, object, text', and T. Lovell, 'Subjective powers? Consumption, the reading public, and domestic woman in early eighteenth-century England', both in Bermingham and Brewer (eds), *The Consumption of Culture*, pp. 1–20, 23–41.

41. J.S. Mill, *Principles of Political Economy, with Some of Their Applications to Social Philosophy*, vol. 1 (1852; London: Routledge & Kegan Paul, 1968), p. 52. See also J.S. Mill, 'II. Of the influence

given to issues of production within economics, arguing that wealth was a function entirely of productive capacity, but he also set out certain rules for consumption. According to Mill gold lace, pineapples and champagne were unproductive because 'these things give no assistance to production, nor any support to life, or strength, but what would equally be given by things much less costly'.[42] Furthermore, he suggested that it is often better not to consume, as the purchase of fancy goods will only benefit the rich, while the direct expenditure of one's income on labour will put money in the pocket of the working man who will then spend it on necessities which will further profit working people. Similarly, later in the century, Alfred Marshall conceived consumption as a moral activity, in the benefits it gave the consumer as worker. He contended that one must consume efficiently and effectively: 'You clearly have, in short, a duty to the rest of us to select consumables which yield "solid, unostentatious pleasure of a wholesome kind" – and to eschew those "impure" forms of consumption which lead to debasement of character as approximated in no small measure by impaired productivity.' Consumption was, in fact, both an act of aesthetic appreciation and a duty to the nation: 'your body belongs at least in part to your nation, and you would appear to have a social duty to the rest of us to decorate rather than pollute the High Street which we share'.[43]

These duties were taken up by John Ruskin and famously inverted in his *Unto This Last* so that useful consumption became not that which added to Mill's productive wealth, but that which added to the experience of life, or Ruskin's notion of wealth: 'the possession of the valuable by the valiant'.[44] Ruskin wanted a market regulated by 'order and reason, instead of demand and supply' and a system of distribution which was 'not absolute but discriminate; not of every thing to every man but of the right thing to the right man'. He looked to the state to set the example with public manufactories competing alongside private firms. The state would set fair standards of work and a level of prices that private firms would have to follow to keep pace: 'The state would in effect, use its economic power to

---

of consumption on production', and 'III. Of the words productive and unproductive', in *Essays on some Unsettled Questions of Political Economy* (London: Thoemmes Press, 1992), pp. 47–74, 75–89; S. Hollander, *The Economics of John Stuart Mill, Vol. 1: Theory and Method* (Oxford: Blackwell, 1985), especially pp. 264–72.

42. Mill, *Principles of Political Economy*, p. 52.

43. A. Marshall, *Principles of Economics* (1890; London: Macmillan, 1961), pp. 63–70, 83–91; D. Reisman, *The Economics of Alfred Marshall* (London: Macmillan, 1986), pp. 25–43; D. Reisman, *Alfred Marshall's Mission* (Basingstoke: Macmillan, 1990).

44. J. Ruskin, *Unto This Last: Four Essays on the First Principles of Political Economy* (1860–61; Orpington: George Allen 1898), p. 125. See also his *Munera Pulveris: Six Essays on the Elements of Political Economy*, 1862–63, in E.T. Cook and A. Wedderburn, *The Works of John Ruskin*, vol. 17 (London: Allen & Unwin, 1903–1912).

moralise the market'.[45] This attack on the usual liberal support for Free Trade[46] was followed by William Morris. He believed that workers turned to the 'vulgarities and shabby gentilities' of the market because their senses had been dulled in the factory. 'Useful work', which would occur in Morris's pastoral communist utopia, would lead to the 'building up [of] the ornamental part of life – its pleasures, bodily and mental, scientific and artistic, social and individual'.[47]

The Morrissian and Ruskinian traditions fed through into a more comprehensively argued economic theory in the work of J.A. Hobson. Hobson called for a mixed economy because the individualism inherent to consumption meant that not all industries could be mechanized and rationalized: 'consumers refuse to conform to a common standard and insist more and more upon a consumption adjusted to their individual needs and tastes . . . such individuality in consumption must impose a corresponding individuality in production and machinery will be dethroned from industry.'[48] He aimed, therefore, to free up working class incomes in order to direct the economy through their individual consumption decisions. Money had to be taken away from the rich whose 'underconsumption' meant the economy was too often run at an inefficient level. In a socialist version of Smith, Hobson argued that it was better to make the poor richer as they would expend all their incomes on consumption and drive the economy. The incomes of the wealthy elites, however, were at such a level that they surpassed that which was necessary for their 'natural' level of consumption, and were therefore inefficiently wasting the rest on savings.[49]

Much of this discussion of liberal economic theory is quintessentially British, but it also inspires wider historiographical considerations. For too long, E.P. Thompson's eighteenth-century 'moral economy' has been posited as the crowd's alternative to political economy and historians have sought to identify similar instances of moral distribution in periods and places as diverse as medieval England and twentieth-century Africa.[50] Thompson's moral economy should however be

45. N. Thompson, *The Market and its Critics: Socialist Political Economy in the Nineteenth Century* (London: Routledge, 1998), pp. 163–7.

46. F. Trentmann, 'Wealth versus welfare: the British Left between Free Trade and national political economy before the First World War', *Historical Research*, 70 (1997), pp. 70–98.

47. Thompson, *The Market and Its Critics*, p. 194. See especially W. Morris, *How we Live and How we Might Live* (1885), *Useful Work and Useless Toil* (1884), and *News from Nowhere* (1890), all in A. Briggs (ed.), *William Morris: Selected Writings and Designs* (1962; Harmondsworth: Penguin, 1977), pp. 117–35, 158–78, and 183–301.

48. J.A. Hobson, *The Evolution of Modern Capitalism*, quoted in N. Thompson, 'Hobson and the Fabians: two roads to socialism in the 1920s', *History of Political Economy*, 26 (1994), pp. 203–20.

49. M. Freeden (ed.), *J.A. Hobson: a Reader* (London: Unwin Hyman, 1988), pp. 106–18; M. Freeden (ed.), *Reappraising J A. Hobson: Humanism and Welfare* (London: Unwin Hyman, 1990), especially chapters 1–4.

50. The classic essay is E. P. Thompson, 'The moral economy of the English crowd in the eighteenth century', *Past and Present*, 50 (1971), pp. 76–136, though his own comments on the extension of his

viewed as just one example of how different moralities can come to influence the workings of the market. A successor to the moral economy might then be the 'spiritual economy' of G.M. Trevelyan's Ruskinian appreciation of the arts.[51] But in the United States, where critics did not share such a strong condemnation of industrialization and supposedly 'indiscriminate' consumption, it might be better to refer to a 'fair economy'. Labour activists such as Ira Steward sought to reconcile consumption and production in his call for a 'living wage', a monetary amount determined by the quantity of goods and commodities American workers believed they had the right to enjoy.[52] Similar collective conceptions of fairness mobilized working-class Berlin women in the First World War who, in a time of food shortages, were able to make successful political protests by appealing to the 'fundamental rights' of wives and mothers to be able to feed their families.[53] Notions of fairness also motivated the American and European consumer movements referred to in Chapters Ten and Twelve to Fourteen in this book, in the writings of the early twentieth-century French co-operator and consumer advocate, Charles Gide,[54] and in the 'ethical economy' of today's consumer protests and boycotts.

The morality or politics of consumption, within this wider liberal framework, has also been articulated according to reasonably consistent dichotomies. Rights and duties, fairness, the role of the state and ultimately citizenship have been established in terms of binaries such as productive and unproductive, rational and irrational, necessity and luxury, useful and wasteful. Thus in Chapter Two, virtue and egoism are seen to have been pitted against one another in the politics of consumption during the French Revolution. Chapter Three similarly identifies the clash of perceived 'real' and 'false' wants in early nineteenth-century socialist thought, polarities which were still very much in evidence in the minds of East

---

concept can be found in his E.P. Thompson, *Customs in Common* (London: Merlin, 1991). For the most recent discussions of 'moral economy' and its wider application, see A.J. Randall and A.Charlesworth (eds), *Markets, Market Culture and Popular Protest in Eighteenth-Century Britain and Ireland* (Liverpool: Liverpool University Press, 1996), especially 'Introduction'; D. Hay, 'The state and the market in 1800: Lord Kenyon and Mr Waddington', *Past and Present*, 162 (1999), pp. 101–62; A.Randall and A.Charlesworth (eds), *The Moral Economy and Popular Protest: Crowds, Conflict and Authority* (Basingstoke: Macmillan, 1999).

51. G.M. Trevelyan, *Must England's Beauty Perish? A Plea on Behalf of the National Trust for Places of Historic Interest or Natural Beauty* (London: Faber & Gwyer, 1929).

52. L.B. Glickman, *A Living Wage: American Workers and the Making of Consumer Society* (Ithaca: Cornell University Press, 1997); L. Glickman, 'Workers of the world, consume: Ira Steward and the origins of the labour consumerism', *International Labour and Working Class History*, 52 (1997), pp. 72–86.

53. B. Davis, 'Food scarcity and the empowerment of the female consumer in World War I Berlin', in de Grazia and Furlough (eds), *The Sex of Things*, pp. 287–310; B. Davis, *Home Fires Burning: Food, Politics, and Everyday Life in World War I Berlin* (Chapel Hill: University of North Carolina Press, 2000).

54. Williams, *Dream Worlds*.

German economists in the second half of the twentieth century (see Chapter Nine). When formal systems of distribution have been advocated, debates have been polarized between individual and collective consumption (Chapter Seven) or between municipal and private provision (Chapter Four). Efficiency, use and the rationality of the consumer were rhetorically positioned in opposition to inefficiency, waste and the irrationality of the shopper by the post-Second World War consumer movements (Chapter Twelve). Finally, Chapter Ten argues that the response of the United States' governments to consumer society was one of creating customer-consumers as opposed to the more politically-engaged citizen-consumers.

The balance between these binary oppositions must always be dependent on precise historical circumstances. Thus in periods of war or scarcity, the consumer had a moral or legal obligation to limit desires to necessities – a term open to constant testing and redefinition. As the converse, the state had a duty to intervene to ensure the basic needs of all citizens were met, which might entail replacing the market as the more efficient allocative device. There is also an important distinction to be made between times of affluence and times of poverty. Economic hardship makes more real the politics of consumption, encouraging citizens to set out their rights to basic entitlements whether through the guarantee of a 'living wage', social provision by the state or a radical utopian experiment. Periods of economic depression might create situations in which consumers were called on to buy the economy's return to prosperity. And on the other hand, periods of affluence might stimulate fears that materialism was subverting control of the self and undermining the social hierarchy. To some, self-denial and asceticism became virtues against the hedonism of a consumer culture; to others, the extension of material goods was a sign of democracy and egalitarian incorporation. Consumption always entailed moral issues, which are sometimes only apparent through close inspection of legal and cultural codes, but which in certain circumstances enter mainstream political debate.

The Politics of Material Culture

How we are to understand the history of the morality of consumption is through a history of material politics. The first aspect of material politics refers to those general ideologies brought to bear on consumption: that is, the wider politics of material culture. One example of these broader concepts emerges from the very dichotomies examined in the previous section. Moral statements of use and abuse, rational and irrational, real and false, necessity and luxury give rise to general theories of consumption in which certain groups speak for the consumer, constructing him or her as an abstract object lacking its own subjective consciousness. Consumption has thus been politicized as liberal reformers have identified waste, abuse, excess and lack of discrimination among the mass of the population. This explains the duties of many liberals on both sides of the Atlantic to reform leisure and popular culture in the nineteenth century, prohibiting 'low', 'uncivilized' forms of entertainment and encouraging instead 'rational recreation' and a greater appreciation of the 'morally uplifting'.[55] These attitudes were developed into a later disdain for mass culture, among both left- and right-wing cultural critics across Europe and America, which saw, most explicitly in the writings of F.R. Leavis, a contempt for the perceived indiscriminate tastes of the masses who ought, instead, to have been led by a 'minority culture' of cultural aesthetes.[56] The tradition has arguably been continued through the work of the Frankfurt School which has shared a similar pessimism about the false, manipulated desires of the 'culture industry'.[57] This school of thought flourished most prominently and persistently in America, in the condemnation of the advertising industry led by Vance Packard and in the exposés of industries such as the car and funeral businesses by Jessica Mitford and Ralph Nader, though these post-Second World War commentators have followed an American tradition stretching back to the reaction to Upton Sinclair's 1906 description of the meat-packing industry in *The Jungle*.[58]

Such polarized discussions of consumption can offer powerful political rhetoric, but it has also added to the general under-theorization of consumption which Noel Thompson sees as emerging in the early nineteenth century. Thompson argues that early socialist writers 'put at the heart of their political economy a symbiosis between social opulence and private asceticism', reconciling a role for consumption within the politics of the Left that has not been matched since J.A. Hobson's emphasis on the 'transformative power of discriminating consumption'. However, an uneasiness with consumption also emerged, as natural – as opposed to false – desires were linked to rationality, thereby identifying irrational or luxurious

55. J. Walvin *Leisure and Society 1830–1950* (London: Longman, 1978); P. Bailey, *Leisure and Class in Victorian England: Rational Recreation and the Contest for Social Control* (London: Routledge & Kegan Paul, 1978); P. Bailey, *Popular Culture and Performance in the Victorian City* (Cambridge: Cambridge University Press, 1998). H. Cunningham, *Leisure in the Industrial Revolution c. 1780–c. 1880* (London: Croom Helm, 1980). B. Harrison, *Drink and the Victorians: The Temperance Question in England, 1815–1872*, 2nd edn (Keele: Keele University Press, 1994).

56. F.R. Leavis, *Mass Civilisation and Minority Culture* (Cambridge: Minority Press, 1930). See also J. Carey, *The Intellectuals and the Masses: Pride and Prejudice Among the Literary Intelligentsia, 1880–1939* (London: Faber & Faber, 1992); T.J. Lears, *No Place of Grace: Antimodernism and the Transformation of American Culture, 1880–1920* (Chicago: University of Chicago Press, 1994); D. Horowitz, *The Morality of Spending: Attitudes Towards the Consumer Society in America, 1875–1940* (Baltimore: Johns Hopkins University Press, 1985); J. Naremore and P. Brantlinger (eds), *Modernity and Mass Culture* (Bloomington: Indiana University Press, 1991).

57. M. Horkheimer and T. Adorno, *Dialectic of Enlightenment* (1944; London: Allen Lane, 1973), 'The culture industry: enlightenment as mass deception', pp. 120–67.

58. J. Mitford, *The American Way of Death* (London: Hutchinson, 1963); R. Nader, *Unsafe at Any Speed: The Designed-in Dangers of the American Automobile* (New York: Grossman, 1965); U. Sinclair, *The Jungle* (1906; Harmondsworth: Penguin, 1965).

consumption as unnatural, and not the driving force of the economy as Adam Smith would have had it. Answers to social ills thus took the form of creating utopian, supposedly more natural, communities instead of embracing the world of goods. Arguably, the legacy still remains and consumption continues to be discussed according to rather straightforward moral and economic categories.

A politics of material culture which in many ways avoided a polemical attitude to the consumer was the co-operative movement. Emerging out of the traditions of solidarity and collective action involved in mutual insurance and friendly societies, co-operative stores were pragmatic responses to the high costs of bread and other essentials in the new industrial communities of Britain, France, the Low Countries and the German states. Originally created as utopian social experiments along the lines set out by Robert Owen, Henri Saint Simon and Charles Fourier, the intention was to secure the collective ownership of the means of production for the workers. Even the Equitable Pioneers of Rochdale, set up in 1844, who established the principle of consumer co-operation through issuing membership shares and the 'dividend', saw themselves first and foremost as an establishment for the raising of capital to purchase the means of production which would then be organized on workers' co-operative principles. The focus on the consumer was therefore a means to an end, and it was not until J.T.W. Mitchell reformulated the principles of co-operation later in the century that the consumer, rather than the worker, became the basis and focus of political action. Although viewed with suspicion by many figures within the trade union and labour movements, leading to an occasionally uneasy relationship between co-operators and socialists, consumer co-operation had become a truly international movement by the early twentieth century, co-ordinated as it was by the International Co-operative Alliance. Furthermore, a number of co-operative theorists, including Percy Redfern and Beatrice Webb in Britain, Richard Ely in the United States, Charles Gide and Jean Prudhommeaux in France and Louis de Brouckère in Belgium, began to see the possibilities of a 'Co-operative Commonwealth' which would emerge from an expanding consumer consciousness that would result in the overthrow of capitalism, the birth of a new democracy and even world peace.[59]

The unwillingness of the consumers' co-operative movement to negotiate with the institutions of the state, however, arguably led to its demise as the voice of the

---

59. E. Furlough and C. Strikwerda, 'Economics, consumer culture and gender: an introduction to the politics of consumer co-operation', in Furlough and Strikwerda (eds), *Consumers Against Capitalism*, pp. 1–65; Furlough, *Consumer Co-operation in France*; Gurney, *Co-operative Culture*; D. Frank, *Purchasing Power: Consumer Organising, Gender, and the Seattle Labour Movement, 1919–1929* (Cambridge: Cambridge University Press, 1994); M. Prinz, *Brot und Dividende: Konsumvereine in Deutschland und England vor 1914* (Göttingen: Vandenhoeck and Ruprecht, 1996); M. Purvis, 'Societies of consumers and consumer societies: co-operation, consumption and politics in Britain and continental Europe, *c.* 1850–1920', *Journal of Historical Geography*, 24 (1998), pp. 147–69.

consumer interest. Instead, business and capitalism were able to ensure that the politics of material culture was centred on the private individual as the basis of customer, not consumer, citizenship. By the inter-war period, appeals were being made to the consumer as a political entity around which the democratic process revolved, ensuring that the ability to engage in private acts of consumption was a badge of citizenship. In America, the self-proclaimed purpose of F.D. Roosevelt's creation of a number of consumer representative bodies in the New Deal era was a reflection of a 'new principle in government' that consumers had the right 'to have their interests represented in the formulation of government policy'.[60] And in Britain, Stanley Baldwin, during the period of the National Government, appealed to the readers of the *Daily Mail* and *Daily Express* as the new citizens of the 'public' through the use of overtly consumerist rhetoric: 'Every housewife knows what inflation means in prices'.[61] But so entrenched was the relationship between individual consumption and the modern state by the 1930s that even the authoritarian regimes of Europe were never able to ignore consumption entirely. Although Hitler used consumption as a site for Nazi propaganda, the Women's Bureau Division of Political Economy–Home Economy seeking to Nazify the entire German menu, issues of individual desire also had to be addressed.[62] As Chapter Eight shows, Hitler was aware of the power of advertising and used it to suggest that higher standards of living were waiting just around the corner, while at the same time allowing some symbolic consumption to take place amidst a general policy of diverting resources to rearmament. In that discussion, Berghoff suggests that this 'constant juxtaposition of enticement and deprivation' first saw the movement towards Western consumerism which was then suppressed in order to reallocate raw materials to producer goods instead of consumer goods. Not all the advertising was successful and consumers were unwilling to develop a 'political stomach', though in other areas, such as the consumption of the symbols of modernity – cars, radios and holidays – the Nazis were able to trade on a policy of 'virtual consumption'. For instance, in 1938 consumers were encouraged to put their money into a state saving scheme to obtain a Volkswagen beetle in four years' time. Consumption was virtual as the money was then redirected to other purposes. The point, however, is that citizens' private consuming desires had to be taken into account, whether or not Hitler was able to manipulate them according to his own improvised economic strategy.

60. L. Cohen, 'The New Deal state and the making of citizen consumers', in Strasser *et al.* (eds), *Getting and Spending*, pp. 120–1. See also the essay by C. McGovern, 'Consumption and citizenship in the United States, 1900–1940', pp. 37–58.
61. Gunn, 'The public sphere, modernity and consumption', p. 23.
62. N. Reagin, 'Comparing apples and oranges: housewives and the politics of consumption in inter-war Germany', in Strasser *et al.* (eds), *Getting and Spending*, pp. 241–61.

Likewise, in the GDR, consumption remained a central element of citizenship, despite the 'grumbling' which formed the basis of the everyday protests against the lack of consumer goods.[63] Chapter Nine argues that there was actually much negotiation taking place between consumers and the state in the 1950s and 1960s, with the ruling party having to take into consideration practical issues to an extent it had never done within its ideology. The image of West German affluence was a constant source of political unrest and the regime was forced to allow wages to expand in order to achieve some degree of political acquiescence. Honecker, however, put in place a more comprehensive collection of consumer measures, as consumption reached the top of the political agenda. Supply policies were changed, investment spending was redirected, pricing measures were re-examined, and a black market was officially sanctioned from as early as 1948 when 'free shops' (*Handelsorganisation*) allowed goods to be purchased without the use of ration cards. Furthermore, in 1961 and 1966, 'Exquisit' and 'Delikat', two luxury shops dealing in high-quality, expensive and often imported goods, were established to satisfy what was acknowledged to be a very real demand. As Heldmann concludes in Chapter Nine, such a political recognition of the private, individual consumption desires of its citizenry was actually crucial to the survival of the East German regime.

Was this recognition of the consumer interest, however defined, reflective of the corporatist nature of the modern state? Were consumers organized and recognized as a political body which negotiated with other political interests through the institutions of the modern state? Across Europe, during and after the First World War, labour was incorporated into the political process,[64] but it seems that consumers themselves played little direct role in state formation, in the sense that there was a clearly demarcated and specifically consumers' movement representing a precise interest group. At the other extreme, however, it was unlikely that state formation and the construction of the consumer interest within political discourse was the direct consequence of business interests. Rather, it is likely that the notion of the consumer as a rationally behaving individual economic unit, or what Chapter Ten identifies as the customer-citizen as opposed to the citizen-consumer, emerged from various sites of expertise. The consumer was not so much an active agent or product of a corporate state, but a category constructed throughout the institutions and discourses of modern government. Consumers played a role in the definition of their own interests, but just as often the meaning of consumerism and consumption emerged out of the official negotiations between other subjects – workers, unions, business, public health officials, local administrators and the

---

63. I. Merkel, 'Consumer culture in the GDR, or how the struggle for antimodernity was lost on the battleground of consumer culture', Strasser *et al* (eds), *Getting and Spending*, pp. 281–99.

64. C. Maier, *Recasting Bourgeois Europe: Stabilisation in France, Germany, and Italy in the Decade after World War I* (Princeton: Princeton University Press, 1975).

professions – all of whom claimed to speak for the consumer. In part, the consumer, in being spoken of as an object through the discourses of consumption created by other interests within the broader nexus of government, became a knowable subject with, potentially, its own agency.[65]

One example of this process, is the ability of many apparently production-minded labour leaders to speak on matters of consumption. In Chapter Seven, on early twentieth-century Britain, Frank Trentmann claims that working-class leaders would never have failed to recognize and articulate their interests as both workers and consumers. The politics of household provisioning ensured that issues of supply and demand, of wages and prices, were ever foremost in the campaigns of the labour and co-operative movements. Trentmann sees the Consumers' Council of the First World War as a pivotal moment in the relationship between consumption and citizenship, as splits appeared between those who favoured a classic liberal Free Trade organization of the economy, and those who demanded protection and government intervention to ensure fair prices and fair quantities of bread and milk for the mass of the population. Earlier, however, the consumer had come to be defined through local, as well as national, political discourse. This is apparent in Chapter Four, which deals with the politics of material culture of public utilities, and especially gas. Here, the claim to represent the consumer was disputed by various groups within the arena of local politics. Both industrialists and the town council were major consumers of gas, and attempted to define themselves as representing the wider consuming public. Meanwhile, the private companies could claim to represent the small private householder against large-scale consumers. The tensions between shareholders for profits, and different classes of consumers for low prices, might have been resolved by ensuring that owners were also consumers. In practice, the disputes between owners and consumers were adjudicated by lawyers and engineers, adjusted by automatic accounting principles, and eventually removed by municipalization which turned consuming citizens into owners. Individual consumers played little role in these debates, but it was through these debates that their subjectivity was defined. Similar debates over the relationship between forms of ownership and consumer interests were fought out over other services, from railways to telephones and financial services.

Despite these different ways in which the politics of material culture were formulated, the ideal of the consumer as a rational, privately-acting individual

---

65. M. Foucault, *The History of Sexuality. Volume I: an Introduction* (Harmondsworth: Penguin, 1979); 'On governmentality', *Ideology and Consciousness*, 6 (1979), pp. 5–22; T. Johnson, 'Expertise and the state', in M. Gane and T. Johnson (eds), *Foucault's New Domains* (London: Routledge, 1993); M. Dean, *Critical and Effective Histories: Foucault's Methods and Historical Sociology* (London: Routledge, 1994), especially chapter 9, 'Governmentality'; N. Rose, 'Governing "advanced" liberal democracies', in A. Barry, T. Osborne and N. Rose (eds), *Foucault and Political Reason: Liberalism, Neo-Liberalism and Rationalities of Government* (London: University College London Press, 1996); M. Dean, *Governmentality: Power and Rule in Modern Society* (London: Sage, 1999).

came to predominate. Even the relative incorporation of labour interests into the state apparatus in the early twentieth century – and the subsequent introduction of piecemeal anti-trust legislation, state-sponsored competition and government regulation of industry – especially during times of war, helped construct the consumer as customer, rather than as citizen. In Chapter Ten's examination of American consumer politics, Lizabeth Cohen outlines three key stages. In the first stage, the Progressive Era from the 1890s to 1920, the consumers' position with civic life was established, the consumer here being understood to be as much a political entity as a purely economic category. In the second stage, the New Deal era of the 1930s, these citizen consumers were incorporated into the political process as the National Industry Recovery Act formally brought consumer representatives into the institutions of the state. At the same time, however, consumers' economic roles were also being stressed as Americans were encouraged to purchase their way out of the Depression. After the Second World War – Cohen's third stage – citizen consumers who pushed for price and rent controls were defeated by corporate interests (including business and labour interests) which demanded a return to full-scale free enterprise. Out of this emerged a 'new post-war ideal', as the 'customer as citizen' 'simultaneously fulfilled personal desire and civic obligation by consuming'. In the new 'Consumers' Republic' the economic aspects of consumption were championed over the political rights of consumers in the new age of affluence and mass prosperity. In Chapter Eleven, Meg Jacobs shows that the promise of plenty could mobilize cross-class alliances in the first half of the twentieth century, creating a state-supported collective bargaining machinery which pressed for high wages against large-scale corporations and underwrote mass consumption. But the alliance fractured as the demands of unions led to inflation which hit the middle class, and allowed the corporations to claim to speak for the consumers, protecting them against the selfish demands of organized labour and offering the benefits of efficient production. The internal divisions within consumer-citizenship led to its own demise, and allowed business corporations to speak for customer-citizens.

A similar history might be identified in British consumer politics. Chapter Twelve argues that in a period of relative consumer poverty before the Second World War, the politics of consumption acquired a more radical edge and consequently a more collectively-based notion of citizenship. By way of contrast, the consumer movement of the post-Second World War period encouraged consumers to think of themselves as individual, private economic agents. This construction of the consumer interest was not purely a result of the largely business interests which examined consumer protection issues in the Molony Committee and which directed competition policy in the 1950s and 1960s,[66] since consumers too played their

66. H. Mercer, *Constructing a Competitive Order: the Hidden History of British Anti-Trust Policy* (Cambridge: Cambridge University Press, 1995).

part. The Consumers' Association mobilized middle-class rational customers from the late 1950s onwards according to a model of consumer politics which acted more as a 'watchdog' to business rather than a radical alternative to it. It was therefore relatively simple for the Consumers' Association to become voluntarily incorporated into the state apparatus through the proliferation of 'quangos' that has marked the expansion of the British state throughout the post-war period.

The difficulty of applying an overarching causal explanation for the emergence of post-Second World War consumer politics becomes apparent in Chapter Thirteen. The experiences of France and Germany do not exactly match the events in Britain and America. In France, consumer politics emerged out of radical and activist traditions. French consumerism can be viewed as a political movement in which consumers have sought greater protection and have been ready to criticize industry. But because it is a movement of consumers, fragmentation has also occurred with trade unions setting up consumer groups in realization that consumer politics can reinforce class politics. This has led to a situation in which French politics of consumption have not been as prominent within mainstream political debate as they have been in Germany where there was much less of a grass-roots movement but where there was much more of a corporatist framework ensuring that the consumer interest was consistently heard at state level. In Germany, there has been greater amicability between business and consumer groups, partly because the state-created consumer organizations have sought to negotiate with industry to build 'a fair domestic marketplace for quality goods'. Despite German consumerism emerging from the top down, then, moderate consumer affairs have always, much more than in France, remained within central political debate, though the existence of EEC protection rules since the 1970s has seen the issues taken beyond the level of the nation state. What the distinction between France and Germany does do, however, is to return us to the issue of who it is that speaks for the consumer. In France, consumers themselves have played a much stronger role in voicing their concerns, while in Germany the articulation of a consumer consciousness has to some extent emerged from above.[67]

The tension between the consumer as subject expressing his or her own interests and the consumer as object about which other groups speak has persisted throughout the history of the politics of consumption. Chapter Fourteen highlights the fact that although the free market has undoubtedly triumphed in Chapter Ten's 'Consumers' Republic', moral agendas still regulate consumption, or 'corral' the market, and that rationality remains as politically loaded a concept as ever. America, as well as other states, has continued to restrict aspects of consumption such as

---

67. This analysis also recognizes the earlier attempts by both French and German consumers to form their own movements, in the Ligue Sociale d'Acheteurs and the Käuferbund Deutschland: W. Breckman, 'Disciplining consumption: the debate on luxury in Wilhelmine Germany, 1890–1914', *Journal of Social History*, 24 (1991), pp. 485–505; Reagin, 'Comparing apples and oranges'.

alcohol, drugs, gambling, shop hours and business zoning. The primary means by which markets have been limited is through appeals to the private rights of parents and the 'innocence' of their children. Innocence restricts the recognition of the full liberal rights and duties of rational individualism and is a powerful force for encouraging the intervention of the state in the running of the free market. It not only applies to the child, however, and can be used to refer to the manipulation of the uninformed and those denied free choice through physical and psychological addiction. Gary Cross argues in Chapter Fourteen that concern for the child has remained 'paramount' and provides the only consistent bulwark against the encroachments of the mass market and, as such, the only general theory of the politics of consumption to act against that of the citizen as customer. His conclusion that childhood is 'the surviving rhetoric of restraint' perhaps explains why the intrinsically linked concepts of innocence and limited rationality are aired so frequently by those who still seek to impose alternative politics of material culture according to their own moral criteria.

The Material Culture of Politics

What Cross's concluding comments demonstrate is that these general politics of material culture have been articulated, reinforced, strengthened and reinvigorated through discussions of the specific, through the material culture of politics. His interpretation has an overall coherence when these single-issue campaigns are examined collectively as attempts to 'corral' the market. For the consumer actors, the politics of consumption is frequently understood only in terms of specific campaigns or with reference to the meaning of a single commodity. Thus it is important to remember that Cross's interpretation is predicated on political discussions which have focused on such controversial commodities as alcohol and tobacco. The same, too, might also be said for all the other chapters of this book: for instance, Trentmann's analysis in Chapter Seven centres upon the specific and local concerns about the price and quality of bread and milk; the Molony Committee discussed by Hilton in Chapter Twelve took particular care not to set any general principles in consumer politics and therefore referred to only one product at a time; Daunton's discussion in Chapter Four revolves around the debates over a specific municipal service; and the consumer politics of Nazi Germany and the GDR outlined by Berghoff and Heldmann in Chapters Eight and Nine respectively are rendered knowable only through the discussion brought to bear on particular goods or classes of goods, be that the Volkswagen beetle or the complaints directed at the lack of availability of certain consumer items.

This concentration on the specific sites of consumption is witnessed in Chapter Two: as Rebecca Spang shows, despite the urgent issues of revolution and war, members of the French National Convention spent much of their time in detailed discussion of the meanings of particular items of material culture. This could be a matter of life and death: to hoard a necessity was a capital offence. In 1793, the discovery of eight barrels of rum in Pierre François Joseph Robert's cellar provoked a series of debates as to the definition of rum, whether it was a luxury or necessity, and who could determine such matters. The General Maximum, a decree of the revolutionary period that regulated prices and wages from September 1793 to December 1794, may well have been motivated by a general principle that certain goods were fundamental to human existence, but the actual workings of this law were only ever decided with reference to specific commodities. The National Convention was petitioned from all over France, each locality eager to define its staple forms of consumption as necessaries to both their own economy and the nation as a whole. Defining rights through material culture was a theoretically simple measure, but the complex politics of consumption that were then released proved to make the regulatory system unworkable.

Likewise, in Chapter Six on citizenship law, state form and everyday aesthetics in France and Germany, Leora Auslander argues that the fundamental need of the modern state to instill a sense of loyalty in its citizens involved the style of everyday goods such as furniture and fabrics. The state played a role in the teaching of taste, which took different forms in France and Germany, with their different notions of belonging to the state. In France, citizens were made as much as born, and the state encouraged a homogenous French style for everyday goods, rooted in the French past, excluding foreign forms and creating a single national style to which immigrants and the regions would conform. In Germany, citizens were born rather than made, and there was also a strong regional autonomy. As a result, style was much more varied and eclectic, with both regional and foreign, historicist and modern expressions. The taste of everyday goods was simply less significant in the creation of a sense of German identity, for citizenship was transmitted through genealogy. The form of everyday objects therefore expressed notions of citizenship and national identity, affecting cultural policy in different ways in the two countries. The design of chairs and tables, wallpaper and kitchens, were matters of political importance.

Many of these specific instances of consumer politics have provided the site for the articulation of wider political identities, based on the lines of class, gender, ethnicity and nation. The ideals of aesthetic appreciation and cultural enlightenment have proved particularly strong in the British context. The National Trust, or the consumption of the past, was inspired by Ruskinian notions of beauty, art and heritage.[68] Similarly, the Council for Art and Industry, although often appearing

---

68. M. Waterson, *The National Trust: The First Hundred Years* (London: The National Trust, 1994); P. Weideger, *Gilding the Acorn: Behind the Façade of the National Trust* (London: Simon & Schuster, 1994); R. Hewison, *The Heritage Industry: Britain in a Climate of Decline* (London: Methuen, 1987).

patronizing in style and even elitist in manner, has attempted to improve the aesthetic content of, for instance, the working-class home.[69] The BBC, operating in one of the most commercialized sectors of the modern mass market – home entertainment – began as an institution imbued with Reithian ideals of cultural direction and education.[70] And, just as the National Convention devoted hours to the discussion of the aesthetic and social merits of certain goods, so too did the British government during and after the Second World War. Different goods were rationed according to distinct criteria and taxed at rates according to their classification as necessity or luxury, and the government created a Utility Scheme to standardize production and consumption according to by now established notions of 'good' design.[71]

Issues of gender were often central to the material culture of politics of single-issue campaigns. Women in Britain and America purchased brooches, badges, ribbons, pins, buttons and jewellery bearing the legend, 'Am I not a man and a brother', in order to protest against the slave trade in the 1790s.[72] Accused of merely purchasing items to engage in fashionable dispute rather than contributing directly to the public sphere of political debate, women brought the private into the public as they went on to boycott sugar, the virtue of abstinence incapable of being dismissed quite so readily as a mere 'feminine trifle'.[73] Women have continued to play a central role in the history of consumer politics. They have been at the forefront of co-operative movements, in the Women's Co-operative Guild in Britain and in supporting their trade-union husbands in America.[74] In the early twentieth century, the suffragette Teresa Billington Greig even articulated a feminist consumer agenda as she urged women to enter the public world of politics

---

69. Council for Art and Industry, *The Working-Class Home: Its Furnishing and Equipment* (London: Council for Art and Industry, 1937). See also, P.J. Maguire and J.M. Woodham (eds), *Design and Cultural Politics in Post-War Britain: The Britain Can Make It Exhibition of 1946* (London: Leicester University Press, 1997); F. MacCarthy, *A History of British Design, 1830–1970* (London: Allen & Unwin, 1979).

70. D.L. LeMahieu, *A Culture for Democracy: Mass Communication and the Cultivated Mind in Britain Between the Wars* (Oxford: Clarendon, 1988).

71. On the classification of goods for taxation, see M. Daunton, *Just Taxes: Britain, 1914–79* (Cambridge: Cambridge University Press, forthcoming); on design of goods, see A. Forty, *Objects of Desire: Design and Society, 1750–1980* (London: Thames and Hudson, 1986); the Utility scheme drew on elements of the earlier arts and crafts movement with its links to Morris: see S.K. Tillyard, *The Impact of Modernism and the Arts and Crafts Movement in Edwardian England* (London: Routledge, 1988).

72. C. Midgley, *Women against Slavery: The British Campaigns, 1780–1870* (London: Routledge, 1992).

73. K. Davies, 'A moral purchase: femininity, commerce, abolition, 1788–1792', in E. Eger and C. Grant (eds), *Women and the Public Sphere: Writing and Representation 1660–1800* (Cambridge: Cambridge University Press, 2000).

74. G. Scott, *Feminism and the Politics of Working Women: The Women's Co-operative Guild, 1880s to the Second World War* (London: UCL Press, 1998); Frank, *Purchasing Power.*

through their role as consumers in an overtly suffragist strategy.[75] Just as women's involvement in nineteenth-century moral crusades paved the way for a more general politicization of women in the suffragette movement, so too did women's role as consumers provide an opportunity for involvement in government in the First and Second World Wars which preceded a wider participation in state bureaucracy and citizenship.[76]

Nationhood, class and ethnicity have also been crucial to the history of the material culture of politics. McGovern has argued for the importance of the consumerist ethic to American national identity in the twentieth century, but the consuming communities created in the eighteenth century through distant markets have been argued by T.H. Breen to have played an important role in developing a revolutionary consciousness, and not merely through the commodity's ability to symbolize issues of taxation.[77] From the consumer's point of view, purchasing decisions could express a commitment to a nationalist agenda as they did in Dublin in the eighteenth century and yet the state might also use consumption as a form of propaganda, the activities of the British Empire Marketing Board in the late 1920s and early 1930s being just one instance of this.[78] In nineteenth-century France, the rational male defined his consumption as the more public-spirited 'collecting', making his purchasing of use to the state, while women's consumption of items of domestic beauty were said to represent the aesthetics of the nation.[79] Similarly, in Britain and America, masculine enjoyment of tobacco, wine and clothing was regarded as 'connoisseurship' in deliberate distinction to 'consumption'.[80] And in terms of racial politics, black American consumers boycotted

75. T. Billington Greig, *The Consumer in Revolt* (London: Stephen Swift, 1912).

76. Reagin, 'Comparing apples and oranges'; B. Davis, 'Food scarcity'; J. Hinton, "Militant housewives: the British Housewives' League and the Attlee government', *History Workshop Journal*, 38 (1994), pp. 129–56; I. Zweiniger-Bargielowska, 'Bread rationing in Britain, July 1946–July 1948', *Twentieth Century British History*, 4 (1993), pp. 57–85; J. Hinton, 'Voluntarism and the welfare/ warfare state: Women's Voluntary Services in the 1940s', *Twentieth Century British History*, 9 (1998), pp. 274–305; I. Zweiniger-Bargielowska, *Austerity in Britain: Rationing, Controls, and Consumption, 1939–1955* (Oxford: Oxford University Press, 2000).

77. McGovern, 'Consumption and citizenship'; T.H. Breen, 'An empire of goods: the Anglicisation of colonial America, 1690–1776', *Journal of British Studies*, 25 (1986), pp. 467–99; T.H. Breen, '"Baubles of Britain": the American and British consumer revolutions of the eighteenth century', *Past and Present*, 69 (1988), pp. 73–104.

78. S. Foster, 'Consumer nationalism in eighteenth-century Dublin', *History Today*, 47 (1997), pp. 45–51; S. Constantine, '"Bringing the Empire alive": the Empire Marketing Board and imperial propaganda, 1926–1933', in J.M. Mackenzie (ed.), *Imperialism and Popular Culture* (Manchester: Manchester University Press, 1986), pp. 192–231.

79. Auslander, 'The gendering of consumer practices in nineteenth-century France', in de Grazia and Furlough (eds), *The Sex of Things*, pp. 79–112; L. Auslander, *Taste and Power: Furnishing Modern France* (Berkeley: University of California Press, 1996).

80. M. Hilton, *Smoking in British Popular Culture, 1800–2000* (Manchester: Manchester University Press, 2000); C. Breward, *The Hidden Consumer: Masculinities, Fashion and City Life, 1860–1914* (Manchester: Manchester University Press, 1999).

discriminating white store owners ('Don't Shop Where You Can't Work') and often supported instead black-owned co-operatives.[81]

All three themes of class, gender and ethnicity are brought together by Margot Finn in Chapter Five, on the Scotch itinerant drapery trade. As well as providing an important reminder of the significant role played by less spectacular forms of distribution to the creation of the mass market, Finn also introduces the rulings and laws of the lower courts into her analysis of the politics of consumption. In the debates over the abolishment of county-court imprisonment for consumer debt, numerous images of the consumer were constructed. The English working-class wife was viewed as an innocent victim of the Scotch traders' seductive charms, whereas the drapers presented themselves as respectable, honest retailers who claimed the English labourer lacked the habits of thrift, frugality and self-denial which marked out the consumer in Scotland. Accordingly, the absence of a law in Scotland which could imprison husbands for their wives' debts had not led to a misuse of the credit laws, as the character of the Scottish working class precluded any uncontrolled temptation to purchase every new fashion. Such work builds on Rappaport's and Finn's own earlier studies of consumer law which demonstrated how local and specific manipulations of the law had important class and gender repercussions in the development of the material culture of politics.[82]

Conclusion

It is precisely these particular workings of the politics of consumption which continue today, creating new sites of action for the consumer and bringing further concepts and wider ideologies to the act of purchasing. Indeed, the four themes highlighted in this introduction – the morality of consumption, the contest for the consumer voice, the structure of the market, and the relationship between states, consumers and citizens – are as apparent today as they have ever been in the last two centuries. Certainly, dominant notions of consumerism and the consumer interest continue to inform the organization of the state and economy. A common critique in recent years has been to point to both the internalization of consumerist discourses within the institutions of the European and American state and the spread of Western commercialism to the global level. Well before Margaret Thatcher's

81. C. Greenberg, '"Don't Buy Where You Can't Work"', in Glickman (ed.), *Consumer Society in American History*, pp. 241–73; F. Kornbluh, 'To fulfil their "rightly needs": consumerism and the National Welfare Rights movement', *Radical History Review*, 69 (1997), pp. 76–113.

82. M. Finn, 'Working-class women and the contest for consumer control in Victorian county courts', *Past and Present*, 161 (1998), pp. 116–54; E. Rappaport, '"A husband and his wife's dresses": consumer credit and the debtor family in England, 1864–1914', in de Grazia and Furlough (eds), *The Sex of Things*, pp. 63–187.

cultural revolution of the 1980s, Raymond Williams complained that the term 'consumer' was extending into fields such as health, education and politics and that its meaning was allowed to be that which was formulated by 'manufacturers and their agents'.[83] Certainly, this would seem to be the case in Britain's National Health Service which has, ever since its inception, been keen to organize patients in bodies similar to consumer defence organizations.[84] But the rise of multinational corporations, whose price-fixing and market-sharing arrangements often exist beyond the confines and legislation of the single nation state, has also meant their models of the consumer have been transferred to countries previously outside the sphere of liberal economics and politics. The developing world is now experiencing the mass consumption of manufactured commodities and it will be interesting to gauge the extent to which consumers are created as political entities in these nations.[85]

However, the dominance of hegemonic discourses also gives rise to the creation of new sites of resistance and the spread of globalization also involves the expansion of consumers' information networks which can lead to the forging of new political alliances and agendas. While Miller has called for the articulation of a new general theory of consumer politics, it is more likely that the politics of consumption will continue to thrive through the local and the specific, whether that be a politics based on environmentalism, human, civil or animal rights, ethical concerns and a preference for the small-scale producer over globalized industry. To reiterate, material politics continues to be constituted by both the politics of material culture and the material culture of politics. Many of these recent issues fall within the ongoing history of the rights and duties attached to liberal citizenship. These rights and duties are forever changing. If in Mill, consumers were expected to add to national wealth; if in Ruskin, consumers were told to develop instead the 'art of life' not 'illth'; and if in co-operative thought, consumers were urged to band together for the collective, democratic commonwealth, then today our rights and duties have further developed our sense of self and our knowledge of the global economy. It is now something of a duty to explore personal identity through consumption, encouraging the formation of lifestyle politics based on gender,

83. R. Williams, *Keywords: a Vocabulary of Culture and Society* (London: Fontana, 1976), pp. 69–70, 'Consumer'.

84. C.J. Ham, 'Power, patients and pluralism', in K. Barnard and K. Lee (eds), *Conflicts in the National Health Service* (London: Croom Helm, 1977), pp. 99–120.

85. B. Orlove (ed.), *The Allure of the Foreign: Imported Goods in Postcolonial Latin America* (Ann Arbor: University of Michigan Press, 1997); T. Burke, *Lifebuoy Men, Lux Women: Commodification, Consumption, and Cleanliness in Modern Zimbabwe* (London: Leicester University Press, 1996). On globalization more generally, see D. Blake and R. Walters, *The Politics of Global Economic Relations*, 4th edn (London: Prentice-Hall International, 1992); R. Goldman, *Nike Culture: Sign of the Swoosh* (London: Sage, 1998); G. Ritzer, *The McDonaldization of Society* (London: Sage, 1995); G. Ritzer, *Enchanting a Disenchanted World* (London: Sage, 1999).

sexuality, ethnicity and the presentation of the healthy body more generally. Our consuming duties, although seemingly eclipsed by purely and narrowly defined rights-based protection legislation, are now extending beyond the nation state to incorporate the protection of the environment and the producers of the developing world. The context may have changed, the issues might now be different, and the commodities may have changed beyond all recognition, but Ruskin's comment from *Sesame and Lilies* appears to be as true today as when he wrote it in 1865: 'The consumers of the products of labour must exercise care in the pains they put on whom their comfort rests.'[86] And if it is true, as numerous cultural critics attest, that we define ourselves today not through the labour we engage in, but through the commodities we consume, then it is only to be expected that the politics of consumption will continue to act as the fulcrum around which citizenship is defined and as the site through which political action takes place.

86. Quoted in Thompson, *The Market and its Critics*, p. 164.

2

What is Rum? The Politics of Consumption in the French Revolution

Rebecca L. Spang

By anybody's estimation, subsistence commissioner Brunet did not have an easy job. Appointed in October 1793, Brunet and two colleagues were set the task of overseeing the supply of food and other necessities across revolutionary and wartime France. With their staff of five hundred, the commissioners were to do much more than monitor the harvest, encourage the cultivation of potatoes and answer petitions from local authorities.[1] Assigned the daunting task of 'generalizing circulation, accelerating production ... and re-establishing commerce in all its forms', they were also instructed to compile tables indicating the place of production of 'goods of prime necessity' and to determine the costs of those goods in 1790. They then were to calculate a standard transportation cost for each of those goods, such that their research could be used as the basis of a nationwide programme of wage and price controls (the General Maximum). All this they were to do within the next month, if possible.[2]

Given the slowness of communication and transportation in eighteenth-century France, and considering that such difficulties were exacerbated by conditions of war, civil war and popular unrest, it is really rather remarkable that the Subsistence Commission completed its tables by the following February. In presenting them to the National Convention, Brunet hinted at the 'labyrinthine' nature of the task just completed and made it evident that the members of the Commission remained anxious about the path they had found through the maze. 'Some enlightened men may be angry', conceded Brunet, 'to find that our dictionary of natural and industrial products does not follow the system of scientific classification created for those who are accustomed to scholarship.'[3] The taxonomy of Linnaeus or even

---

1. P. Caron (ed.), *La Commission des subsistances de l'An II: Procès-verbaux et actes* (Paris: Documents inédits sur l'histoire économique de al Révolution française, 1925); J.-P. Gross, *Fair Shares for All* (Cambridge: Cambridge University Press, 1997), pp. 78–83.

2. *Archives parlementaires de 1787 à 1860. Recueil complet des débats législatifs et politiques des chambres françaises* (Paris: 1862–), 78:144 (hereafter, *A.p.*)

3. *Ibid.*, 85:310; compare the comments made by Coupé in introducing the General Maximum, 75:14–15.

the alphabetical order of the *Encyclopédie* – neither had won the Commission's approval, because 'a law made for all should be written for all'. Therefore, the tables of the Maximum 'follow not the order found in collections of precious curiosities, but that of the shops where citizens buy those things indispensable for man's principal needs'.[4] (Hence 'tobacco' was a subheading of 'drugs and groceries' and two dozen sorts of paper were included in the category 'clothing'.[5])

The detailed tabulations of the General Maximum remind us that, for ordinary people, consumption – be it of political pamphlets or Equality Bread or tricolour bonbons – was one of the most important ways in which the Revolution was lived.[6] Indeed, in the arguments of some legislators, it was economic policy as it affected consumers that actually defined the Revolution and served as an index of how far they had succeeded in shaping a new regime. Pierre Samuel Dupont de Nemours, a noted economic theorist, asserted that it was 'respect for the Rights of Man' that prompted his fellow members of the Constituent Assembly to abolish the Old Regime's taxes on consumer goods; nearly two years later, representative of the people Jacques Antoine Creuzé-Latouche hailed the 'progress of the human spirit' to which revolutionary France had been witness, but bemoaned attitudes toward the grain trade that, he said, 'seem to take us back in time two centuries'.[7]

Throughout the revolutionary decade, consumption was a crucial concern in a vast array of contexts.[8] The *cahiers de doléances*, the famous grievance lists compiled by electoral assemblies in advance of the meeting of the Estates-General in May 1789, detailed consumers' complaints about meat prices, salt taxes and adulterated wines. Every year, municipal authorities and national legislative bodies repeatedly confronted the problem of keeping markets provided with sufficient wheat and the population supplied with suitable bread. During 1793–1794, the imposition of a ceiling on both prices and wages involved the revolutionary state

4. *A.p.*, 85:310.

5. *Ibid.*, 86:78.

6. The expanded volume of this decade's *petites affiches,* or classified advertisements, may be an indication of this. On those of the Old Regime, see C. Jones, 'The great chain of buying: medical advertisement, the bourgeois public sphere and the origins of the French Revolution', *American Historical Review*, 101 (1996), pp. 13–40. On the vagaries of the market for printed works, see C. Hesse, *Publishing and Cultural Politics in Revolutionary Paris, 1789–1810* (Berkeley: University of California Press, 1991); for an advertisement of 'national' candies, see *Affiches, annonces, avis divers*, 1 January 1790, p. 6; on Equality Bread, see Gross, *Fair Shares*, pp. 88–91.

7. *A.p.*, 24:446, 54:682. For an illuminating discussion of how a certain understanding of economic life came to be considered more modern than others, see G. Faccarello, 'L'Evolution de l'économie politique pendant la Révolution: Alexandre Vandermonde ou la croisée des chemins', in *Französische Revolution und Politische Ökonomie* (Trier: Karl Marx Haus, 1989), pp. 75–121.

8. Many of this paragraph's points are explored further below. See also Gross, *Fair Shares*; J.A. Miller, *Mastering the Market* (Cambridge: Cambridge University Press, 1999); R.L. Spang, *The Invention of the Restaurant: Paris and Modern Gastronomic Culture* (Cambridge, Mass.: Harvard University Press, 2000), chs 4–6.

in an ambitiously comprehensive effort at economic regulation that affected producers and consumers alike. The rejection of such policies by governments after Thermidor was one of many factors that contributed to the runaway inflation of 1795 and the truly bitter satires of 'Fat and Lean' that remained such a fixture in French social and political commentary throughout the first half of the nineteenth century.

The theme of consumption has been most familiar to historians of the Revolution as part of this visceral struggle between the 'haves' and the 'have-nots'. Since Dickens's *A Tale of Two Cities,* the desperate misery of France's haggard millions has gripped readers' imaginations and inspired a host of empirical studies. Popular agitation over the cost of bread and a few other items (most notably, wine) has been extensively scrutinized for indications of the socio-economic motives for political mobilization; one recent article has authoritatively asserted that 'from autumn 1791 through spring 1793, France was nothing but one enormous food riot'.[9] Yet for all the enduring popularity of this interpretation, the trend in the past two decades of so-called 'Revisionist' scholarship has been to emphasize the overwhelmingly discursive nature of Revolutionary politics.[10] From that perspective, an emphasis on the material aspects of political life may seem simplistic, a naive attempt to reduce complex cultural formations to the status of mere epiphenomena. In this new orthodoxy, it is the Revolution's role in the shaping of *modern* political culture that is emphasized – and food riots are rarely (rightly or wrongly) identified as especially modern developments.

Approaching the politics of consumption from a somewhat different perspective, this chapter considers how consumption was understood, measured and debated within national political bodies and how pressure was brought to bear on these bodies by those whom they were intended to represent. In other words, this chapter focuses on consumption in order to begin to work through the apparently irreconcilable opposition between the 'political culture' and the 'social conflict' interpretations of the Revolution. This question has been partially addressed by William Sewell, who argues persuasively that the sans-culotte obsession with subsistence was as much a tool of effective polemic as it was an echo of grumbling bellies. In his 'The Sans-Culotte Rhetoric of Subsistence' (1994), Sewell makes

9. For classic examples, see A. Soboul, *The Parisian Sans-Culottes and the French Revolution, 1793–1794,* trans. G. Lewis (Oxford: Clarendon, 1964); G. Rudé, *The Crowd in the French Revolution* (Oxford: Oxford University Press, 1959); R.B. Rose, 'Tax revolt and popular organization in Picardy, 1789–1791', *Past and Present,* 43 (1969), pp. 92–108. More recently, see C. Bouton, 'Les Mouvements de subsistance et le problème de l'économie morale sous l'ancien régime et la révolution française', *Annales historiques de la Révolution française,* (2000), pp. 71–100, quote from pp. 89–90.

10. F. Furet, *Interpreting the French Revolution,* trans. E. Forster (Cambridge: Cambridge University Press, 1981); K.M. Baker, *Inventing the French Revolution* (Cambridge: Cambridge University Press, 1990); K.M. Baker, *The French Revolution and the Creation of Modern Political Culture,* 4 vols (Oxford: Pergamon, 1987–1994).

the case for a 'publicly available and widely employed rhetorical system' deployed within various domains by political actors from no single 'social condition, class, or group'. Section militants, radical journalists and crowd-pleasing Jacobins could all vilify the Revolution's opponents for trying to starve the Republic out of existence.[11] Elsewhere, Colin Jones and I have suggested that the era's heated political debates over subsistence should also be seen in the broader context of the drastic eighteenth-century expansion of available consumer goods. Sugar and coffee, we noted, may both have been exotic novelties in 1690 but, by 1790, they had become daily necessities – at least for some people.[12] People, even French people, do not live by bread alone: the crowds who in the winters of 1792 and 1793 looted grocers' shops, demanding sugar and coffee, may well have felt that their survival was at stake.

Recent studies of the eighteenth-century 'consumer revolution' have focused largely on Great Britain, long considered the birthplace of modern industrial society.[13] This chapter's concentration on France brings the study of consumption into dialogue with debates over the emergence of modern political culture and the construction of national identities in the era of the Great Revolution.[14] There is more at stake here than simply a shift of national contexts. Much of the recent scholarship on consumption has endeavoured to trace the development of modern 'consumer society' and has seen its origins in the commercial expansion of the mid- to late seventeenth century. Historians have hence been more interested in buttons, baubles and the Dutch tulip mania than in food or drink. For the latter categories are, of course, also at the heart of the pre-modern period's so-called moral economy, which analysts often posit as modern economic life's exact opposite. Modern consumption has been characterized as a move away from the

11. W.H. Sewell, Jr.,'The sans-culotte rhetoric of subsistence', in K. Baker (ed.), *The Terror,* vol. 4 of *The French Revolution and the Creation of Modern Political Culture* (Oxford: Pergamon, 1994), pp. 249–70, quote from p. 253.

12. C. Jones and R. Spang, 'Sans-culottes, *sans café, sans tabac*: shifting realms of necessity and luxury in eighteenth-century France,' in M. Berg and H. Clifford (eds), *Consumers and Luxury: Consumer Culture in Europe, 1650–1850* (Manchester: Manchester University Press, 1999), pp. 37–62.

13. Since N. McKendrick, J. Brewer and J.H. Plumb, *The Birth of Consumer Society: The Commercialization of Eighteenth-Century England* (Bloomington: Indiana University Press, 1982), this field has developed dramatically and the literature is now quite extensive. For good introductions see J. Brewer and R. Porter (eds), *Consumption and the World of Goods* (London: Routledge, 1993), and Berg and Clifford, *Consumers and Luxury.* For a thoughtful review of the literature on consumption and a critique of its Occidentalist tendencies, see C. Clunas, 'Modernity global and local: consumption and the rise of the West', *American Historical Review,* 104 (1999), pp. 1497–511.

14. For other studies of consumption in the French context, see D. Roche, *A History of Everyday Things: The Birth of Consumption in France,* trans. B. Pearce (Cambridge: Cambridge University Press, 2000); A. Pardailhé-Galabrun, *La Naissance de l'intime* (Paris: Presses Universitaires de France, 1988); L. Auslander, *Taste and Power: Furnishing Modern France* (Berkeley: University of California Press, 1996).

subsistence economies of earlier centuries and as an extraordinary growth in the world of goods. Today, consumption 'in general' and consumption in a literal sense do not often sit well within a single historiographical or analytic framework. As Sidney Mintz has written, 'food is bothersome to theorists of consumption'.[15] But the most comprehensive consumption law of the French Revolution – the General Maximum that regulated wages and prices from September 1793 through December 1794 – covered linens, candles and leathers as well as salt cod, wine and butcher's meat.[16] Consideration of the culture and politics of consumption during the French Revolution may help us to understand the relationship between the literal and figurative senses of the word.

In September 1793, as civil war raged within France and as foreign armies threatened the year-old Republic, militants from the Paris 'section' (local administrative district) of 'Théâtre Français, dite de Marseille et de Marat' charged Pierre François Joseph Robert, a member of the National Convention and one-time editor of the *Mercure national*, with hoarding 'a good of prime necessity'. This was a serious business, for the Convention had several months earlier made the hoarding of necessities a crime punishable by death.[17] But it was also a complicated matter, for it was eight barrels of rum that the local commissioner had found in Robert's cellar and rum did not appear on anyone's list of necessities.[18]

Robert responded by saying that the section's charges against him were trumped up, an effort by the remnants of one political faction (the Girondins, who had been purged from the Convention in May) to discredit the most stalwart of its opponents (the Montagnards). But even if Robert was correct and the local militants were simply looking for some petard on which to hoist him, it is worth reflecting on the one they found. They denounced him neither as a heretic nor as a Jew; they did not dream of calling him a witch. These would have been potent accusations in early modern France, but they had all become 'imaginary crimes' under the Constitution of 1791. Nor did the section stain Robert's public reputation by labelling him an alcoholic or an adulterer, a wife-beater or a manic-depressive. Today, these are all effective ways of discrediting political enemies, but they were largely meaningless in autumn 1793. We might also note that the sans-culottes of the Left Bank did not directly denounce Robert as a royalist or a traitor. This is

---

15. S.W. Mintz, 'The changing roles of food in the study of consumption', in Brewer and Porter (eds), *Consumption and the World of Goods.*

16. *A.p.,* 75:321–3.

17. By the law of 26 July 1793.

18. I base the following discussion largely on documents published in *A.p.,* 75:258–9; 76:215–21, 237–9, 259–62; 77:369, 378. See also H. Calvet, *L'Accaparement à Paris sous la Terreur* (Paris: Commission de recherche et de publication des documents relatifs à la vie economique de la Revolution, 1933), pp. 164–8; A. Mathiez, *La Vie chère et le mouvement social sous la Terreur* (Paris: Armand Colin, 1927), pp. 512–20.

curious, for while the former charge would have been unlikely to stick to a man who had called for a republic eighteen months before the monarchy was abolished, the latter charge had been (and would be) used successfully against men with Revolutionary credentials at least as solid as Robert's. What is important here is that the section members made the charge material, physical: not a matter of the ideas he had in his head or the beliefs he cherished in his heart but the bushels, baskets and barrels he held in his basement.

No legislation had, however, pronounced rum to be a 'good of prime necessity'. Robert therefore quickly took the matter outside the jurisdiction of his local section, appealing to the municipal government of Paris to lift the seals slapped on his rum by the section's zealous Commissioner for Hoarding, Frédéric-Pierre Ducroquet. The city police administrators, when summoned, hedged their bets, asserting that if the liquor in the barrels was rum then it certainly was 'a caprice' (rather than a necessity) but that, for all they knew, it might not be rum in the barrels at all. They recommended that experts be summoned 'in order to determine if the liquor really is rum as declared'. Six days later, Ducroquet returned to Robert's cellar accompanied by two members of his section's Committee of Public Safety. Tasting a sample from each barrel, they declared the contents to be rum and hastened to report their findings to the full section. The section meeting, in turn, effectively ignored the question of the barrels' contents by concluding that no individual should have so much of any liquor and dispatching Ducroquet and two other colleagues to replace the seals that very evening. Then, things became somewhat chaotic. Robert's wife, the noted author Louise de Kéralio, brandished letters from the committee that had composed the original law on hoarding; his child's nurse fainted and his cook may have had an epileptic fit.

To hear Robert tell the story to the Convention, he had been the victim of a political smear campaign that had eventually brought a crowd of several thousand troublemakers to invade his house and steal his rum (all under the pretence of making a necessary good available to the people of Paris). As a patriot, he knew the law by heart and knew that rum was not a regulated substance. He hence begged the Convention to reject the petition presented by the section and to act swiftly to guarantee public order across Paris. In their denunciation, however, the section members said that Robert was sitting on a supply of high quality 'sugar brandy' (sugar and brandy both being catalogued as necessities).[19] The powerful Committee of General Security, to which the Convention initially referred the case, discussed it for hours, only to conclude that it was beyond its members to answer the fateful question: 'what is rum?' When the matter returned for discussion to the entire Convention, it occasioned heated debate but little clear policy. Was 'rum' just a foreign word for 'eau-de-vie', as Gilbert Romme asserted (they were both made,

19. *A.p.,* 76:216.

he said knowledgeably, from sweet products) or was it, as Jean Henri Voulland claimed, 'a luxury liqueur . . . made at great expense and never drunk by sans-culottes'? One representative of the people said he knew nothing about rum; another said the word was vague but the alcohol should not be stockpiled. Tempers frayed, dramatic poses were struck, and the ground shifted from attempting to define 'rum' to interrogating the word 'hoarding'. Did collections of all sorts (say of books, paintings or scientific instruments) constitute hoarding?

The narrative of Robert's rum has so far been given at some length, in order to convey the complexities of revolutionary efforts to police consumption. At stake, clearly, were several interrelated questions: What was rum? Who had the right to answer this question? On what basis could this question be answered? Rum was, perhaps, an especially problematic substance for it was neither produced in France nor routinely consumed there.[20] The Old Regime, in attempting to protect French brandy producers, had prohibited the import of rum in 1689; in 1752, this law had been slightly relaxed in order to permit Caribbean rum to pass through the port of Bordeaux on its way to West Africa as part of the slave trade. Rum was not exclusively a product of the British Empire – in 1770, the French colony of Saint Domingue exported 900,000 gallons (as much rum as Jamaica) – but it was almost certainly a comparative rarity in France.[21] What was a national law, intended to be applied on a national basis and to ensure that no region had more resources than another did, to do with imported goods?

The question of imports was particularly charged when it focused on the products of the French Empire (the *denrées coloniales* that occasioned protests during the winters of 1792 and 1793). Far from being foreign, these products had been integral to the wealth of Bordeaux and Nantes in the eighteenth century.[22] Yet they were not grown in Europe and it was possible for proponents of the Rousseauean virtue of self-sufficiency to overlook their role in the French economy. In the National Convention's brief July 1793 discussion of the status of sugar, Joseph G.F. Le Bon opined that it could not be a necessity for French people because it 'was not harvested in France'.[23] Like many of his contemporaries, Le Bon sought a perfect balance between the production and consumption of goods. His was a closed system, into which 'new needs' could not penetrate.

---

20. The entry for 'rhum' in Diderot and D'Alembert's *Encyclopédie* explains a way of harnessing horses to pull canal barges and has nothing whatsoever to do with distilling; the word 'rhum' does not appear in the dictionary of the Académie Française until 1835.

21. J. McCusker, *Rum and the American Revolution* (New York and London: Garland, 1989), vol. 1, pp. 320–2.

22. R.L. Stein, *The French Sugar Business in the Eighteenth Century* (Baton Rouge: Louisiana State University Press, 1988).

23. *A.p.*, 69:594. This was not the first time that members of the national political assemblies had discussed sugar; see also *A.p.*, 37:552, 612–7.

Distilled in the debate over rum's status were many of the fundamental difficulties faced by those charged with enforcing the Revolution's most draconian consumption laws. In a famous speech in early December 1792, Robespierre argued that past governments had tried to control the trade in luxury but it was a republic's task to legislate concerning necessity.[24] The affair of Robert's rum occurred almost simultaneously with the Convention's most ambitious effort to do just that, in the form of the Law of the General Maximum. An earlier law had ordered each department to set its own ceiling on grain prices, but the law passed on 29 September 1793 required administrative districts to set uppermost prices for a far greater variety of consumer goods. Although the French term for 'goods' (*denrées*) is derived from the same root as the word for 'teeth' (*dents*), the General Maximum's list of 'goods of prime necessity' included boots, copper, woollens and any number of other objects unlikely to be literally chewed or devoured. Like the Law on Hoarding under which Robert was denounced, the language of the General Maximum asserted that certain goods were fundamental to human existence and that the trade in these had to be regulated, lest some unscrupulous scoundrel accumulate more necessities than he actually needed. Straightforward in appearance, neither of these two laws proved simple in practice.[25]

Rabelaisian verbosity flies in the face of the genre conventions governing 'necessity'; it is hardly surprising, therefore, that the Maximum and the Law on Hoarding were both concise in their initial enumeration. The laws' brevity posed immediate difficulties, however (which the tables compiled by the Subsistence Commission were intended, in part, to resolve). For if the barrels in Robert's cellar were a particularly vexed case, they were hardly the only occasion on which the Convention or one of its committees was required to determine whether a given item or product was a 'good of prime necessity'. Wallpaper manufacturers petitioned to be exempted from the ban on exporting paper; citizen Maille (of mustard fame) pleaded that his scented and flavoured vinegars were 'of no use to the army'; the vermicelli-makers of Paris asked for a special shipment of white flour, so they could prepare their pastas for the ill and infirm.[26]

A seemingly simple binary distinction – that of necessity from luxury – structured these petitions and the responses to them. The Convention's efforts to regulate consumption resulted in a formulation that is initially clear: French men and women

---

24. *Ibid.*, 54:46.

25. On the difficulties of enforcing the General Maximum, see: Mathiez, *Vie chère*; R. Cobb, *The People's Armies*, trans. M. Elliott (New Haven: Yale University Press, 1987); M. Darrow, 'Economic terror in the city: the General Maximum in Montauban', *French Historical Studies,* 17 (1991), pp. 498–525.

26. *A.p.,* 72:536, 75:171; F. Gerbaux and C. Schmidt (eds), *Procès-verbaux des comités d'agriculture et de commerce* (Paris: Imprimerie Nationale, 1906–1910), vol. 4, pp. 196, 219, 232, 249.

were legally allowed to acquire luxury items in whatever quantities they desired but were required to keep their purchase of necessities within certain limits. If rum had been a necessity, then no individual should have had so much as Robert did. If it was a luxury, then stockpiling it was legally allowed (albeit morally suspect). But what sort of luxury is it than can be accumulated in great quantities? A qualitative, rather than quantitative, model for separating necessities from luxuries underpinned this logic. The Law on Hoarding rested on the assumption that certain goods – such as embroidered silks or fruit-flavoured vinegars – were intrinsically luxuries. Luxuriousness was a property inherent to goods themselves and not a side effect of their cost. In other words, the designation was a comment on use-value (luxuries were things for which the Republic had little use) and not related to exchange-value.

The necessity/luxury dichotomy was not a creation of the French Revolution. Commentaries on the danger of luxury date back to Antiquity and had been revived with particular insistence by cultural commentators throughout the eighteenth century. For Enlightenment writers, understanding what was necessary was part of the project of accepting natural laws; the critique of luxury so common in this period was the reverse side of this, and meant that luxury was not only unnecessary but also unnatural.[27] In this way, the necessary, in many accounts, became synonymous with the sufficient while luxury constituted a dangerous surplus. The excessiveness of luxury was a moral issue but, as the *cahiers de doléances* of winter 1789 remind us, it was a fiscal and political question as well.[28] Confronted with the evidence of state bankruptcy, nobles in Angoulême, clergymen in Champagne and commoners in Besançon were all fast to blame 'luxury' and propose its taxation as a remedy for the nation's ills.[29]

Sarah Maza has argued that the Old-Regime condemnation of luxury allowed commentators to bemoan the blurring of social distinctions and the increasing pace of cultural change while maintaining an effectively universalist understanding of France as an integrated whole, marked by organic unity rather than class division.[30] If this is true, then both the stridency of the critique and the difficulty of turning it into policy are understandable. As a matter of principle, taxing 'luxury' was acceptable to nearly everyone but there could be no clear agreement as to what belonged in the category. Precisely because the criticism of luxury responded to broad-based social, economic and cultural change, it could not be given a stable

---

27. C. Berry, *The Idea of Luxury* (Cambridge: Cambridge University Press, 1994); J. Ehrard, *L'Idée de Nature en France* (Paris: S.E.V.P.E.N., 1963), vol. 2, pp. 657–736.

28. J.-P. Gross, 'Progressive taxation and social justice in eighteenth-century France', *Past and Present*, 140 (1993), pp. 79–126.

29. *A.p.*, 2:5, 341; 6:292; for other examples, see *A.p.*, 2:279, 321; 6:16, 27–8, 73, 283, 299.

30. S. Maza, 'Luxury, morality, and social change: why there was no middle-class consciousness in pre-revolutionary France', *Journal of Modern History*, 69 (1997), pp. 200–29.

material form. The *cahiers,* for example, identified a bewildering variety of luxuries (some more easily taxed than others), ranging from 'packs of hounds and superfluous lackeys' to 'coffee, hair powder, and other things of this sort' and 'dangerous superfluities and hazardous excesses'.[31]

Historians have most often treated the Maximum and the Law on Hoarding as integral elements of an 'economic Terror' conceded by the Convention in order to appease the populace.[32] In such accounts, these laws represent a brief-lived and unstable alliance of 'bourgeois' Jacobins with ordinary working people (especially Paris section militants). The moralizing condemnation of 'luxury', common in the rhetorical flourishes by which these laws were accompanied, seems to support this analysis and to demonstrate that the Maximum's attack on 'excess' and the tribunals' hounding of 'aristocrats' were but two components in a single plan for national austerity and regeneration.[33] But when we reintegrate Montagnard economic policy with the Enlightenment analysis of necessity and luxury, a more nuanced picture emerges. As long as the laws on consumption are viewed as the Convention's response to pressure from the streets, the Maximum represents a drastic change of direction in Jacobin economic policy, which, according to most historians, had been resolutely liberal until late spring 1793.[34] This is, however, a questionable conclusion to draw. Undoubtedly, if one looks at Revolutionary economic debates in terms of schools of thought that became polarized in the nineteenth and twentieth centuries (laissez-faire *or* state intervention, liberal bourgeois capitalism *or* social welfare state), then the Maximum constitutes a rejection of the previous year's endorsement of free trade.[35] But if one considers

31. *A.p.*, 2:336, 279; M. Boiloiseau, *Cahiers de doléances du Tiers Etat du bailliage de Rouen* (Rouen: Imprimerie Administrative de al Seine Maritime, 1960), vol. 2, p. 174.

32. It is therefore partially hailed by the Marxist Mathiez and utterly mocked by the neoconservative F. Aftalion, *The French Revolution: An Economic Interpretation*, trans. M. Thom (Cambridge: Cambridge University Press, 1987). Gross, *Fair Shares,* argues for distinguishing the Terror that used economic policy to political ends (Fouché's Equality Bread) from Jacobin economic policies that were not 'terroristic' (Romme's Equality Bread). In other words, not all Equality Bread is equal. See too, J.A. Miller, 'Politics and urban provisioning crises: bakers, police, and Parlements in France, 1750–1793', *Journal of Modern History*, 64 (1992), pp. 227–62.

33. It is important to note, however, that the consumption policies of the so-called 'economic Terror' led to barely a handful of executions, while the various forms of political Terror resulted in the loss of 20,000 lives. Even in the trouble-ridden department of Paris, violation of the Law on Hoarding resulted in only eleven indictments, or 0.5 per cent of the total; D. Greer, *The Incidence of the Terror during the French Revolution* (Cambridge, Mass.: Harvard University Press, 1935), pp. 17–18, 148–52.

34. F. Furet, 'Maximum', in Furet and M. Ozouf (eds), *Dictionnaire critique de la Révolution française* (Paris: Flammarion, 1988), pp. 596–602; F. Hincker, 'Y eut-il une pensée économique de la Montagne?' in G. Faccarello and P. Steiner (eds), *La Pensée économique pendant la Révolution française* (Grenoble: Presses Universitaires de Grenoble, 1990), pp. 211–24.

35. In December 1792, the Convention ordered an address to the people detailing the benefits of *libre circulation, A.p.*, 54:704–6. Miller notes quite rightly that 'free circulation' is not necessarily synonymous with 'free trade,' see her 'Politics and urban provisioning crises', p. 231.

that these nineteenth- and twentieth-century polarities may not have been so stark in eighteenth-century heads, then this notorious volte-face becomes much less obvious.

The Convention's policies on hoarding and prices need to be re-positioned within the context of the imperative 'right to subsistence' that had been a feature of economic and fiscal debates from the earliest days of the National Assembly.[36] Anxiety about subsistence may have fitted very well within the paranoid language of denunciation that was so central to the political Terror, but it did other things as well. Articulating political demands in terms of consumption meant insisting that equality be made material, physical and substantive. (In this, it is quite dramatically unlike the now standard account of the Terror and Jacobinism as driven by abstractions such as virtue and the General Will.) It cannot be doubted that petitions and denunciations made use of Sewell's violent 'sans-culotte rhetoric of subsistence'. They execrated blood drinkers, vampires and greedy speculators; they accused the Revolution's enemies of dumping grain, poisoning wine and slaughtering pregnant cows. Nor can it be doubted that this language was spoken within the Convention as well.[37] Members of the Subsistence Commission or of the Convention's Committee on Agriculture, Commerce and Industry were immersed in this sea of gory images (imported wholesale from the famine plot persuasion of the moral economy), but many were also familiar with models and metaphors from eighteenth-century political economy.[38]

The Montagnard Convention's decrees on hoarding and pricing partook of the Manichaean 'rhetoric of subsistence' that saw treachery behind every price hike and aristocrats at the bottom of every poisoned chalice, but the implementation of these laws hinged on developing strategies for measuring national levels of production and consumption. This is perhaps counter-intuitive, for on first consideration it seems evident that the General Maximum was a product of sans-culottisme and an effort on the part of the Convention to impose a 'moral economy' on a national basis. Like the early-modern moral economy, the Maximum established 'fair' prices and attacked individuals who dared to profit 'unfairly'. Like most instances of popular price-setting, the Maximum was a response to social uncertainty and cultural unrest rather than a product of absolutely dire want. The Law of 29 September 1793 left responsibility for setting prices with the local administrative districts (all 600 of them) and hence, like Old-Regime *taxation populaire*, worked within a community framework.

36. L. DiCaprio, 'Women workers, state-sponsored work, and the right to subsistence during the French Revolution', *Journal of Modern History*, 71 (1999), pp. 519–51.

37. See for instance Thuriot's speech of 3 September 1793 (*A.p.*, 73:358–9) and the accusations made in winter 1794 by the Commune of Paris (*ibid.*, 86:91).

38. E.P. Thompson, 'The moral economy of the English crowd in the eighteenth century', originally published in *Past and Present*, 50 (1971) and reprinted in his *Customs in Common* (London: Merlin, 1991); S. Kaplan, *The Famine Plot Persuasion* (Philadelphia: American Philosophical Society, 1982).

The analogy of the Maximum with the moral economy cannot be taken too far, however, for the mechanism by which it operated was radically different. When crowds in Lyon in 1789 overturned customs barriers and tax booths, they sold the wine confiscated at a traditional fair price: 'Third Estate wine, four *sols* the bottle', they proclaimed.[39] The Maximum, in contrast, set uppermost prices on the basis of a uniform calculation for all goods concerned: one-third was to be added to what the price had been in 1790, regardless of how much prices had varied since then.[40] Moreover, the charts of the Maximum were to be printed and publicly displayed, so that the fair price was not so much traditional or intuitive as it was visible and quantifiable. When Bertrand Barère, so-called 'spokesman' of the Committee of Public Safety, introduced the revised Maximum and the Subsistence Commission's accompanying charts, he directed the Jacobins' Rousseauean language of transparency into all nooks and crannies of daily expenditure. The Maximum, said Barère, was a *réverbère* (one of the Revolution's famous street lamps from which traitors had been hanged). But he also spoke of it as collecting diffuse knowledge (*lumières éparses*) and conveying it to all citizens; the eight columns of details provided by the Maximum were, he said, humanity's 'vitality tables'.[41]

The economic policy of this era was a last-ditch effort to make the distinction of necessity from luxury something intelligible, tangible and material. Using a language of subsistence to describe an economy of superfluities, the members of the Subsistence Commission faced an unimaginably daunting task. For throughout the Revolution, cultural policies and political upheaval created a host of new needs (of which the blue-white-red cockade required by law is only one obvious example). Reading these debates, it is evident how expansive the definition of 'necessity' had become (in the General Maximum, for instance, it covered several kinds of butter, many types of dry fish, and a remarkable variety of textiles) and how nebulous was that of 'luxury'. Efforts to stabilize or universalize the definitions cost revolutionary political bodies countless hours of committee work but yielded little in terms of either general rulings or easily applied laws.[42]

In the early months of the Revolution, new norms of fashionable simplicity had rendered some sorts of luxury easily identified. During the heady months of summer and autumn 1789, people eagerly volunteered to sacrifice their own bit of excess

39. Archives Municipales de Lyon (413), cited by G. Bossenga, 'City and state: an urban perspective on the French Revolution', in K.M. Baker (ed.), *The Political Culture of the Old Regime*, vol. 1 of *The French Revolution and the Creation of Modern Political Culture* (Oxford: Pergamon, 1987), pp. 115–40.

40. *A.p.*, 75:15.

41. *A.p.*, 85:311–16.

42. Crane Brinton long ago commented on the practical difficulties this posed for the General Maximum: see his *A Decade of Revolution* (1934; New York: Harper and Row, 1963), pp. 135–6.

for the good of the nation. In the most famous instance, members of the National Assembly hastened to give up the privileges of the First and Second Estates; ordinary French men and women participated in a more literal fashion by donating ornate jewellery and silver tableware to the Nation's coffers.[43] Transferred from private ownership to the state, such goods lost their luxury status and transmuted into the precious metals perceived to be necessary for restoring fiscal equilibrium. This was feasible, even mildly enjoyable, in the beginning, for people could rely on the conventions of Rousseauean sensibility (simplicity of dress, naturalness of diet, impetuosity of emotion) to help them recognize the 'surplus' that they both did not need and did not want. Even before the Revolution had begun, Marie Antoinette had traded her ornate court robes for more austere (if no less expensive) dresses inspired by pastoral fantasies about the life of shepherdesses; now other women were content to trade their gold and emeralds for a polished fragment of the Bastille.[44]

As the needs of the Nation became more pressing, however, it made more weighty demands. Successive revolutionary governments had to determine what sacrifices individuals could be expected to make for the greater good. Some individuals sacrificed everything and provided the Revolution with its own cult of martyrs, but even the usually less melodramatic topic of taxation required posing a comparable question: how much would people be willing to pay before they protested that they were being deprived of necessities?

Several recent works have examined the place of direct taxation in eighteenth-century political controversy. Opposition was especially strong among the privileged groups who were historically exempted from paying the older direct taxes (such as the *taille*) but were nonetheless obliged to pay the newer inventions such as the *capitation* and *vingtième*. By the time that the *cahiers de doléances* were drafted in early 1789, 'no taxation without representation' had become a rallying cry of considerable effectiveness.[45] But direct taxation actually represented

43. *A.p.*, 8:588–92, 9:99; V. Cameron, 'Approaches to narrative and history: the case of the Donation of September 7, 1789 and its images,' in L.E. Brown and P. Craddock (eds), *Studies in Eighteenth-Century Culture* (East Lansing, Michigan: Colleagues Press for American Society for Eighteenth-Century Studies, 1989), pp. 413–32. The literature on the abolition of 'privilege' is vast, but for a good account of the personal choices involved in the Night of August Fourth, see T. Tackett, *Becoming a Revolutionary* (Princeton: Princeton University Press, 1996).

44. For the description of a brooch made from a small bit of the Bastille, see H.M. Williams, *Letters Written in France in the summer 1790 to a Friend in England*, 5th edn (London: T. Cadell, 1796), p. 36. See also J. Jones, 'Repackaging Rousseau: femininity and fashion in old regime France', *French Historical Studies*, 18 (1994), pp. 939–67, and R. Spang, 'Rousseau in the restaurant', *Common Knowledge*, 5 (1996), pp. 92–108.

45. M. Kwass, 'A kingdom of taxpayers: state formation, privilege and political culture in eighteenth-century France', *Journal of Modern History*, 70 (1998), pp. 295–339; see also, P. Hoffman and K. Norberg (eds), *Fiscal Crises, Liberty, and Representative Government, 1450–1789* (Stanford: Stanford University Press, 1994).

a smaller proportion of state revenue in 1788 than it had in 1700. At the end of the Old Regime, the bulk of the tax burden consisted of indirect taxation on goods and services.[46]

The full complexities of Old-Regime taxation can hardly be addressed here, but it is important to recall certain key features. Throughout the eighteenth century, the monarchy's efforts to increase the scale of direct taxation had been partially rebuffed by powerful political actors such as the Parlements, the Church and the nobility. Nonetheless, state expenditure grew considerably, and it was therefore the burden of indirect taxation that increased most dramatically and unevenly. Excises on goods such as wine, tobacco and hides were most easily and efficiently collected at city gates, and hence fell somewhat less heavily on those who lived in the countryside. Most municipalities added their own taxes as well, but the peasants were as convinced as the town dwellers 'that they had never been so heavily taxed'.[47]

Inequality in taxation was exacerbated by tremendous regional differences, the result of treaties and charters granted when various provinces became part of France. So, for example, salt was untaxed in Brittany and in Lille, but in most of the remainder of northern France it was heavily taxed and its sale was a state monopoly. A pound of salt in the province of Anjou (where it was taxed at 866 per cent) sold for nineteen times more than a pound of salt in neighboring Brittany.[48] Moreover, so crucial was the salt tax to state finances (accounting as it did for 40 per cent of all indirect taxes), that individuals living in those areas where it was levied were *required by law* to purchase a certain quantity of salt every year.[49]

It is hardly surprising that the salt tax (*gabelle*) was decried in 59 per cent of both the Noble and the Third-Estate *cahiers de doléances*.[50] While some *cahiers*

46. For concise overviews, see G. Bossenga, 'Impôt', in Furet and Ozouf (eds), *Dictionnaire* pp. 586–95, and R. Mousnier, *Les Institutions de la France sous la monarchie absolue* (Paris: Presses Universitaires de France, 1980), vol. 2, pp. 413–52. For a more detailed account of the most important indirect taxes, see G.T. Matthews, *The Royal General Farms in Eighteenth-Century France* (New York: Columbia University Press, 1958).

47. P.M. Jones, *The Peasantry in the French Revolution* (Cambridge: Cambridge University Press, 1988), pp. 34–42.

48. J.C. Hocquet, 'L'Impôt du sel et l'etat', in Hocquet (ed.), *Le Roi, le marchand, et le sel* (Lille: Presses Universitaires de Lille, 1987), pp. 27–49, see also his *Le Sel et le pouvoir, de l'an Mil à la Révolution française* (Paris: A. Michel, 1985).

49. In some areas, this was calculated on an individual basis (everyone over the age of eight in Sainte Ménénould, for instance); in others, on a household basis; see Hocquet for details.

50. G. Shapiro and J. Markoff, *Revolutionary Demands: A Content Analysis of the cahiers de doléances of 1789* (Stanford: Stanford University Press, 1998), p. 277. Shapiro and Markoff note that the duty charged on official documents and registry acts was even more unpopular than the *gabelle* – in some future study, it would be interesting to consider how French people came to see themselves as consumers of services.

iterated separate grievances against each of the indirect taxes,[51] others combined the complaints about indirect taxation into a single item that decried the taxation of all 'goods of prime necessity'. In the words of the parish *cahier* of Ternand (Forez), 'salt, which is so useful for men and animals, tobacco, wine and other similar products' should all be allowed to circulate freely within France.[52] But in what ways are the three items mentioned – salt, tobacco, wine – similar (*semblables*)? Certainly the similarity lay neither in how they were produced nor in how they were consumed, nor in any tangible quality (colour, size, nutritional content) of the goods enumerated. It was, of course, the taxes to which these goods were subject that gave them their great similarity. During the fiscal crises and social unrest of the 1770s and 1780s, it was by being taxed so heavily and inequitably that tobacco, wine and salt were polemically identified as a set of goods to which consumers had natural rights.

Opposition to indirect taxation was one of the chief ways in which the category 'goods of prime necessity' came to have political, as well as moral, significance.[53] The tax protests of 1788–1789, which sacked customs houses and confiscated goods, worked largely within the register of the moral economy but once the Constituent Assembly had abolished indirect taxation (or was perceived to have done so), any effort to collect the *gabelle* or *aides* met with indignance and appeals to the Declaration of the Rights of Man and the Citizen.[54] Revolutionary emphasis on legal equality gave ideological impetus to a new way of thinking about goods and how people related to them. In abolishing privilege, the revolutionaries of summer 1789 made it logically inconceivable that some people had some needs (kings needed ermine trim, for example) and some people had others (cheap bread being the classic example). Such an argument was no longer politically viable; when a deputy proposed that priests and physicians should be exempt from paying the new tax on saddle and carriage horses (since their horses enabled them to do work of 'public utility'), he was quickly reminded that 'we did not abolish the old privileges just to create new ones.'[55]

---

51. In the parish-level *cahiers* from the *bailliage* of Rouen, for example, it is not uncommon for indirect taxation of salt, tobacco and wine to constitute the first three grievances: see Boiloiseau, vol. 2.

52. E. Fournial and J.P. Gutton (eds), *Cahiers de doléances de la province de Forez* (St Etienne: Centre d'etudes foreziennes, 1975), vol. 2, pp. 379–80; numerous *cahiers* refer to 'goods of prime necessity': for examples, see *A.p.*, 2:232, 240, 360.

53. Compare Sewell, 'Sans-culotte rhetoric', pp. 266–7.

54. 'It is easy to see . . . that the immortal declaration of the Rights of Man cannot be reconciled with the immoral regime of [city] trade barriers': E. Chevalier, speech of 15 February 1791, cited in R. Dion, *Histoire de la vigne et du vin en France des origines au XIXe siècle* (Paris: n.p., 1959), p. 503.

55. *A.p.*, 20:18.

The abbé Sieyes's famous pamphlet, 'What is the Third Estate?' examined the categories of Old-Regime political representation and found they did not coincide with the world of production he saw around him. For those who lived under the consumption laws of 1793–1794, and for those who tried to enforce them, the world was full of goods and objects that had to be scrutinized just as carefully. The contested politics of consumption during the French Revolution highlights the inadequacy of the analytic models that people had at their disposal. In a world where so many things were available and people lived in so many different ways, the language of necessity/luxury fits especially poorly with social and economic realities. Empiricist reliance on evidence provided by the senses was of little help in this quandary, for it led to a proliferation of details (such as tasting reports on each of eight barrels of rum) and further stymied the Convention's efforts to legislate on a national basis. For while it may have been the case that any local community could have eventually agreed on its own list of goods of prime necessity, doing so for the entire nation was fraught with contradictions. Olive oil was a staple in Marseille; butter was a staple in Rouen; that much was clear. But did that mean that both butter and oil were necessities in 'France'? Petitions and letters to the National Assembly and the Convention inevitably began with reference to fraternal feeling and the universal right to subsistence, but they nearly always deployed that language in arguing that additional provisions should be sent immediately to the authors' hometowns.[56]

By abolishing internal trade barriers and reassigning employees from internal customs offices to national frontiers, laws and decrees from the earliest moments of the Revolution had moved in the direction of making consumption national.[57] Yet in the autumn of 1793, when the passage of the General Maximum set price ceilings for all 'goods of prime necessity', there were actually six hundred maximum prices for any given good (one for each administrative district). The evidence of people's senses, in addition to the poor condition of roads and the force of local politics, told them that while butter in Normandy was cheaper (and better) than butter in Provence, the reverse was true for olive oil. For centuries, walnuts had been grown around Grenoble – how could they sell for the same price there and in Brittany? Attention to detail and regional difference seemed the only empirically sound basis on which to set maximum prices and yet it did not work as the Convention expected, for 'scoundrels and the Revolution's enemies' took advantage of the price differentials to make unexpected profits. When Barère presented revisions to the Maximum in February 1794, he therefore insisted that one price be set across the nation. 'A uniform national Maximum will re-establish circulation', he said, and he praised the Subsistence Commission's detailed charts

---

56. For examples, see Miller, *Mastering the Market,* pp. 131–2.
57. Gerbaux and Schmidt, vol. 1, p. 263.

and tables as a 'course in public education for consumers and producers . . . a map of . . . political-practical economy'.[58] Like many of his colleagues in the Convention, Barère had effectively imagined the nation, and even identified several of its key visible manifestations (maps, charts, uniform currency).

But social and economic inequality in a single town or district was addressed by inhabitants in an insistently material and dogmatically literal fashion that cared little for the charts and graphs so laboriously produced in the capital. Paris radicals argued for only one size of cockade; the people of Périgueux insisted that bakers only be allowed to produce a single type of bread; the Jacobin Club of Dijon demanded that the local kosher butcher be shut down since 'all citizens without distinction' should eat the same meat.[59] Articulating the demand for equality in material terms also meant conceiving of equality in terms of perfect, unachievable, identity.

58. *A.p.* 85:311–6, quotation from p. 315.

59. *Ibid.*, 61: 461; Gross, *Fair Shares,* especially pp. 88–91; L. Hugueney, *Les Clubs Dijonnais sous la Révolution* (Dijon: Nourry, 1905), p. 117 cited in P. Higonnet, *Goodness beyond Virtue* (Cambridge, Mass.: Harvard University Press, 1998), p. 237.

3

Social Opulence, Private Asceticism: Ideas of Consumption in Early Socialist Thought

Noel Thompson

It is really only in the past two decades that British socialists can be said to have sought to integrate the individual consumer and the business of personal consumption into their political economy with any degree of conviction and enthusiasm. Building on the theoretical basis of a bastardized postmodernism and a more nuanced post-Fordism, many in the 1980s and 1990s came to see the discriminating consumer of customized quality products as the archetype of a new revolutionary vanguard; effecting a transformation in the position of labour by demanding goods produced by non-alienated, polyvalent artisans, in small computer-resourced workshops, characterized by co-operative and democratized decision-making. For these post-Fordist socialists it has been the discriminating consumer, not the hardy-handed producer, who can be relied upon to precipitate those revolutionary changes in the organization of production which will lay the basis for a liberated proletariat within a socialist economy and polity.[1] Not only can rich consumers enter the New Jerusalem; their activity in the shopping malls of England's green and pleasant land would prove instrumental in its construction. A Benetton Britain can be a socialist Britain[2] and, of course, given the relative attractions of Benetton and socialism in the 1980s this was a proposition which, in some quarters, had considerable political significance. Nowhere was the spirit of this new consumer

---

1. Such views have their origins in the works of the French regulationists and in that of the American writers Charles Sabel and Michael Piore. See for example C. Sabel, *Work and Politics* (Cambridge: Cambridge University Press, 1982) and M. Piore and C. Sabel, *The Second Industrial Divide* (New York: Basic Books, 1984). For a rendition by British writers see for example P. Hirst and J. Zeitlin, 'Flexible specialisation vs post Fordism: theory, evidence and policy implications', *Economy and Society*, 20 (1991), pp. 1–56; P. Hirst, *Associative Democracy: New Forms of Economic and Social Governance* (Amherst: Massachusetts University Press, 1992), for an elaboration of these ideas and a discussion of some of their political implications and potentialities.

2. I borrow the epithet from R. Murray, 'Benetton Britain: the new economic order', in S. Hall and M. Jacques (eds), *The Politics of Thatcherism* (London: Lawrence & Wishart, 1983).

socialism more fervently embraced than in the pages of *Marxism Today*, which entered into the spirit of what, with unnerving originality, they termed 'New Times' by launching their own credit card and range of consumer goods, giving the impression that, as one critic put it, 'where you st[ood] on consumption' was 'becoming a litmus test of the whole issue of socialist renewal'.[3]

But all this is a recent development. Of course there were British socialists prior to this who warmed to the place of consumption in a socialist scheme of things. And there were those whose lifestyles testified to a practical not to say sybaritic enthusiasm for the business of consuming. In addition, if post-Fordists read their Hobson they would realize that most of what they had to say on the transformative power of discriminating consumption was prefigured in his *Evolution of Modern Capitalism*.[4] But then home-grown socialism has rarely possessed the radical chic and intellectual cachet of one whose meta-history has a continental and/or transatlantic provenance. In general though, mavericks apart, the consumer and the nature of consumption have occupied a subsidiary theoretical place in the socialist scheme of things, even if it was frequently attested that securing a substantial increase in working-class consumption was a primary reason for constructing a socialist economy.

To explain why this has been the case would require not one but a series of studies, so in this chapter I will limit myself to a consideration of whether it is possible to trace back to the early nineteenth century the theoretical and ideological roots of an uneasiness with consumption which certainly characterized British socialist political economy from the late nineteenth to the late twentieth centuries.

Certainly one does not have to delve far into the socialist economic literature of the early nineteenth century to detect a disquiet with the activity of consuming and what surrounded it. To begin with there is the concern to distinguish 'productive' from 'unproductive' consumption. As regards the latter, the concept tended to embody one or both of two notions. On the one hand there was the idea that it entailed the consumption of goods other than those produced to satisfy what were termed the 'natural wants of society'.[5] On the other hand it involved the notion of consumption by those who gave 'no profitable labour in exchange for the maintenance they receive' or 'those who consume and do not furnish an equivalent product of mind or matter in return for what they consume'.[6] So unproductive

---

3. J. Saville, '*Marxism Today* : an anatomy', *Socialist Register, 1990* (London: Merlin, 1990), p. 36.

4. See my 'Hobson and the Fabians: two roads to socialism in the 1920s', *History of Political Economy*, 26 (1994), pp. 203–20.

5. For a use of this term see W. King, *To the Makers of Wealth, the Useful Working Population* (London, 1831), p. 1.

6. J.F. Bray, *Labour's Wrongs and Labour's Remedy, or the Age of Might and the Age of Right* (Leeds, 1839), pp. 86–7; H. McCormac, *An Address to the Working Classes* (Belfast, 1830), p. 10.

consumption referred both to categories of good and to categories of consumer. It was, of course, possible for consumption to be productive in one sense but not the other; as when consumption involved the gratification of 'natural wants' by those who furnished nothing in return for what they consumed. More often, though, the two conceptions of unproductive consumption were combined in 'the rich non-productive consumer' who 'can and does turn the labourer from the production of the necessaries of life, to that of hurtful and useless superfluities'.[7]

As regards 'natural wants', these were variously defined but few would have disagreed with John Gray's view that they entailed a demand for 'everything which tends to improve the condition of the human race physically, morally or intellectually'.[8] More concretely, the gratification of natural wants was usually seen as involving the consumption of 'food, clothing, lodging and the objects of conveniency or the articles which are used or consumed in supplying these.'[9] The problem was that under existing economic and social arrangements where demands were mediated by money, and where the distribution of income and wealth was profoundly skewed, wants were likely to acquire an unnatural, and consumption an unproductive, character, resulting in a substantial demand for goods the real utility of which was negligible or nil; a demand for 'unsocial objects, objects disgraceful to humanity'.[10]

In such circumstances consumption had a number of consequences. To begin with it precipitated a fundamental misallocation of resources. As William King had it, 'the producing classes are set in motion not to supply the natural wants of society, but only as their labour can be rendered profitable to the possessors of money' and likewise, 'the wants of mankind are at present supplied in proportion to their supply of money and not in proportion to the usefulness of their occupations'.[11] Contemporary consumption therefore precipitated the 'manufacture of articles of utter inutility'. 'This is wasteful labour, it is consumption without useful production'.[12] And resources wasted in this manner were, of course, not available for the production of those goods which were needed to service the natural wants of the greater part of the population. In effect, the satisfaction of unnatural wants, which in general meant the consumption of luxuries, diminished the economy's

7. H. McCormac, *An Appeal on Behalf of the Poor* (Belfast, 1830), p. 6.

8. J. Gray, *A Lecture on Human Happiness* (London, 1825), Preface.

9. A. Combe, *The Sphere for Joint Stock Companies, or the Way to Increase the Value of Land, Capital and Labour* (Edinburgh, 1825), p. 114.

10. Anon., *An Essay in Answer to the Question, Whether does the Principle of Competition with Separate Individual Interests or the Principle of United Exertions with Combined and Equal Interests Form the Most Secure Basis for the Formation of Society* (London, 1834), p. 43.

11. King, *To the Makers of Wealth*, p. 1; W. King, *To the Useful Working Population* (London, 1831), p. 2 n.

12. W. Hawkes Smith, *The Errors of the Social System, being an Essay on Wasted, Unproductive and Redundant Labour* (Birmingham, 1834), p. 21.

capacity to furnish the necessities of life. So, given the nature of contemporary consumption, there were many whose natural wants were left unsatisfied. For 'the rich, non-productive consumer can and does turn the labourer from the production of the necessaries of life, to that of hurtful and useless superfluities'.[13]

As importantly, market imperatives to satisfy unnatural wants meant the imposition of unnecessary toil. Of course this is a theme which predates the early nineteenth-century socialists. It is expressed with particular force, for example, in Godwin's *Political Justice* where he wrote of 'costly gratifications . . . purchased with considerable labour and industry'; luxuries which gratified because of the 'love of distinction' which they satisfied or, in more modern parlance, positional goods which distinguished the affluent and successful from the *hoi polloi*.[14] 'How many individuals have been condemned to slavery and sweat, incessant drudgery, unwholesome food, continual hardships, deplorable ignorance and brutal insensibility', he wrote, 'that [they] may be supplied with these luxuries?'[15]

Similarly, early nineteenth-century socialists recognized that consumption imposed toil. Unnecessary or unnatural consumption imposed unnecessary and unnatural labour. Desire gratified too often meant labour exacted with no equivalence between the relative real utilities and disutilities of work and consumption. William Thompson intimated in *Labor Rewarded* that where what was wanted demanded incessant toil on the part of its producers, 'no [such] articles of wealth, though all enjoyed by the producer, could be worthy of so dear a purchase'; while Owen wrote of the 'innumerable evils' suffered by labour in consequence of the production of 'that which is of little real value to society'.[16] There was, in effect, under existing economic arrangements, a fundamental mismatch between the social utility of consumption and the social disutility of labour.

It is, indeed, in such a context that one should understand the determination on the part of early nineteenth-century socialists that goods should exchange according to the labour time which they contained. For this was clearly a means of overtly linking consumption to the labour effort entailed by the production of what was to be consumed. Exchange conducted on such a basis drove home to consumers the toil involved in the gratification of desire. In demanding labour for labour it also secured a closer approximation between the disutility of effort and the utility of consumption. The equitable labour exchanges of Birmingham and London were, in effect, practical expressions of such ideas. In such institutions, it was considered

13. McCormac, *An Appeal on Behalf of the Poor*, p. 6.

14. W. Godwin, *An Enquiry Concerning Political Justice and its Influence on Morals and Happiness* (Harmondsworth: Pelican, 1976 [1793]), p. 704.

15. *Ibid.*, p. 712.

16. W. Thompson, *Labor Rewarded, the Claims of Labor and Capital Conciliated, or How to Secure to Labor the Whole Product of its Exertions* (London, 1827), p. 30; R. Owen, 'A letter published in London newspapers, 25 July 1817', in *The Life of Robert Owen written by Himself*, 2 vols (London, 1857–8), Appendix 1A, p. 68.

that none but those prepared to suffer the diseconomies of labour were allowed to consume the products available and, because the basis of exchange was labour effort/time, some restraint was thereby put on material appetites that could otherwise prove destructive in terms of the burden of incessant and degrading toil which they imposed. What labour exchanges did in part and what co-operative communities, through their effective abolition of exchange did, *in toto*, was to focus attention on the use-value of goods or, as early nineteenth-century socialist writers often phrased it, their 'intrinsic worth'.[17] This done, it was believed that consumption would once again become oriented to the gratification of natural wants.

The early nineteenth-century socialist antipathy to money and the exchange of goods according to money prices can also be understood in these terms. For money obscured the nature of the relationship between consumer and producer. Not only did it conceal the kind and extent of the labour which consumption imposed, it served to hide the social utility or otherwise of what it called forth. To take an example sometimes used by early nineteenth-century socialist writers: the money price of lace gave no idea of what its production entailed and, because that price was high, also conveyed an inaccurate idea of its real social utility. Like Marx, these writers recognized that in a capitalist market economy 'the exchange of commodities [was] evidently an act characterised by total abstraction from use-value'; in consequence, it became impossible to judge the relative utilities and disutilities of consumption and effort.[18]

It was the case too that, during the Revolutionary and Napoleonic wars and the period which followed, the volatility of the price level gave an evanescent quality to the value of money. Like the Jacobins discussed in Chapter Two, therefore, this caused early nineteenth-century socialists to call into question its capacity to convey what they believed should be a stable notion of a commodity's real worth. Here again money price could not be trusted to convey a consistent and accurate sense of social utility and was in this respect contrasted adversely with the seeming stability of the labour-embodied estimates of value used by the Labour Exchanges.[19]

The attitude of early nineteenth-century socialists to consumption also explains, in part, their generally critical view of the benefits to be derived from international trade. As they saw it, commerce provided virtually limitless opportunities for the indulgence of unnatural wants. As one writer stated, 'by foreign trade the capitalists contrive to outwit *nature*, who had put a thousand *natural limits* to their exactions, and to their wishes to exact; there is no limit now, either to their power, or their

17. For example, R. Owen, *An Explanation of the Cause of Distress which Pervades the Civilized World* (London, 1823), p. 2.

18. K. Marx, *Capital, a Critical Analysis of Capitalist Production*, 3 vols (London: Lawrence & Wishart, 1974), vol. 1, p. 50.

19. See Chapter Two, pp. 40, 43–4.

desires, but impossibility'.[20] Thus while domestic resources might set bounds to the artificial demands which could be indigenously satisfied, trade made possible the export of what was produced to gratify the insatiable caprices and whims of the wealthy. Again this was seen as having adverse repercussions for the availability of necessities which were viewed as the goods primarily exported to furnish the luxuries required. Thus Britain was seen as sending 'to other Countries, the articles of consumption and real utility, that it may procure others which . . . are of little or no intrinsic value in promoting happiness'. In Ireland in particular 'the inhabitants . . . [were] condemned to unending toil to ship from their harbours cargoes of grain and all other staple productions of their country, while they themselves are cursed with an over flow of pauperism and starvation. The herds bleat and low around them but not for them. They furnish neither their larder nor their clothes chest'.[21] The corollary was, of course, that where unnatural wants were no longer forthcoming or indulged, where one could secure the 'disuse of many needless and pernicious articles', the volume of foreign trade would diminish to a point where it became of 'comparatively little account'.[22] Such would certainly be the case with the establishment of co-operative communities which were conceived of as essentially autarchic and as engaging in trade to a minimal extent even within the domestic economy. In early nineteenth-century socialist political economy, therefore, a suspicion of consumption was integrally related to a scepticism as to the social utility of foreign trade.

The nature of the consumption entailed by the satisfaction of unnatural wants was also seen as imparting a unnerving volatility and uncertainty to economic life which manifested itself, in particular, in crises resulting from periodic deficiencies in demand. Where, however, demand was the expression of natural wants no such instability would exist. Then, as within co-operative communities, 'the demand for labour would be simple and uniform not, as at present, complex and uncertain, influenced by all the intricacies of whim, fashion and duplicity'.[23] Indeed 'a community would be very careful how it directed its surplus labour to the production of any articles, however glittering the immediate profit, for which the *real and regular wants of society* did not guaranty something approaching to a permanent demand'.[24] Consumption which took the form of satisfying the 'real and regular wants of society' was, therefore, the kind of consumption which would provide that stability so signally absent from contemporary economic life.

20. Anon., *The Source and Remedy of the National Difficulties Deduced from Principles of Political Economy in a Letter to Lord John Russell* (London, 1821), p. 18, my emphasis.

21. Combe, *The Sphere for Joint Stock Companies*, p. 119; 'Proposals for a change of system in the British Empire', *New Moral World*, 21 March 1835, p. 163.

22. W. Hawkes Smith, *Letters on the State and Prospects of Society* (Birmingham, 1838), p. 57.

23. *New Moral World*, 31 October 1835, p. 2.

24. W. Thompson, *An Inquiry into the Principles of the Distribution of Wealth* (London, 1824), pp. 424–5.

If there were fundamental social diseconomies attached to the indulgence of unnatural wants, then most socialist writers of the period were also critical of the moral diseconomies involved in the constant and intensifying inducement to consume which characterized competitive capitalism. Here again many of the sentiments they expressed were prefigured by Godwin, who wrote of the 'tradesman . . . stud[ying] the passions of his customers, not to correct but to pamper them'.[25] Thus, for its successful functioning, capitalism actually required the calculated creation of 'unnatural wants' and that in turn required a deliberate cultivation of humanity's worst instincts, irrational passions and corrupting material desires. To induce consumption, dissimulation as regards the competitive merits of products was also required, with those engaged in the business of selling, necessarily acquiring 'strong powers of deception' with 'truth and sincerity' sacrificed 'to dishonesty and misrepresentation'.[26] The whole business of consumption in a capitalist market economy was, therefore, fraught with moral dangers both for seller and consumer. With the 'higgling of the market', a necessary prelude to consumption, it was certain there would be 'highly injurious effects on the disposition, mind and conduct of each individual' which would 'lower the character and make hypocrites of buyers and seller'.[27] Under existing arrangements consumption was integrally related to the art of calculated deception.

Once, however, unnatural wants had been constrained or eliminated, once demand became in effect the articulation of natural wants, consumption would be set on a rational basis and much else became possible. Most importantly this would open up the possibility of a material abundance and all that followed from that. Here it is important to stress that for early nineteenth-century socialists abundance was not synonymous with an absolute surfeit induced by limitless production. Rather abundance, or potential abundance, was conceived of in relation to 'real needs', 'rational desires', 'natural wants', 'the wants of human nature'.[28] 'Limited' in this way, material desires no longer tyrannized over the producer; consumption no longer demanded incessant and degrading toil; resources were no longer wasted on 'unsocial objects' and the 'manufacture of articles of utter inutility' and the spirit of avarice and greed intrinsic to an overweening passion for consumption would be effectively exorcized.[29] It was this 'limitation' of consumption to the gratification of natural wants, in conjunction with a rapidly growing capacity to produce, which had created the means of furnishing a material abundance; making

25. Godwin, *An Enquiry Concerning Political Justice*, p. 726.

26. R. Owen, *Observations on the Effect of the Manufacturing System* in *A New View of Society and other Writings* (London: Dent, 1927 [1815]), p. 122; Thompson, *Labor Rewarded*, p. 16.

27. 'Catechism of the New Moral World', *New Moral World*, 3 January 1835, p. 76

28. For example Abram Combe wrote of '*a superabundance* of all that is either requisite or desirable *for supplying the wants of human nature*', *The Sphere for Joint Stock Companies*, p. 157, my emphasis.

29. *An Essay*, p. 43; Smith, *The Errors of the Social System*, p. 21.

it 'now practicable, by proper arrangements, to create a superabundance of all that is either requisite *or desirable for supplying the wants of human nature*'.[30] Abundance was seen as a function of disciplined desire not jaded palates.

What eventuated from the creation of such an abundance in relation to natural wants was seen as profoundly liberating. It would then become possible to place 'all men on a footing of equality'; for 'if men were placed in a situation where, by moderate occupation, without care or agitation of mind, they could procure the necessaries and comforts of life in abundance, they might be trained to dispute as little about the division of them as they now do about the commonly attainable products of nature'.[31] The advent of abundance would lay the material basis for an end to social antagonism and conflict. Contention was intrinsic to scarcity. Where resources were limited in relation to competing ends then dispute over what those ends should be was inevitable. Further, in such circumstances, there was both rationale and imperative to possess what was in limited supply, both to obviate the threat of impoverishment and to ensure that the ends to which scarce resources were put were those which satisfied one's own wants. However where 'wealth would everywhere and at all times superabound beyond the wants or wishes of the human race [then] . . . all desire for individual accumulation or inequality [would] cease'.[32] The end of scarcity would obviate the need for acquisitive individualism and thence the accumulation of property and property itself would become a burden rather than a source of satisfaction.

Seen in this light individual property would have lost not only its coercive authority but, in some senses, its hold on the mind of humanity; something which many socialist writers considered a prerequisite for human liberation and fulfilment. As Owen put it in 'Two memorials on behalf of the working classes', 1818, because of the nation's capacity to create a material abundance, 'the dominion of wealth and the evils arising from the desire to acquire and accumulate riches are on the point of terminating'. 'Individuals [would] not trouble themselves with the possession or useless care of property'; their creative abilities, their truly productive potentialities, their capacities and enthusiasms could now be directed to a higher order of things than the sordid grinding pursuit and accumulation of material wealth.[33] Moreover the lightness of labour would release the time and the energy requisite for this, with labour entailing 'no more exertion than that which every sensible man . . . takes in order to preserve the healthy action of their normal functions'.[34] So the capacity to produce a material abundance would, paradoxically,

30. Combe, *The Sphere of Joint Stock Companies*, p. 157, my emphasis.

31. *Ibid.*; Owen, 'A letter published in the London newspapers', p. 70.

32. 'The book of the New Moral World', *New Moral World*, 27 August 1836, p. 345.

33. R. Owen, 'Two memorials on behalf of the working classes', 1818 in *Life of Robert Owen*, p. 211.

34. Smith, *Letters on the State and Prospect of Society*, p. 20.

signal a diminution in the perceived importance of material acquisition and consumption.

But all this was predicated not just on the expansion of the nation's productive capacity, which Owen and others certainly celebrated, but also on the limitation of demand to natural wants. Or, put another way, human liberation lay in no small measure in the simplification of desire. Here again, there is something quint-essentially Godwinian and, given the extent and nature of Godwin's influence on early nineteenth-century anti-capitalist and socialist writers, that should come as no surprise. For Godwin, one of the hallmarks of a society perfected by human reason was to be its simplicity, in terms of both its social and economic organization and the needs and demands of its members. He looked, in effect, to the emergence of a frugal agrarian economy[35] and, in some important respects, this idea of the simplification of demand to the expression of natural wants can be seen as taking early nineteenth-century communitarian socialists in a similar direction. Certainly, the whole emphasis on natural wants, and the aim of matching productive capacity with these, meant that communities were almost invariably conceived of as fundamentally agrarian.

There is, though, one other relevant point to be made here about the agrarian emphasis in early nineteenth-century communitarian socialism which has a particular relevance for their attitude to consumption. The consumption of manufactured goods and, specifically, the demand for cheapness drove entre-preneurs towards a progressive subdivision of labour to raise productivity and reduce unit labour costs. For many socialist writers the consequences of this were what Adam Smith had foretold in the *Wealth of Nations*. The division of labour had 'rear[ed] an immense number of industrious men, who are utterly ignorant, except of the minute details of their own small department or art, and who are altogether useless and helpless, except when combined under one employer. If not counteracted in its effects, by an extensive education it renders the workmen incapable of properly discharging their duties . . . as members of society by leaving them ignorant of everything except their own narrow department of trade'.[36] In short, intellectual atrophy and a diminution in the capacity to fulfil social responsibilities were a likely consequence of the demand for cheap manufactures. Where, however, demand had assumed a natural form, where it was primarily a demand for the means of subsistence and thence for the products of agriculture and, therefore, where agriculture was the predominant form of economic activity, such social and intellectual diseconomies might be obviated. Agriculture, as Smith

---

35. There are clearly echoes here of the 'Rousseau-inspired frugality' which, as Chapter Two (p. 45) indicates, found expression in Jacobinical attitudes to luxury and the business of consumption.

36. J. Thimbleby, *Monadelphia: or the Formation of a New System of Society, without the Intervention of a Circulating Medium* (Barnet, 1832), p. 27.

had pointed out, and as communitarian socialists reiterated, did not lend itself to an extensive and progressive subdivision of the workforce and so labour would not find its attention confined, as in manufacture, to one small fragment of the production process. Labour so engaged could thus escape that intellectual atrophy characteristic of a workforce in an economy driven by an insatiable demand for cheap manufactured goods. Many early nineteenth-century socialists were therefore alive not just to the incessant toil which unnatural demands could impose but also to the degraded nature of the labour which it could and did exact. Again, there is an acute sensitivity to what, for the producer, different types of consumption might bring in their wake; a sensitivity which, as we shall see, was also to inform the political economy of John Ruskin later in the century.

All that said, it is certainly the case, as one commentator has written, that Owen's avowed objective was 'to put the productive forces unlocked by modern science into the service of collective production and distribution'[37] but the fact remains that the primary natural want was seen as being that for food, and the theorization, portrayal and practice of communities reflected this. Robert Owen wrote of the need for 'a judicious arrangement of spade cultivation with *manufactures as an appendage*' and of 'communities . . . *having their basis in agriculture*'; while William Thompson likewise stressed that 'the grandest step by far of capitalist-laborers in securing to themselves the product of their labor . . . is in *the acquisition of land*'.[38] Also in the engravings, woodcuts and architectural plans of communities the scene is invariably a pastoral one, innocent of the blemish of smoking factory chimneys or signs of industrial enterprise.[39] The imagined community of the Owenite socialist John Minter Morgan was, for example, one where 'numerous flocks of sheep were browsing on the side of the mountains, herds of deer were seen in various directions and the cattle were grazing in the richest pastures. The meadows and fields resembled gardens and parks. . . The white stone of the buildings seen through the foliage of the trees; the various temples and colonnades, the hanging woods, the intermixture of knolls and crags of rock, and the elegant vessels and boats upon the lake, formed a picture surpassing description'.[40]

Adherence to the principle of satisfying natural wants and those which did not involve a degraded, mentally-atrophying human labour, therefore, implied for many

37. M. Beer, *A History of British Socialism*, 2 vols (London: Allen & Unwin, 1953), vol. 1, p. 162.

38. R. Owen, *A Report to the County of Lanark of a Plan for Relieving Public Distress* [1821] in *A New View of Society*, p. 259, my emphasis; Thompson, *Labor Rewarded*, p. 96.

39. For one such depiction see S. Whitwell, *Description of an Architectural Model . . . for a Community upon a Principle of United Interests* (London, 1830).

40. J.M. Morgan, *The Revolt of the Bees*, 5th edn (London, 1831), pp. 346–7. Here, and elsewhere, in prose and graphic representation, romanticism was to leave its imprint on the imaginations of early nineteenth-century socialists.

a regime of pastoral simplicity.[41] But one should be careful about drawing the parallel with Godwin too closely. What was envisaged was an agrarian community but not, in most instances, a frugal agrarian community. It is true that, in theory and practice, some early nineteenth-century communitarian socialists did embrace the notion of frugality and asceticism. The communitarians of Ham Common subsisted, for the most part, on a regime of fresh air, basic food, vigorous exercise and cold water.[42] Similarly, individual communitarian socialists such as James Pierrepont Greaves advocated and practised vegetarianism and cold-water therapy, while most of the communities which were established 'had their vegetarians, teetotallers, non-smokers and fresh-air-and-cold-water faddists'.[43] So frugality and asceticism were aspects of the attitude to consumption of early nineteenth-century communitarian socialists; tied up with notions of the tyranny of material demands and the corrupting and effeminizing consequences of luxury expenditure.

And yet, when we look at descriptions of communities, real and imagined, there is clearly another, very different, attitude to consumption apparent in them. G.J. Holyoake wrote of Queenwood Hall, the central building of the Owenite socialist community established near Tytherly, in Hampshire, in the late 1830s, that 'no cathedral was ever built so reverently . . . Hand-made nails, not machine made, were used in the work out of sight . . . The great kitchen was wainscotted with mahogany half-way up the walls'.[44] Further, we know that expenditure on the building was on such a scale as to create major financial difficulties for the community and elicit strong criticism on the part of many communitarian socialists who were not directly involved in the project.[45]

Consistent with such social opulence a visitor to J.M. Morgan's imagined co-operative community remarked to a resident communitarian on 'the full supply of everything essential, not only to comfortable but even luxurious subsistence; the beauty of your walks, the fertility of your fields, gardens and parks; the convenient and elegant accommodations of every description; and above all, the extent and magnificence of your buildings, notwithstanding the very temperate labour, or rather employment, of the inhabitants'. In like vein he describes the rooms of the community as 'lofty with circular ceilings, and in each were suspended two magnificent chandeliers of exquisitely cut glass, which in winter were lighted with

---

41. In practice too 'all the communities were agricultural colonies, in which farming was carried on collectively. In most cases it was subsistence farming and in no community was large-scale commercial agriculture undertaken'. J.F.C. Harrison, *Robert Owen and the Owenites in Britain and America, the Quest for the New Moral World* (London: Routledge & Kegan Paul, 1969), p. 190.

42. On the Ham Common transcendentalists see W.H.G. Armytage, *Heavens Below: Utopian Experiments in England, 1560–1960* (London: Routledge & Kegan Paul, 1961), pp. 178–9.

43. Harrison, *Robert Owen and the Owenites*, pp. 129, 179.

44. G.J. Holyoake, *A History of Co-operation* (London, 1908), pp. 640–1.

45. 'Harmony Hall at Queenwood was a most handsome building in which no expense was spared in the materials and fittings'. Harrison, *Robert Owen and the Owenites*, p. 191.

gas, producing a splendid effect; the panels of the rooms were fawn colour with gold beading, and the curtains of a rich crimson, tastefully disposed in festoons with deep fringes. The roof was entirely of oak, and carved in imitation of the richest Gothic fretwork . . . There were wines and liqueurs of various kinds . . . they were, however, but seldom asked for . . . the earthenware was brought to such great perfection as to be superior to that of the Chinese . . . Between the windows were slabs of the finest marble, supported by bronze figures: upon these marbles were placed large vessels of gold, filled with spring water and at each corner of the room was a marble figure holding a Roman lamp suspended by a chain'.[46] So no bracing whiff of asceticism here. One suspects, indeed, that the vegetarians and fresh-air-and-cold-water immolators of the flesh would have felt singularly ill-at-ease in such sumptuous surroundings; though they might take some comfort that these wines and liqueurs would be '*but seldom asked for*'. Clearly a prevailing, if non-judgemental, preference for teetotalism was assumed.

So where does that leave the notion of consumption as the satisfaction of natural wants and the argument that, for early nineteenth-century socialists, liberation lay in a material culture alive to the toil which consumption imposed and to the need to circumscribe material desires ?

The crucial point, of course, is that this is collective, not individual, consumption. The labour that it requires is not enforced by the demands of others but democratically decided upon and sanctioned by the community as a whole. It is therefore, by definition, not the consumption of 'unsocial objects'. Further, the community would collectively determine the scale of social consumption by balancing the resultant social benefits against the diseconomies of labour. With respect to the material magnificence described above a communitarian averred that because '*all derive gratification* from the result . . . *it has always been considered useful* to render the public rooms as attractive as possible'.[47] Some rigorous social cost-benefit-analysis in relation to a carefully constructed social welfare function were therefore considered a necessary preliminary to any collective consumption. Here communitarians circumvented the difficulties confronted by those, such as the Jacobins discussed in Chapter Two, who sought to differentiate luxuries from necessities by reference to a product's physical attributes.[48] Working in microcosm, with collectively determined and accepted notions of social utility, they believed it possible to tackle the problem of what should be produced and consumed by reference not to such attributes but by reference to what would approximate to a communitarian felicific calculus. What they proposed here therefore represented a solution to what Spang refers to in Chapter Two as the Jacobins' lack of a fixed referrant in relation to which the binary opposites "necessity" and "luxury" might

---

46. Morgan, *The Revolt of the Bees*, pp. 357, 397.
47. *Ibid.*, p. 398, my emphasis.
48. Chapter Two, pp. 37–45.

be determined. For within a co-operative community while the distinction between luxury and necessity would shift over time in relation to productivity, output and changing collective demands, the fixed referrant would be there in the form of what we might term, if somewhat anachronistically, its social welfare function.[49]

Labour to satisfy communitarian consumption is not forced but collectively embraced. Consumption of this kind is thereby stripped of the alienating and coercive characteristics which attach to it in a capitalist market economy. Consumption ceases to be the expression of individual economic power and an assertion of success in the competitive race; it is no longer about the possession of positional goods. Where the personal consumption of such artefacts would be essentially divisive, their collective consumption becomes a source of unity; a celebration of collective identity, endeavour and achievement – 'all derive gratification from the result'.[50] Consumption of this kind is also free of the ethical diseconomies which infuse that acquisitive instinct which personal consumption always threatens to inflame. What is collectively owned and collectively consumed is also free from the insecurity and anxieties inevitably attaching to individual possession. Thus, 'far from exclusive possession adding to happiness, under the old system it generally impaired the pleasures to be derived from the things possessed'.[51]

Yet clearly for a communitarian socialist such as Morgan, collective opulence and ostentation was to have its limits. The whole point of 'the co-operative state' was that 'by supplying with facility under comprehensive arrangements, the whole of its members with food, raiment and dwelling' it 'bestow[ed] upon mankind abundant leisure to improve their higher faculties and promote the happiness of the species'.[52] As envisaged, communitarian socialism would bring about a qualitative change in the nature of consumption not simply as regards the balance between the collective and the individual, but also, crucially, in relation to the form which consumption would assume. For communitarians, the satisfaction of material needs was to be seen as merely a prelude to the satisfying of the demands of humanity's 'higher faculties'. Thus a visitor to Morgan's ideal community was impressed that 'although you could produce by many degrees a greater quantity of articles than were formerly manufactured, still you [give your time to] literary and philosophical pursuits ... music and other recreations'.[53] Similarly, for Morgan's communitarians, it was a cause of substantial satisfaction not just that 'all [their] wants are readily supplied' but also that they had 'access to libraries, museums, concerts ... superior to those which any private fortune ... could command'.[54] Also while, as has been suggested, little was said by socialist political

49. Chapter Two, pp. 41, 44, 48.
50. Morgan, *The revolt of the Bees*, p. 398.
51. *Ibid.*
52. *Ibid.*, p. 357.
53. *Ibid.*, pp. 359–60.
54. *Ibid.*, p. 400.

economists about the manufacturing aspect of the communitarian economy, specific mention is made, in John Minter Morgan's *Revolt of the Bees*, 1831, of the community's 'type foundry, and a paper manufactory' 'connected with [which] . . . was a printing and binding establishment'.[55] Insofar then as personal consumption was expected to expand over time, it was believed that it would assume an increasingly intellectual character. If natural desires could be considered limitless, it was insofar as they assumed this immaterial form.

One should not, therefore, understate the scale of the consumption which Morgan and others anticipated that communitarians would enjoy. Communitarian civilization would not rest on a frugal agrarian economy of a Godwinian kind. Private, material self-abnegation there might be but in tandem with social opulence. In the eidetic world of the communitarian visionary, and in the reality of Queenwood Hall, the co-operative community was possessed of the artefacts, decor, architecture and ambience of the English country house, not the squalid spartan asceticism of the English public school. Collective consumption would be a celebration of community values, creativity, achievements and aspirations, not merely a testimony to frugal self-restraint.

Later in the century many of these ideas on consumption were to resurface in the work of John Ruskin and, through William Morris and J.A. Hobson among others, were to percolate back into the socialist political economy of the late nineteenth and early twentieth centuries. In particular the critique of that consumption which imposed unnecessary or destructive and demeaning labour was central to *Unto this Last* (1862), but also found powerful expression in works such as *Munera Pulveris* (1872), *Sesame and Lilies* (1865) and *The Crown of Wild Olives* (1866).

For Ruskin, as for the early socialists, consumption had profound ethical implications and individuals should see themselves as responsible for the consequences of what they consumed. Consumption should not therefore involve the simple gratification of desire; rather it should be an activity undertaken with precise cognizance of the nature of the labour it demanded and therefore an understanding of the relative social and personal utilities and disutilities it involved. It would be a consumption too which, for Ruskin, would take account of its impact on the natural environment.[56]

As regards maximising the utility to be had from what labour furnished, demand should be for things 'which serve either to comfort the body, or exercise rightly the affections and form the intelligence'[57] and here there is a strong parallel with

---

55. *Ibid.*, p. 389.

56. On this, see for example W. Henderson, *John Ruskin's Political Economy* (London: Routledge, 2000), pp. 38ff.

57. J. Ruskin, *Munera Pulveris* (1905), in E.T. Cook and A. Wedderburn (eds), *The Works of John Ruskin*, 39 vols (London, Allen & Unwin, 1903–12), vol. 17, p. 150.

the early nineteenth-century conception of natural wants which, to quote John Gray again, were of those things which 'tend[ed] to improve the condition of the human race physically, morally or intellectually'.[58] In this regard Ruskin wrote that 'you can never be wrong in employing any labour to produce food, house-room, clothes and fuel'.[59] *Per contra*, the utility generated would be minimal, and labour therefore wasted, when productive activity was geared to servicing the frivolous whims and desires of the self-indulgent, idle rich. For Ruskin, 'of all wastes, the greatest waste you can commit is the waste of labour'[60] and, like the early socialists, he evinced a profound distaste for luxury expenditure and a concomitant espousal of a measured asceticism. Thus he enjoined the middle classes that 'the less your keep costs the better. It does not cost money only it costs degradation. You do not merely employ people you also tread on them . . . It cannot be helped . . . but see that you tread as lightly as possible'.[61]

It was the consumer's responsibility to minimize the disutility of labour, 'the consumers of the products of labour must exercise care in the pains they put upon those on whom their comfort rests'. But also, as Ruskin opined in *The Seven Lamps of Architecture*, 'we should think of the manner of life which our demand necessitates'.[62] In this regard consumers must acquire 'a right understanding of what kinds of labour are good for men'; secondly, they must seek to demand such products as eventuate in 'healthy and ennobling labour' and, finally, they must be prepared to make 'a determined sacrifice of such convenience, or beauty, or cheapness as is to be got by the degradation of the workman'.[63] Here Ruskin was concerned in particular with the cheapness secured by rendering labour mechanical by way of the division of labour and the mechanization of the productive process; for this robbed labour of the creativity and expressiveness which, wherever possible, should be at its core.[64] 'It is a good and desirable thing truly to make many pins in a day. But if we could only see with what crystal sand their points are polished – sand of human soul – we should think there might be some loss in it also; but to brighten, to strengthen, to refine or to form a single living spirit never enters into our estimate of advantage'.[65]

Early nineteenth-century socialists would have demurred at none of this. However, while Ruskin looked to an ethical transfiguration of individual behaviour the early socialists saw adherence to such principles of consumption as being

58. see n.8 above.
59. Ruskin, *Munera Pulveris*, p. 278.
60. J. Ruskin, *The Crown of Wild Olives*, in *Works*, vol. 18, p. 426.
61. J. Ruskin, *Time and Tide by Weare and Tyne*, in *Works*, vol. 17, p. 424.
62. J. Ruskin, *The Seven Lamps of Architecture*, in *Works*, vol. 8, p. 264.
63. J. Ruskin, *The Stones of Venice*, in *Works*, vol. 10, p. 196.
64. For a meticulous dissection of Ruskin's view of labour see P.D. Anthony, *John Ruskin's Labour: A Study of Ruskin's Social Theory* (Cambridge: Cambridge University Press, 1983).
65. Ruskin, *Stones of Venice*, in *Works*, p. 196.

collectively implemented and policed. While for Ruskin it was for ethical consumers to calculate the balance of utilities and disutilities involved in their expenditure,[66] for the early nineteenth-century socialists it was the community's responsibility to make such judgements. That aside, there is a remarkable similarity between the ethically-informed consumption decisions which both anticipated being made; decisions which would lead back to a simpler and more pastoral economy as the basis for, and consequence of, the social transformation they desired.

As many commentators have noted, such themes were also to find extended expression in the work of Morris. Less commented upon is the manner in which they infused Hobson's approach to consumption, particularly in the revised 1906 edition of his *Evolution of Modern Capitalism*. The general impact of Ruskin on Hobson has of course been frequently discussed.[67] In particular, the imprint of Ruskin's work can be seen in Hobson's moral critique of capitalism, his rejection of the narrow atomistic utilitarianism of mainstream economics and his own attempt to formulate an organic, social economics.[68] Of Ruskin Hobson wrote that he would 'rank as one of the greatest social teachers of his age, not merely because he has told the greatest number of important truths upon the largest variety of vital matters, in language of penetrative force but because he has made the most powerful and the most felicitous attempt to grasp and to express as a comprehensive whole the needs of human society and the processes of social reform'.[69]

More specifically, Hobson responded positively to Ruskin's exposure of one of the 'deepest destructive maladies of modern industrial society', namely 'the prevalent mechanisation of work and life',[70] expressing concern in his own political economy at the creativity-atrophying consequences of routine and mechanical labour. These he saw, however, as being circumvented in a manner very different from that of Ruskin. For Ruskin such labour would only diminish with the emergence of a moral sense in consumers as regards the consequences of their expenditure. Only the ethically-informed consumer could be expected to consider the social and individual diseconomies of mechanical production; only such

66. As Henderson has phrased it, for Ruskin, 'every wealthy consumer is expected to be his or her own guardian rather than a mere utilitarian hedonist', *John Ruskin's Political Economy*, p. 104; on this see also J. Sherburne, *John Ruskin, or the Ambiguities of Abundance* (Cambridge, Mass.: Harvard University Press, 1972), p. 179.

67. See for example H.C.G. Matthews, 'Hobson, Ruskin and Cobden', in M. Freeden (ed.), *Reappraising J.A. Hobson: Humanism and Welfare* (London: Unwin Hyman, 1990), pp. 11–30; J. Townsend, *J.A. Hobson* (Manchester: Manchester University Press, 1990), pp. 47–9; J. Allett, *New Liberalism: The Political Economy of J.A. Hobson* (Toronto: University of Toronto Press, 1981), pp. 5–6, 17–19.

68. '. . . he has laid a true scientific foundation of a science and art of social economics', J.A. Hobson, *John Ruskin, Social Reformer* (London: Nisbet, 1899), p. 309.

69. *Ibid.*, pp. V–vi.

70. *Ibid.*, p. 309.

consumers would be likely to orient their expenditure to products which allowed the exercise of craftsmanship and conscious creativity. In this regard the moral consumer was the discriminating consumer.

For Hobson, while the objective was the Ruskinian one of maximizing creative labour, the means by which this would be achieved were very different from those envisaged by Ruskin. His position on consumption was predicated upon a critique of the contemporary emergence of unearned rental income from the exercise of monopoly power.[71] This maldistribution of incomes, as Hobson saw it, resulted in oversaving, overinvestment and overproduction in relation to effectual aggregate demand. Hobson looked therefore to a redistribution in favour of earned income and thence the working class, and suggested a number of expedients to effect such an outcome. This would bring about an increase in aggregate demand and eliminate the problem of underconsumption, excess productive capacity and unemployed labour, which was an endemic feature of contemporary capitalism.

In terms of its macroeconomic consequences such an increase in aggregate consumption was to be welcomed. However, it was also the case that Hobson saw this improvement in living standards as something to be welcomed for other reasons. For, as he stated in *The Evolution of Modern Capitalism*, 'the improved character of consumption', which would result from rising levels of earned income, would also prove a 'guarantee of social progress'. This was so because it would lead to a demand for 'higher forms of wealth' which in turn were likely to transmute labour from the mechanical to the artistic as demand became more individualized and discriminating.[72] For while there would continue to exist, for some considerable time, a demand for mass-produced goods furnished by routine and mechanical production methods, the growth of individualized consumption would ultimately ensure the emergence of large areas of industry which necessarily eschewed the mechanization and standardization of production. Here Hobson had in mind manufacturing activity tailored to differentiated human needs where craftsmanship and skill were the crucial factor inputs.

So, as society in general became more prosperous, individuals would spend a diminishing proportion of their income on mass-produced essentials and a growing proportion on quality products of a non-standardizable kind, with salutary consequences for the nature of production and thence the kind of labour demanded of the producer. 'Just suppose', wrote Hobson, 'that consumers refuse to conform to a common standard and insist more and more upon a consumption adjusted to their individual needs and tastes . . . such individuality in consumption must impose

71. For a full exposition of Hobson's position here see, for example, *The Economics of Distribution* (London, 1900).
72. J. Hobson, *The Evolution of Modern Capitalism: A Study of Machine Production* (London: Walter Scott Publishing Co., 1906), p. 424.

a corresponding individuality in production and machinery will be dethroned from industry'.[73]

Hobson therefore anticipated a 'division of labour' which would 'apportion machinery to the collective supply of the routine needs of life and art to the individual supply of individual needs'.[74] Thus the unskilled, routine, alienated labour involved in standardized mass production would be minimized while the creative skilled labour involved in satisfying differentiated consumption would increase in line with living standards. History, or more accurately economic history, was taking humanity in the direction of the Ruskinian ideal without any prior moral transformation of society. En route the interests of consumer and producer, given the requisite equitable distribution of wealth, would be rendered harmonious. Measures such as the 'living wage', which Hobson and the ILP advanced in the 1920s, could therefore be portrayed not only as just but also economically expedient, aesthetically pleasing and profoundly humanizing.[75] The parallels here with the socialist political economy predicated in the 1980s and 1990s upon the triumph of flexible specialization are embarrassingly stark.

Because of its impact on producers and the nature of work, the acquisitive and self-regarding instincts it could unleash, the divisions between producers and consumers it could engender, the narrow and corrupting materialism it might encourage, its environmental repercussions and its tendency to celebrate the sensual rather than the cerebral, consumption has always posed problems for socialists and socialist political economy. Some, in consequence, have sought the moralization and education of consumers; some have preached the virtue of asceticism or at least restraint; some such as William Morris have looked to the emergence under socialism of a desire constrained by the growing recognition of the worthlessness of an unthinking pursuit of the material; while with Hobson, and what has been termed 'flec spec' socialism, we have the expectation that a discriminating consumption will satisfy worthy demands through the mobilization of high-skilled, polyvalent, creative and fulfilling labour. However, few writers have dealt as satisfactorily with the problems which consumption poses for socialists as those who, in the early nineteenth century, had at the heart of their political economy a symbiosis between social opulence and private asceticism. For them consumption was to be, above all else, an expression of social purpose and a celebration of society's achievements, not a degrading, desperate and self-regarding assertion of personal identity.

---

73. *Ibid.*, p. 425.
74. J.A. Hobson, *The Crisis of Liberalism* (London: King, 1909), p. 132.
75. See for example J.A. Hobson *et al.*, *The Living Wage* (London: I.L.P., 1926).

4

The Material Politics of Natural Monopoly: Consuming Gas in Victorian Britain

Martin Daunton

One of the most influential interpretations of British history in the eighteenth and early nineteenth centuries has been Edward Thompson's account of the decline of a 'moral economy' of fair prices and just wages set by a paternalistic elite, and its replacement by a 'political economy' which left prices and wages to the unfeeling laws of the market.[1] Recent research on both the eighteenth and nineteenth centuries suggests that such a simple account of binary oppositions obscures many important features of the intellectual and political response to capitalism. Many historians have queried the concept of a 'moral economy' in the eighteenth century, and have argued instead that society was permeated by notions of commercial exchange which were sustained by social values of obligation, trust, sociability and politeness.[2] Similarly, a more nuanced understanding of nineteenth-century attitudes to the market is emerging. Margot Finn, for example, has suggested that 'the sway of free-market ideology was ... undercut by contemporaries' understanding of the growth of the consumer market'. She indicates that judges used the new county courts 'as a public forum in which to articulate their own distinctive conception of a moral economy insulated from the full force of market mechanisms'. Whereas the labour market was considered to be a male domain of free

---

1. 'The moral economy of the English crowd in the eighteenth century', *Past and Present,* 50 (1971), pp. 76–136

2. For alternative views on riots and unrest, see D.E. Williams, 'Morals, markets and the English crowd in 1766', *Past and Present,* 104 (1984), pp. 56–73. For more recent accounts which stress the emergence of a culture of commerce, see C. Muldrew, *The Economy of Obligation: The Culture of Credit and Social Relations in Early Modern England* (Basingstoke: Macmillan, 1998); G. Clark, *Betting on Lives: The Culture of Life Insurance in England, 1695–1775* (Manchester: Manchester University Press, 1999); P. Langford, 'British politeness and the progress of western manners', *Transactions of the Royal Historical Society,* 6th series, 7 (1997), pp. 53–72; P. Clark, *British Clubs and Societies, 1580–1800: The Origins of an Associational World* (Oxford: Oxford University Press, 2000).

exchange, consumption was conceptualized as female with a need for the courts to protect women – and their husbands' incomes – from exploitation by merchants. As she remarks, there is a need to rethink the supposed 'demoralization' of the market by political economy.[3]

This chapter extends the approach of Finn to another area of the market: the provision of transport, water, gas, and electricity by large-scale enterprises which are often characterized as natural monopolies. These services were crucial in resolving the serious problems of under-investment and rising mortality in British towns in the second quarter of the nineteenth century. The solution rested, in part, on removing barriers to *public* investment,[4] but it also depended on large-scale *private* investment with the attendant danger that monopolists might exploit consumers in precisely the same way as the old chartered companies. In the second quarter of the nineteenth century, the East India Company was stripped of control over tea and other goods from the east, but one set of 'artificial' monopolies might merely be replaced by another. Merchants might be free to use any ship only to make them captives of railway companies able to charge high freights. Tariffs on raw materials might be abolished, only to place producers at the mercy of companies able to charge high prices for other vital commodities. The power of the railway companies was feared by many commentators. As Herbert Spencer remarked, the corporate conscience of a railway company was inferior to the conscience of an individual and a group of men might collectively undertake an act which each as an individual would find repellent.[5]

A similar argument was developed by John Stuart Mill, who was concerned that monopolistic companies were not accountable. In theory, shareholders had power over the directors of companies; in practice, their input was often minimal. By contrast, government agencies – whatever their failings – were more accountable

3. M. Finn, 'Working-class women and the contest for consumer control in Victorian county courts', *Past and Present,* 161 (1998), pp. 154, 119–20, 128–9. An excellent analysis of the legal position of married women as creditors, which shows the importance of the law and gender in shaping consumption, is provided by E. Rappaport, '"A husband and his wife's dresses": consumer credit and the debtor family in England, 1864–1914' in V. de Grazia and E. Furlough (eds), *The Sex of Things: Gender and Consumption in Historical Perspective* (Berkeley: University of California Press, 1996), pp. 163–87.

4. See S. Szreter and G. Mooney, 'Urbanisation, mortality and the standard of living debate: new estimates of the expectation of life at birth in nineteenth-century cities', *Economic History Review,* 51 (1998), pp. 84–112; and S. Szreter, 'Economic growth, disruption, deprivation, disease and death: on the importance of the politics of public health for development', *Population and Development Review,* 23 (1997), pp. 693–728.

5. P.S. Atiyah, *The Rise and Fall of Freedom of Contract* (Oxford: Clarendon, 1979), p. 281, quoting H. Spencer, 'Railway morals and railway policy', 1854, from *Essays: Scientific, Political and Speculative,* iii (London: Williams & Norgate, 1891), p. 60. On the regulation of railways, see T.L. Alborn, *Conceiving Companies: Joint-Stock-Companies in Victorian England* (London: Routledge, 1999), chapters 7–9; and F. Dobbin, *Forging Industrial Policy: The United States, Britain and France in the Railway Age* (Cambridge: Cambridge University Press, 1994).

to electors. As Mill saw it, any 'delegated management' was likely to be 'jobbing, careless and ineffective' compared with personal management by the owner, whose own reputation was at stake. However, the faults of delegated management were even greater in the case of large companies than the state. Despite the dangers that a powerful state bureaucracy would keep citizens in a child-like condition, Mill felt that the threat posed by company control of gas and water was still greater: 'a government which concedes such monopoly unreservedly to a private company does much the same thing as if it allowed an individual or an association to levy any tax they chose for their own benefit, on all the malt produced in the country, or on all the cotton imported into it'. What was needed, therefore, was strict regulation over the private companies, to control their prices and profits or to give the right of public purchase at fixed intervals.[6] On such a view, the railway and utility companies were a threat to a freely competitive market, and control was needed to complement the removal of customs duties and chartered monopolies. The politics of natural monopolies were therefore formulated in the same way as the politics of taxation: electors and their representatives needed to pay close attention to the spending and taxing powers of the government; and consumers of gas and water needed to pay close attention to the ability of companies to 'tax' through their charges for essential services. In both cases, the 'franchise' – the voice of the person purchasing or consuming services – should be carefully devised to provide effective controls, and to prevent the state or the companies from levying taxes or charges on one group to the benefit of another. As Mill put it, 'The question is not between free trade and a Government monopoly. The case is one in which a practical monopoly is unavoidable; and the possession of the monopoly by individuals constitutes not freedom but slavery; it delivers over the public to the mercy of those individuals.' The issue was how the government should best protect the public and secure their liberty.[7]

The weakening of older forms of monopoly might therefore simply give way to newer forms of what economists term 'natural' monopolies. The cost of providing a gas supply or water system, a railway line or telegraph service, was high and a large initial investment was needed. Even where competition did exist, concerns were likely to collude or merge in order to protect their investment with its high ratio of fixed to variable costs. But the notion of 'natural' monopolies can mislead. The concerns could only operate by obtaining powers from parliament, and the terms were the subject of considerable political and intellectual debate, influencing

6. J.S. Mill, *Principles of Political Economy* (first edition 1848, last major revision 1865), chapter XI of Book IV.

7. J.S. Mill, *Public Agency v Trading Companies: The Economical and Administrative Principles of Water-Supply for the Metropolis* (London, 1851), reprinted in J.M. Robson with an introduction by Lord Robbins, *Collected Works of John Stuart Mill, V: Essays on Economics and Society* (London: Routledge & Kegan Paul, 1967), p. 434.

the mode of operation of the companies and the allocation of profit between shareholders, consumers of various types, and the public good. Such issues were central to the wide question of intellectual and political responses to an industrial, urban capitalist economy.

In the opinion of Atiyah, the period from 1770 to 1870 was marked by the rise of freedom of contract, of which one important feature was the doctrine of *caveat emptor*. This rejected the assumption that the payment of a 'fair' price for a commodity implied a warranty, and argued that the price reflected any risk that the commodity might be defective. In the absence of an explicit warranty or proof of actual fraud, it was up to the buyer to beware. However, Atiyah is careful to qualify the extent to which freedom of contract was dominant. Many judges were pragmatic, highly skilled in using equity and precedents, or reading implications into contracts, in order to offer some substantive justice. Hence there was no more than a 'brief flirtation' with the doctrine of *caveat emptor* in the early nineteenth century, and even then some judges argued that the courts should establish whether contracts were fair – a position generally accepted by the 1860s.[8] Further, statute law challenged notions of freedom of contract. The notion of *caveat emptor* always excluded fraud, and parliament was willing to control any commercial behaviour which might make it more feasible. Hence measures were enacted on adulteration, weights and measures, hall-marking and assay, merchandising marks, and even hackney carriages.[9] But Atiyah does not consider another important area, the relationship between the owners of 'natural' monopolies and consumers. There was little point in the buyer of gas being wary if the supplier had a complete monopoly of the local market. Further, any estimation of quality depended on scientific tests of illuminating power and chemical composition, and the measure of quantity depended on the reliability of meters supplied by the producer. Freedom of contract was an illusion in these circumstances, implying a constant threat to liberty by a despotic, exploitative power. The consumer needed scientific knowledge, validated by 'experts', which entered the negotiation of relationships between provider and consumer, however defined.

The introduction of free trade in early Victorian Britain was not intended to lead to an unfettered play of economic forces; rather, it implied a removal of barriers to free association by all members of society in a world of small firms and voluntary societies designed to generate moral and civic virtue and not merely individual self-interest.[10] The political economy of Victorian Britain was not simply an act of destruction of what has been called, somewhat misleadingly, 'old corruption'.

---

8. Atiyah, *Freedom of Contract*, Part I *passim*, and especially pp. 398–405; and 178–80, 471–9 on *caveat emptor*

9. *Ibid.*, pp. 544–61.

10. F. Trentmann, 'Political culture and political economy: interest, ideology and free trade', *Review of International Political Economy*, 5 (1998), pp. 218–19, 232.

It was also an act of construction of new forms of organization – co-operatives, friendly societies, trade unions – and preservation from the dangers of what may be called 'new corruption'. Free trade promised to defend the 'consumer' from exploitation by tariffs erected in favour of producers. The dominant assumption in the political economy of free trade was that unorganized consumers must have priority over organized producers, especially when producers claimed to be trading in the public good. As Trentmann remarks, 'the political nation was defined as a nation of consumers, represented in Parliament', and the consumer was defined as the 'public interest' rather than an atomistic individual seeking satisfaction of material wants. The debates over the corn laws and navigation laws set selfish interests against the consumer and the public, and the same rhetoric could easily be extended to the new circumstances of public utilities in British cities.[11]

The issue was how best to ensure that consumers or the 'public' should be guarded against exploitation by utilities, and specifically by gas companies which provide a good case study of the material politics of a commodity as it became the site of debate over cultural meanings and economic benefits. It might be through encouraging competition; by using courts and arbitrators to define acceptable prices and profits; by devising an automatic accounting mechanism to allocate benefits between shareholders and consumers; or by transferring private firms to public ownership. There was also the matter of how to define consumers. They might be public bodies purchasing gas for street lights; they might be industrialists eager for cheap gas to light their factories; they might be shopkeepers wishing to display their wares and tempt customers into their store; or individual householders anxious to obtain small amounts of gas at low prices for domestic comfort. The definition of the 'consumer interest' might therefore be constructed through rhetorical appeals to represent the consumer or public in a way which masked self-interest: a factory owner might claim to speak for the consumer in general and in the process seek a tariff structure which benefited large users. Often, the consumer was someone for whom others claimed to speak, rather than an interest with his or her own voice. Public bodies were often anxious to ensure that the power of monopolies was constrained so that shareholders did not exploit consumers, an interest to which politicians appealed as synonymous with citizens, the voters, or the public.

Many of these issues were considered by Arthur Johnes, a barrister who ended his career as one of the county court judges studied by Finn, seeking to define the morality of commercial transactions. Twenty years earlier, as a barrister in London, Johnes pondered another set of questions concerning commercial morality and

---

11. *Ibid.*, p. 229. Of course, protectionists countered that the best way of creating prosperous domestic consumers was by maintaining a balanced economy of agriculture and trade, which protected producers in order to create employment. See A. Gambles, *Protection and Politics: Conservative Economic Discourse, 1815–52* (Woodbridge: Royal Historical Society, new series, Boydell Press, 1999). But from about 1850 to the 1890s, the free trade rhetoric was in the ascendant.

the relationship between consumers and the market. In 1847, Johnes and Samuel Clegg, a London-based civil engineer, were appointed by the Commissioners of Woods, Forests, Land Revenues, Works and Buildings to make 'preliminary enquiries' into local bills for gas lighting in Wolverhampton, Ashton-under-Lyne, Shipley, Bingley and Wakefield.[12] Johnes and Clegg had a clear set of assumptions about the relationship between companies and consumers. Although different groups of local residents articulated conflicting rhetorical appeals to represent the consumer, Johnes and Clegg presented themselves as the true voice of consumers and recommended a major change in company structure to ensure that their interests were protected. In 1846, the repeal of the corn laws prevented exploitation of consumers by agriculturalists; in 1847, Johnes and Clegg proposed measures to prevent exploitation of consumers by gas companies.

The debate over the powers of gas companies was cast in the same terms as discussion over the franchise for public bodies, with an explicit link between control over commercial firms and that over elected authorities. Many local commissions for lighting and watches formed in the eighteenth and early nineteenth centuries allowed all ratepayers or owners above a certain threshold to serve as a commissioner on taking an oath. When parliament laid down general procedures for establishing commissions in the 1830s, two different approaches were adopted. In the first, larger owners and occupiers had more votes in order to ensure that power was in 'responsible' hands; in the second, each ratepayer had one vote. The franchise for these commissioners was therefore a subject of controversy and considerable variation, which affected the extent to which they could speak with any authority for the consumer or the 'public'.[13]

The question faced by Johnes and Clegg in 1847 was whether, given the nature of the franchise, the commissioners were representative of the consumers of gas. The commission might have fallen into the hands of large consumers who would press for a tariff offering them a lower price at the expense of small consumers. The commission itself might obtain lower prices for gas for street lighting at the expense of other consumers. Similarly, the 'franchise' of the gas company was the subject of debate. If shares were held by large consumers, they could make sure that the tariff favoured them with heavy discounts for large purchases; if the owners came from outside the town, they might simply maximize their profits at

---

12. Finn, 'Working class women and the contest for consumer control', pp. 126–7. They were appointed under 9 and 10 Vict. cap 106, 'An act for making preliminary inquiries in certain cases of applications for local acts'.

13. For the debates over these different franchises, see J. Prest, *Liberty and Locality: Parliament, Permissive Legislation and Ratepayers' Democracies in the Nineteenth Century* (Oxford: Clarendon, 1990), pp. 8–9, 12–13 and also P.M. Ashbridge, 'The power and the purse: aspects of the genesis and implementation of the Metropolitan Poor Act, 1867', PhD thesis, University of London, 1998, chapter 2.

the expense of the consumers. These issues were most explicit in the case of Ashton-under-Lyne, where the surveyors heard extensive evidence from local interests.

The gas company in Ashton claimed that it was more representative of the consumers than the local police commission established in 1827 as a self-elected body which represented larger ratepayers. Consequently, small consumers would not benefit from transferring ownership to the commission. Indeed, the company argued that in Manchester – where gas *was* supplied by the police commissioners – the outcome was high prices for consumers, with profits used to reduce local taxes for large ratepayers. The company therefore claimed that 'public' ownership placed the works under the control of a select and selfish body rather than the general body of the consuming public. It followed that the Ashton gas company (at least in its own estimation) was more accountable and democratic, and that 'the interests of the whole body of consumers are more likely to be regarded by a company like the Gas Company, who can have no interests to serve except those of the consumers generally, than by vesting them in any other body'. The company argued that its new bill offered effective protection of the consumers' interest. Not only would dividends be limited, but the 'franchise' of shareholders would prevent a few wealthy individuals from taking control of the company by limiting shareholders to a maximum of 13 votes so that large owners could not dominate the company through large blocs of votes. Further, new shares would not be offered to existing shareholders at par with the danger of creating a 'closed' company, but would be sold at public auction so that any resident of the town had the opportunity to become a shareholder with a vote. Not surprisingly, the commissioners were sceptical of the company's claims to represent the consumer. In their opinion, the bulk of shareholders came from outside the town, and the commissioners argued that no individual should be permitted to own more than 50 shares, regardless of voting rights. The control and ownership of gas companies were therefore fought out in similar terms to debates over the franchise, with similar concerns about the precise relationship between owners and consumers, taxpayers and beneficiaries.[14]

Johnes and Clegg were sceptical of the claims of both the company and the commission, and they proposed an alternative approach. Their starting point was that competition was wasteful and that amalgamation would offer greater efficiency and lower prices for consumers – always assuming that monopoly did not lead to exploitation of consumers or to lack of care in the use of capital. They opposed

---

14. PP 1847 XXII, *Minutes of evidence . . . on a preliminary enquiry respecting the Ashton Gas Amendment Bill*, Qq 903–89, 996, 999–1020; on the ownership of shares, see Qq 480–520 and the list of owners on pp. 211–12. The criticism of the Manchester police commissioners had some force: the Manchester Police Act, 1828, gave a vote to only 8.5 per cent of adult males by 1835, and gave the wealthier districts a disproportionate number of commissioners. Disputes over gas prices, and the use of profits, formed a major political issue in the town: see M.J. Turner, 'Gas, police and the struggle for mastery in Manchester in the Eighteen-twenties', *Historical Journal*, 67 (1994), pp. 301–17.

discriminatory pricing for different categories of consumers, arguing that the lower prices paid by large consumers such as mill-owners or public bodies for street lights could only entail higher prices to other consumers and reduce the tax burden on well-to-do ratepayers. Above all, Johnes and Clegg argued that discriminatory pricing was socially harmful by limiting the benefits of new technology, for 'those very classes to whom economy in every branch of their affairs is of the most vital moment, have been in a great measure excluded from this important discovery'. After all, 'in a northern climate, a cheap and good light is of great importance to the working classes of towns. Without an economical artificial light, it must be next to impossible for them, in the winter months, to preserve cleanliness in their persons, on in their dwellings. Moreover, we may remark, that the attractions of the gin-palaces of our populous districts chiefly consist in the contrast which they present to the dark and comfortless homes of the poor'. Most gas consumers were, at this stage, commercial and public users in shops, public houses, factories, railway stations, and streets. In Wolverhampton in 1847, street lamps consumed 4.4 million cubic feet, commercial users 27.8 million and households only 0.7 million, and working-class households only became significant consumers with the introduction of pre-payment slot meters in the 1890s. [15] Johnes and Clegg felt that the poor were being excluded by artificially high prices, and their argument was similar to Sir Robert Peel's complaint in 1830 that high customs and excise duties excluded the 'humbler classes' from the 'comforts . . . of civilised society' whose possession 'would form the best guarantee that the higher classes could have for the possession of their property and their power'.[16] The market for gas was 'moralized', linked with a wider strategy of creating a democratic world of goods; pricing – and taxation – were intimately connected with social improvement and the desire to bring workers within a new world of consumption. In reality, the debate over gas consumers involved commercial and public users and most residents of towns were not individual consumers.[17]

In Johnes and Clegg's opinion, the fault lay with the provision of gas by 'Companies composed of private individuals, uncontrolled by any public authority'. Their solution was to buy the existing companies on fair terms and sell them to consumers of gas resident in the district who would each be limited to a small

15. PP 1847 XXII, *Local Acts: preliminary enquiries,* 'Observations or General Report on the existing system of lighting towns with gas by Messrs Johnes and Clegg . . .', pp. 95–8; consumption in Wolverhampton from p. v. For a discussion of the market for gas and the spread of slot meters, see Daunton, *House and Home in the Victorian City: Working-Class Housing, 1850–1914* (London: Edward Arnold, 1983), pp. 238–41.

16. *Parliamentary Debates* ns 23, 19 March 1830, col. 658.

17. For an interesting discussion of the moral effects of gas, as a source of metropolitan improvement and also of urban degradation, see L. Nead, *Victorian Babylon: People, Streets and Images in Nineteenth-Century London* (New Haven and London: Princeton University Press, 2000), Part 2, 'Gas and Light'.

number of shares, with a dividend of no more than 5 per cent. 'In short, we conceive it to be desirable that the members of the Gas Company should, as far as possible, be identical with the gas consumers.' Discriminatory pricing would be banned; and where the actual cost of supplying small consumers *did* prove to be high, the difference should be explicitly and consciously covered by the community from taxes. To ensure that gas works were run efficiently and without waste of capital, the government should employ an officer to examine the works and accounts in order to enforce the limitation of dividends laid down by private acts, which could easily be evaded without expert inspection of the books. This officer would have power to hear complaints from consumers, which would both protect the managers of gas works from ill-informed criticism and provide consumers with scientific authority, without which they would have no effective control over the companies.[18] In other words, protection of the consumer depended on expert chemists and accountants who understood the complexities of the chemical composition of gas and the technicalities of accounts. *Caveat emptor* could not apply, for the individual purchaser could not make an informed decision, and was not able to find an alternative supplier. The report of Johnes and Clegg was a major statement about the politics of company structure and the relationship between owners and consumers, and many of the issues addressed by their report were to recur over the following thirty years.

In response to Johnes and Clegg's report, parliament adopted a set of model clauses to be used in future gas bills. The Gas Works Clauses Act, 1847 fixed a maximum dividend, usually of 10 per cent per annum, with the right of companies to make up any previous deficiency and to place any profit above the upper limit in a reserve fund of up to a tenth of the nominal capital of the concern. Any two 'gas ratepayers' – a term suggesting the connection with debates over the local government franchise – could apply to the Quarter Sessions (or sheriff in Scotland) to appoint an accountant to report on the state of the concern. Where the dividend and the reserve reached their upper limits, the court could order such reduction in prices as it thought proper, provided that the company was ensured a profit as close as possible to the maximum dividend.[19] The Act therefore accepted that competition was wasteful, and that consumers should be protected from exploitation by setting a statutory limit on dividends, with a right to apply to the Quarter Sessions for a reduction in the price of gas. Whether the Act offered sufficient protection to the consumers was open to question.

In some towns, consumers (or at least individuals who appropriated that identity) took action into their own hands by creating 'consumer' gas companies to challenge

18. PP 1847 XXII, 'Observations . . . by Messrs Johnes and Clegg . . .', pp. 2, 98–100.

19. 10 Vict. cap 15, 'An act for consolidating in one act certain provisions usually contained in acts authorizing the making of gasworks for supplying towns with gas'.

the existing concerns. For example, the Surrey Consumers Co. was established in 1849 to supply south London. However, the costs soon proved too great, and the consumer companies succumbed to the economic imperatives for local monopolies. In London, the gas companies agreed to end competition by dividing the metropolis into 'districts', to the south of the Thames in 1853 and to the north in 1857 – and these arrangements included the consumer companies.[20] By the late 1850s, the gas companies were facing serious criticism from consumers who were largely commercial users and public bodies. The protection offered by restriction on dividends was limited, for the company could simply offer new shares to existing owners at par, which could be sold at a premium or retained to earn generous dividends. Critics of the companies complained that they had little reason to borrow money at low interest rates, or to improve their efficiency. The issue was taken up by the South London Gas Consumers' Mutual Protection Association in 1855, which presented a list of complaints against the companies. Prices were too high, and the benefits of 'districting' were not passed to consumers. There were suspicions that the illuminating power of gas was not constant, and that meters recorded excessive consumption.[21] As a result of pressure from the Association and local vestries, Select Committees were appointed to consider the supply of gas in London in 1858 and 1859, and the Metropolitan Board of Works (M.B.W.) drafted a bill to control maximum *prices* as well as dividends, with provision for auditing accounts and enforcing quality. The aim was to create a sliding scale so that dividends could only be increased on condition that the price of gas to the consumer was reduced; any increase in price would entail a drop in dividends. Consequently, a company could only pay a higher dividend by cutting prices through greater efficiency in the use of capital and the adoption of new technology. The benefits of technical change would therefore be divided between consumers and shareholders by an automatic accounting procedure, so creating symmetrical interests without, as Johnes and Clegg proposed, making owners and consumers coterminous.

When the M.B.W.'s bill reached the Commons in 1860, the companies succeeded in removing the sliding scale. Instead, the Metropolis Gas Act, 1860 limited dividends to 10 per cent, with the right to make up any deficiency over a period of six years. Competition was admitted to be inefficient, and the district agreements were recognized and brought under public control. The M.B.W., vestries, and any twenty householders supplied with gas could complain about the quality or quantity of gas to the Home Secretary, who could appoint an inspector with power to examine the gasworks. If the complaint was sustained, the Home Secretary would

---

20. D. Matthews, 'Laissez-faire and the London gas industry in the nineteenth century: another look', *Economic History Review,* 2nd ser., 39 (1986), p. 256; PP 1859 III, *Report from the Select Committee on Gas (Metropolis)*, Qq 3–19.

21. PP 1859 III, *Select Committee on Gas (Metropolis)*, Qq 25–237 and evidence of W. Crosley.

give notice to the company to remove the grievance, on penalty of a fine of £50. The illuminating power, maximum level of chemical components such as ammonia and sulphuretted hydrogen, and the precise form of tests, were laid down with considerable precision. The companies were to provide an experimental meter a thousand yards from the works, and each local authority was to supply instruments and pay an examiner to test the gas. When the company failed the tests, it was liable to summary conviction and payment of a fine. The price of gas was not to rise above 4*s*. 6*d*. per 1,000 cubic feet, unless justified by an increase in costs, in which case the local authority had the right to object to the Home Secretary who sent the proposal to arbitration. In this respect, individual consumers had no power of objection, and the act used the term 'consumers' as interchangeable with 'local authority' - a significant shift in the definition of who spoke for consumers. In any event, the price for gas was not to rise above 5*s*. 6*d*. per 1,000 cubic feet. The maximum dividend was now complemented by some attempt to impose a maximum price, which could only be breached with the agreement of arbitrators appointed by the Home Secretary.[22]

This act laid down standards of illuminating power and chemical composition in order to provide the consumer with some explicit measure of quality. There was also the serious issue of how to measure the quantity consumed, for meters were supplied by the producers and consumers were not sure that they were not cheated. This issue was tackled by the Sale of Gas Act, 1859.[23] The precise definition of a cubic foot of gas and the method of measurement formed one element in the Victorian obsession with metrology, the construction and dissemination of standards. The great physicists William Thomson and James Clerk Maxwell realized in the 1870s that precise units of measurement were needed for electricity, both for experimental observation and for exchange. As Maxwell remarked, standards were 'national treasures'. 'The man of business requires these standards for the sake of justice, the man of science requires them for the sake of truth, and it is the business of the state to see that our . . . measures are maintained uniform'.[24] A similar process applied to gas. The Act of 1859 laid down a legal standard for a cubic foot; the Exchequer's office of weights and measures was to obtain accurate standard equipment which could then be used to verify copies throughout the country. All new domestic meters were to be 'stamped' as accurate, and all existing

---

22. 23 and 24 Vict. cap 125, 'An Act for better regulating the supply of gas to the Metropolis'; D.A. Chatterton, 'State control of public utilities in the nineteenth century: the London gas industry', *Business History*, 14 (1972), pp. 70–2. On the polluting and tarnishing effects of gas lighting in domestic interiors, see 'Refracting the gasolier: understanding Victorian responses to domestic gas lighting', in I. Bryden and J. Floyd (eds), *Domestic Space: Reading the Nineteenth-Century Interior* (Manchester: Manchester University Press, 1999), pp. 84–102.

23. 22 and 23 Vict. cap 66, 'An Act for regulating measures used in sales of gas'.

24. Quoted in S. Schaffer, 'Accurate measurement is an English science', p. 136, in M. Norton Wise (ed.), *The Values of Precision* (Princeton: Princeton University Press, 1994), pp. 136–72.

meters within ten years. The Astronomer Royal, George Biddle Airy, was consulted about the construction of these measuring devices, but he pointed to a further problem. A meter might be accurate in measuring the passage of a cubic foot of gas, but the 'wheel work' recording consumption on dials could be extremely inaccurate and make the Act 'nugatory and useless'. This remark offered an opportunity for the Treasury to propose the repeal of the Act and to re-assert the principle of *caveat emptor*. In their view, it was better 'to leave the detection of fraud and the means of preventing it to the acuteness of the individuals interested, and to the ordinary operation of competition, rather than to endeavour to guard against fraud by legislation of such minute detail'. The Privy Council for Trade was not convinced, arguing that gas was an exceptional case and that the correct measurement should be laid down in law. 'A purchaser of goods by yard measure or pound weight, if he suspects that he has not obtained full measure, can readily find an authentic test, and if dissatisfied can in most cases resort to another dealer.' Gas was different, for there was no competition and a legal standard with properly verified instruments was essential. The Treasury's case was rejected, and Airy's doubts were easily resolved. The Act required meters to 'register' the amount of gas, and the term was held to cover the wheel-work and dials. Accordingly, the Act was implemented and standard measures were supplied throughout the country.[25]

The process of creating standardized weights and measures was therefore extended to gas, and the conceptual and engineering problems of accurately measuring and indicating the consumption of an invisible commodity were resolved.[26] The principle of *caveat emptor* was overruled. Nevertheless, the failure to link prices and dividends through an automatic sliding scale meant that the M.B.W. and the City of London corporation doubted whether consumers had sufficient protection. The result, it seemed, was simply to allow companies to increase their dividends to the maximum of 10 per cent without passing on the benefits of monopoly and 'districting', and they could still issue new shares at par in order to circumvent the limitation on dividends.[27] Consequently, in 1866, the City of London corporation proposed to establish its own company unless the price were reduced to 3s. 6d. The proposal was referred to a Select Committee, which also reconsidered the terms of the act of 1860. The Select Committee

---

25. PP 1860 LIX, *Copy of the Report of the Astronomer Royal . . . on the instrumental equipments of the Exchequer Office of Weights and Measures, as regards the measures for preventing fraud in the sale of gas to the public . . .*, pp. 573–83; PP 1860 LIX, *Copies of all correspondence between the Lords Commissioners of HM Treasury and the Board of Trade, the Controller of the Exchequer and the Astronomer Royal . . .*, pp. 585–99; PP 1860 LIX, *Copies of all correspondence . . . on the subject of the Sale of Gas Act . . .*, pp. 603–51

26. On the development of standardized weights and measures, see J. Hoppit, 'Reforming Britain's weights and measures, 1660–1824', *English Historical Review,* 108 (1993), pp. 82–104.

27. *Parliamentary Debates* 3rd ser. 186, 11 April 1867, col. 1578.

accepted that 'regulated monopoly' offered 'economy of administration and the convenience of the consumers', but that the regulations should be much tighter, with a reduction in the maximum price and improvement in the quality of supply. The Select Committee proposed that a Chemical Board should be established at the expense of the companies to report to the Home Secretary on the procedures for a daily analysis of gas, to be undertaken by officials appointed by the local authorities. Further, the right to make up deficiency of dividends should be restricted to three years. The gas companies were appalled, complaining that they had not made adequate representations to the Select Committee, in the mistaken belief that they had no cause for concern.[28]

When the new Conservative government came to power in 1867, it was faced by the report of the Select Committee and by deputations from the M.B.W, City of London corporation, and vestries as well as unspecified 'gentlemen representing the consumers'. The President of the Board of Trade, Stafford Northcote, claimed that the government was merely a disinterested arbiter wishing to create a 'friendly agreement' between the gas companies and consumers of London. Indeed, the Board of Trade had a strongly held view of its position. In 1876, T.H. Farrer, the permanent secretary of the Board of Trade, suggested that the Board represented the public in acting as a fair arbitrator between the companies and the consumers. Although it might take the side of consumers where they had a clear grievance, the task of representing the consumers fell to the M.B.W. and City of London corporation.[29] However, compromise proved impossible and the government presented its own bill following the lines of the Select Committee. It would create a 'metropolitan gas board' to test the quality of gas, reduce the maximum price to 3s. 6d. at a dividend of 7 per cent, and introduce a sliding scale so that the dividend could increase when the price fell below 3s. 6d. Northcote proposed – in an unusual procedure – to refer the bill to a Select Committee after the second reading, when the companies would have a chance to make their views known. The companies were not reassured and – not surprisingly – interpreted the bill as an attack on their dividends. One Member of Parliament denounced the bill for introducing an unprecedented principle of confiscation by devaluing gas shares, and the interests of consumers and shareholders collided. Northcote complained that 'he had received letters without numbers from clergymen and widows stating that the Bill would ruin them, would destroy all the foundations of property throughout the country, and that its privileges were infinitely more to the advantages of the consumers than of the companies'. The water and railway companies took up the campaign, sending out circulars and forms en masse for signature and presentation

---

28. PP 1866 XII, *Report from the Select Committee on the London (City) Corporation Gas etc Bills*, pp. 67–8.
29. PP 1876 XI, *Report from the Select Committee on the Metropolis Gas (Surrey Side) Bill*, Qq 4–6.

to parliament. Northcote accused them of misusing the power of petitioning parliament in a way 'which was unfair and not in the spirit of the constitution', and he was in turn attacked for his despotism. The debate was a prime example of the 'politics of joint-stock', the tussle between shareholders and consumers which had different outcomes in different circumstances. In the case of railways, local users had problems in organizing against the power of shareholders and directors with a national voice and parliamentary presence. In the case of gas, the coincidence of the customer base with local authorities meant that shareholders and directors were less likely to dominate, and local authorities, as the voice of the public interest, had more chance of success.

Northcote was forced to compromise with the London gas companies, abandoning the proposed maximum of 7 per cent and retaining a maximum dividend of 10 per cent. However, the draft bill did not specify the maximum price or the illuminating power which would be inserted as a result of bargaining on the Select Committee. Neither had a firm decision been made about the adoption of a sliding scale, which made the composition of the Select Committee a matter of great significance. A.S. Ayrton, the Liberal M.P. for Tower Hamlets, felt that the government had given way to the gas companies at the expense of the metropolis and its inhabitants, and without consulting the local authorities. He argued for a large committee to include London representatives – a claim denounced by his opponents for simply adding members 'with preconceived opinions, half advocates, half witnesses, and entire partisans'. In the event, a small Select Committee was appointed, and was duly attacked by Ayrton for failing to represent consumers.[30] The case for the consumer was therefore put to the Select Committee by the M.B.W. and the City of London corporation, as petitioners against the bill rather than through any consumer representation on the Committee.

The Select Committee started from the assumption that the terms granted to companies to employ their capital were sacrosanct and 'a compulsory and unconditional interference with the prices already conceded to the producer, is not the weapon by which Parliament is accustomed to secure the rights of the consumer'. Although the Select Committee seemed to be taking the side of the companies, it admitted that circumstances had changed. In 1847, parliament assumed that the power of the companies would be limited by competition; now, it was accepted that an exclusive supply reduced costs. Accordingly, the Committee recommended further amalgamations 'if accompanied by conditions securing the consumer against the evils to which monopoly, unrestrained by sufficient regulations, is calculated to give rise'. The committee needed to reconcile the claims

---

30. *Parliamentary Debates* 3rd ser. 186, 4 April 1867, col. 1107–8; 11 April 1867, cols 1576–9; 2 May 1867, cols 1914–24; 3rd ser. 187, 9 May 1867, cols 362–3. On the politics of joint stock in the case of railways, see Alborn, *Conceiving Companies*.

of the companies with the 'just expectations of the consumer', and was more critical of the companies than Ayrton expected. It concluded that the terms of 1860 were too favourable to the companies, allowing them to secure 10 per cent dividends unlike in the era of competition. By contrast, the 'interests of the consumer have been very inadequately protected' either by competition or regulations. The consumer would not accept a system under which 'no one who represents his interest has any share in, or control over, the direction of that expenditure'. How should this be achieved?

A period of bargaining ensued and a compromise seemed about to emerge: a reduction in price to 3s. 9d. at 16 candles, with amalgamations under the direction of the Board of Trade, and periodic revision of price and illuminating power to balance the interests of consumers and shareholders. This revision would be implemented by arbitration under the control of the Board of Trade, with audit of accounts and inspection of works. However, agreement broke down over the terms of the arbitration clause. The companies and the metropolitan authorities took different views over the Board of Trade's proposal that the arbitrators should fix a price to give the companies a dividend 'attaining or at least approaching' 10 per cent on condition they showed 'due care and management'. The companies felt that they should be *assured* a dividend of 10 per cent. The committee tended to agree with the metropolitan authorities, arguing that the act of 1847 did not guarantee a statutory dividend of 10 per cent, for it was assumed that profits would be limited by competition. The committee was therefore adamant that the consumer was entitled to stricter regulation of monopoly power and that, failing acceptance of these terms, the City of London corporation and M.B.W. should be allowed to introduce a public supply.[31]

Although a general settlement proved impracticable, piecemeal change was possible. The City of London Gas Act, 1868 introduced these new terms for one company, which were gradually extended to other metropolitan companies. The Act of 1868 fixed the price at 3s. 9d. per 1,000 cubic feet of 16 candle power, with a maximum dividend of 10 per cent and a reserve of 1 per cent. If the City of London corporation or the company wished to change the maximum price, they applied to the Board of Trade which would appoint commissioners to fix an illuminating power and price 'calculated to yield to the Company, with due care and management, a dividend . . . attaining as near as may be, but in no case exceeding, the rate of £10 per centum per annum', as well as preserving the reserve fund. The commissioners were to take account of savings from amalgamations, and were not to fix the price higher than allowed in the act of 1860 (5s. 6d.); the price was to be as low as circumstances permitted. The Board of Trade was also to

---

31. PP 1867 XII, *Special Report from the Select Committee on the Metropolis Gas Bill*, pp. 5–16.

appoint a Board of Gas Referees to decide on the permitted level of impurity in gas and the method of testing to be used by the City's gas examiners.[32]

The Board of Gas Referees was responsible for a stricter definitions of the quality of gas, extending metrological rigour. The tests of impurity and illuminating power established in 1860 had their shortcomings. The existing system of photometry was defective, for examiners varied in their readings by half a candle, which amounted to a large loss to the consumer or a heavy penalty to the company. The referees also found that burners varied by 30 to 50 per cent in the light produced from the same amount of gas, which had serious financial consequences as well as generating heat and vitiating the atmosphere. As they pointed out, manufacturers were not fully aware of the principles affecting the light obtained from gas, and the Referees therefore investigated the principles for the construction of burners 'as a means of economy for the gas-consuming public'. The referees moved in a new direction, away from protecting the public against exploitation by monopolistic companies to advising on the development of best-practice technology, both by the manufacturers of equipment and of gas. The Referees were also given discretion to fix levels of impurities, making highly technical decisions in the interests of the consumer and advising the companies on the techniques of purification. In the case of sulphur compounds, for example, the Referees were aware that the companies could only increase the illuminating power of gas, as required by the legislation, by using coal with more sulphur compounds. In effect, the Referees were moving in the direction of a research institute, undertaking studies to improve methods of production. As they pointed out, the engineers of each company were fully employed in their daily tasks, and each company had different methods; the Referees had power to carry out investigations and to employ men at each works, and could undertake systematic studies in co-operation with the engineers at each works. Consequently, the Referees were extending their concern for the consumer into highly technical assessments of production and chemical composition, working with the companies to develop optimum practice.[33]

Nevertheless, the legislation of 1868 did not fully resolve the disputes over prices and profits. The definition of dividends was more favourable to the companies than the metropolitan authorities wished, and they felt that the act was one-sided. The companies had the right to apply to *increase* the maximum price, but there was no mechanism to *reduce* the price below 3*s*. 9*d*. The company could still

32. Chatterton, 'State control of public utilities', pp. 172–3; 31 and 32 Vict. c 125, City of London Gas Act, 1868.

33. PP 1868–9 LI, *Report . . . by the Referees appointed under the City of London Gas Act, 1868*, pp. 575–93; PP 1870 LIV, *First Report of the Gas Referees upon the Sulphur Question*, pp. 659–72; PP 1871 LVII, *Report . . . by the Gas Referees on the Ammonia Impurity in Gas*, pp. 209–23; PP 1871 LVII, *First Report by the Gas Referees on the Construction of Gas Burner*, pp. 233–57. A comparison may be drawn with more recent debates over the chemical composition of petrol and the use of taxes to alter demand and supply for particular types of fuel, whether lead-free or low-sulphur.

issue new shares at par to existing shareholders in order to pay out more dividends instead of offering lower prices to consumers. And a company earning 10 per cent had little motivation to increase productivity. The problem noted by Johnes and Clegg had not been resolved, and regulated monopoly still did not offer sufficient protection to the consumer. The deal of 1868 was challenged in a way which reactivated some of the concerns of Johnes and Clegg about the 'franchise' of shareholding and the ability of the companies to operate as 'closed' or self-electing corporations. Coal prices rose in the early 1870s and a number of metropolitan companies applied to the Board of Trade to appoint commissioners to revise the price and illuminating power of gas. The debates of 1867 were repeated, for the companies claimed that prices should be fixed in order to sustain what they now termed their 'rightful dividend' of 10 per cent and payments into the reserve fund. The M.B.W. took a different line: the companies were only entitled to 10 per cent when earned at the authorized price and power of gas, and on condition that the company showed 'due care and management'. Further, the reserve fund was discretionary and not a right. The M.B.W. also reiterated the complaint that new shares were offered to existing shareholders, so creating an incentive for excessive capital expenditure and negligence in the operation of plant. Nevertheless, the commissioners concluded that the act *did* give a right to a 10 per cent dividend, and that the companies were showing due care and management in the use of plant. Legal advice from the crown law officers prevented the commissioners from considering whether the method of raising and expending capital showed due care and management. Prices were therefore raised, and the M.B.W. and City of London corporation complained that the companies had secured an absolute right to pay a dividend of 10 per cent, except in cases of the most blatant incompetence.[34] Profits were given priority over prices, and the shareholder over the consumer.

The alternative to arbitration was to adopt a sliding scale, but the form was open to dispute. In 1867, the Board of Trade had proposed a one-way sliding scale allowing the dividend to rise above 10 per cent when the price was cut. This was not acceptable to the M.B.W. and City of London corporation which did not accept that the companies should get more than 10 per cent. In 1875, they suggested a one-way sliding scale based on a cut in the dividend from 10 per cent if the price rose above 3s. 9d. The outcome was a *double* sliding scale: a fall in prices permitted a rise in the dividend and a rise in prices led to a fall in the dividend. This was supported by the Board of Trade and at least some of the companies. In 1874, George Livesey, chief engineer and manager of the South Metropolitan company, suggested that 'the interests of gas companies are so closely bound up

---

34. PP 1874 LVII, *Copies of certificate of commissioners appointed by the Board of Trade in 1873 on an application of the Gaslight and Coke Co. for a revision of the illuminating power and price of gas . . .*; Chatterton, 'State control of public utilities', pp. 173–4.

with the interests of their customers, that the two are really identical'. The companies needed to satisfy the customers in order to retain their position, and his solution was to 'cause the interests of gas companies, and their customers, to run side by side, to make the consumers, in a sense, partners in the gas company, whereby both should participate in any improved or more economical working'. A double sliding scale would share the benefits of efficiency between prices and profits; and he extended his approach to the workforce by introducing profit-sharing. The double sliding scale also appealed to Farrer as preferable to arbitration, for he argued that no department or commissioners 'can succeed in dictating to a trading company the terms and conditions of manufacture on which they can make the greatest amount of profit, and to fix the price of their article accordingly'. The double sliding scale was adopted by the Select Committee under the chairmanship of W.E. Forster. The scheme 'would, without immediate increase of price, give to the companies, who alone possess the requisite knowledge and power, a strong interest to reduce expenditure, whether of capital or income, in lieu of the present system under which they have an interest in increasing the expenditure of capital, and non-interest in keeping down the expenditure of income'. In other words, assessment of 'due care and management' would no longer be left to arbitrators with all the problems of defining and interpreting criteria. Instead, an automatic mechanism was created so that the only way of increasing dividends was through passing on efficiency gains to the consumer. The double sliding scale protected the interests of consumers by securing as low a price as possible and giving an inducement for improvements to secure a higher dividend, so as 'to bring the consumer and the producer into the one common interest of maintaining a low price of gas'. As Forster remarked, the incentive of a greater profit was a better stimulus to good management than enquiries by outsiders were a check to bad management. [35]

The sliding scale was reinforced by steps designed to prevent companies from offering shares at par to existing shareholders. The 'auction' clauses required the companies to sell stock to the highest bidders, so that companies took any premium and the capital charges were reduced. Existing shareholders were no longer able to reward themselves with additional shares paying a generous dividend, and the 'self-electing' corporation gave way to a more democratic system of ownership rather as the Municipal Franchise and Assessed Rates Act, 1869, extended the franchise for local government. The new pattern of 'regulated monopolies' of the Commercial Gas Co. Acts of 1875 and 1876 therefore rested on a combination of sliding scales and auction clauses. As a result, many of the problems noted by

---

35. PP 1918 III, *Report from the Select Committee on Gas Undertakings (Statutory Prices), Report*, pp. 591, 604–8; PP 1875 XII, *Report from the Select Committee on the Metropolis Gas Companies Bill* (Livesey's evidence at Qq 1052–3 and see also the entry in *Dictionary of National Biography*); PP 1876 XI, *Report,Select Committee on Metropolis Gas (Surrey Side) Bill*, pp. 11–51.

Johnes and Clegg in 1847 were resolved, not by making consumers and share-holders coterminous within a company but rather by creating symmetrical interests based on a mutual interest in efficiency. Generous profits were justified by low prices and permitted by the achievement of high productivity. The perils of personal judgement by surveyors, judges, arbitrators or commissioners gave way to the automatic mechanism of the double sliding scale. The result was not a simple reliance on the invisible hand of the market; rather, the outcome depended on contested, politically contingent, and highly visible institutional or accounting arrangements in order to allocate productivity gains between different parties.[36] Of course, the question remained of whether any private concern should be allowed to make high profits and whether these were socially created – an issue which was to become increasingly important in London and national politics.

The sliding scale system only applied to about half the private companies by 1900, and the remainder continued to rely on maximum prices. A further step was to take the firms into public ownership. The political logic had changed since the 1840s, when public bodies could be seen as representing a small proportion of the community. By the later nineteenth century, Manchester City Council had greater claims to represent consumers in general than had the Manchester police commis-sioners in the early nineteenth century – and the number of gas consumers increased with the wider adoption of slot meters which accounted for 37.5 per cent of consumers in the city in 1914. In many towns, there was a close identity between gas consumers and voters, and purchase of the gas company seemed to offer considerable advantages in obtaining profits to reduce local taxes rather than pay dividends to private shareholders. The transfer of trading surpluses to the rates and other municipal accounts was sizeable. As Millward and Ward point out, municipalization did not have a major impact on prices to the consumer, but did direct profits away from private dividends to town councils in order to supplement the rates.[37]

The case study of the gas industry shows that the natural monopolies of early and mid-Victorian cities generated a complex material politics. The market was permeated by notions of fairness and morality, and by distributional contests over the claims of shareholders for profits and consumers for low prices. Consumers might, on occasion, mobilize as a group as in south London in the 1850s, yet they were more often an interest for which others spoke and acted. Departments of the

---

36. See PP 1899 X, *Report from the Select Committee on Metropolitan Gas Companies*, pp. 21–9 and appendix 8, pp. 347–51.

37. On patterns of municipalization, see R. Millward and R Ward, 'From private to public ownership of gas undertakings in England and Wales, 1851–1947: chronology, incidence and causes', *Business History*, 35 (1993), pp. 1–21; R Millward, 'The market behaviour of local utilities in pre-World War I Britain: The case of gas', *Economic History Review*, 44 (1991), pp. 102–27. On the incidence of slot meters, see Daunton, *House and Home*, p. 240. The proportion was higher in London: in 1914, 73 per cent of South Metropolitan consumers had slot meters.

central government varied in their perceptions: the Treasury preferred to rely on *caveat emptor*, whereas the Board of Trade tried to arbitrate between companies and consumers in the public interest. Local authorities were increasingly defined as the representative of the consumer. The discourse of free trade often merged the interest of the consumer into that of the public, and gave consumers priority over producers as the main beneficiary of policy. But it was not simply a matter of rhetoric: real interests were at play and the dominance of a discourse of consumption was challenged. The directors and shareholders of the gas companies could mobilize when their dividends were threatened, and place pressure on national politicians as in 1867. However, politicians were also susceptible to pressure from local authorities, whose electors overlapped with the consumers of gas. And the 'franchises' of the companies and the local authorities were contested, allowing them to speak with greater or lesser authority for the public. Over time, the claims of local authorities to represent consumers became stronger and more difficult for the companies to resist. The outcome in many towns was municipal ownership, where the consumer and owner/elector were largely identical. In London, the lack of clear identity between company districts and the metropolitan boroughs made public ownership problematical – and the M.B.W. or London County Council simply seemed too big and politically dangerous. The outcome in London was therefore different from that in many large provincial cities, with a greater reliance on sliding scales and on the technical advice of gas referees. The debates and legislation constantly referred to the needs of consumers, in terms of prices, profits and the very nature of the commodity offered for sale. *Caveat emptor* was simply inappropriate: how could a consumer of an invisible gas be sure of how much was supplied, or of the appropriate quality? Indeed, it might be asked: What is gas? The sciences of chemistry and metrology were called into service to define the very nature of the commodity upon which the relationship between consumer and producer was based. Such issues were debated in other commodities, in order to define the purity of water or milk or food, or the voltage and current of electricity. The market in Victorian Britain was permeated with notions of morality – they were simply different from those of Hanoverian Britain.

5

Scotch Drapers and the Politics of Modernity: Gender, Class and National Identity in the Victorian Tally Trade

Margot C. Finn

In charting the evolution of 'modern' mass markets in late nineteenth-century western Europe, scholars have emphasized the dramatic expansion of advertising, the use of commercial spectacle to generate consumer desire and the rise of the department store as a locus of anonymous, commodity-oriented acquisition in the public sphere. 'The department stores were highly visible, through their architectural presence and their ostentatious publicity, and this very visibility was one reason why they became a symbol of modernity in much of late nineteenth-century Europe: modernity in design, in sales methods, in the application of new technology to the act of retailing and to the art of attracting customers', Geoffrey Crossick and Serge Jaumain assert.[1] In this triumphal narrative of consumer modernity, new capital-intensive retail structures provide the institutional and the iconographic fulcrum upon which the emergence of the mass market turns, and increasingly abstract, depersonalized exchange relations underpin the creation of a truly modern commodity culture. 'Mass (in the sense of anonymous) marketing appeared, as shopkeepers increasingly sought individual transactions with unknown buyers',

---

1. G. Crossick and S. Jaumain, 'The world of the department store: distribution, culture and social change', in G. Crossick and S. Jaumain (eds), *Cathedrals of Consumption: the European Department Store, 1850–1939* (Aldershot: Ashgate, 1999), pp. 7–8. Along similar lines, see also L.A. Loeb, *Consuming Angels: Advertising and Victorian Women* (New York: Oxford University Press, 1994), M.B. Miller, *The Bon Marché: Bourgeois Culture and the Department Store, 1869–1920* (Princeton: Princeton University Press , 1981), T. Richards, *The Commodity Culture of Victorian England: Advertising and Spectacle, 1851–1914* (Stanford: Stanford University Press, 1990) and R.H. Williams, *Dream Worlds: Mass Consumption in Late Nineteenth-century France* (Berkeley: University of California Press, 1982).

James Carrier argues. 'Customers were increasingly acquiring objects in impersonal interactions in impersonal institutions.'[2]

Closely intertwined with this representation of the mass market is a prevailing historiographical tendency to depict the middle-class female consumer and the department store as the archetypal agents of commercial modernity. For Mica Nava, department stores and 'women's massive participation in the exploding culture of consumption and spectacle' constituted the public arena in which 'the everyday lives of large numbers of ordinary women were most deeply affected by the process of modernity'.[3] Cash transactions loom large in this feminized paradigm of commercialization. Erika Rappaport's analysis of bourgeois women's experience of shopping is characteristic. 'The department stores, which were built upon lower prices and "ready money", were in some sense responding to the legal morass that surrounded selling to a "mass" market of married women', she notes. 'These stores institutionalized cash transactions, introducing a new relationship between buyer and seller, to extricate themselves from older trading practices that essentially protected wealthy shoppers at the storekeeper's expense.'[4]

This emphasis on novel retail outlets selling drapery goods for cash to undifferentiated bourgeois women nicely captures the anxieties of beleaguered small-scale shopkeepers in these decades,[5] but it offers only a partial index to the dominant purchasing practices of the later nineteenth century. To be sure, the new Victorian retail institutions boasted impressive gains in sales, but their proportion of market share remained relatively modest. As late as 1915, department stores, co-operative societies and multiples accounted, respectively, for only 2 per cent, 8 per cent and 8 per cent of all retail activity in fixed shops.[6] Stores, moreover, represented only a portion of the expanding Victorian and Edwardian retail market. In the years from 1831 to 1911, the number of itinerant traders reported in the census rose from 9,459 to 69,347, figures which reflect an increase in the ratio of pedlars to population from 1:1,470 (1831) to 1:520 (1911).[7] As John Benson has remarked

2. J.G. Carrier, *Gifts and Commodities: Exchange and Western Capitalism since 1700* (London: Routledge, 1995), p. 75.

3. M. Nava, 'Modernity's disavowal: women, the city and the department store', in M. Nava and A. O'Shea (eds), *Modern Times: Reflections on a Century of English Modernity* (London: Routledge, 1996), p. 46.

4. E.D. Rappaport, *Shopping for Pleasure: Women and the Making of London's West End* (Princeton: Princeton University Press, 2000), p. 50.

5. For a balanced assessment of the discrepancy between independent tradesmen's perceptions of modernity and the persistence of conventional forms of retailing, see M.J. Winstanley, *The Shopkeeper's World, 1830–1914* (Manchester: Manchester University Press, 1983), esp. p. 217.

6. J. Benson, *The Rise of Consumer Society in Britain, 1880–1980* (London: Longman, 1994), p. 62.

7. D. Alexander, *Retailing in England during the Industrial Revolution* (London: Athlone, 1970), p. 64; J. Benson, *The Penny Capitalists: a Study of Nineteenth-century Working-class Entrepreneurs* (Dublin: Gill and Macmilan, 1983), p. 103.

of this trend, 'the late-nineteenth-century decline of rural hawking and peddling was more than counterbalanced by its expansion in urban areas'.[8]

Undercapitalized and underreported, itinerant trade none the less played a vital role in bringing working-class consumers into the modern market. Although largely insulated from the advertising craze, peddling – particularly the itinerant trade in items of clothing – was central to the expansion of plebeian women's participation in the mass market. Relying on extended lines of credit and personal relations based in the home rather than on anonymous cash transactions conducted in the public sphere, the itinerant drapery trade displayed a very different modernity than did the department store frequented by ladies of the upper and middle class. By offering goods for purchase on the instalment plan, the so-called Scotch traders (also known as credit drapers or tallymen) who dominated this sector of the plebeian market provided consumers with routine access to consumer credit well before the advent of the hire-purchase system. Conspicuous in their use of courts, prisons and trade associations to enforce their credit contracts, Scotch drapers were also at the forefront of political campaigns to protect the collective economic interests of tradesmen. Together these activities, as Gerry Rubin has convincingly argued, constituted an essential component of the 'modernisation programme' of British retailing.[9]

This chapter explores the material politics of Victorian Scotch drapers from the three-fold perspective of class, gender and nation. Building upon Rubin's analysis of the class dynamics of the credit drapery trade and my own work on gender and the consumer market, I examine the instrumental use of national identities in political debates over the relative virtues of cash and credit for working-class consumers.[10] Parliamentary and judicial critics of itinerant traders consistently identified credit drapery with a dangerous female proclivity for luxurious expenditure, a moral failing on the part of working-class women which they contrasted to the supposedly innate thrift of the manly English labourer. Credit drapers, confronted by these efforts to depict their trade as a parasitic imposition upon women and workers, struggled to mobilize their ranks under the banner of an invented Scottish nation distinguished by its modern commercial virtues. Deploying

---

8. J. Benson, *The Rise of Consumer Society*, p. 45. See also D.R. Green, 'Street trading in London: a case study of casual labour, 1830–60', in J. Benson and G. Shaw (eds), *The Retailing Industry*, 3 vols, vol. 1 (London: I.B. Tauris, 1999), pp. 115–31.

9. G.R. Rubin, 'From packmen, tallymen and "perambulating Scotchmen" to Credit Drapers' Associations, *c.* 1840–1914', *Business History*, 28 (1986), p. 206.

10. Rubin, 'From packmen', and *idem*, 'The county courts and the tally trade, 1846–1914', in G.R. Rubin and D. Sugarman (eds), *Law, Economy and Society, 1750–1914: Essays in the History of English Law* (Abingdon: Professional Books, 1984), pp. 321–48; M.C. Finn, 'Working-class women and the contest for consumer control in the Victorian county courts', *Past and Present*, 161 (1998), pp. 116–54.

an amalgam of ersatz Highland tradition, highly professional business techniques and canny political lobbying, the Scotch tally trade successfully protected its members from successive threats of parliamentary intervention. The lineaments of these campaigns provide a salutary reminder of the conflicted character of modernity in the British marketplace. Transacting business on the doorstep of the plebeian home, engaged in protracted, face-to-face contact with their customers and intent to justify their activities through ostensibly timeless ethnic identities, Scotch drapers were located at the very forefront of the construction of a modern mass market in nineteenth-century England and Wales.

Itinerant credit drapery was firmly entrenched in English consumer life from at least the seventeenth century, providing humble purchasers from an early date with an impressive range of goods that included domestically produced linens and imported calicoes as well as haberdashery items.[11] Far from fading as fixed shops multiplied and developed along new institutional lines, the peddling of drapery goods shared in the broader efflorescence of street-trading that marked the later nineteenth century. As weekly and fortnightly wages increasingly supplanted piecework and independent production, cash entered the working-class budget with a new degree of predictability, fostering regular instalment payments for mass-produced textile goods purchased on credit. Declines in the cost of foodstuffs also promoted increasing expenditure on textiles by plebeian house-holds.[12] Clothing, which accounted for only 6 per cent of reported working-class household expenditure in 1845, consumed an estimated 12 per cent of the family budget in 1904.[13]

Comprehensive statistics on the proportion of plebeian clothing supplied by itinerant traders are lacking, but a number of sources attest to the growing significance of the tally trade. Postal and trade directories, which had earlier failed to acknowledge the existence of Scotch drapers, routinely identified credit drapers as a distinct subset within the trade later in the century. The ratio of itinerant traders to fixed-shop drapers varied substantially, but often reached significant levels. Birmingham's forty-four travelling credit drapers constituted over a third of listed members of the trade in 1858; in Preston, nearly half of the drapers recorded in the trade directory were itinerants in 1866, and in Peterborough over a quarter of

---

11. M. Spufford, *The Great Reclothing of Rural England: Petty Chapmen and their Wares in the Seventeenth Century* (London: Hambledon, 1984), p. 145.

12. B.R. Mitchell, *British Historical Statistics* (Cambridge: Cambridge University Press, 1988), p. 738; E. Ross, *Love and Toil: Motherhood in Outcast London, 1870–1918* (New York: Oxford University Press, 1993), p. 40.

13. S. Levitt, 'Cheap mass-produced men's clothing in the nineteenth and early twentieth centuries', *Textile History*, 22 (1991), p. 181.

listed drapers travelled from door-to-door to sell their wares in 1874.[14] Statistics gathered by the House of Commons in 1873 demonstrate the wide consumer base successfully garnered by mid-Victorian credit drapers. The high bailiff of Birmingham's county court estimated that the twenty-eight credit drapers active within the city limits served a total of 51,429 customers. Adam Brown, a town councillor with 37 years' experience as a travelling draper, testified that the Scotch drapers active in Leeds had 72,048 credit customers on their books in 1872.[15]

Initially conducted in tandem with the sale of small parcels of tea, travelling drapery expanded significantly as a trade in its own right from the 1830s, as reductions in the excise duty helped to make the sale of domestically-produced cotton textiles more lucrative than that of tea.[16] From the outset, critics of this burgeoning trade stigmatized its agents and practices along class, gender and national lines. The original derivation of the term 'Scotch' drapery is, admittedly, unclear. Margaret Spufford notes that so-called 'Scotch cloth' – 'which contemporaries, who may have been making scurrilous allegations, said was made of nettle fibre' – served as a cheap alternative to imported calico and was a stock item in the inventories of seventeenth-century itinerant traders. But pedlars' use of nicked or 'scotched' tally sticks to keep accounts and the prominence of Scottish migrants among the ranks of the trade no doubt also contributed to the evolution of the phrase.[17] Regardless of its provenance, by the nineteenth century the association between Scotch drapery and Scottish nationals was firmly established. A commentator in 1894 confidently asserted that whereas 'pedlars and hawkers may be and are English, Scotch, Welsh, and Irish . . . the tally dealers, almost to a man, are born north of the Tweed, although they exercise their vocation in the land of the Saxon'.[18] Entries in trade directories do suggest a disproportionate concentration of stereotypically Scottish surnames in this particular sector of the

14. W.H. Dix and Co., *General and Commercial Directory of the Borough of Birmingham, and Six Miles Round* (Birmingham: printed for the author by James Upton, Sheffield, 1858) [44 of 123 drapers]; *Topography and Directory of North and South Lonsdale, Amounderness, Leyland, and the Town of Southport, &c* (Preston: P. Mannex and Co., 1866), p. 141 [33 of 74 drapers]; Francis Whellan and Co., *History, Topography, and Directory of Northamptonshire*, 2nd edn (London: Whittaker and Co., 1874), p. 645 [8 of 29 drapers].

15. *Report from the Select Committee on Imprisonment for Debt; together with the Proceedings of the Committee, Minutes of Evidence, and Appendix*, Parliamentary Papers, 1873 (348), XV, pp. 173, 181.

16. For the evolution of the trade, see *The Credit Drapers' Gazette*, 17 November 1894, p. 326.

17. Spufford, *Great Reclothing*, p. 89; A. Adburgham, *Shops and Shopping, 1800–1914: Where, and in what Manner the Well-dressed Englishwoman Bought her Clothes*, 2nd edn (London: Barrie and Jenkins, 1981), p. 3; Rubin, 'From packmen', p. 207. The preponderance of Scottish pedlars among itinerant traders in sixteenth-, seventeenth- and eighteenth-century Europe is noted by L. Fontaine, *History of Pedlars in Europe*, trans. V. Whittaker (Durham, NC: Duke University Press, 1996), p. 41, and C. Smout, 'The culture of migration: Scots as Europeans, 1500–1800', *History Workshop Journal*, 40 (1995), pp. 108–17.

18. *Credit Drapers' Gazette*, 17 November 1894, p. 326.

working-class consumer market. In Bristol's directory for 1897, surnames beginning with M', Mc and Mac were prominent among travelling drapers but were rare among other trades serving the plebeian consumer. Of 23 credit drapers, 8 (34.8 per cent) had surnames with these three prefixes; in contrast, only 4 of 254 drapers who traded from fixed shops (1.6 per cent), only 3 of Bristol's 1,302 general shopkeepers (0.2 per cent), 3 of 606 local boot and shoemakers (0.5 per cent) and none of the city's 315 bakers bore such surnames.[19]

Peddling at the doorstep two commodities – tea and apparel – which had been associated with women's promiscuous consumer desires since at least the eighteenth century,[20] Scotch drapers attracted increasingly caustic criticism as their trade expanded in the early Victorian years. The first edition of J.R. McCulloch's *Dictionary, Practical, Theoretical, and Historical, of Commerce* (1832) railed against the prevalence of shop credit but made no reference to the iniquities of credit offered to plebeian consumers by itinerant traders.[21] By 1844, however, the tally system merited its own entry in his *Dictionary*, and McCulloch was careful to underline the confluence of class, gender and national identities that rendered this form of consumer credit exceptionally pernicious. 'The customers of the tally shops are mostly women, consisting principally, of the wives of labourers, mechanics, porters . . . servant girls, and females of loose character', he commented. Notorious for beguiling wives to purchase unnecessary goods in their husbands' absence, McCulloch's tally tradesmen exploited an innate Scottish business sense to the detriment of English consumers and English tradesmen. As he noted dourly, 'The greater number of the small tally concerns are kept by Scotchmen; it is a curious fact, that when a "Tally-walk" is to be sold . . . a Scotchman's walk will bring 15% more than an Englishman's!'[22]

Middle-class commentators repeatedly elaborated upon this critique of the tally trade in the following decades, consolidating Scotch drapers' reputation as a foreign threat to plebeian virtue in England and Wales. In 1876 James Greenwood's depiction of the sales practices of a London credit draper – whom he dubbed 'M'Rooster' – was shot through with sexual connotations. 'He was every inch a

---

19. Even tally drapers without the 'Mc' prefix often boasted suspiciously Scottish names: they included Robert Andrew Ferguson, William Murdoch, David Scott and John Stewart. See *Kelly's Directory of the Counties of Somerset* (1897).

20. For the association between tea consumption and fears about female sexuality, see E. Kowaleski-Wallace, *Consuming Subjects: Women, Shopping, and Business in the Eighteenth Century* (New York: Columbia University Press, 1997), esp. p. 21; the relations among women, finery and sexuality are detailed by M. Valverde, 'The love of finery: fashion and the fallen woman in nineteenth-century social discourse', *Victorian Studies*, 32 (1988–89), pp. 169–88.

21. J.R. McCulloch, *A Dictionary, Practical, Theoretical, and Historical, of Commerce and Commercial Navigation* (London, 1832), p. 421.

22. J.R. McCulloch, *A Dictionary, Practical, Theoretical, and Historical, of Commerce and Commercial Navigation* (London, 1844), pp. 1206–7.

tallyman – tall and slim, with a genteel figure, but a keen-looking blade . . . undoubtedly a man who, amongst a certain class of the more impressionable sex, would be voted a "fascinator"', Greenwood commented. Emphasizing 'the silken sheen' of the 'scented but carefully combed sandy whiskers' 'fondly caressed' by M'Rooster, Greenwood played upon the illicit potential of credit drapers' intrusive marketing activities in the plebeian home. ' "The men don't half like chaps like me . . . calling at the house when they are away from it" ', his archetypal tallyman observed knowingly.[23] Margaret Penn's memoir of village life in Edwardian Lancashire attests to the force and longevity of this association between the itinerant tally trade and domestic consumer seduction. The Scotch draper of her childhood was the antithesis of the anonymous mass market which scholars of consumption argue came to dominate retail relations in this period. The monthly visit of the local credit draper, armed with frocks, pinafores, stays, drawers, chemises, sheets and pillow cases, saw her stepmother's 'will-power slowly drawn from her by the tallyman's dreadful charm . . . tempted beyond all human limits by the dazzling display . . .'[24]

As Victorian philanthropists mapped the distinctive contours of British working-class life, the tally trader became a stock figure in representations of plebeian consumer excess. The trope of domestic seduction pervaded these Victorian critiques of the Scotch draper, which depicted tawdry goods purchased on credit from alluring Scotsmen as emblems of a wider failure of English working-class thrift. Francis Heath, lamenting the incursion of the tally trade into rural regions in 1880, drew a sharp contrast between the beneficent moral effect of charitable clothing clubs on the one hand, and the baneful influence of promiscuous female consumer credit on the other. Members of clothing clubs in Wiltshire received a ticket representing their accumulated savings at the end of each year, but were permitted by the charities to purchase only approved items at the local drapery shop, 'as a precaution against the money being expended on light, useless finery . . .' Scotch drapers in Devonshire, however, had debauched the plebeian female consumer. Here, 'The "tally system", under which so much per week is paid towards an article of dress or cheap jewellery, too often unsuitable and unbecoming, has engendered a taste for finery in the wives and especially in the daughters of our labourers – a taste that, in its results, is sometimes almost grotesque'.[25]

In urban areas, tally traders figured prominently in increasingly racialized narratives of sexual danger and were easily conflated with the quintessential outsider of the Victorian metropolis, the immigrant Jew. Thrifty to a fault, the

---

23. J. Greenwood, *Low-life Deeps: an Account of the Strange Fish to be Found There* (London: Guildford, 1876), pp. 258–9, 265.

24. M. Penn, *Manchester Fourteen Miles*, intro. J. Burnett (Firle, Sussex: Futura, 1979), p. 174.

25. F.G. Heath, *Peasant Life in the West of England*, 2nd edn (London: Sampson, Low and Co., 1880), pp. 298, 300.

Scotchman-as-Jew offered an especially powerful icon of urban degeneration as the century drew to a close, signalling at once the decline of English commerce, domesticity and nationhood. 'England and Wales are the rich, happy hunting grounds for Sandy and Dougal, for Levi and Jacob, the scum and outcasts of their tribe and country,' the *Parish Councillor* raged in a particularly offensive variant of this argument in 1895, denouncing the ability of Scotch and Jewish traders 'to insinuate themselves into the Englishman's home in his absence'.[26] *Reynolds's Newspaper* drew attention to the travelling drapers' commercial perversion of the Scotsman's native thrift in its variation on this theme. 'The travelling draper is generally a cross between an Aberdeen Scotchman and a Jew – the very worst mixture in the world', the paper proclaimed in 1894.[27]

From the 1860s, politicians mobilized this persistent strain of cultural critique alongside parliamentary interrogations of the distinctive roles played by the court system in policing Scottish, English and Welsh petty debts. Established in 1846, the English and Welsh county courts offered creditors a rapid, inexpensive means of enforcing consumer contracts: for a modest fee, the creditor could summon his debtor to court, obtain an order for payment (typically by instalments) and commit the defendant to prison should the payments fail to materialize.[28] Credit drapers were frequent plaintiffs in these tribunals, accounting in some courts for as many as a third of all plaints.[29] Arguably more significant than such statistics in politicizing the practices of the credit drapery trade, however, was the partisan reform of English and Welsh insolvency law in 1869. By permitting debtors capable of paying a ten pound fee to file for personal bankruptcy and thus evade county-court commitment, this legislation effectively abolished imprisonment for upper- and middle-class debtors – thereby extending to affluent English and Welsh consumers legal immunities enjoyed by Scottish debtors of all classes since the 1830s.[30] Against this backdrop, and in the aftermath of the enfranchisement of a significant portion of the male artisanate by the 1867 Reform Act, the Scotch drapery trade emerged as a particularly worthy object of parliamentary scrutiny.

26. Cited in *Credit Drapers' Gazette,* 20 April 1895, p. 129.

27. *Reynolds's Newspaper*, 29 July 1894, p. 2.

28. 'A Solicitor', *County Court Practice Made Easy: or, Debt Collection Simplified* (London: Effingham Wilson, 1902) offers a good introduction to the courts' operation in this period.

29. See for example *Report of the Select Committee of the House of Lords on the Debtors Act; together with Proceedings of the Committee, Minutes of Evidence, and Appendix*, Parliamentary Papers, 1893–94 (HL 156), IX, p. 243.

30. For the transformation of the debt law see G.R. Rubin, 'Law, poverty and imprisonment for debt, 1869-1914', in Rubin and Sugarman (eds), *Law, Economy and Society*, pp. 241–99; and P. Johnson, 'Class law in Victorian England', *Past and Present*, 141 (1993), pp. 147–69. Scottish law had prohibited imprisonment for debts of less that 100 pounds Scots (approximately twelve English pounds) since 1835.

Debate on the insolvency legislation of 1869 established the parameters which structured this conflict for decades. Antagonists to county-court imprisonment repeatedly interwove class interests, national identities and gendered understandings of plebeian consumption in their arguments against the 1869 insolvency act. Married women – immune, under the common-law principle of coverture, from imprisonment for debt – featured in this critique as voracious consumers of drapery whose purchasing activities compromised the supply of male labour by subjecting men to imprisonment for their dependents' unpaid bills. Addressing the Commons in June 1869, Sir Henry Hoare called the proposal to maintain county-court imprisonment for small debts 'a Bill of Pains and Penalties against the working classes', arguing that 'It often happened that the honest artizan was drawn into debt by the imprudence of his wife'.[31] The Liberal M.P. M'Mahon, proposing an amendment to prohibit county-court imprisonment for debts of less than twenty shillings, contrasted the deleterious economic behaviour of Scotch drapers in England with the rational function of the modernized commercial law in Scotland itself. Drawing the House's attention to tally tradesmen's excessive imprisonment of plebeian debtors, M'Mahon charged that 'the power of imprisonment for small debts aided very materially in supporting strikes, by enabling the trader to give credit with safety'. He concluded by adverting favourably to the Scottish abolition of imprisonment for petty debts – a point forcefully reiterated by George Anderson, Liberal M.P. for Glasgow, who described the decision to retain imprisonment for small debts in England and Wales as 'retrograde'.[32]

Although M'Mahon's proposed amendment was unsuccessful, parliamentary antagonism to Scotch drapers' use of county-court imprisonment proved enduring. Michael Thomas Bass, Liberal M.P. for Derby and heir to the highly lucrative Bass brewery of Burton-on-Trent, was particularly instrumental in keeping the plight of the credit drapery consumer in public view. A substantial private philanthropist, Bass played an active parliamentary role in ameliorating working-class life and labour. Leone Levi undertook his exhaustive inquiry into the *Wages and Earnings of the Working Classes* at Bass's behest in 1866; in 1870, Bass was a vocal advocate of the railway servants' agitation to reduce their hours of labour.[33] His hostility to hawkers, criers and itinerant tradesmen was also noteworthy. Bass's 1864 act for the 'Better Regulation of Street Music within the Metropolis' laid the foundations for a series of legislative measures designed to diminish peddling in urban and rural areas alike.[34]

---

31. *Hansard's Parliamentary Debates*, 3rd ser., vol. 197 (22 June 1869), col. 574.

32. *Ibid.*, cols 572–3, 575.

33. *Dictionary of National Biography*, ed. L. Stephen (London: Smith, Elder, 1885), vol. 3, pp. 371–2; L. Levi, *Wages and Earnings of the Working Classes, with some Facts Illustrative of their Economic Condition, drawn from Authentic and Official Sources, in a Report to Michael T. Bass, Esq., M.P.* (London: John Murray, 1867).

34. For Bass's act (27 & 28 Vict. cap 55) and rising middle-class antagonism to itinerants in this period, see Green, 'Street trading in London', esp. p. 122.

By the 1870s, this antipathy for street traders had become intertwined with Bass's hostility to imprisonment for debt, and he emerged as a key parliamentary antagonist of the Scotch drapery trade. June 1872 saw the second reading of Bass's Imprisonment for Debt Abolition bill, legislation predicated on the argument that the 1869 insolvency act had created 'one law for the rich and another for the poor' in England and Wales. Complaining that the English expended half a million pounds per annum 'for the purpose of collecting the debts of Scotch tallymen', Bass ascribed the presence of 'so many Scotch tallymen in England running all over the country' to the retention, south of the Tweed, of the anachronistic legal instruments of imprisonment for debt. The virtues of masculine plebeian thrift were contrasted to the liabilities of feminine credit in this analysis of errant Scotch drapers. 'The labourer at present would have no difficulty in saving a certain moderate sum to go to market', Bass asserted confidently, 'and if a man went with cash in his hand he might buy at thirty per cent less than if he asked for credit'. Bass stressed the role of the man – and William Roden, Liberal M.P. for Stoke-upon-Trent, reiterated this contrast between modern and archaic, masculine and feminine consumer relations in supporting Bass's bill. Arguing that the abolition of imprisonment for debt would not 'stop legitimate credit, but only illegitimate credit – credit incurred by a man's wife really without his authority', Roden concluded that 'the present system was a relic of barbarism . . .'.[35]

Unable to gain sufficient parliamentary support for the passage of his bill, Bass did secure the appointment of a select committee on imprisonment for small debts. Here a succession of witnesses – relentlessly badgered by Bass when they departed from his received views – engaged in a protracted dispute over the commercial practices and legal structures which would best promote an equitable market for the working-class consumer. Conflicting understandings of national character provided a leitmotif for these deliberations, ironically offering Bass an effective means of mobilizing Scottish patriotism against Scotch drapery. Robert Malcolm Kerr, judge of the City of London's small claims court, proved a model witness. Born in Glasgow, Kerr opposed imprisonment for debt as the source of 'a vicious system of credit' and predictably contrasted the tallyman's demoralizing credit dealings with labourers' wives and daughters to the putative virtues of limited credit and the cash nexus. Prodded by Bass to expatiate upon the relative virtues of Scottish debt law, Kerr, 'being a Scotchman', testified that he had 'never found the want of the power of imprisonment was injurious to the small shopkeeper' in his homeland, and conjectured darkly that 'perhaps . . . the Scotch pedlar . . . has come south in consequence of the power of imprisonment for debt in England'.[36]

---

35. *Hansard*, vol. 211 (19 June 1872), cols 1977, 1979–80, 1982.
36. *Report of the Select Committee* (1873), pp. 18, 19, 20, 23, 26. For Kerr's judicial career, see G. Pitt-Lewis, *Commissioner Kerr – an individuality* (London: T. Fisher Unwin, 1903).

George Anderson of Glasgow expanded upon these themes in his testimony, celebrating the moral reform of male and female consumers supposedly effected since 1835 by the abolition of imprisonment for small debts in Scotland. 'The effect, particularly with regard to females, is very great', he claimed. 'They used to be very much beset by traders tempting them with clothes for which they were to pay by instalments, but I am glad to say that the system is nearly knocked on the head.'[37] David Forsyth, town clerk of Elgin and a Scottish debt collector by trade, situated these developments securely within the framework of Scottish legal modernization. 'I think that a process of improvement in our laws has been going on for a considerable period', he noted proudly. 'We have had improvement after improvement, until now there is every influence in favour of the working classes paying ready money.' Pressed to detail the effect of this legal reform, Forsyth claimed that tally traders had been driven from Scottish commerce, with an ensuing decrease in drapery prices of fifteen per cent. 'I should be sorry if they were [active in Scotland] from what I have heard of them', he stated piously. 'I do not think that they ought to have the name of Scotch drapers . . . it must be the worst character of Scotchmen that came to England, I think, as Scotch drapers.'[38]

Confronted simultaneously by the merits of the modernized Scottish legal system and the conspicuous failings of the Scottish itinerants who had colonized English county courts, proponents of imprisonment for debt were compelled to argue that the preservation of this archaic practice in England was necessitated by the inferior moral character of the English labourer. St John Yates, judge of the Stockport and Macclesfield county court, suggested that 'the habits of the Scotch are very different from ours'. Needled by Bass to acknowledge the superior rationality of Scottish law, Yates in exasperation instead justified imprisonment for debt by appealing to the distinctive economies of plebeian national character in Britain. 'I suppose they are as capable, but they are not so provident; they have not the self-denial of the Scotch', he stated. 'The English labourer will not live as the Scotch labourer will.'[39]

Couching its celebration of Scottish law and its denunciation of Scotch traders as a defence of the male worker and his vulnerable consuming wife, the select committee of 1873 strongly endorsed the abolition of imprisonment for small debts in its report,[40] which provided a departure point for a decade of unsuccessful legislative endeavour to equalize the credit laws for rich and poor in England, Scotland and Wales. Parliamentary representations of national, class and gender identities displayed little evolution in this persistent debate on working-class consumption: antagonists rehearsed well established narratives contrasting masculine thrift and female fallibility, Scottish commercial modernism and English

37. *Report of the Select Committee* (1873), pp. 41, 45.
38. *Ibid.*, pp. 237, 238, 239.
39. *Ibid.*, pp. 230, 235.
40. *Ibid.*, pp. viii–ix.

legal archaism, in successive political campaigns against county-court imprisonment. At the second reading of his 1874 bill to abolish imprisonment for small debts, Bass claimed that 'Scotch tallymen' had fled their homeland for England, where 'The course pursued by those tallymen was to travel over this country and to induce men's wives and daughters to get into debt'.[41] Nine years later, George Anderson reiterated yet again the exemplary role of the Scottish legal system in promoting cash sales by abolishing imprisonment for small debts. 'They had driven that class of trader out of Scotland', he noted. 'He was only a Scottish trader because they had driven him out of Scotland, and now he flourished in England only.'[42]

The perspectives offered by legislative committees and debates illuminate an insistent line of political argument about the relations of class, gender and nationality to the modern market. But these parliamentary sources fail to capture the full cultural resonance and strategic utility of Scottish identities in consumer politics. For Scotch drapers themselves actively sought to construct a national identity which would counter the negative perceptions of their trade that pervaded parliamentary discourse on working-class consumer credit. Rhetorically, their campaign to legitimate the tally trade privileged male over female consumers and celebrated supposed Highland cultural attainments over stereotypical Lowland business acumen. Organizationally, these Scotch drapers worked to establish a reticulation of modern commercial associations which would protect their trade against the depredations of plebeian purchasers while insulating their practices from public scrutiny in the Commons and the county courts.

Organizations of Scotch drapers appeared in England from the 1830s, drawing sustenance from the expansion of credit drapery and from two parallel developments in later eighteenth-century British associational life: the establishment of expatriate Scottish societies and the creation of so-called Guardian Societies. Promulgating a mythical Highland culture as the unifying historical force of the wider Scottish nation, affluent Scots were inspired to cultivate Celtic song and dance, to acclaim the validity of the concocted epics of Ossian and to attire themselves in kilts and tartans in an anachronistic celebration of Caledonian heritage.[43] A constant southward migration encouraged the instantiation of these ersatz sentiments in Anglo-Scottish societies. Twenty-five 'Highland gentlemen', 'inspired by a desire . . . to cherish and perpetuate a national spirit', formed the Highland Society of London in 1778, and gathered thereafter at regular intervals,

---

41. *Hansard*, 3rd ser., vol. 219 (14 April 1874), cols 546–7.

42. *Ibid.*, vol. 280 (27 June 1883), col. 1627.

43. H. Trevor Roper, 'The invention of tradition: the Highland tradition of Scotland', in E. Hobsbawm and T. Ranger (eds), *The Invention of Tradition* (Cambridge: Cambridge University Press, 1983), pp. 15–41.

clad in kilts, as living proof that 'Highlanders have always been attached to their ancient garb'.[44]

The Victorian era saw this 'Highlandolatry' reach new cultural heights. The Caledonian Society of London, established in 1837, cultivated a reverence for 'national character' among middle-class professionals 'of Scottish blood'. Invoking the memory of Burns and 'the patriotic deeds of our ancestors', the Caledonian Society worked to fix Scottish nationality securely within the firmament of British patriotic politics. Its annual festival conspicuously drew attention to Scottish loyalty in toasts to 'The Queen, our Sovereign, and Prince Albert her Consort', 'The Prince of Wales, Lord of the Isles', 'The Army and Navy', 'The Land we live in', 'The Land o' cakes', and 'The Garb of Old Gaul'.[45] This access of Celtic patriotism 'made it possible for a surprisingly wide range of people to express sentiments of national identity simply by focusing on the fripperies which the new imaginary Highlands so readily supplied', Theodore Hoppen has argued. 'The more Scottish culture embraced a Celtic area which had had most of its linguistic and cultural teeth pulled, the more easily a sanitized vision of "Scottishness" impressed itself upon . . . consciousness'.[46]

Distinct in origin and purpose but emerging contemporaneously with these Highland societies were the English Guardian societies, which developed in response to the expansion of commerce. The first of these associations was the London Society of Guardians for the Protection of Trade against Swindlers and Sharpers, established in 1776. For an annual subscription of a guinea, members of the London Guardian Society received descriptive information about metropolitan swindlers – particularly persons who used false identities to obtain goods on credit.[47] Provincial Guardian societies developed in the north of England from the 1820s, with the Manchester Guardian Society for the Protection of Trade enjoying particular success. Issuing weekly reports on poor credit risks in the locality, the Manchester Guardian Society established a debt-collection department to assist its members in 1850, a development which other Guardian associations were quick to follow. From the 1830s, the Manchester Guardians also played an active role in policing legislative activity. The secretaries of a number of local Guardian associations began to meet annually in London to co-ordinate their political efforts in 1851; the National Association of Trade Protection Societies,

---

44. *The London Scotsman: A Weekly Journal of Anglo-Scottish News*, 17 August 1867, p. 128.

45. D. Hepburn, *The Chronicles of the Caledonian Society of London, part I, 1837–1890* (London: Waterlow and Sons , 1923), pp. 4–5, 9–20.

46. K.T. Hoppen, *The Mid-Victorian Generation, 1846–1886* (Oxford: Oxford University Press, 1998), p. 541.

47. *Rules and Orders [of] The Guardians: or Society for the Protection of Trade against Swindlers and Sharpers. Established March 25, 1776* (London, 1816).

active in lobbying parliament to retain imprisonment for debt, was established in 1864.[48]

In this two-fold institutional context, the creation of local Scotch drapers' associations allowed the beleaguered tally trade to capitalize upon a growing British fascination with Highland 'traditions' while embracing the novel instruments of business and political organization pioneered by the English Guardian societies. The first wave of specialized credit drapers' associations appeared in Birmingham, Nottingham and Sheffield in the 1830s; Northampton, Worcester and Wolverhampton established associations in the following decade.[49] Parliamentary efforts to abolish imprisonment for small debts lent new political urgency to this expansion from the 1860s, and the second half of the century saw the foundation of a host of new associations. In the 1870s, efforts to co-ordinate political lobbying precipitated a number of national credit drapery conferences, a development much advanced in 1882 by the appearance of George Woodhead's monthly *Credit Drapers' Gazette and Trade Informant*.[50] By 1886, Woodhead's publication could list forty-seven affiliated credit drapers' associations in England and Wales, and an additional thirty-three towns boasted a local correspondent.[51]

Whereas Guardian societies downplayed sectional identities, the credit drapers' associations deployed a particularistic patriotism to bolster the legitimacy of their trade practices. Social activities designed to highlight Scottish contributions to British culture and politics became a prominent feature of these associations, as they established a regular annual cycle of festivities – typically culminating in January, with celebrations of the birth of Robert Burns. Echoing the patriotic toasts voiced at meetings of the elite London Highland societies, credit drapers' associations underscored their allegiance to monarchy, state and empire and worked sedulously to incorporate Scottishness into an all-encompassing British national identity. At the annual dinner of Bristol's credit drapery association in 1885, a delegate offered 'The Land We Come from' – a toast which 'would commend itself to all present, whether of English, Welsh, or Irish nationality' – and concluded by asserting that 'Scotland was a land that none should be ashamed of'.[52] At the Leicester society's annual dinner in 1894, a participant proposing 'The Land o'

---

48. *Manchester Guardian Society for the Protection of Trade, 1826–1926* (Manchester, 1926), pp. 11–15.

49. *Report of the Select Committee, 1893–94*, pp. 170–1 [Birmingham]; *Credit Drapers' Gazette*, 27 February 1892, pp. 62–4 [Nottingham and Sheffield]; 10 February 1894, p. 44 [Northampton]; 10 March 1894, p. 78 [Worcester]; 15 February 1886, pp. 55–6 [Wolverhampton].

50. The appointment of the 1873 select committee on imprisonment provided a powerful incentive to the conference movement, as testified by the *Abstract Report of a Conference of Delegates Representing the Northern Central Credit-Drapery Association, held at the Clarence Hotel, Spring Gardens, Manchester, April 17th and 18th, 1873* (Manchester, [1873]).

51. *Credit Drapers' Gazette*, 15 April 1886, p. 118.

52. *Ibid.*, 1 February 1885, p. 33.

Cakes' asserted that 'Patriotism . . . was a very good thing, and Scotchmen . . . were not behind the rest of the world in their patriotic feelings'. The tallyman McClean, toasting 'The Land We Live in', insisted that 'Scotchmen were looked upon in England as part and parcel of that great empire, and that feeling was reciprocated in Scotland'.[53]

In the highly-charged atmosphere generated by parliamentary and judicial antagonism to the tally trade, patriotic pronouncements such as these readily acquired a polemical spin. As credit drapers sought to construct an effective Scottish economic identity with which to combat attacks on their trade, a Celtic commercial patriotism that inverted the reasoning of Michael Bass and his political allies emerged as a central component in the tally trade's rhetorical armoury. At the annual meeting of the Kent Credit Drapers' Association in 1886, toasts by the tallyman McClure to 'The Land o' Cakes', 'The Land We Live in', and 'The Immortal Memory of Burns' preceded the proud claim that Scotch drapers 'worked hard and at small expense [so that] they could give their clients good value, and under easy terms of payment, enabling them to maintain a respectable appearance in the society in which they moved'.[54] At the Hereford Caledonian Society's annual dinner in 1892, toasts to the Queen and 'The Immortal Burns' led up to Watson Morrison's ironic panegyric to 'The Land We Live in'. Amid laughter from his audience, Morrison speculated 'that the Scotch had done some good in coming to England to help the English people to get on . . . for he was sure that if it had not been for some of the Scotchmen in Hereford the trade of the city and country would not have been as actively carried on as it was'.[55] In this manner, credit drapers' associations offered a patriotic reading of their contribution to British economic growth as an overt challenge to the dominant conflation of Scottish and Jewish trade practices. Addressing the Merthyr Caledonian Society's annual banquet in 1892, the speaker neatly co-opted and then reversed the valence of this reigning cultural logic. 'Scotchmen invariably got to the top of the tree wherever they went', he proclaimed. 'They were pretty shrewd men, but it was said that the shrewdest man in the world was a cross of American and Scotch blood just with a dash of Jew in it (Laughter).'[56]

Partisan cultural claims and calculated patriotic rhetorics clearly played a central part in Scotch drapers' efforts to displace the pejorative commercial connotations of their national identity in these decades, but organized political and business

---

53. *Ibid.*, 13 January 1894, pp. 4–5. Toasts to 'The Land o' Cakes', in the interpretation of the London Caledonian Society, were freighted with connotations of Scottish thrift. As Dr McLaren noted in proposing this toast in 1869, 'our fathers coined this phrase, admonishing to frugal living and thrift, to discipline and self-denial': Hepburn, *Caledonian Society*, p. 46.
54. *Credit Drapers' Gazette*, 15 March 1886, p. 80.
55. *Ibid.*, 13 February 1892, pp. 49–50.
56. *Ibid.*, 30 January 1892, p. 32.

strategies were also vital to the function of their trade societies. To advance the interests of the tally trade, Scotch drapers' societies inundated parliament with data designed to weaken the association between Scotch drapery and the imprisonment of labourers for their wives' debts. At a conference of credit drapers convened in 1873, delegates underscored their unwillingness fully to exploit the legal instruments at their disposal. Here statistics provided by 63 Scotch drapers who traded with 146,103 customers in Manchester demonstrated that local tallymen initiated county-court suits at a rate of only one plaint per 42 customers and imprisoned only 0.03 per cent of their debtors per annum.[57] Coupled with this statistical information was the trade's rhetorical claim that its development over time had witnessed a shift from dependent female to independent male consumers. A delegate from Rochdale insisted 'that, so far from doing business with wives, in the absence of their husbands, three-fourths of their trade was done in articles of men's apparel'. In his testimony before Bass's Select Committee, Adam Brown of the Leeds Scotch Drapers' Association similarly declared that the drapers' supposed seduction of wives was 'a great fallacy' and estimated that three-quarters of the goods sold by Scotch drapers in north Staffordshire was items of male apparel.[58]

Statistically credit drapers' efforts to demonstrate their reluctance to impose county-court imprisonment on debtors was not without foundation. Gerry Rubin has argued that Scotch drapers were the 'numerically dominant body of creditors' in the county-court system,[59] but this assertion accurately describes litigation in only some jurisdictions. The examination of witnesses before the select committees of 1873 and 1893–94, indeed, suggested that grocers and shopkeepers – plaintiffs against whose legal activities there was little public outcry – were at least as prominent as Scotch drapers in the courtroom. George Russell, judge of the Staffordshire circuit that included Bass's home town, Burton-on-Trent, was an avowed antagonist of the tally trade's use of the debt law. But when pressed to document abuses in his jurisdiction, Russell conceded that grocers figured more prominently in suits against his debtors than did credit drapers. William Wake, a Sheffield solicitor hostile to imprisonment for debt, likewise acknowledged that shopkeepers were responsible for far more county-court commitments in his locality than Scotch drapers.[60]

Testimony such as this, although no doubt statistically satisfying to Scotch drapers, was of only limited value in the public sphere, where the pronouncements of county-court judges themselves repeatedly undercut tradesmen's efforts to legitimate their practices. Possessing wide-ranging legal authority in their jurisdictions and commanding ready access to the press, county-court judges enjoyed

57. *Abstract Report of a Conference of Delegates*, pp. 8–9.
58. *Ibid.*, pp. 11–12; *Report of the Select Committee* (1873), pp. 192–3.
59. Rubin, 'From packmen', p. 322.
60. *Report of the Select Committee* (1873), pp. 59, 144, 147.

a privileged position in the discursive construction of the tally trade.[61] Confronted by a barrage of abusive commentary from this quarter, the credit drapers' societies of the 1880s and 1890s sought to bypass the litigation of their debts in the county courts altogether. Borrowing tactics from the English Guardian societies, tally traders increasingly augmented Scotch drapery organizations' political and cultural work with formalized debt-collecting activities.

The development of debt-collecting facilities within credit drapers' societies marked a significant developmental stage in the modernization of the trade. By delegating responsibility for the collection of bad debts to salaried agents who charged all members a uniform commission, debt-collecting departments worked to distance itinerant traders at once from the personal processes of door-to-door debt collecting and from the intrusive, moralizing gaze of the county-court bench. Celtic culture and credit enjoyed a symbiotic relationship in these new debt-collecting agencies. At the annual meeting of the Leamington and Warwickshire Caledonian Society in 1892, an announcement of the annual Burns celebration vied for members' attention with discussion of accounts sent in for collection; credit drapers in Portsmouth interwove the discussion of their bad debtors with convivial conversation at their 'annual dinner and "a nicht wi' Burns"' in 1899.[62] The sums collected through these shared activities could be substantial, offering tradesmen a considerable financial incentive to membership in Caledonian societies. In Manchester, where George Woodhead, editor of the *Credit Drapers' Gazette*, assumed duties as a salaried debt collector in 1885,[63] the press of debt-collecting business at the annual meeting in 1886 was so great that a lecture on Burns was postponed to a later date. By 1891, the Manchester society was processing 1,100 claims a year for its members.[64]

The campaigns waged by Victorian credit drapers offer a range of insights into the creation of a politics of material life in England and Wales. Shaped by persistent themes of gender and economic vulnerability, contemporary understandings of the tally trade were also informed by competing conceptions of national character. Scottish nationality acquired divergent meanings in these debates on the tally trade. Observers hostile to their colonization of the county courts depicted itinerant Scotch traders as an impediment to the emergence of putatively 'modern' cash relations in England and Wales. But proponents of imprisonment by the county courts

---

61. For the county-court judge as a public spokesman, see P. Polden, 'Judicial selkirks: the county court judges and the press, 1847–80', in C.W. Brooks and M. Lobban (eds), *Communities and Courts in Britain, 1150–1900* (London: Hambleden, 1997), pp. 245–62, and Finn, 'Working-class women and the contest for consumer control'.

62. *Credit Darpers' Gazette*, 16 January 1892, p. 17; 7 January 1899, p. 8.

63. *Ibid.*, 1 February 1885, p. 38.

64. *Ibid.*, 15 February 1886, pp. 49–50; 21 May 1892, p. 177.

emphasized the need to recognize, and maintain, legal distinctions among the three British nations. Henry Stonor of Marylebone county court testified eloquently to this effect before the select committee of 1893–94. Asked to comment on the applicability of Scottish debt law to England, Stonor revealed the extent to which English understandings of *homo economicus* were undercut by conceptions of nationality. 'I think there is a difference in the national character', he pronounced. 'The Scotch, I think, are more frugal and thrifty, and also more independent, and I do believe they have a great natural reluctance both to lending and borrowing, and that they are in fact very different from what we are.'[65]

The Scottish identities invoked by credit drapers displayed a correspondingly broad (and conflicted) series of associations with nationality and modernity. Wedded through their trade protection societies to a school of Celtic cultural representation that was strongly coloured by conceptions of Scottish backwardness,[66] Victorian credit drapers nonetheless insistently claimed to be the harbingers of modern consumer democracy. In a lecture entitled 'Our Past Contributions and Present Obligations to the Public Weal', a Lancashire Scotch draper articulated this argument with great clarity in 1894. Telling the assembled Scotch traders that 'As true men of that country, your nation has the right to expect you to maintain its honour before an English people', he explicitly compared the routine extension of consumer credit to workers by Scotch drapers with the extension of the political franchise to artisans by John Bright in 1867.[67]

Although credit drapers' rhetorical claims to embody the spirit of consumer democracy smack of special pleading, the discursive and substantive contributions made by their trade to the emergence of modern consumer mentalities in Britain were arguably significant. Playing a leading role first in the routine provision of plebeian credit and then in the routine collection of plebeian debts, Scotch tallymen were articulate, vocal participants in the processes by which contemporaries attempted to conceptualize and implement anonymous market relations in the later nineteenth century. Where department store magnates equated modernity with the anonymous bourgeois mass market, credit drapers simultaneously engaged in highly personalized relations with their working-class consumers, drew attention to venerable ethnic identities and enthusiastically adopted modern contractual relations. In the imagined world view promoted in their polemics, all persons figured as responsible contracting agents and all goods could be reduced to exchange equivalents. An editorial in the *Credit Drapers' Gazette* captured these

---

65. *Report of the Select Committee* (1893–94), pp. 66, 70.

66. For conceptions of Scottish backwardness in nineteenth-century historical writing, see C. Kidd, 'Teutonist ethnology and Scottish national inhibition, 1780–1880', *Scottish Historical Review*, 74 (1995), pp. 45–68.

67. *Credit Drapers' Gazette*, 21 April 1894, pp. 117–19.

contractual sentiments in 1883 when it railed against judges' use of their discretionary powers to discipline Scotch drapers in English and Welsh county courts. 'How can "dealing with female relatives" in a matter of clothing be any more reprehensible than dealing with them in groceries?', the paper asked rhetorically. 'Why should *women* be allowed to go "Scot free"?'[68]

In analyzing the evolution of modern retail structures, historians of consumption have unduly discounted the pragmatic historical role of itinerant traders in the provision of goods and credit. By neglecting this conspicuous body of traders, they have constructed a narrative of modernization which fails to account for the internal disruptions and inconsistencies – and thus the historical texture – of the emergence of mass markets for consumer goods in England, Scotland and Wales. Miles Ogborn, critiquing the totalizing tendencies of modernization theory, has suggested that modernity is most usefully conceptualized 'as a matter of hybrid relationships and connections between places'.[69] The evolving history of Scotch drapery in England and Wales offers abundant material for a case study of this uneven process of hybridization, attesting at once to the political significance of divergent sexual, national and cultural identities in the emergence of the modern working-class consumer in Britain.

---

68. *Ibid.*, 1 November 1883, p. 103.
69. M. Ogborn, *Spaces of Modernity: London's Geographies 1680–1780* (London: Guildford, 1998), p. 17.

6

'National Taste?' Citizenship Law, State Form, and Everyday Aesthetics in Modern France and Germany, 1920–1940

Leora Auslander

Introduction

All modern nation-states, because of their dependence upon mass popular armies for their defence, taxation for their economic survival, and mass suffrage for their legitimacy, need to instil a sense of belonging, of shared responsibility, and of loyalty in their citizens. Because few nation-states have the coercive capacity to enforce co-operation on such a scale, they rely on voluntary compliance and participation. Citizens must, somehow, come to identify with people whom they have never met and will never meet, to be willing to pay for them and die for them. They have to trust that others will pay, and die, for them in turn. A nation's citizens must decide, at times, to do things that are not in their own or their family's, or their town's, or their region's best interest. This identification with strangers and a willingness to put the interests of an abstraction called the nation ahead of one's own does not come to people naturally; it must be learned. All modern nation-states face this pedagogic task, but differing histories of state formation and criteria for citizenship have shaped how they approach it.

In this chapter, and in the larger project of which this is an overview, I suggest that in modern nation-states, conceptions of citizenship, in combination with understandings of the relation between the local and the national, shape national cultural policy and how the nation is lived in the everyday lives of a nation's inhabitants. Grasping the self-understanding of historical actors is, of course, notoriously elusive. I would like to propose that a productive point of access to these domains is the design and consumption of everyday goods 'of style', including furniture, flatware, architecture, fabric and jewellery. Taste in such objects is particularly revealing in modern consumer societies because it is both inevitable and not entirely a matter of conscious volition. No one in late nineteenth- and twentieth-century Europe could completely avoid making judgements of taste; everyone bought clothing, basic housewares, furniture, linen, cutlery, and china. Everyone had opinions on what styles they found more or less desirable, but few knew exactly *why*. Other signs of group or national belonging may be coerced; purchases in a liberal state at peace are not, although they are obviously constrained by economic means.[1]

Goods are, furthermore, not merely *reflective* of identifications; through their repetitive use, through their utility and inevitability, these objects come to *shape* perceptions and even unconsciously influence people's identification of soulmates or strangers. The objects chosen help to *generate* a sense of individual and collective identity as they ally their owners with other possessors of like things and distance them from others who display alien taste.[2] Given particularly the potential role of goods in modern capitalist nation-states, these objects provide a privileged means of grasping the place of the abstractness that is the State in the concreteness that is everyday life.

More specifically, this study demonstrates that the national State plays a different role in the teaching of taste, and taste itself is different, in nation-states – such as Germany – in which citizens are understood to be born rather than made and in which town and region are seen as mediating between the immediacy of emotional attachments to kin, neighbours, friends, and children and the abstraction of the national State than in nation-states – such as France – in which citizens are understood to be as much made as born and in which town and region are understood to compete perniciously for the affection and loyalty properly given to the national State. This juxtaposition of taste, citizenship law and state form elucidates why people made certain aesthetic judgements and not others. More significantly, perhaps, analysis of those judgements allows us to better understand the implications of the two foundational criteria for national belonging in the modern world – *jus sanguinis* and *jus soli* – as well as the two foundational forms of state – federal and jacobin.

The project starts, then, with an analysis at the level of the law and the State. It examines the logics of citizenship law and State form and how both influenced cultural policy and institutions in each nation-state. But because the experience and practice of everyday aesthetics are as important to grasping this dynamic as law and policy, the study has been further grounded empirically in the two capital cities – Paris and Berlin – and in a study of a group particularly interesting from

---

1. For concise and incise presentations of the meanings of consumption, see the introductions by V. de Grazia in her edited volume *The Sex of Things: Essays on Gender and Consumption* (Berkeley: University of California Press, 1996).

2. For a brilliant demonstration of objects' generative capacity, see N. Kamil, *Fortress of the Soul* (Baltimore: Johns Hopkins University Press, 2000).

the standpoint of this problematic – the Jews. The capitals were chosen rather than two more 'typical' towns because insofar as each nation-state attempted to shape a national culture, its efforts were particularly energetic in the capital.[3] Jews are a good 'test case' because both France and Germany had significant emancipated, bourgeois, native Jewish populations in this period (although that of Germany was much larger than that of France). They were fully citizens of their respective nation-states and yet were not unmarked. A detailed study of Jews as consumers of goods of style enables one to assess both the importance of different conceptions of citizenship and of the nation-state to everyday life and experience and the ways in which individuals and groups make their own ways within those constraints and possibilities.[4]

Citizenship Law, State Form, and the Making of a 'National Aesthetic' in Republican France

In the decades following its founding in 1871, the regime that would govern France for the seventy years bracketing the turn of the century – the Third Republic – faced three crises. It faced a serious challenge to its *political form* from monarchist forces, a serious challenge to its claim to people's *loyalty* from their local and regional ties, and a *population crisis*. The majority of the population was not yet firmly convinced of the virtues of republicanism, and despite centuries of centralized government, many French men and women felt stronger ties to their village or town than to the nation-state. Those commitments were enacted by, for example, a refusal (or inability) to speak French, draft resistance, and attachment to local priests and notables. Finally, France's defeat in the Franco-Prussian war was attributed, in part, to its considerably slower rate of reproduction than that of other European nations. Both political and economic survival were understood to be threatened by the lack of enough French citizens. In their quest for solutions to these problems, politicians inevitably looked to earlier (and enduring) political, legal, and cultural forms, particularly those of the Revolution of 1789 and the previous two republics, for their solutions.

The Revolution of 1789 had combated regional and other identifications, affiliations, and loyalties by establishing the principle of an unmediated relation between the individual and the nation. The principle – strong during the Old Regime and in other modern democracies – that people who share a profession, a gender, a religion, a status, or a neighbourhood also share a particular interest was denied.

3. On the particular place of Paris for French Republicans see A. Ben-Amos, 'The sacred center of power: Paris and Republican state funerals', *Journal of Interdisciplinary History*, 22 (1991), pp. 27–48.
4. The larger project also addresses the question of Jews as producers.

People were no longer entitled to political representation as a member of a collectivity, but as individuals. The system of political representation was now designed so as to emulate as much as possible the workings of direct democracy. Corollaries of that principle were the creation of weak local and regional governments and the undermining of loyalty to institutions or groups other than the national state and its citizenry. Thus, new administrative districts were created, breaking up the old regions, and mayors and other local government officials were most usually appointed by the central government. The central government also took responsibility for education and other forms of culture. Thus, from 1789 onwards, although private philanthropists could, and did, create their own cultural institutions, the national State had a quasi-monopoly on public culture. When local institutions were founded, either privately or publicly, they most often found themselves ultimately taken over by the national State or depending upon it for financing.

In the domain of citizenship, Third Republicans inherited from the Revolution an emphasis on territory (*jus soli*) and an individual's expressed desire to participate in the nation over inheritance (*jus sanguinis*). In part because 'Frenchness' was conceived by such influential philosophers as Condorcet as a universal value, not only to be inculcated within the borders of France, but to be spread abroad, a particular weight was given to the place of culture in the making of citizens. Thus, during the First Republic, those born in France of foreign parents were assumed to absorb French culture through their everyday lives and to thereby become French; and in the process the foundations were laid for France's imperial *mission civilisatrice*.

The balance among *jus soli*, *jus sanguinis*, and volition varied across the nineteenth century, but genetics never entirely trumped culture. This faith that foreigners could be *made* French encouraged politicians concerned with the relatively slow growth of France's population to turn to State-sponsored *immigration* as a solution. Legislation passed in the first thirty years of the Third Republic tended to ease naturalization requirements and to see in Italians, Poles, and Russians not only potential *labour* but also potential *citizens*. Foreigners were, of course, in need of linguistic and cultural education if they were to become both French and Republican, but in the mind of many politicians of the Third Republic, those needs were shared by many of the native-born who were perceived to have monarchist tendencies, too strong an attachment to the Catholic Church, and/or too strong an attachment to their local or regional interests.

In their efforts to combat both monarchism and regionalism, the Third Republic turned to strategies first used during the Revolution – the transformation of the rituals, forms, and patterns of everyday life. During that revolution, the calendar, the system of weights and measures, clothing design, naming habits, decorative patterns were all made over so that they would be shared by *all the French* and so that through them people's *hearts* and not just their *minds* would cleave to the Revolution and new Republic, abandoning previous loyalty to the King and monarchism as a political form. This theme was repeated by Republican thinkers long after babies were once again named for saints and weeks were once again seven days long. In 1846 for example, just before the Revolution of 1848 brought the Second Republic into being, the staunch republican Jules Michelet argued that 'In this great body of a nation . . . [a] certain idea enters by the eyes (fashion, shops, museums, etc.), another through conversation, by the language which is the grand depository of common progress. All receive the thinking of all, perhaps without analyzing it, but they nonetheless receive it.'[5] According to Michelet and other Republican thinkers, it was in the small unnoticed moments of life that the people internalized both national sentiment and political ideology.

The Third Republic had the means and the reason to put into place a network of national cultural institutions designed to eradicate local languages and cultures and to create a homogeneous French culture. Key to that project was central administration of education and rendering primary schooling obligatory. Teachers (who were civil servants of the national State) were sent to parts of France distant from their home towns so as to spread the French language, a single French accent, and a single French republican culture.[6] The work of the schools was seconded by state-sponsored Universal Expositions and by the state appropriation of the libraries and museums created by private philanthropists earlier in the century.[7] These institutions, through the style of goods they displayed or books they owned, as well as public lectures and publications, were thought to help shape a more uniformly French culture.

Producing such cultural uniformity was not, of course, a simple task. Many cultural forms and everyday practices were in fact marked by local, regional, and class differences and the colonial project further complicated the story. Inhabitants of Lorraine, or Auvergne, or Normandie did not necessarily *want* to dress, eat, speak or write alike. Intrusions of what was perceived to be not only a cultural programme of the central government but a *Parisian* cultural programme were deeply resented and helped spark regionalist (often anti-Republican) movements.

---

5. J. Michelet, *Le Peuple* (Paris: Libraire Marcel Didier, 1946 [1846]), p. 231 and p. 233, n. 2.

6. The classic account of this story is E. Weber, *Peasants into Frenchmen: The Modernization of Rural France, 1870–1914* (Stanford: Stanford University Press, 1976). For an argument for how, even in France, nation and region could be mutually reinforcing, see A.-M. Thiesse, *Ils apprenaient la France: L'exaltation des régions dans le discours patriotique* (Paris: Editions de la Maison des sciences de l'homme, 1997).

7. Different parts of this story may be found in P. Mainardi, *The End of the Salon: Art and the State in the Early Third Republic* (Cambridge: Cambridge University Press, 1993); D. L. Silverman, *Art Nouveau in Fin-de-Siècle France: Politics, Psychology, and Style* (Berkeley: University of California Press, 1989), particularly part III; and my *Taste, and Power: Furnishing Modern France* (Berkeley: University of California Press, 1996), Part III.

Republicans responded to this resistance by repression on the one hand – punishing children who spoke Basque or Breton in school – and by the efforts to find more subtle means – through use of the market – of influencing the taste of the French on the other. The centralization and power of the national State was essential to these strategies. Thus, even though local loyalties, languages and styles did not completely die out, the State did succeed in radically weakening them.

Predictably perhaps, the aesthetic outcome of these interventions and ruminations was somewhat surprising to both contemporaries and historians. In the domain of interior decoration, a vast majority of French homes in the last years of the nineteenth century and early decades of the twentieth were furnished with goods that strongly echoed those of the pre-Revolutionary Old Regime. While art historians tend to condemn these furnishings as bad copies of dead styles, they were in fact new inventions of a particular sort – historicist pastiche. Furniture makers borrowed historical forms and altered their curves, angles and colours, thereby inventing new furniture reminiscent of, although distinguishable from, the old.[8] These nineteenth-century versions were based on ideal types, rather than concrete embodiments, of particular ancien régime styles combined with contemporary forms. These new versions of old styles were often very distinctive, sometimes playful, and sometimes ironic. Some producers were, in fact, explicit about what they were doing. 'French manufacturers have often been reproached for not having created a modern style. One can respond that none of the furniture which we make resembles antique furniture, that if we, in effect, use ornaments from all styles, we create from all these pieces, forms appropriate to *our tastes*, and furthermore, a style can not be invented, because a style emerges from the customs and the social system of an epoch . . . While we have been inspired by the documents of the period of Louis XV, we have modernized the general form.'[9]

A particular characteristic of late nineteenth-century French historicism was that these styles were understood to belong to the nation as a whole, to be reappropriated and imbued with new meanings as needed by contemporary French society. These styles, named after kings, were in fact detached from their monarchist heritage. The Revolution of 1789 and the definitive establishment of Republicanism in France in the 1880s, made it possible to reconfigure these styles as *French*, part of the *French patrimony*, styles that could link *all* the French of whatever region, gender, place of birth or class into one family, one nation.

This historicist pastiche was the dominant style in France throughout the Third Republic. By the end of the nineteenth century, however, this national style was

8. For contemporary discussion by woodworkers of the role of old techniques and old forms in the creation of new work, see 'Planche 3: Porte Louis XV', *Journal de menuiserie,* 3 (1965), pp. 28–9.

9. Bibliothèque Historique de la Ville de Paris. Archival collection: Ameub 120 N–R, Perol s.d. c. 1900.

challenged, not only by designers, decorators and artisans, but also by the ever growing internationalization of consumer goods, and by the first attempts to find a *new* style appropriate to the age – variously known as moderne style, *style 1900* and art nouveau – and finally by art déco in the 1920s and 1930s.[10] Art nouveau had clear aspirations to 'modernity', but was characterized by organic forms, decorative elements borrowed from nature, extensive use of natural materials, luxurious woods, fabrics and production techniques, and heavy borrowings from Japan and from French historical referents. Almost every country in Europe had a national version of this style, from the earliest arts and crafts movement in England and Scotland, to Jugendstil in Germany and Austria, to the Liberty style in Italy. Art nouveau was a very important aesthetic development in France but had only limited commercial impact. It posed an aesthetic challenge; it was an indication of dissatisfaction with the versions of historicism then being used; but it did not replace them. Another option was presented to French taste – the modernism of the Eiffel tower, constructed for the Universal Exposition of 1889 – a modernism that gloried in industrial materials, linearity, exposure of the underlying structure, and the absence of historical referent. The response to the modernity represented by the Eiffel tower was even less enthusiastic than that to art nouveau. It is one of the ironies of design history that the globally recognized symbol of France is a style which never won much popularity among the French. Nor were the more thoroughly modern styles, elaborating the impulses behind the Eiffel tower (art déco and the work of Le Corbusier) that succeeded art nouveau, much more commercially viable. Despite active support by the State's cultural apparatus, these styles were purchased only by a small elite, often themselves employed in architecture or the arts. The relative unpopularity of either form of modernist design and the persistence of historicist pastiche, along with the continued refusal of foreign styles, can be explained at least in part by the place of the aesthetic of the everyday in the republican French nation-state.

I would argue that the ahistoricism of modernist design of the inter-war period, its distance from nature and natural forms, and its emphasis on mechanical production were fundamental to its very definition. They were all characteristics that stressed the detachment of goods from particular contexts whether of region, of nation, or of time. In their distanciation from natural materials they were also distant from place. In their emphasis on forms derived from geometry rather than nature, or individual imagination, they further aspired to universalism. It was a style produced out of the reality of the development of an international market and was explicitly conceived as *challenging* national taste and style. As Le Corbusier put it in 1925: 'The machine, a modern phenomenon, is bringing about

10. N. J. Troy, *Modernism and the Decorative Arts in France: Art Nouveau to Le Corbusier* (New Haven: Yale University Press, 1991).

a reformation of the spirit across the world. Tangible proof that the evolution which has begun is far from complete is the continuing lack of a universal language, which would break down the cardboard barriers erected along frontiers.'[11]

Why was modernist style resisted in France? Why did most French people in the first third of the twentieth century live surrounded by goods with a very powerful and obvious historical referent? How was the French engagement with historicism different from that of other countries? Finally, why was there so little consumption or appropriation of foreign styles in France?

I would like to suggest that the answer to all of those questions lies in France's powerful central State and its conception of citizenship. France's assimilationist citizenship policy necessitated the nationalization of the everyday, and one way in which that could be accomplished was the construction of a very strong linkage between the national present and the national past. There was a sense of a shared *national* past, that could be taught to others, even to those whose ancestors had not participated in it. Historicist design was a way of constituting an everyday that was distinctively French – forms were not borrowed from the past *in general*, but from the *French* past. The reconfiguring, recombining of those forms – the fact that this style was historicist pastiche, and not reproduction – liberated it from its monarchist origins and made it usable for a republic. Peasants, Italians and Poles could all become French by sitting on Henri II chairs and sleeping in Louis XVI beds. All people could thus incorporate the nation's past into their very beings. And, in the imperial version of this vision, potentially, even those living outside the territory could absorb Frenchness and republicanism through the things of everyday life. The day when Frenchness became global would, of course, be the end of Frenchness per se and the beginnings of true universalism.

Citizenship Law, State Form, and the Making of a 'National Aesthetic' in Imperial and Weimar Germany

The situation in Germany was very different because of its genealogical definition of citizenship, low rates of immigration and high rates of out-migration, late unification, and a federal rather than a republican model that entailed an endorsement of strong regionalism.

Although 1871 marked the shift from an Imperial to Republican regime in France, the core geographic area covered by the term 'France' had not changed for centuries. By contrast, the creation of the Kaiserreich in 1871 brought twenty-two monarchies and three republics together into a new Empire. This new Germany

---

11. Le Corbusier, *The Decorative Art of Today* (Cambridge, Mass.: MIT Press, 1987 [1925]) trans. and intro. by J.I. Dunnett, p. 110.

was governed by a common constitution but one that left considerable autonomy to the member states. In stark contrast to circumstances in France, '[e]ducation, policing, law and order, health and social welfare, taxation, commercial and economic policy . . . and a host of other matters were left largely to the discretion of the federated states . . .'.[12] These federated states were also marked by religious difference, with the dominant Prussian state forming part of the Protestant majority against a significant Catholic minority.[13]

The Prussian state, dominant within the German Reich and the site of the new capital city of Berlin, at first attempted to deal with regional and religious diversity by repression, launching what became known as the *Kulturkampf*. This threat to local autonomy provoked dramatic resistance and ultimately failed in its ambitions. The compromises that brought the *Kulturkampf* to an end in fact both reinforced regional power and underscored the role of the local states as mediators between the individual and the national. Local sovereignty over cultural matters and the compatibility of regional and national identities were never challenged by the national State in the same way again. Thus, for example, in Württemberg little changed after 1871. The textbooks, stamps, railroad system remained as they had been, and Württembergers even served in their own unit in the German army.[14] The degree of acceptance of the idea of Germanness as the sum of regional difference can be seen in the domain of law by the fact that, until 1934, 'citizenship of the Länder which made up the German Reich had priority. One became a citizen of a Land (Hessen, Hamburg, etc.) . . . and only on this basis, a member of the German Reich.'[15] The states even nominated the members of the upper house of parliament, the political body that initiated legislation.

The difference between French and German conceptions of the relation between the local and the national in the domain of culture may be summed up in the word *Heimat*. While both French and German have words for nation (*la nation* and *die Nation*), for the national State (*l'état* and *der Staat*), and for native-country (*la patrie* and *das Vaterland*), there is no French equivalent of *Heimat*. The closest French comes to *Heimat* is *le pays*. But while *Heimat* essentially always includes (in its dictionary and other uses) a collective identity and feeling, both the 1865–1873 and the 1937 editions of a standard French dictionary define *le pays* primarily in objective criteria as the place where one was born, or a geographic

12. R. Evans, *Death in Hamburg: Society and Politics in the Cholera Years, 1830–1910* (Oxford: Clarendon, 1987), p. 2.

13. A.J. Hoover, 'German nationalism and religion', *History of European Ideas,* 20 (1995), pp. 765–71 and especially H.W. Smith, *German Nationalism and Religious Conflict: Culture, Ideology, Politics, 1870–1914* (Princeton: Princeton University Press, 1995).

14. A. Confino, *The Nation as a Local Metaphor: Württemberg, Imperial Germany, and National Memory, 1871–1918* (Chapel Hill: Univesity of North Carolina Press, 1997), p. 21.

15. N. Räthzel, 'Germany: one race, one nation?', *Race and Class,* 32 (1990), p. 42.

area characterized by a particular climate.[16] And, while regionalist movements around a *pays* did develop in France in the last third of the nineteenth century, they did so *in opposition* to the national republic. In Germany, by contrast, as the historian Celia Applegate put it, 'Those who created and promoted *Heimat*, consciously or not, were suggesting a basic affinity between the new, abstract political units and one's home, thus endowing an entity like Germany with the emotional accessibility of a world known to one's own five senses . . . *Heimat* was both the beloved local places and the beloved nation; it was a comfortably flexible and inclusive homeland, embracing all localities alike.'[17] Loyalty to the new German nation did not require withdrawal from one's affective ties with the local but was rather built on those ties. Both *Heimat* and the German nation were made at home, in the village square, while restoring the local church, and visiting the regional museum. Germany's citizenship law facilitated this acceptance of the importance of local affect, of cultural diversity, and the capacity to imagine them as non-threatening to national cohesion.

Following unification in 1871, the new German state endorsed the principle of essentially pure *jus sanguinis*: those born of German parents were German regardless of where they were born, and those born of non-German parents were not German regardless of how long they had lived on German territory. And, just as the French State further endorsed its principles of *jus soli* when it revised its nationality code in 1889, so the German State endorsed *jus sanguinis* when it revised its code in 1913.[18] Discussion of the origins of this conception of national belonging lies beyond the scope of this chapter, but it is crucial to bear in mind both the extensive out-migration from Germany of those deemed ethnonationally like (and desirable) and the fear, and to a limited extent reality, of immigration of those deemed undesirable and unlike – Slavs and Jews from the East – in the late nineteenth and early twentieth centuries. By 1894, the pan-German league was attempting to make it easier for ethnic Germans abroad to retain citizenship and even more difficult for those who immigrated to get it. The reform of 1913 in fact enabled those living abroad (and their children) to remain German indefinitely. An assumption behind the idea that all those born of German blood, even if raised in a different culture, and the exclusion from Germanness of those raised in a

---

16. *Grand Dictionnaire Universel. Larousse* (Paris, 1865–76) p. 454; *Larousse du XXe siècle* (Paris, 1932), vol. 5, p. 432. For *Heimat*, see *Meyers Grosses Universal Lexicon* (Berlin, 1982), Band 6, p. 386. I am grateful to Geoffrey Crossick for bringing the question of *pays* to my attention.

17. C. Applegate, *A Nation of Provincials: The German Idea of Heimat* (Berkeley: University of California Press, 1990), pp. 10–11; 11.

18. This discussion follows chapter 6 in R. Brubaker, *Citizenship and Nationhood in France and Germany* (Cambridge: Harvard University Press, 1992). For a close analysis of the law of 1913 that productively complicates this story see: D. Gosewinkel, 'Die Staatsangehörigkeit als Institution des Nationalstaats: Zur Enstehung des Reichs- und Staatsangehörigkeitsgestzes von 1913', in R. Grawert, B. Schlink, R. Wahl and J. Wieland (eds), *Offene Staatlichkeit: Festschrift für Ernst-Wolfgang Böckenförde zum 65. Geburtstag* (Berlin: Duncker and Humbolt, 1995), pp. 359–78.

German culture if of foreign blood was that Germanness was genetically transmitted: even if a person of German parentage had never set foot on German soil, nor spoken a word of German, nor eaten a German meal, they would nonetheless be German, morally, intellectually, and emotionally.

While it is easy to underemphasize the foundational and persistent importance of *jus sanguinis* in France, the differences in the citizenship laws of the two countries are indeed significant. The emphasis on blood-ties between individuals and the nation in Germany meant that there was little emotional pedagogy needed or possible. Those born of non-German parents would remain foreign (as would their children) and those born of German parents would, in a way very unlike the French, already always have known how to be German. A consequence of all of these differences – in the conceptual foundations of citizenship, high rates of emigration and low rates of immigration, and the relation between the local, the regional, and the national – is that far less was invested by the German national State than by the French in everyday aesthetics intended to inculcate national sentiment into the inhabitants of the German lands. The national French State had the power to take over private and local institutions and a political reason to do so. The German State had neither the power nor the need.[19]

I do not mean, however, to imply that the genetic definition of citizenship, a relatively weak national State and low immigration produced only silence on the definition of German culture.[20] There was lively discussion on the topic, and that from early in the nineteenth century, well before the existence of the German nation-state. That early discussion in many ways paralleled that in France – it was a discourse constructed by the *Bilderbürgertum*, those bourgeois elites of various political orientations, who saw engagement in the reconciliation of class strife as their duty to the nation. They were very active at the municipal and local state level, creating museums, writing in decorating magazines, fostering trade schools. Likewise certain rulers and politicians, most notably Wilhelm II, were active patrons of the arts and engaged in discussions on the definition of German culture. As they participated in these institutions, they debated the virtues of different historicist styles and the question of whether there should be *a* modern, German style – in large part, however, in the context of seeking *class* reconciliation, and *expressing* rather than *creating* national character. It follows, therefore, that the moment when the German national State became most intensely involved with taste was for the Universal Expositions. The Expositions were conceived as moments for the

19. On German cultural institutions see M. Abelein, *Die Kulturpolitik des Deutschen Reiches und der Bundesrepublik Deutschland. Ihre verfassungsgeschichtliche Entwicklung und ihre verfassungsrechlichen Probleme* (Köln and Opladen: Westdeutscher Verlag, 1968).

20. For a classic example of an effort (although a private one) to reform German culture in this period see J. Campbell, *The German Werkbund: The Politics of Reform in the Applied Arts* (Princeton: Princeton University Press, 1978).

showcasing of national industrial and aesthetic traditions. The German State's preoccupation with taste was largely externally directed. As the historian Joan Campbell has argued, in the inter-war period members of the Werkbund went so far as to argue that Germany could regain an honourable place in the community of nations through good design.[21] Constructing a viable German taste was therefore more a matter of diplomatic *representation* of the nation than of its domestic *construction.*

The stylistic corollaries of this very different history of State- and nation-making, and the place of taste within it, was that historicist, regionalist, foreign and (to a lesser extent) modernist styles all flourished in Germany during the first thirty years of the twentieth century. Historicist design in Germany was closely linked with particular regional styles, rather than with a (non-existent) shared national past. Thus, styles were labeled by period – gothic, renaissance, baroque, biedermeier – at times with place-name modifers: Danziger (or English or Dutch) Baroque, for example.

Most striking is the continued importance and presence of foreign styles, particularly French, English and Italian, in late nineteenth- and early twentieth-century bourgeois German households. Many Berliners were living surrounded by objects constructed to represent other national identities.[22] While the mix of German regional historicist styles is consistent with national belonging being constructed from a multiplicity of localities, the presence of so many foreign things is symptomatic of the relatively unimportant place taste was understood to occupy in the construction of the German nation. Even if there was little worry that sleeping on a French bed, or sitting at an English table, would weaken German citizens' ties to the nation, art critics were, however, concerned in Germany about the need for a new, modern aesthetic.

Germany's version of the early attempt to create a 'modern' style in the form of *Jugendstil*, more or less contemporaneous with *art nouveau* in France. Like *art nouveau*, organic forms, the use of rich wood and fabric, and hand labour characterized *Jugendstil*. Unlike in France, however, the perceived limitations, indeed the (in some respects) anti-modern impulses of *Jugendstil* inspired the creation of two (private) institutions specifically devoted to the invention of a *truly modern* style – the Werkbund in 1907 and the Bauhaus a few years later. Both were institutions devoted particularly to the elaboration of a decorative art that wasn't one; that is to the invention of a non-decorative, 'honest', modern form of interior decoration. It may perhaps be argued that the 'mature' version of modernist design was a German project; in fact Le Corbusier himself found the direction of his work altered after a study visit to Germany in 1914.

21. *Ibid.*, p. 49.
22. See the files in 243–04 series in the Landesarchiv Berlin.

I would like to suggest that it was possible, perhaps even necessary, for a true stylistic eclecticism, including extensive appropriation of foreign styles, to reign in Germany because there was no common German national past – no repertoire as in the French case. Germany's past and, to some extent, Germany's present were characterized by strong segmentation into regions, religions, classes, and collective organizations or *Vereine*. There was also no stark revolutionary break (neither 1848 nor 1918 held a place in German politics comparable to that of 1789 in France) to mark the end of an old regime and the beginning of a new. Old Regime styles in France were truly of the past when they were appropriated and reused. Regional styles, historical styles in Germany – even those of the very distant past, such as the Gothic – were still of the present, or of a particular past. Making a *new* Germany, a *modern* Germany, a Germany with a new history and a new present to contrast with the old disunity was therefore possible. But that modernism could and did coincide with continued strength of regional traditions and a willingness to import foreign forms both because of the impotence of the national State in matters of culture and the relative unimportance of that impotence given Germany's genetically defined citizenship.

The differences in citizenship law and state form had obvious implications for the cultural policy of national-level government. What is less obvious are how these differences were lived and experienced by inhabitants of the two nation states. While there could be many ways of grounding a study of the relationship of citizenship and everyday aesthetics in the modern nation state, I would like to suggest that a study of the ways in which Jews in France and Germany positioned themselves in relation to the aesthetics of everyday life is particularly fruitful. By the early twentieth century, Jews in both countries were both highly acculturated and marginalized. They generally understood themselves as loyal citizens of their nation state and expressed surprise (in fact often astonishment) as well as anger when the limitations to their acceptance by their fellow citizens and by the institutions of state and civil society were made explicit. The structural situation in which Jews in the two countries found themselves was not identical, however, nor was their strategy for negotiating the simultaneity of their ethnic and national locations. It is that simultaneity, and Jews' relative consciousness of it, which makes them an especially appropriate group to study in this context.

Jews, Citizenship, and the Aesthetics of the Everyday in France and Germany

It would seem that, given the different fundamental logics of the nation in France and Germany, Jews ought to have been more thoroughly – more seamlessly – incorporated into the French than into the German nation and state. In fact the story is much more complicated. French Jews had, of course, been emancipated much earlier – in 1791 rather than 1871 – than those in Germany. But the path to full incorporation into polity and society was linear in neither country, nor did Jews anywhere behave as a bloc. Origins, wealth, piety and politics internally differentiated the Jewish communities of both Paris and Berlin. Despite this diversity, however, on the basis of analysis of the contents of hundreds of homes of Parisian and Berlin Jews in the 1930s, certain generalizations may be made concerning the two communities and their aesthetic choices.[23] The presentation here sketches the broad outlines of these stories; their details must await another context.

Recent historiography has made a powerful argument for the inaccuracy of the concept of 'assimilation' for both German and French Jews, arguing rather that their insider-outsider position is better captured by the term 'acculturation'. The historian Marion Kaplan, for example, argues that German Jews saw no contradiction between their Jewishness and their Germanness, conforming to the norms of their class in public life insofar as they were able, while maintaining specific religious practices, participating in Jewish organizations, and creating a unique German-Jewish culture.[24] While some authors suggest that assimilation is by contrast the right concept in the French case, others, including the historian Paula Hyman, make a persuasive case for the doubled identities and cultures of French Jews as well.[25] Given the continual existence of Jewish communities and patterns

23. The discussion below is based on research in the series AJ38 in the Archives Nationales in Paris and the series 243–04 (Oberfinanzpräsident) in the Landesarchiv Berlin. The AJ38 series contains thousands of files of household inventories written up by Jews who had been forced to flee Paris during the war (or their heirs) as part of the post-war restitution process. They include inventories written before the war for insurance purposes as well as those done from memory after war's end. Households range from the very poor to the very wealthy, from all parts of Paris. They are obviously a complex source; some may have exaggerated what they had owned, some may have forgotten. The series 243–04 in the Landesarchiv Berlin is composed of the auction records of both 'aryan' and 'non-aryan' residents of the city who put up some or all of their goods for auction between 1935 and 1942. This source obviously also must be read with care and caution. For my purposes here the most problematic aspect of both these sources is that the definition of 'Jew' is that of the Nazi regime, not of those whose goods were expropriated and whose lives were taken as a result of that categorization. Thus, in another source in the Landesarchiv, while all replied 'yes' to the question 'Are you a Jew?' the replies in the blank following 'religion' were far more varied, including Catholic, Evangelical, Jewish, nothing, and blank. For further discussion of these sources see my article, '"Jewish Taste"? Jews, and the aesthetics of everyday life in Paris and Berlin, 1933–1942', in R. Koshar (ed.), *Histories of Leisure* (Oxford: Berg, 2000). See also my 'Remembered homes: The work of memory in postwar Paris'.

24. M.A. Kaplan, *The Making of Jewish Middle Class: Women, Family, and Identity in Imperial Germany* (New York: Oxford University Press, 1991), p. 10.

25. For the assimilation model see for example M. Marrus, *The Politics of Assimilation: A Study of the French Jewish Community at the Time of the Dreyfus Affair* (Oxford: Oxford University Press, 1971). For the acculturation argument see for example P.E. Hyman, *From Dreyfus to Vichy: the Remaking of French Jewry, 1906–1939* (New York: Columbia University Press, 1979) and her *The Jews of Modern France* (Berkeley: University of California Press, 1998).

of sociability in the two nations, Jews were all also always, in their choices of everyday style and life practices, addressing at least two audiences; their Jewish friends, colleagues and relatives and the non-Jewish world in which they lived. The degree to which Jewish construction of distinctive practices was voluntary or a response to quiet roadblocks or to overt anti-Semitism has been a matter of controversy among historians. My preoccupation here, however, is less with the cause of the making of German-Jewish and French-Jewish culture than with their content and the implications of those cultures for German and French strategies of nation-building.

Most native-born Parisian Jews under the Third Republic seem at first glance to have embodied, in the style of their everyday lives, the French republican vision of unmarked individualism. They dressed in the same clothes as all other French people of their class, they sent their children to public schools, they ate French food, and they worked on Saturday. Parisian Jews' staunch adherence to the signs of Frenchness, of republicanism and of secularism, seems to have grown even stronger from the 1880s through the early years of the twentieth century as waves of Eastern European Jews arrived, bringing distinctive dress, orthodox religious practice, and radical – socialist – politics with them. These new Jews were clearly foreign, and clearly threatening to French Jews' arguments that they were, in public at least, French like everyone else. Any impulse most established French Jews might have had to create a publicly visible distinctively Jewish culture would have been inhibited by this influx of Jews from Eastern Europe, and the expansion of rightwing nationalism and anti-Semitism – including the Dreyfus Affair – in France. Most French Jews defended their place in the nation by reinforcing their historicity, their locatedness, and their adherence to a common, distinctively French culture.[26] This strategy seems to have been effective. By the late nineteenth century, as the historian Pierre Birnbaum and others have argued, more Jews in France than in any other polity had achieved positions of real political power. They had become deputies, ministers, judges, city councillors, mayors and even military officers.[27] They achieved success in civil society as teachers, professors, literary critics, lawyers and doctors.

Within this narrative of conformity to French norms (and success within them), however, are an interesting and significant array of sociological and aesthetic anomalies. With a few very notable exceptions – the Perreires and Rothschilds among them – Jews were not the leading figures in France's economic and industrial expansion, nor did they ever come to play an important role in industry. And,

---

26. This was paralleled by the reluctance of French Jews to become Zionists. See C. Nicault, *La France et le sionisme 1897–1948: Une rencontre manquée?* (Paris: Calmann-Lévy, 1992).

27. P. Birnbaum, *Les fous de la République: Histoire politique des Juifs d'État de Gambetta à Vichy* (Paris: Fayard, 1992) and P. Birnbaum and I. Katznelson (eds) *Paths of Emancipation: Jews, States, and Citizenship* (Princeton: Princeton University Press, 1995).

despite their general success in the liberal professions, native-born French Jews did not tend to become architects, decorators, designers or artists.

In terms of their social lives, Jews were highly endogamous and very few converted to Christianity. Many contributed to, and participated actively in, Jewish charitable organizations as well as belonging to a synagogue. The significance of these choices in a national climate in which secularism was highly valued and particularism disparaged is very great.[28] It would, therefore, appear that the assimilationist pressures of the French state and French society, while indeed powerful, did not succeed in eradicating all difference between French Jews and their secular, Catholic, or Protestant compatriots. This balance between likeness and difference can be seen in Jews' aesthetic choices.

Just before the outbreak of World War I, for example, an Orthodox congregation in the Marais, the old Jewish ghetto, hired the famous *art nouveau* architect Hector Guimard to design their new synagogue. In a neighbourhood dominated by seventeenth-century architecture, and among French synagogues generally built in a vaguely orientalist style, this synagogue stands out. The surprise diminishes, however, when one learns that the congregation consisted almost entirely of recent poor immigrants from Eastern Europe. As the art historian Dominique Jarrassé argues, their preoccupation in building their synagogue was twofold: it needed to be inexpensive and it needed to attract their children who were fleeing orthodoxy. The concerns of this group, then, were less with *their* place in the French nation than with *their children's* relation to Judaism. Their greatest worry was not that they themselves would appear foreign – they felt that was inevitable and irrelevant – but that their children would find their religious practice archaic and would therefore abandon it.[29] In contrast to most French Jews most of the time, therefore, they chose the most 'modern' design they could. This aesthetic choice was strongly minoritarian, however.

In the 1940s, then, when French Jews found themselves very publicly marked by the Vichy regime, household inventories reveal them to have been largely committed to French aesthetic norms, with important themes and variations. Thus the vast majority of those Parisians identified by the Vichy government as Jews furnished their homes in French historicist style. Whether they lived in a luxurious private home in the elegant suburb of Neuilly, or in a modest apartment in a working-class neighbourhood, their homes were furnished in pastiche versions of

28. On these points see particularly E. Benbassa, *Histoire des Juifs de France* (Paris: Editions du Seuil, 1997); M. Graetz, *Les juifs en France au 19e siècle: De la révolution française à l'Alliance Israélite universelle* (Paris: Le Seuil, 1989); Hyman, *From Dreyfus to Vichy*; A. Chouraqui, *Cent ans d'histoire: L'Alliance israélite universelle et la renaissance juive contemporaine (1860–1960)* (Paris: PUF, 1965); and L. M. Leff, '"The sacred tie of solidarity: French Jews and world Jewry, 1790–1890', (PhD dissertation, University of Chicago, 1999).

29. D. Jarrassé, *Une histoire des synagogues françaises. Entre occident et orient. Essai* (Arles: Actes Sud, 1997).

(and occasionally authentic) Henri II, Louis III, XIV, XV, and XVI and First Empire. Mme Cojocaru, for example, who lived in a two-room apartment at 14, rue Guénot in the working-class 11th arrondissement, wrote that she had had a 'Louis XV bedroom set in veneered walnut . . . and a walnut Henri II dining table'.[30] Monsieur and Madame Joseph Cohen, who clearly had far more means to indulge their taste, living in a luxurious six-room apartment in an elegant part of 17th arrondissement, showed a similar aesthetic. They had a bedroom furnished in Louis XVI and a living room in Louis XV, while the husband's study was largely seventeenth-century (although with a modern desk).[31]

Of the thousands of extant household inventories in which the styles of the furniture is indicated, the vast majority was French historicist pastiche, a significant number of the wealthy households possessed French Renaissance, Baroque and eighteenth-century antiques, a small but significant proportion owned some art déco or other 'modern' styles, and essentially none had furniture identified as foreign in origin. Very, very few owned (or acknowledged owning) specifically Jewish objects, whether religious or cultural. Equally few acknowledged owning representations of the Madonna and Child, or other Christian objects.

The French State appears, then, to have been relatively effective in its effort to encourage the creation of a homogeneous French style of everyday life, which would be both accepted by native-born citizens – of diverse class and religious origins – and appropriated by immigrants to the hexagon. That style was deeply rooted in the French past and exclusive both of explicitly religious and explicitly foreign forms. I would like to suggest that most French Jews' expression of this 'French taste' is an indication of the power of the French state's dependence on a common culture to create a common nation. The majority of French Jews, I believe, understood that they could not afford to mark themselves off from the national project, could not participate in the undermining of the national project, by participation in the creation of a distinctive aesthetic of everyday life. And I suspect, furthermore, that the vast majority had no desire to do so. It is important to underscore, however, that that 'national taste' was not as hegemonic as the above might imply.

Jews, and other French people, *did* buy modernist and foreign furniture and other objects. Everyday taste does not, cannot, simply mirror larger political or economic structures. While it seems that the dominant trend among Jews matched that of French designers and consumers in general – thereby demonstrating the force of the French assimilationist model – that trend was only a trend with room for individual and collective variation. This pattern of conformity and idiosyncrasy is revealing of the dynamic of the intersection of law and everyday aesthetics in

30. Archives Nationales, 38 AJ 5912, D30.
31. *Ibid.*

France. That intersection becomes even clearer when juxtaposed to the German case.

Despite earlier efforts, Jews in the German lands had to wait for unification in 1870 for their systematic legal emancipation. Individual states had, at various moments since the late eighteenth century, passed legislation improving the status of Jews as a class, and individual Jews had negotiated full emancipation for themselves and their families for years. Despite this lack of political freedom and rights, German Jews had benefited from the economic boom years of mid-century, and from their – non-voluntary – concentration in the fields of finance and commerce. By the 1880s many had prospered, with perhaps half having entered the ranks of the middle class. Those who found it difficult to earn a living joined the waves of out-migration from Germany to America and elsewhere. Consequently, despite legal restrictions, the German Jewish community in the nineteenth century was overall wealthier than that in France. By the time of emancipation in 1871 there was, therefore, a large German-Jewish bourgeoisie who saw the acquisition of legal rights as the last step in their acquisition of full Germanness. They appear, in fact, to have responded with relative indifference to this full entry into the state.[32]

Their indifference may have been reinforced by the difficulties German Jews faced as they attempted to move into politics and even into the civil service. Thus, in some senses, the German and French cases were mirror images. French Jews seem to have found the public world of the state relatively open and the private world of commerce and society relatively closed. The comparative openness of society in Germany is attested to by the high rates of intermarriage, by the relative closure of politics and other domains of the public sphere, and by the high conversion rates.[33] In France, conversion was not needed to acquire public office or a post in the civil service and endogamy there appears to have been voluntary – a means of keeping one's Jewishness alive. Finally, given the importance and acceptability of mediating institutions – whether based on region, religion, or profession – in the German polity and society, German Jews created far more specifically Jewish organizations than did their co-religionists in France.[34] Those organizations included ones organized to further the Zionist cause and others oriented towards the creation or retrieval of an 'authentic' Jewish culture.[35] Neither cause found many adherents in France. Despite these differences, however, Berlin

32. W.E. Mosse, 'From "Schutzjuden" to "Deutsch Staatsbürger Jüdischen Glaubens": the long and bumpy road of Jewish emancipation in Germany', in Birnbaum and Katznelson (eds), *Paths of Emancipation*, pp. 59–93.

33. Between 1911 and 1915 22 per cent of Jewish men and 13 per cent of Jewish women married non-Jews and between 1880 and 1919 about 23,000 converted (of a total Jewish population of approximately 550,000). Kaplan, *The Making of Jewish Middle Class*, p. 7.

34. M.P. Birnbaum, *Staat und Synagoge, 1918–1938: Eine Geschichte des Preußischen Landesverbands Jüdischer Gemeinden* (Tübingen: J.C.B. Mohr, 1981).

35. *Ibid.*

Jews like their Parisian counterparts seem generally to have followed national norms in their taste in interior furnishings.

Most Jews in Berlin in the 1930s seem to have decorated their homes with an eclectic assortment of German, French, English, and 'oriental' goods and styles. Thus one household in the bourgeois Charlottenburg district of Berlin, when forced by Nazi legislation to leave their apartment, auctioned off (among other things) two mirrors in Louis XVI style, a Chinese lacquered bowl, a Japanese woodcut, a Russian Icon, and an Empire incense-burner.[36] Another couple had had an even more eclectic décor, combining a study and dining-room in Queen Anne style, a modern bedroom in white lacquer, a Louis XVI table and porcelain and crystal from all of the major manufacturers in Germany.[37] Essentially no households were composed of entirely German goods, and most mixed different national styles and different periods freely. Likewise, in a culture in which glassware, flatware, and china were all important, essentially all households combined various European manufacturers with Chinese and Japanese products. A few people had also acquired some modern-style furnishings or lamps. This eclecticism seems to have mirrored that of the society around them, as did the widespread ownership of Christian artefacts – paintings and sculptures of the Madonna and Child, of the Apostles, of Christ. One couple, for example, for whom we have particularly precise document-ation, chose to sleep under a very large painting of the Madonna and Child.[38] These Christian objects may have been collected for their aesthetic qualities, some of their owners may have been Christian ('Jews' only in the Nazi classification scheme), or they may have been acquired to conform to norms. In general, then, Berlin Jews seem to have, like their counterparts in Paris, shared the aesthetic norms of their fellow citizens.

In both Berlin and Paris, however, a fraction of the Jewish community chose to live in a modernist dwelling, or to surround themselves by objects in that style. In both countries, most of those who made that choice appear to have earned their livings in the arts – as painters, architects, writers, or critics. In France, a very substantial proportion of them seems to have been migrants from Eastern Europe.[39] And in Berlin as in Paris, Jews seem to have been somewhat more inclined to worship in a modernist synagogue than to dwell in a modernist house. Thus, two important Jewish communities commissioned Bauhaus style designs for their synagogues (at a time when no church had yet been built in that style) and a Jewish

36. Landesarchiv Berlin 243–04 46. (Note that German archive law prohibits providing the names from these files.)

37. *Ibid.*

38. Landesarchiv Berlin, Baupolizei, Bezirk Tiergarten/Baupolizei und Straßenpolizei. 105 A Pr. Br. Rep. 030 Bln C Nr. 820 a.

39. K.E. Silver and R. Golan, *The Circle of Montparnasse: Jewish Artists in Paris, 1905–1945* (New York: The Jewish Museum, New York and Universe Books, 1985).

architect provided radically modern designs for a series of Berlin department stores.[40]

Both German and French Jews, like their fellow citizens, were inevitably shaped by the political and legal structures in which they lived. Thus, most French Jews thought that the greatest threat to their place was that they be perceived as unrooted, insufficiently assimilated, and cosmopolitan and they therefore fled association with modernism. German Jews were more worried about seeming archaic and uncivilized and tended therefore to avoid the same aesthetic trend. While acculturation is surely a more accurate concept than assimilation, it can only be given adequate content through investigation of the society into which historical actors were being 'acculturated' and what form the acculturation actually took. The research strategy I am proposing here broadens the relevant aspects of the dominant society and polity to include citizenship and state form and it broadens the relevant aspects of the minority society to include taste in everyday goods. That broadening, in a comparative context, should help clarify the consequences of differences in legal and political history in modern capitalist nation states, including how those differences are lived.

Acknowledgements

Versions of material in this chapter have been presented at the Max Planck Institut für Geschichte in Göttingen, the University of Hannover, the Einstein Forum in Berlin, the University of Texas, and Harvard, Emory, and Cornell Universities as well as the conference at Cambridge University that generated this book. I am grateful to the participants in all of these contexts for their insightful comments. I would like particularly to thank Steven L. Kaplan for his very close reading and David Blackbourne, Geoffrey Crossick, Karin Hausen, Tom Holt, Peter Jelavich, Dominic LaCapra, Alf Lüdtke and Adelheid von Saldern for their suggestions. Finally I would like to express my gratitude to the staff of the Landesarchiv Berlin, and particularly Frau Erler, for their help.

40. M. Brenner, *The Renaissance of Jewish Culture in Weimar Germany* (New Haven: Yale University Press, 1996), pp. 181 and 184.

7

Bread, Milk and Democracy: Consumption and Citizenship in Twentieth-Century Britain

Frank Trentmann

In 1903 several thousand women gathered at the Free Trade Hall in Manchester to voice their opposition to tariffs.[1] Held under the auspices of the Women's Co-operative Guild (WCG), this mass meeting was part of the movement that defeated Joseph Chamberlain's imperial tariff reform crusade and preserved Britain's unique Free Trade system. The cheap white loaf was the central icon to radicals and liberals alike. It represented the material benefits of cheap 'necessaries' and the growth of citizenship rights, pacific sentiment, democratic accountability, and secondary associations that were traced to the repeal of the corn laws (1846).[2] When the time came to celebrate the centenary of repeal, this configuration of consumption and citizenship had unravelled. 1946 brought bread rationing but no Free Trade revival. On the one hand, some former Liberals supported anti-rationing campaigns by Conservatives and organized housewives' campaigns, but here the meaning of consumption had narrowed to a defence of individual 'choice', divorced from earlier societal and international ideals.[3] On the other hand, the co-operative, Labour, and progressive women's movements – the former heart and soul of radical Free Trade – now embraced a vision of consumption and citizenship which demanded regulated, not unregulated, trade. The standard of living was no longer guaranteed by 'cheapness' and the market but by state-sponsored entitlements and

---

1. *Manchester and Salford Co-operative Herald*, December 1903, p. 199.

2. See F. Trentmann, 'Civil society, commerce, and the "citizen-consumer"', in *idem* (ed.), *Paradoxes of Civil Society* (Oxford and New York: Berghahn, 2000) and Trentmann, 'The erosion of free trade' (Harvard PhD thesis, 1999), ch. 1. For the Victorian background, see A.C. Howe, *Free Trade and Liberal England* (Oxford: Clarendon, 1998).

3. And from policy systems too, for post-war Conservative governments did not champion Free Trade all-round; see J. Tomlinson, '"Liberty with order": Conservative economic policy, 1951–64', in M. Francis and I. Zweiniger-Bargielowska (eds), *The Conservatives and British Society, 1880–1990* (Cardiff: University of Wales Press, 1996), pp. 275–88.

'fair', 'steady' prices. The 'necessary' foodstuff central to this new mode of consumer politics was no longer the cheap white loaf, but 'clean' free milk.

The shift in consumer politics from the white loaf to clean milk, this chapter argues, is interesting beyond its immediate and often noted connection to public health. It reveals a larger reconfiguration of consumption and citizenship, a process in which social movements redefined the meaning of 'consumption', their identity as 'consumers' vis-à-vis producers, and their position in civil society in relation to the British state and international political economy. During and after the First World War, organized consumers gradually reworked the radical-liberal picture of self-organized consumers, freed by Free Trade from state domination, trusts, high prices, and everyday hunger, into a vision of healthy and employed consumers protected by the state against profiteers, market fluctuations and scarcities, unemployment and disease. To follow the changing political purchase of the Free Trade loaf and welfare milk, then, is also to focus attention on the broader dynamics of change in the history of consumer politics. How, when, and what aspects of 'consumption' have been politicized in the past? And how have collective actors changed their identity as 'consumers' and 'citizens' over time? To understand the shift from a radical-liberal to a social-democratic vision of consumption and citizenship, we need to retrieve the changing world views of organized consumers themselves.

The importance of food and consumption in the creation of identity and community has been a long-standing theme in anthropology.[4] Many historians, too, disillusioned with male-centred narratives of class and production, have turned their attention to mothering, shopping, nutrition, domestic economy, public health, and food science.[5] Notwithstanding their historiographical significance, however, most accounts tend towards fragmented pictures of consumption, focusing either on the material and social dynamics of the household or on the emerging community of food scientists in relation to state and industry. Yet the symbolic centrality of 'necessaries' such as bread and milk in political culture stemmed precisely from their power to communicate between the experience of the everyday

4. M. Sahlins, *Culture and Practical Reason* (Chicago: University of Chicago Press, 1976), pp. 166–79; M. Douglas and B. Isherwood, *The World of Goods* (London: Allen Lane, 1979).

5. J. Lewis, *The Politics of Motherhood* (London: Croom Helm, 1980); E. Ross, *Love and Toil* (Oxford: Oxford University Press, 1993); V. Fildes, L. Marks and H. Marland (eds), *Women and Children First* (London: Routledge, 1992); S. Koven and S. Michel (eds), *Mothers of a New World* (London: Routledge, 1993); D.F. Smith (ed.), *Nutrition in Britain* (London: Routledge, 1997); C. Geissler and D.J. Oddy (eds), *Food, Diet and Economic Change Past and Present* (Leicester: Leicester University Press, 1993); R. Floud, K. Wachter and A. Gregory (eds), *Height, Health, and History* (Cambridge: Cambridge University Press, 1990); D.J. Oddy and D.S. Miller (eds), *Diet and Health in Modern Britain* (London: Croom Helm, 1985); D. Oddy and D. Miller (eds), *The Making of the British Diet* (London: Croom Helm, 1976); J. Burnett, *Plenty and Want* (London: Nelson, 1966); J. Vernon, 'The citizen as consumer', paper read at the 1999 North American Conference of British Studies.

and the individual body and larger ideas about political economy and the social body. This is not to say that maternalist discourses did not also assign values to milk, or to ignore the contribution of nutritionists or food engineers to new types of knowledge and marketing strategies for 'healthy' enriched foods, but it is to contest the explanatory primacy assigned to these variables. Bread and milk were not single issues, short-lived protest symbols or instances of food policy. Rather they served in popular politics as central constituents of two different configurations of consumption and citizenship. It was through the debates about the cheap loaf in the Edwardian period and about 'clean' milk during and after the First World War that organized consumers defined themselves in relation to state and economy and acquired knowledge about the nature of local and international political economy. And it was the beliefs, knowledge and mobilization created first around bread, then around milk that facilitated first the defence of Free Trade, then its challenge, and finally its replacement with the consumer politics of the welfare state. In brief, to trace the shift from bread to milk is to reconnect the history of consumption to the history of politics, and by doing so suggest a new way of linking the local, material, and everyday to the global, civic, and utopian.

Consumers in modern societies have been active constituents of political economy, not merely atomistic purchasers of goods produced in a commercial system beyond their control. The burgeoning literature on modern consumer society has evolved around two quite different lines of inquiry. The first is interested in the relationship between political economy and consumption but traces the development of modern consumer societies to changing systems of production and distribution, such as corporatism, Fordism, advertising, economic nationalism and demand management.[6] Here the key subjects are firms and states. 'The consumer' is either an abstract aggregate, a pliant creature who (fully aware of Say's law) absorbs an ever-expanding deluge of goods, or the object of an increasingly anonymous (and Americanized) commercial world inducing meaning-less tastes and desires – the target of the Frankfurt school.[7] Whether positive or

6. For a wide-ranging critique of universal accounts of consumer society in terms of consumer taste or industrial development, see B. Fine and E. Leopold, *The World of Consumption* (London: Routledge, 1993) which argues for a vertical analysis of the different 'systems of provision' of commodities, but unfortunately does not say much about consumer politics.

7. Habermas early on counterpoised culture and consumption as incompatible, see his 'Konsumkritik', *Frankfurter Hefte*, 12 (1957), pp. 641–5. His development of theories of public sphere and communicative action since continues to leave little room for consumer politics. Consumer protests fit poorly a view of consensus-oriented discursive reasoning as the defining mode of communication in the public sphere: see B. Davis, 'Reconsidering Habermas, politics, and gender', in G. Eley (ed.), *Society, Culture, and the State in Germany, 1870–1930* (Ann Arbor: University of Michigan Press, 1996). Most fundamentally, by separating civil society from political economy, Habermas locates consumption within the self-driving system of the economy to which social movements respond rather than assigning consumers a more active role within civil society: J. Habermas, *Between Facts and Norms* (Oxford: Polity, 1996). For further discussion, see Trentmann, 'Paradoxes of civil society', in *Paradoxes of Civil Society*, pp. 24 ff.

negative in evaluation, this set of approaches tends towards a linear narrative of expanding consumerism, in which consumer politics follow on the heels of affluence and commodification.[8] The second strand of approaches has focused on new sites of consumption, such as the department store, as sites of empowerment.[9] If these studies have restored agency to the individual consumer, especially women, they have at the same time widened the gulf to consumer politics. Here the interest lies with the individual self and immediate acts and dreams of consumption, opportunities for transgression, and the changing boundaries between public and private, rather than the collective voice of the consumer and the meanings assigned to consumption in political culture and economy.

Notwithstanding their many refreshing contributions to consumer studies, these dominant strands have left us with historical blindspots. Alongside the uncritical consumer deplored by the Frankfurt School and the transgressive consumer celebrated in post-colonial readings, large movements of consumers entered the political stage at certain times in history (and disappeared at others). By nature all human beings are consumers, but the political meaning and identity attached to consumption varies in history. This chapter will try to reappraise one such episode in which the political meanings of consumption changed as labour, progressive liberals, co-operatives, and women's organizations moved from the cheap loaf and Free Trade in the decades before the First World War to clean milk and social-democratic ideals thereafter.

Retrieving the connection between political meanings, social norms, economic knowledge and the material dimensions of consumption opens up several new perspectives for consumer studies. To explain how a policy of laissez-faire that

8. The productivist bias is even evident in some of the best work on the subject, see S. Strasser, C. McGovern and M. Judt (eds), *Getting and Spending* (Cambridge: Cambridge University Press, 1998); V. de Grazia (ed.), *The Sex of Things* (Berkeley: University of California Press, 1996). See also A. Gerschenkron's classic *Bread and Democracy in Germany* (Berkeley: University of California Press, 1943) with its almost exclusive focus on state and producers; for an analysis of consumer issues in Wilhelmine party politics, see now C. Nonn, *Verbraucherprotest und Parteiensystem im wilhelminischen Deutschland* (Düsseldorf: Droste, 1996). Many studies of early consumer politics, such as the white label campaign of the National Consumers' League in America, have focused on their connection to the sphere of production: K. Kish Sklar, 'The consumers' White Label Campaign of the National Consumers' League, 1898–1918', in Strasser *et al.,* (eds), *Getting and Spending*, ch. 1. For exceptions, see L. Cohen, 'The New Deal state and the making of citizen consumers', in *Getting and Spending*, ch. 5; B. Davis, 'Food scarcity and the empowerment of the female consumer in World War I Berlin', in de Grazia (ed.), *Sex of Things*, ch. 9; E. Furlough and C. Strikwerda (eds), *Consumers Against Capitalism?* (Lanham and Oxford: Rowman and Littlefield, 1999). Tellingly, the most original recent exploration of the links between cultures of consumption and citizenship has been for ancient Greece, not 'modern' consumer societies: J. Davidson, *Courtesans and Fishcakes* (London and New York: HarperCollins, 1997).

9. J. Walkowitz, *City of Dreadful Delight* (Chicago: University of Chicago Press, 1992); S. Buck-Morss, *The Dialectics of Seeing: Walter Benjamin and the Arcades Project* (Cambridge, Mass.: MIT Press, 1989); M. Miller, *The Bon Marché* (Princeton: Princeton University Press, 1981).

today stands condemned by democrats, women, and consumers all over the world was able to attract popular support in late Victorian and Edwardian Britain, it is necessary to recognize consumption as something more than just the economic other of production and restore its links to social and political ideals. The movements for the cheap loaf and for pure milk point to an alternative narrative to those of free market consumerism, Fordism or economic nationalism dominating the literature. In Britain, consumer politics did not follow on the heels of the unprecedented age of prosperity and mass consumption beginning in the 1950s, but preceded it. The politicization of milk partly reflected a new concern with nutrition that transformed the meaning of essential foodstuffs and linked food and trade policy to public health. Equally important was the changing popular knowledge of the workings of the economy and the role of private and public organizations communicated through a re-examination of food prices, supply, and distribution. Consumer movements conducted an intense debate during and after the First World War about how best to interpret developments within states and business organizations (such as trusts) and the most appropriate response by organized consumers nationally and internationally. The shift from the cheap loaf to pure milk went hand in hand with a more balanced vision of the reciprocal rights (and duties) of producers and consumers, a more sceptical sense of the relationship between civil society and freedom of trade, and a more positive view of economic regulation by the state and international organizations as an instrument for advancing domestic and global welfare and peace.

Consumption and Citizenship in Free Trade

The comparatively unique strength of Free Trade in Victorian and Edwardian Britain was a product of political culture rather than a mere reflection of economic 'interests'.[10] The popularity of Free Trade and the cost of living were inversely related. Although many working-class families still spent up to 60 per cent of their budget on food at the turn of the century[11] and thus had good reasons to be sceptical of tariffs, British society had benefited significantly from the fall in prices in the late nineteenth century and was less dependent on cheap food for survival than preceding generations or other Europeans at the time. It was the interlacing of citizenship and consumption that translated material needs into larger social,

---

10. The following section draws on my discussion in 'Commerce and civil society', in *Paradoxes of Civil Society*; 'The erosion of free trade'; and 'Political culture and political economy', *Review of International Political Economy*, 5 (1998), pp. 217–51 which see for further discussion and references.

11. D.J. Oddy, 'A nutritional analysis of historical evidence: the working-class diet, 1880–1914', in Oddy and Miller (eds), *Making of British Diet*, p. 216. The percentage was lower in high rent areas such as London: see Ross, *Love and Toil*, p. 41.

moral, and political concerns. Free Trade became the thread in a narrative of a civilizing process, buttressed by assumptions about nationality, the educational role of trade, and the threat of modern mass society.

Civil society and consumption mutually reinforced each other in the popular Free Trade revival before the First World War. For radicals and liberals, the repeal of the corn laws in 1846 marked the birth of independent social movements and the freedom of society from the state. After decades of oppression, the old co-operator George Holyoake told audiences, labourers gained 'rights which should be respected . . . [and] interests which should be consulted'.[12] Free Trade, in this view, strengthened the self-regulating powers of society and insulated it against organized interests, be it the state, aristocracy or trusts.[13] Indeed, Free Trade could be defended as a quasi-constitutional arrangement providing virtual representation to all members of society, including groups without formal representation. Liberal posters and propaganda appealed to women as consumers and portrayed protectionism as an invasion of the female sphere of the household (and purse) by the state. For women co-operators, the 'fiscal controversy' about food duties showed just how critical politics was to 'the women with the basket' and reinforced their demand for enfranchisement. The Women's Co-operative Guild (WCG) saw Free Trade as a framework for the growth of civil society in which co-operatives would expand and act as 'a training ground' in democratic citizenship and community self-help.

The historical myth of the 'hungry forties' – constructed and popularized in the Edwardian debate – told a quasi-biblical story of the emancipation of the English people from the horrors of starvation attributed to the corn laws. The white loaf which was waved from political platforms symbolized the civilizing achievement of Free Trade. This dietary story of advancing liberal democracy was sustained by inflated accounts of hungry Germans reduced by protectionism to a diet of black bread, horseflesh, and dog-meat.[14] The contrast between British and German diet came to symbolize the apparently unbridgeable divide created by different fiscal systems between democracy, wealth, and upright, peaceful citizens under Free Trade, on one hand, and autocracy, poverty, militarism and the disempowered mob

---

12. G. Holyoake, 'In the days of protection', in H.W. Massingham (ed.), *Labour and Protection* (London, 1903), p. 112. For the co-operative movement, see P. Gurney, *Co-operative Culture and the Politics of Consumption in England, 1870–1930* (Manchester: Manchester University Press, 1996); G.D.H. Cole, *A Century of Co-operation* (Manchester, 1945).

13. F. Trentmann, 'The transformation of fiscal reform', *Historical Journal*, 39 (1996), pp. 1025 f.

14. Free Trade Union, *Tales of the Tariff Trippers* (1910). In fact, wheat and rye flour production were almost evenly balanced in imperial Germany at this time (47.9 per cent to 52.1 per cent). German wheat consumption had increased in the protectionist era and more rye went into exports; see K.P. Ellerbrock, *Geschichte der deutschen Nahrungs- und Genussmittelindustrie* (Stuttgart: Franz Steiner Verlag, 1993), pp. 380 ff.

under tariffs on the other. 'We are at the parting of the ways', Lloyd George typically reminded Edwardian audiences: 'We are choosing between free Britain and bound, shackled Germany.' 'If this country wanted German tariffs, it must have German wages . . . German militarism, and German sausages.'[15]

This language of consumption should not be confused with consumerism. Victorians and Edwardians held paradoxical views of consumption that fit uneasily the older historiographical picture of a nineteenth-century divide between morals and markets, when, in E.P.Thompson's famous account, a 'traditional moral economy' was being swept aside by the new 'demoralised' political economy of free markets.[16] Free Trade was believed to insulate society against materialism, which, like capitalist trusts, was traced to the selfish culture of protectionism. Radicals and Liberals drew a stark distinction between different forms of consumption. The case for Free Trade was that it guaranteed cheap necessaries for the poor, not that it would increase demand for commodities all-round. Free Trade instilled a sense of 'reciprocity' into individuals, making them active citizens, with a sense of responsibility towards each other.[17] 'New liberal' Free Traders, such as J.A .Hobson, thus looked forward to the evolution of 'citizen-consumers', peace-loving, co-operative individuals with a social conscience and individual taste for 'higher' forms of consumption, who would regenerate civic life and stop the drift of modern society towards the dehumanising, bureaucratic world of corporatism, commercialism, and jingoism.

The Transvaluation of Necessaries

The associations between the pure white loaf, Free Trade, social justice and the 'purity' of politics began to unravel during the First World War. The war gave rise to popular demands for state controls and a more interventionist food policy, and prompted a new understanding of trusts and profiteering. Radical, labour, socialist and some co-operative groups campaigned for the state to take over milk supply and distribution to guarantee its citizens an essential foodstuff at fair prices. By

15. House of Lords Record Office, Lloyd George Papers, A/12/2/49 speech at Perth (20 November 1904); A/13/1/4 (30 January 1905).

16. E.P. Thompson, 'The moral economy of the English crowd in the eighteenth century', *Past and Present*, 50 (1971), pp. 76–136; Thompson acknowledged that the older moral economy of provisions lived on for a while in the 'bowels of the Co-operative Wholesale Society' (p. 135), but was entirely blind to the new moral horizon and popular appeal of the 'new political economy' of Free Trade. For the middle classes' ambivalence towards consumer culture, see M.C. Finn, 'Working-class women and the contest for consumer control in Victorian county courts', *Past and Present*, 161 (1998), pp. 116–54.

17. This educational function can be traced back to the enlightenment: see R. Gordon 'Hegel, Smith, and the market', in my *Paradoxes of Civil Society*, ch. 3.

the end of the war, milk had become recognized as 'this most necessary food', a 'prime necessity'[18] to which people had a right, in the words of the Food Controller, George Roberts, and H.M. Hyndman, a socialist on the advisory Consumers' Council.

The political transvaluation of 'the people's food' in the war and post-war years built on earlier campaigns for food reform but now grafted the new dietary knowledge of nutritional science onto the older Victorian campaign against adulteration. A divide emerged between the material and political worlds of consumption. The white loaf continued to dominate Britons' diet but became marginalized in consumer politics. White bread had become the principal diet of the British people by the early nineteenth century and formed 95 per cent of bread consumption by weight in 1900, and still 80 per cent in 1970.[19] Brown bread advocates and food reformers, such as the Bread and Food Reform League, focused from the 1880s on the white loaf's threat to national fitness and dental health, and highlighted the dangers of bleaching and of extracting the wheat berry in the milling process.[20] Co-operative mills and commercial companies such as Hovis introduced brown bread and mixed flour in the 1890s, but well into the late twentieth century, their impact on the national diet remained small and disproportionally weighted towards pensioners and higher income groups.[21] The political capital of the white loaf developed in the opposite direction, and had been depleted by the inter-war years. Co-operative women in 1930 confessed that it had become difficult to stir up public interest in 'the loaf', a problem explained away (a little too easily) with reference to falling prices and a slimming craze favouring brown bread over white bread.[22] Interestingly, there were now consumers, such as Mrs Wilson, the wife of a London artisan, who ate the cheaper white bread but readily told the Royal Commission on Food Prices in 1925 that brown bread was 'more nutritious to the children [and] I think it would be better if they had less pure white bread'.[23]

18. British Library of Political and Economic Science [BLPES], Coll Misc. 92 [Beveridge, Food Control Collection], XIII/11, Roberts, 'Future Food Problems' memo by the Food Controller; Manchester Labour History Museum [MLH], Consumers' Council Papers [CC] CC/REF/86, minutes 1 June 1920 (Hyndman).

19. Burnett, *Plenty and Want*, pp. 2 ff.; E.J.T. Collins, "The consumer revolution' and the growth of factory foods', in Oddy and Miller (eds), *Making of the British Diet*, p. 28.

20. MLH, CC/CP.152, 'A Standard for Meal, Flour and Bread', by May Yates, the honorary secretary of the League.

21. B. Fine, M. Heasman and J. Wright, *Consumption in the Age of Affluence* (London, 1996), pp. 224 ff.; Collins, 'Consumer revolution', pp. 29ff. CWS flour mills sold six different brown bread flours, including Hermes, Sun, and Star, in addition to its white flour selection.

22. *Co-operative News*, 6 December 1930, p. 12.

23. The Commission's findings were popularized in an edition of extracts from the evidence of housewives, *Why Your Food Costs More* (London, 1925), cit. at p. 27. According to the Bread and Reform League, the price of brown bread often exceeded that of white bread in poorer areas: see MLH, CC/CP 153, Memorial to C. Addison, p. 10.

The catalyst for the political fall of the white loaf was the German navy's pressure on Britain's wheat imports in the First World War. The pressure on shipping space and the need to maximize the nutritional intake from foodstuffs provided the previously missing opening for the brown loaf. The British state avoided bread-rationing by raising the milling standard from the customary pre-war 70 per cent to 73–78 per cent.[24] As studies of the national food supply demonstrated, the 70 per cent standard led to a tremendous waste of resources. Ideally, humans were able to utilize over 90 per cent of the energy contained in bread. A low milling standard led to a significant waste because only part of the extracted wheat berry fed as offal to cattle or pigs was left in the meat that eventually ended up on the dining table. In the last year of the war, the Food War Committee of the Royal Society experimented with a series of 'special breads' made of wheat flour of 80 per cent or 90 per cent extraction and a small admixture of maize and rice. For two months in a series of carefully monitored experiments, groups of chemical workers, laboratory attendants, children, and patients suffering from pulmonary tuberculosis ate the 'pale golden yellow' and 'light brown' breads and had their faeces weighed every morning. The results were astonishing. The breads were 'well digested' even by children and even when eaten in large quantities. In 'certain cases health seemed to improve during its use'. The 'bread was stated by all to be palatable, and no one complained of becoming tired of it . . . as was feared by some members of the Committee'. Indeed, the browner bread was so popular that the patients, of whom many had 'more or less impaired digestions', asked to receive it in future and supply it to others. The sixty-one employees of the West Riding Chemical Co. Ltd even composed a memorial, recording their appreciation of the experiment from which 'we derived great benefit' and asked for further supply of the wholemeal bread, 'as we do not wish to resume the use of the ordinary flour, which we are convinced contains deleterious materials.'[25] The Bread and Food Reform League used these experiments to step up its campaign to put the white loaf on a blacklist of dangerous adulterated foods. For the sake of future citizens and democratic survival, its scientists urged the Lloyd George coalition, the state should regulate the people's bread rather than relying on the operation of the free market.[26]

The co-operative movement joined food reformers in the critique of the white loaf and extended the fight against adulteration into a new nutritional politics.

24. This raised the percentage of wheat milled ending up as flour (rather than as offal fed to animals) by 20 per cent and 22–7 per cent.

25. BLPES, Coll Misc. 92, XX/4, Food War Committee, Royal Society, Report on the Digestibility of Breads, March 1918, pp. 4, 34 f.

26. MLH, CC/CP 153, Memorial to C. Addison; the League's scientists also emphasized the part played by calcium phosphates in the wheat berry, an important constituent of teeth and bones. CC/CP.152, 'A Standard for Meal, Flour and Bread'. See also CC/CP 151, Bread and Reform League to the Consumers' Council, 22 March 1920.

The WCG began to promote 'Food Purity' in the mid-1920s. They contrasted, for example, the use of unbleached flour in co-operative flourmills and the adulteration by 'unscrupulous bakers' who were using various phosphates to beautify inferior flour, thereby causing dermatitis. Most importantly, this literature popularized knowledge of vitamins and the germ theory of disease among the largest organized consumer movement, the co-operatives. Bread handled improperly by too many hands carried a 'real danger of infectious diseases'. Basic nutritional lessons introduced members to the terminology of carbohydrates and proteins, and, especially important for our concerns, to the importance of vitamins, a term born in 1912. Pure white flour was devoid of the vitamins contained in the germ and outer skin of the grain, notably vitamin B, known as the 'the anti-neurotic vitamin', important for growth, especially of the nervous system. The Co-operative Wholesale Society's (CWS) wholemeal flour, by contrast, one woman co-operator explained, contained vitamins as well as iodine, 'one of the elements which in minute quantities has lately been discovered to be of great importance in human diet'.[27]

The marginalization of the white loaf was accelerated by the growing attention to an essential foodstuff that fit more squarely the new nutritional foundations of consumer politics. The war and post-war period saw the redefinition of necessaries in terms of scientific knowledge rather than culture and history. Customary notions of what type of food was a necessary part of decent life, well reflected in associations of brown bread with slavery or oppression, gave way to a new focus on quantifiable bio-chemical units (rather than foodstuffs and their appearance and taste) and their physiological functions, thought to apply to human needs across cultures.[28]

More than any other aspect of consumer politics, it was the campaign for pure milk that harnessed new nutritional knowledge to the enfranchisement of women and children in a new democracy of consumers that turned to the state rather than the free market. Efforts to increase and improve milk consumption had pre-war origins, such as the co-operative sale of 'pure milk' in its new branches in poorer districts (Sunderland), the WCG's pressure for special maternity allowances, the 1906 Education (Provision of Meals) Act and the 1912 Act preventing the use of

27. F. Ranson, *Food Values*, WCG pamphlet (nd [1926]), p. 13; see also F. Ranson, *Food Purity*, WCG Pamphlet (1926), pp. 9 f. These popular lessons on food science and food purity even told readers that wholemeal bread contained the 'anti-rachitic' vitamin A.

28. The nutritional standards laid down by the League of Nations and the work of scientists such as Boyd Orr and Crawford in the mid-1930s have become main reference points in the literature, so it might be worth stressing that the transvaluation of necessaries from a cultural to a nutritional basis had already begun in consumer politics during and after the First World War. Boyd Orr's work on diet and poverty was so remarkably influential in the 1930s and 1940s precisely because organized consumers had weaned themselves from the food politics characteristic of Free Trade culture and begun to turn to a new configuration of food entitlements and citizenship. Cf. the volumes on nutrition and diet cit. above, n. 5 and the prominence of individual scientists therein compared to the absence of consumer politics.

preservatives in milk. It was the combination of material scarcity and human sacrifice in total war that turned the 'milk question' into a fundamental issue connecting the rights of social citizenship to the redesign of political economy. As 'the most important health industry', milk illustrated that the interests of the consumer called for controls, not laissez-faire, the *Co-operative News* concluded in June 1918: 'If men could be commandeered for the Army, surely milk ought to be commandeered for the benefit of the health of the community.'[29] A year after the armistice, one thousand women marched towards the council house in Bristol protesting against the high price of milk with mottos such as 'We Want Cheaper Milk' and 'God Save the Babies'. If there were no food riots as in Germany,[30] it was protests such as these that established a new popular discourse about consumer rights and fair prices as a domain of the state.

Dirt, disease, waste, high prices, scarcity, insufficient consumption – what were common features of the milk trade before the war became an unacceptable indictment of liberal political economy during the war. Milk had been the principal offender in adulteration before the war.[31] The Local Government Board's inspection of 90,000 samples of food before the war revealed that over 9 per cent were adulterated, of which milk was the highest single culprit (12.5 per cent). Water was added freely, cream removed liberally. Yet the main source of danger stemmed from the atomized, uncontrolled nature of production and distribution in many areas. Outside of London (where by 1900 there had developed an integrated, semi-monopolistic milk trade with large wholesalers who had access to depots and railway supplies from as far away as Derbyshire), milk was still sold directly via hand carts or horse floats by small retailers who were either small producers themselves or bought from local farmers.[32] The long chain from cow to consumer made milk a haven for bacilli, most dangerously those responsible for tuberculosis. Wartime attempts to maximize available milk supplies revealed an astounding

29. *Co-operative News*, 22 June 1918, p. 453.

30. I know of one riot only, in Ipswich over the price of butter, *Co-operative News*, 3 August 1918, p. 526.

31. This casts doubt on the presumed success of anti-adulteration legislation. See the positive picture painted in Burnett, *Plenty and Want*. For a reassessment, see J. Phillips and M. French, 'Adulteration and food law, 1899–1939', *Twentieth-Century British History*, 9 (1998), pp. 350–69. Part of the problem was that British legislation was uniquely permissive and relied on local initiative and voluntary improvements by the food industry, rather than on a national system of inspections and controls. Moreover, the 1875 Sale of Food and Drugs Act made it necessary to prove the guilty knowledge of sellers of adulterated goods. For a historical assessment, a lot depends on how adulteration is defined. Whereas pre-war legislation focused on 'cheating', such as watering down milk, it is clear that consumers also faced a principal health danger from contamination with the tubercle bacilli, something on which anti-adulteration policies before the First World War were silent. Arguably, the increase in milk consumption prior to pasteurization in the 1920s means that consumers became more not less vulnerable in this period.

32. E. Whetham, 'The London milk trade, 1900–1930', in Oddy and Miller (eds), *Making of British Diet*, pp. 65 ff.

degree of chaotic distribution, costly production, and unhygienic handling of milk. Consumers were either unable to obtain or pay for milk, especially in poorer neighbourhoods, or they stood a good chance of consuming milk that had gone sour, had been improperly pasteurized, or had become infected with tuberculosis. Before the commercial turn to pasteurisation in the 1920s, British society faced the worst of both worlds: a significant group went short of fresh milk and Vitamin A, the rest consumed milk that carried disease or was safe but no longer had nutritional value. The disproportionate consumption of condensed milk by working-class families exacerbated the problem, especially for children; small children did not have the enzyme necessary for splitting and absorbing the particular sucrose and were especially vulnerable to die through diarrhoea caused by bacteria carried by flies attracted to opened tins of the sweetened milk often kept in an unsanitary environment.[33]

Across Britain, milk consumption increased gradually in the late Victorian and Edwardian eras, a trend that resumed in the 1920s. Milk was already by the Edwardian period part of the British diet and its health benefits appreciated, not least by those groups who only managed to consume it infrequently. Yet overall consumption remained below that of many other European societies.[34] In 1904, according to the Board of Trade, families consumed between 5.5 and 12.6 pints of milk per week. Consumption was uneven not just across class but age and region, gradually becoming more uniform in the next half-century. According to D.J. Oddy's survey of working-class budgets, workers increased their weekly consumption of milk in the thirty years before the First World War from 1.4 to 1.8 pints per head.[35] This was less than half of what New Yorkers and Parisians consumed at the time.[36] Children and expectant and nursing mothers needed more than a pint per day, as contemporaries stressed; unlike their social superiors, working-class

33. Buchanan, 'Infant feeding, sanitation and diarrhoea in colliery communities, 1880–1911', in Oddy and Miller (eds), *Diet and Health in Modern Britain*, pp. 148–77; F.B. Smith, *The People's Health* (London: Croom Helm, 1979), pp. 92 f.

34. Consumption patterns defy generalizations such that urban workers barely ever saw any fresh milk or that milk only became popular in the 1930s thanks to the campaign of nutritionists; F. McKee, 'The popularisation of milk as a beverage during the 1930s', in Smith (ed.), *Nutrition in Britain*, pp. 123–41. Ross, *Love and Toil*, p. 143. British consumption in 1900–2 was 14.5 gallons per capita per annum and 16.3 in 1910–12: see J.B. Jefferys, *Retail Trading in Britain, 1850–1950* (Cambridge: Cambridge University Press, 1954), p. 227; cf., in 1902, Saxony (46 gallons), Sweden and Denmark (40) and France (16), cit. Burnett, *Plenty and Want*, p. 158.

35. Oddy, 'Nutritional analysis', in Oddy and Miller, *Making of British Diet*, p. 221. Edward Smith's survey of 1864 found that urban workers consumed less than one pint per week in 1864: see Burnett, *Plenty and Want*, p. 143. In 1902 the weekly consumption of milk among rural working families ranged from 4 pints of fresh milk and 9 ½ pints skimmed in Eastern counties to 6½ pints of fresh milk in Northern counties: Burnett, *Plenty and Want*, p. 132.

36. For New York: Clean Milk Society; for Paris: T. Bonzon, B. Davis, 'Feeding the cities', in J. Winter and J.-L. Robert (eds), *Capital Cities at War* (Cambridge: Cambridge University Press, 1997), p. 317, who cite 1.6 lbs of milk per head for Londoners in 1913.

mothers breast-fed their babies for the first six months if possible and then gradually switched to hand feeding, which would frequently include breadstuffs mixed with fresh or condensed milk and water.[37] In some towns and rural areas prices or supply networks put milk beyond the reach of the poorest groups. The problems in Bradford were not atypical. In 1913, 22 per cent of the homes in the city did not get any milk at all; the remaining households consumed 1.31 pints per day. Most streets were served by half a dozen different milk dealers. A good deal of the milk was sour or infected. The city council in 1916 saw here the 'causes of abnormal malnutrition, infantile sickness, and unnecessary death' and called for municipal control and reorganization of the milk trade.[38]

Growing awareness about vitamin deficiency was reinforced by knowledge of bacteria and the success of public health reforms abroad, and co-operative, labour, and nutritionists campaigns to provide subsidized milk did much to popularize this knowledge. The National Clean Milk Society, founded in 1915, campaigned for higher standards of hygiene and publicized the nutritional importance of milk through a series of educational pamphlets, posters, and 'Clean Milk Films' which were shown during labour conferences.[39] These portrayed bacteria as well as the unhygienic 'small milkboy who was seen carefully straining milk through his pocket handkerchief on somebody's doorstep'. Drawing on investigations by medical officers and the Lister Institute as well as on American public health reports, the Society painted a terrifying picture of rampant disease and death. Milk was richer in bacteria than the sewage of British cities. Of a London sample of milk, 99 per cent had traces of cow dung. West End shops revealed a higher number of bacteria than those in the East End. Milk supplied to babies at schools for mothers and hospitals carried bacilli coli (indicating the presence of manure) and several million bacteria per cubic centimetre, a terrifying number considering the 60,000 considered hygienically possible at the time. As was pointed out again and again, virtually all British milk would have been outlawed as unfit for human consumption in New York City, where authorities had pioneered a system of municipal licensing and grading.[40] The introduction of dairy controls in American cities provided the

37. Buchanan, 'Infant feeding', pp. 148–77; Ross, *Love and Toil*, pp. 141 f.; V. Fildes, *Wet Nursing* (Oxford: Blackwell, 1988), pp. 201 ff.

38. *Yorkshire Observer*, 13 December 1916.

39. See the 19th London Labour Conference at the YMCA Tottenham Court Road on 22 July 1920, MLH, CC/MIL/166.

40. For comparison, in New York City in 1911, the year when grading was introduced, the percentage of milk with less than 10,000 bacteria per cubic centimetre was 15 per cent in raw milk and 44 per cent in pasteurized milk; an additional 26 per cent in raw milk and 42 per cent in pasteurized milk had more than 10,000 but less than 100,000 bacteria. Of the 48 samples of milk supplied to London hospitals and schools of mothers, only one was in that category, and only barely (98,000 bacteria): the National Clean Milk Society, *Report of Investigation* (1918). For municipal reforms in America and the rapid growth in milk consumption (by 85 per cent in New York City, 1890-1924), see E.E. Vial, 'Milk supply', in *Encyclopaedia of the Social Sciences* (New York: Macmillan, 1933), pp. 475 ff.

British debate with additional evidence about the human cost of an unregulated milk trade. In Cincinnati, the mortality rate of infants (under one) fell from an average of 139 per 1,000 births before milk supervision to 93 after. As 'A Short Talk to Mothers on Milk' by the Society concluded in June 1919, mothers in New York had been taught that milk was a necessary and bought high-grade milk in consequence. The appeal to nutritional utility (rather than cheapness) now merged with a language of the rights of consumers:

> Remember it is not so much what you pay as what you get for your money that counts . . . British mothers too have a right to clean milk for their children, and the government must see to it that arrangements are made, not only for the proper housing of the people, but also for the proper production and handling of the children's food – clean milk.[41]

The New Consumer Politics of Milk

The 'milk question' became an increasingly explosive political subject during the First World War, as the gulf between rising consumer consciousness and falling milk production steadily widened. Milk, unlike wheat, was almost exclusively a domestic product and could be politicized as a terrain of direct conflict between domestic producers and consumers. It thus posed a direct potential challenge to the legitimacy of the state as a guardian of citizens' interests.

Britain had entered the war with the lowest number of milk cows per capita in Europe (excepting France),[42] a bad situation made worse by rising costs of war-time production. An already short supply of milk shrank further as producers followed the signals of the market and turned to cheese or slaughtered their cows for more profitable meat. Three years into the war, Britain faced a 'milk famine'.[43] The state responded with four sets of reforms. Most immediately, the government began to fix prices for producers and set maximum retail prices. In November 1917 the food controller introduced a maximum price of 2s. 8d. (more than twice the pre-war price), raised further to 3s. 4d. the following year. Second, it granted powers to the Local Government Board to regulate conditions of sale and

41. MLH, CC/MIL/123, National Clean Milk Society, June 1919.

42. In 1871, there were 8 cows per 100 people in the United Kingdom; by 1914 the number of cows was down to 7: see BLPES, Coll. Misc. 92, XX/10 h 'Memorandum on the Permanent Control of the Milk Trade', 14 May 1919, Ministry of Food, 2.

43. For the winter 1918–19, for example, the total amount of liquid milk was estimated at ¼ pint per day per person. The situation was made worse by the fact that cows' milk production was cyclical, reaching a low in winter. In December 1918, for example, 63 per cent of dairy cows were in milk in England, 37 per cent were dry, compared to 81 per cent and 19 per cent respectively in June 1918: see BLPES, Coll. Misc.92, XXIV, minutes of the Food Council, 4 June 1919.

distribution of milk to assure sanitary standards and prevent the addition of water and colouring.[44] 'Grading' was now officially recognized through special licences to sell milk above the maximum price if the herds had passed a tuberculin test.[45] Third, in October 1918, the Ministry of Food took control of the wholesale trade to ensure a more equitable distribution of milk, shifting it away from industrial uses (cheese, condensed milk, chocolate) to liquid milk.[46] Finally, it gave local authorities permissive powers to distribute milk at reduced prices to mothers and children.[47]

This last policy was a milestone in the recognition of the special nutritional needs of children and their mothers and was, partly, a response to the WCG's campaign for maternity care and free milk. In the course of the war the WCG produced a series of influential studies that documented how mothers and children were the first to suffer from higher prices and illustrated the causal link between malnutrition, mothers' milk giving out, the unaffordability of liquid milk, and disease and death.[48] This episode can be partly understood in the context of maternalist ideas and public health, but it was also part of larger debate among social movements about the relationship between state, economy, and civil society. For organized consumers (men and women), the milk question went to the heart of the need to reform Britain's political economy. Between 1917 and 1920, the demand for purer milk from labour and co-operative movements evolved into a campaign for nothing less than price subsidies and the comprehensive reordering of the milk trade, in national, municipal or co-operative hands. The popular activism for milk reform, then, was intimately tied to a discussion of the failure of the competitive market and the rise of trusts, combines, and profiteering. Thinking about the type and instruments of control needed to protect consumer interests forced labour and co-operative groups to rethink their assumptions about the relationship between civil society and the state. To protect the consumer against

44. Wartime and post-war legislation for milk is a good indication of the limited effectiveness of earlier anti-adulteration legislation: the Adulteration Act of 1872 had already set a minimum standard for fats and solids to prevent watering.

45. Milk and Dairies (Consolidation) Act 1915. Grading licences were introduced by the Food Controller in 1918.

46. Wholesale Milk Dealers (Control) Order, 1918; Use of Milk (Licensing) Order, 1918.

47. Milk (Mothers and Children) Order, February 1918: the expenses under this policy were covered half by local rates, half by a grant from the Local Government Board. Maternity and Child Welfare Act, 1918. Under the Milk (Local Distribution) Order, December 1918, the priority scheme for children, mothers, and invalids was further improved. The local food-control committee could order retailers to provide infants under six months and expectant mothers on medical certificate with up to one pint per day.

48. See the 1916 Memorandum by the WCG detailing the dietary suffering of 58 families, in BLPES, Coll. Misc. 92, III/42; and WCG, *Maternity: Letters From Working-Women* (London, 1915). The WCG campaigned for a comprehensive policy of subsidized milk whereas the government's legislation merely granted certain permissive powers to local authorities.

increasingly organized economic forces, now led to a call for creating bridges between state and civil society.[49]

Profiteering played an instrumental part in the debate about the control of food supplies, and milk in particular, for it tied together a critique of high prices with a new emphasis on the inevitable rise of trusts in capitalist society.[50] In autumn 1917, for example, the London Food Vigilance Committee asked its affiliated trades unions, co-operative societies, and the Labour party to consider the new fixed price of milk as a decisive issue for the survival of labour and co-operative movements. 'Milk', it explained, 'is not subject to the manipulations of foreign markets, or the dangers of the submarine, or the difficulties and high freights of sea transport: those three great dopes that have served to keep the people quiet and accept the great increase in prices.' Upon whose evidence did the government decide that a 100 per cent price increase was warranted for 'a home product of such vital importance as that of milk?' Here was

a direct challenge to the consumer [and] in so far as Labour comprises the bulk of the population, it is a direct challenge to Labour . . . [Had] the 'Milk Combine,' which has practically secured control of London's milk supply, whilst the husbands and sons of mothers are suffering and dying in France, nothing to do with the increased price?

If they were not able to stop '**this clear issue of legalised profiteering**', the Committee warned, workers would go hungry during and after the war. They had only two options. Either prices would in future be fixed in public (if necessary enforced by 'direct action'), with a majority representation of consumers and workers on all controlling authorities, or, '[i]f the claims of loyal citizenship are not to be recognised, then the questions of food supplies and prices are of such vital moment to the people that in self-preservation the Labour and Co-operative Movements will have to consider what other means they shall adopt to secure control'.[51]

49. The turn towards a stronger state as an ally of civil society casts doubt on the somewhat monochromatic picture of stronger state but weaker social movements painted by S. Koven and S. Michel, 'Womanly duties', *American Historical Review,* 95 (1990), pp. 1076–108, a view rightly challenged by P. Thane in Koven and Michel (eds), *Mothers,* pp. 343ff. This argument was typical of a notion popular in Europe in the 1970s–1980s of an inherent antagonism between state and social movements. As subsequent work has shown, this is a problematic assumption: see J. Keane, *Civil Society* (Cambridge: Polity, 1999); J. Hall (ed.), *Civil Society* (Cambridge: Polity, 1995); Trentmann (ed.), *Paradoxes of Civil Society.*

50. The centrality of profiteering in popular politics has been oddly ignored or misunderstood; e.g., in his otherwise magisterial *Classes and Cultures* (Oxford: Oxford University Press, 1998), Ross McKibbin presents it as a middle-class issue (pp. 53 f, 553), a view at odds with evidence from labour, co-operative and radical movements. For a comparative iconographic analysis, see J-L. Robert, 'The image of the profiteer', in Winter and Roberts (eds.), *Capital Cities at War,* pp. 104–31.

51. MHL, War Emergency Workers' National Committee [WNC] WNC 17/4; London Food Vigilance Committee, 'Milk. A Challenge to Labour' (n.d. [Oct. 1917?]), emphasis in original.

Throughout the period 1917-1920, there were protests against the scarcity and high price of milk and pressure for controls and anti-profiteering measures. Local Trades and Labour Councils protested against price increases.[52] Over 50 branches of the WCG took action about the price and supply of milk; some tried to secure their own municipal distributing centre.[53] In Bristol and several other areas consumers took to the streets to demonstrate.[54] Women's groups put pressure on the authorities, as in Edinburgh where the Women's Citizen Association demanded that the food commissioner take over the Scottish milk supply.[55] These local demonstrations culminated in a mass rally in Hyde Park in September 1919 that brought together an estimated 100,000–250,000 people calling for food controls, lower prices and a fight against trusts. Milk profiteering was a central topic at the rally.[56]

The milk question easily spilled over into questions about the legitimacy of the political and economic system. At a South-Western conference of food committee members in September 1919, Dr Winter of Torquay likened politicians to

an orange – the more they squeezed them the more they would give away. But, unlike the orange, they did not give away of their own, but gave away the rights of the community by further taxing the community. Milk was an essential food, and it was wicked to put up the price beyond the figure that it *legitimately* should be put to.[57]

Several local food committees did in fact attempt to circumvent the price orders by keeping prices low, as in Chelmsford in October 1918 where retailers in turn went on strike refusing to deliver milk. Here as elsewhere, the presence of co-operative stores as alternative suppliers ultimately helped to lower prices, an experience cheered by co-operators for showing 'the way of progress to a better system of dealing with the necessaries of life'.[58] In other places, consumers tried to set their own legitimate price and sabotage retailers who refused to sell below the maximum price. At Chertsey, housewives organized a 'silent strike', boycotting fresh-milk retailers for a week. At Staines women pursued a 'muddling strike', buying a lot one day and nothing the next, to confuse producers and traders. Both consumer strikes were successful and the price of milk was dropped from 1*s.* to

52. MLH, WNC 19/1.

53. WCG, *36 Annual Report* (May 1918–April 1919), p. 15; the WCG had at this time expanded to 716 branches with 32,908 members.

54. *Co-operative News*, 8 November 1919, p. 12.

55. MLH, CC/MIL/79, 18 March 1919.

56. *Co-operative News*, 27 September 1919, pp. 1, 4; MLH, WNC/ADD/15.

57. MLH, CC/MIL/143, *Exeter Express and Echo*, 9 September 1919.

58. *Co-operative News*, 12 October 1918, p. 670; Chelmsford tried to sell milk at 8*d.* rather than 9*d.* a quart. For other examples, see *Reynolds*, 6 October 1918, p. 3.

10*d*.[59] Only the elimination of private interests from the milk trade, women co-operators emphasized, could ultimately resolve the milk question at a national level.

Here was a type of consumer politics that, unlike the middle-class women's National Consumers' League in America,[60] reached a broad social spectrum and brought together labouring men, women, and housewives in collective actions primarily concerned with the rights of consumers, rather than improved working conditions, as with boycotts of bad employers. The notion that consumers had a right to a fair price, moreover, was not some echo of an eighteenth-century paternalistic 'moral economy', but was now tied directly to demands for permanent controls and for consumer representation in economic decision-making to ensure greater transparency in pricing mechanisms and profits.

Just as the state had resisted popular demands for food controls and rationing in the first half of the war, so it now resisted such pressures for constitutional reform. An advisory Consumers' Council was established in January 1918 partly to contain the growing mobilization of consumer grievances. The Council was composed of the principal labour, co-operative and women's movements, representing the majority of Britons, as well some non-organized consumers and leading socialists. Although the Council was nominally advisory, its weekly meetings became an important source of information and assistance for the Ministry of Food, sometimes leading to the modification of orders. Above all, the Consumers' Council gathered unprecedented information about markets and business organizations at the national and international level. In its three years of existence, it thus became the principal forum for discussions of the place of the consumer in political economy in general as well as about food politics more specifically.

The milk question functioned as a crucial transmitter between information about costs and prices, views of profiteering and trusts, and, ultimately, political pressure for economic controls. Delegates of the Council were appointed members of the travelling commission inquiring into the cost of milk production in December 1918 and gained first-hand knowledge of different methods and costs of production. The Council protested against a further price increase as incorporating excessive profit. The protest reinforced both the association of profiteering with the coalition government and the argument that the consumer would be better served by national controls and the elimination of competitive trade.[61] Profiteering became linked to the apparently unstoppable spread of private monopolies, trusts, and combinations, such as the 'Milk Combine', which, next to the American Meat Trust, became the

59. *Co-operative News*, 15 November 1918, p. 12.
60. See Kish Sklar, 'White Label Campaign'; cf. Cohen, 'The New Deal state', pp. 113 f.
61. See for example Mrs Cottrell in *Co-operative News*, 17 May 1919, p. 12. Cottrell was one of three representatives of the Women's Industrial Organizations on the Consumers' Council and the travelling commission.

most hated capitalist villain. By the end of the war, three years after its foundation, United Dairies Ltd (the London 'milk combine') controlled 80 per cent of the milk supply of greater London.[62] As a Ministry of Food memorandum noted, '[i]f the State stands aside this growth will continue unchecked, placing the consumer at the mercy of a powerful monopoly controlling an essential food.'[63]

By 1918 the growing power of rings and combines had become a core issue of consumer politics. This not only undermined the pre-war belief that Free Trade naturally prevented trusts and cartels, it also prompted a review of the changing nature of capitalism. Thomas Killon aimed his inaugural address as president of the co-operative congress in May 1918 at the 'small rings of vested interests [that] have had a more disastrous effect upon the home of the people than the war itself'.[64] The radical press ran weekly reports on the 'menace' of concerns consolidating their resources to gain control of the economy. Britain was in danger of being Americanized. Women, in particular, were the 'practically helpless victims of this evil system'.[65] Returning to an 'open market' after post-war reconstruction, the *Co-operative News* argued in 1919, was a 'fraudulent' notion, for 'how can there be an "open" market when so many sources of supply are controlled in financial interests by various trusts and rings?'[66] Consumer representatives such as the co-operator Watkins sat on the Committee on Trusts. And C.A. McCurdy himself, the parliamentary secretary to the Ministry of Food chairing the committee, lectured the Consumers' Council on the end of the era of free competition and the unstoppable growth of international trustification of basic commodities, from boots to meat and eggs: the British state could no longer afford a laissez-faire attitude.[67] The majority of the Consumers' Council shared McCurdy's insistence in February 1920 that, in an age of trusts, '[c]ompetition among traders could no longer be regarded as any real protection to the consumer'.[68]

62. United Dairies was founded in 1915 as an amalgamation of three leading wholesalers, and, offering large-scale economies at a time of scarcity, expanded rapidly. After a year and half, it already had a capital of £1m. In 1918 it acquired multiple-shop retail branches and, by 1920, controlled 470 shops; Whetham, 'London milk trade'; Jefferys, *Retail Trading*, pp. 227 ff.

63. BLPES, Coll Misc. 92, XX/10h, 14 May 1919. Ben Davies, a director of United Dairies, after the war contested the idea that prices were kept artificially high or that United Dairies, which organized distribution, was a combine with the power to control prices: *The Food Council: The Consumers' Council Bill and Milk Distribution* (London, n.d. [1930]). The Astor Committee appointed in 1917 had already found United Dairies to have monopolizing tendencies and recommended in turn state control of supplies and distribution.

64. *Co-operative News*, 25 May 1918, p. 370.

65. E.g., *ibid.*, 17 August 1918, p. 550; 18 January 1919, p. 48; and the Midlands conference of trade unionists and co-operators in May 1919, reported in *ibid.*, 10 May 1919, p. 11. *Daily News*, 'Profiteer's Harvest: Necessaries of Life Three Times Their Former Cost', 11 June 1919, p. 1.

66. *Co-operative News*, 22 February 1919, p. 125.

67. MLH, CC/Gen/135, 16 July 1919, 'Address by Mr McCurdy, M.P. on the operations of Trusts'.

68. Speech at Northampton on 24 February 1920, reported in *National Food Journal*, 10 March 1920, p. 29.

The future of food control after the war became inseparable from the general question of how to transform a market political economy. The Consumers' Council's opposition to de-control in 1919 was spelled out by T.W. Allen, a director of the Co-operative Wholesale Society (CWS). The rise of trusts and combines in the preceding four years showed that 'freeing the trade may be the bondage of the consumer'. The interests of consumers, Allen emphasized, therefore lay with a strengthened Ministry of Food, 'the one Department of State that has had the confidence and blessing of the consuming public'. The Council advocated a separate department of state for the protection of consumers against trusts and powers of control 'with regard to supply, with regard to sufficiency of produce, with regard to home production, and to standard of quality, and in respect to proper weights and measures'.[69] State-guaranteed 'good food at proper prices' would merely be the first step in a comprehensive programme of consumer protection that would develop from milk and meat to include other commodities such as clothes as well. Rather than reminiscing about the Free Trade system before the war, the Consumers' Council emphasized the 'complete chaos' that had existed in the public's food supply, when 'the consumer was practically at the mercy of profit-making enterprises'. Instead of decontrol, the Ministry of Food needed to become a permanent department exercising 'full powers over production, distribution, and prices of food . . . includ[ing] . . . [t]he Control of Milk [and the] Supervision of supplies of all necessary food both at home and abroad, with power to secure fairness of distribution and reasonable level of price'.[70]

The discussion about trusts and prices did not stop with the question of regulating domestic markets but, inevitably, forced consumers to rethink assumptions about international trade. We can only note in passing the remarkable convergence of the new consumer politics with ideas and policies developed by 'new inter-nationalist' thinkers and civil servants who were looking towards international bodies of economic co-ordination, as well as with proposals articulated in the Labour party for state import boards and purchasing agencies as means of stabilizing prices and supplies. A concern with entitlements and social justice, in short, prompted plans for commanding distribution. Already in December 1918 the Consumers' Council concluded that war shortages had demonstrated that 'control of prices without control of distribution is of little, if any use'. It called for a monopoly of state purchase of imported foodstuffs in peacetime as a weapon against excessive price fluctuation, scarcity, and foreign trusts and shipping rings.

69. BLPES, Coll. Misc. 92, XIII/8, Proceedings of a meeting of the Consumers' Council at Westminster, 9 April 1919, 6.

70. MLH, CC/PP/52, Report Adopted by the Consumers' Council on the Future of the Food Ministry, 14 May 1919, p. 3.

The experience of inter-allied controls added an important international instrument of regulation.[71] The WCG, like other co-operative and labour groups, urged the additional development of inter-allied controls into an international economic organization whose task would be to co-ordinate the equitable distribution of scarce and key raw materials and to 'maintain equality of supply and a reasonable basis of cost'.[72] The lessons of the domestic supply of an essential commodity (such as milk) were now extended to the international sphere and essential resources (such as oil): trade regulation was needed to prevent international tension and economic nationalism.

Consumers Divided

If the war gave rise to a new vision of political economy among organized consumers, the 1920s proved the difficulties of translating this vision into reality. Pressure for 'decontrol' from business groups and from the Conservative and Liberal parties was overwhelming, and the general fall of prices from the end of 1920 helped to lessen (though not kill) the agitation against profiteers. It would be simplistic, however, to explain the relative failure of new consumer policies solely in external terms or by reference to some generic disadvantage of consumers in overcoming the costs of collective action. Part of the explanation lies with a division within consumer politics that manifested itself in the winter of 1919/20 and preceded the resignation of the Consumers' Council in December 1920. This division reflected two competing strategies for protecting consumers against trusts, scarcity, and high prices, and was ultimately premised on two different conceptions of the relationship between civil society, state, and economy.

The big blow to the Consumers' Council and its united call for further controls came in December 1919, when the CWS, one of its constituents, decided in favour of decontrol. Through its 1,470 distributive societies, the CWS represented one third of Britain's population; in 1918 its sales amounted to £249 million. Like many of its commercial rivals, the CWS trading committees saw state controls as disadvantaging established traders. It became convinced 'that unfettered operations and supplies would result in stabilising the market, and that the CWS could, under decontrol, manufacture and make purchases on terms more favourable to the consumer than is the case under the existing system of control'.[73] But what about trusts, scarcities, and the much-hated profiteer? The majority on the Consumers'

71. BLPES, Coll. Misc. 92, XIII/3, Consumers' Council Sub-Committee on controls in peace time (n.d. [December 1918?]); MLH, CC/CP/94, 'Food Supplies and International Control', 28 May 1919, Consumers' Council Sub-Committee report.
72. WCG, *36 Annual Report*, p. 18.
73. *Co-operative News*, 27 December 1919, p. 5.

Council, including labour and women's organizations, looked to national and municipal controls as the only way to protect the consumer from these enemies. Even Allen, a wholesaler, told the co-operative congress in 1919 that the co-operative movement was not strong enough to resist food trusts: consumers had to choose between state control or trust control.[74] It was this line of reasoning that the majority in the CWS came to reject.

Whereas most members on the Council turned to political controls as a stepping-stone to economic co-ordination, price stabilization and consumer power, the CWS saw them as a barrier. A heated exchange at a Consumers' Council conference in February 1920 laid bare an unbridgeable gulf. Marion Phillips, the Labour women's representative, argued that in an age of trusts and scarcities, the abolition of the Ministry of Food would mean that 'we go back not to the pre-war chaos with regard to food supplies, but to chaos infinitely worse'. After further speeches in favour of controls, the co-operator Gallacher rose in protest. Decontrol, he insisted, would assist, not hurt the consumer of milk. Gallacher strongly disputed Phillips's view of pre-war political economy: 'We think that food was cheaply and well handled before the war.' As socialization was not a practical proposition with a capitalist Government in power, the interest of the consumer lay with setting the CWS free. The Parliamentary Committee of the Co-operative Congress and the English and Scottish CWS recorded a minority vote against the resolution to establish the Ministry of Food as a permanent department.[75]

For the CWS, the co-operative movement remained the only viable opponent of trusts. Social agencies, not the state, would transform political economy and guarantee the rights and interests of consumers as citizens. From the vantage point of the early twenty-first century, after the decline of the co-operative movement and the globalization of capital, this vision might look naïve, but at the time there were good reasons one branch of organized consumers found it persuasive. For one, trusts could be interpreted as a sign of a historical trend towards concentration which could benefit co-operatives, enabling them to absorb small retailers.[76] Co-operative societies had increased their share of retail sales between 1900 and 1920

74. *Co-operative News*, 14 June 1919, p. 6. For the split in the co-operative movement, see the debate in the *Co-operative News*, 29 November 1919, pp. 2, 4, 8, and 20 December 1919, pp. 2 f., 6.

75. MLH, CC/CP.126, 19 February 1920, Report of proceedings, pp. 7, 10. The conference brought together representatives of its constituent organizations. The majority for the resolution (8 bodies to 4) included the Co-operative Union as well as the Labour Party, WNC, and the Joint Committee of Industrial Women's Organizations. The WCG abstained.

76. For an early instance of the notion that the trust movement was not all bad because it showed small traders that they were doomed anyhow, thus preparing the expansion of co-operatives, see Mrs M. O'Brien Harris, *Co-operators and the Trust Movement* (Manchester, 1903). P. Gurney has rightly stressed that many co-operators before the war genuinely believed they were building a co-operative commonwealth in the midst of their society, 'Labour's great arch', in Furlough and Strikwerda (eds), *Consumers Against Capitalism?*, pp.151 ff.

from 7 per cent to 9 per cent, while department stores and multiple shops had respectively grown from 2 per cent to 4 per cent and 5 per cent to 10 per cent.[77] Any controls that constrained the co-operatives' expansion would disadvantage them in the advancing battle with commercial giants. In addition, the centrality of basic foodstuffs in consumer politics still highlighted those commodities where the co-operative movement was strongest and where working-class spending was highest. Thus, the WCG looked upon the wartime experience of capitalist combines as being as much a lesson as a threat: it 'taught us very clearly what this capitalist consolidation means to the woman in the home . . . touch[ing] her every week as she lays out the family income', and provided the movement with a golden opportunity to incorporate angry consumers and make a big leap forward towards the co-operative commonwealth.[78]

Milk served as the showcase for co-operative economics and, for many organized consumers, offered practical proof that the movement could reform political economy without state assistance. The success of co-operatives in distributing milk and holding down prices during the war, as well as their campaign for maternity care and cleaner and more abundant milk, laid the foundations for the co-operative take-over of much of the milk trade in the inter-war years. Through the co-operatives, organized consumers played an important role in introducing health standards in production and distribution, long before the state ruled in favour of compulsory pasteurization. Co-operators threw themselves into rationalizing the milk trade, introducing some of the first registered pasteurization facilities and sterilized bottling plants, and promoting the grading of milk and the testing of herds. Like United Dairies, the co-operatives made the best of the milk grading and testing orders of 1922–23 which favoured large-scale concerns. They gave incentives to farmers to produce cleaner milk, established central depots and, already by 1920, had purchased 47,000 acres of pasturage. It was a co-operative society which introduced white overalls and peaked caps as symbols of its clean milk and awarded prizes for the best-kept milkcarts and ponies.

The co-operative milk trade expanded by leaps and bounds in the inter-war years. By 1925, some 200 co-operative societies supplied milk. The biggest was in London with 65,000 gallons a week, rising to 460,000 gallons per week by the late 1930s.[79] In Leicester the co-operative controlled 40 per cent of the trade, in

---

77. Small retailers' share declined by 8 per cent: Jefferys, *Retail Trading in Britain*, p. 73.

78. WCG, *Co-operation's Great Opportunity*, issued by the central committee for sectional conferences in spring 1919, p. 2.

79. London Co-operative Society, *20 Years Later* (1940), pp. 63 ff. By 1953, co-operative sales in milk amounted to £88 million or 12 per cent of its total business: *Democracy in Action* (Co-operative Study Guide, n.d. [1953]), p. 13.

Derby even 60 per cent.[80] One the eve of the Second World War, the co-operatives commanded over a quarter of the national milk market.[81] It is against this background that the logic of a type of consumer politics looking towards social agencies (not the state) must be understood. For the WCG, the co-operative milk campaign was a direct path to greater consumer power, eliminating the middleman and obliging farmers to improve their methods: 'All who desire to remove this essential foodstuff from the control of profiteers should concentrate their efforts on increasing its sale by co-operative societies. This is by far the surest way of securing its control by the community.'[82]

Answering the milk question, then, meant redefining the place of the co-operatives in the envisaged new social order. To put milk under national or municipal control, women co-operators agreed with the CWS, was a risky business. As Honora Enfield argued in 1920, public controls did not guarantee the material or physiological interests of consumers. It was dangerous to trust public health committees to inspect their own milk. Reactionary groups might gain control of local councils and abandon interest in good quality and low prices – a suspicion borne out a few years later in Sheffield, where a change in local government led to an overhaul of the municipal milk supply. Even well intentioned municipalities lacked the network of the CWS necessary for large-scale production and equitable distribution at the national level. Nationalization was rejected because it would make the central state even bigger and 'absolutely irresistible', with disastrous consequences for international as well as domestic peace.[83] To nationalize foodstuffs in a capitalist world would force Britain to trade with competitive businesses, and thus fuel the competitive causes of war. Only international trade between co-operative producers and consumers could guarantee peace and stable, fair prices for all – from this perspective, free trade policies remained conducive to co-operative internationalism.[84] British co-operators looked with a great deal of hope to the expansion of the international co-operative alliance and entered into a series of trade and purchasing agreements with co-operatives in the Dominions and Russia after the war. Next to the more regulatory, interventionist consumer politics born during the First World War, then, many co-operators

---

80. Women's Co-operative Guild, *The Milk We Want* (London, 1925), pp. 4–9.

81. The co-operative share of total sales was 26 per cent compared to 22 per cent of multiple shops, and 52 per cent to other retailers: Jefferys, *Retail Trading*, p. 238.

82. Women's Co-operative Guild, *The Milk We Want*, p. 10.

83. H. Enfield, *The Place of Co-operation in the New Social Order* (London, 1920), pp. 9 f.

84. [M. Llewellyn Davies and L. Harris], *After the War: the Work of Co-operation* (London, 1916), pp. 9 f.; A.H. Enfield, *International Co-operative Trade* (London, n.d. [1920]). Of course, this view of Free Trade must be distinguished from the more dynamic eighteenth- and nineteenth-century notion that the commercial act of exchange itself created a network of wealth, welfare, and international solidarity.

continued to associate pluralism, freedom, and economic reform with civil society in separation from the state.[85]

Consumers in Social Democracy

The inter-war period saw the gradual narrowing of these two visions in radical politics and their ultimate fusion in a social-democratic consumer politics. The social-democratic configuration of consumption and citizenship deserves attention not only for its relevance to British Labour politics but also because it suggests a more contingent and richer picture of consumer politics in the West than a simple divide between the New Deal (Fordist mass production, organized labour, big business) and neo-mercantilist regimes on the European continent (cartelized distribution, corporatism, crafts).[86] Significantly, social-democratic consumer politics evolved around basic foodstuffs, rather than around mass-manufactured consumer durables such as cars or washing machines and the productivist politics and advertising and retailing revolution associated with them. The politics of milk illustrates how organized consumers did not merely respond to changes initiated by producers or retailers, but themselves encouraged changes in production (sterilization, bottling stations) and distribution (centralized depots). And, their demand for a more equitable and stable distribution of healthy foodstuffs also left its imprint on the political economy of the British welfare state after the Second World War. Social movements on the left now associated the interests of the citizen consumer with price controls, subsidies, and trade regulation, rather than free trade, and supported a more self-sufficient agricultural policy and national economic planning. Finally, in the evolution of social-democratic consumer politics, a concern with public health and distributional justice became tied to a new internationalist food programme that laid the ideological foundations for subsequent campaigns against world hunger.

The view that consumer interests required trade regulation, already articulated by the majority of the Consumers' Council in 1918–20, gained a growing number

85. In 'any kind of Society, capitalist or socialist', Enfield tellingly argued, 'the individuals comprising it have many different sides. They are citizens in relation to other individuals; producers in relation to their work; consumers in relation to their food, clothes, and other possessions . . . The same individual may desire one thing as a citizen, another as a consumer, another as a producer. If we give all power and authority over all sides of life to a single organisation like the State, these different interests get little opportunity of expression'. At times of crisis, the interests of individuals might need sacrificing to the strongest interest', Enfield continued, but in general it was this dualism that would 'secure the largest and freest life for each individual and so the best possibility of progress for the community'. *Place of Co-operation*, p. 11.

86. See the important discussion in V. de Grazia, 'Changing consumption regimes in Europe', in Strasser *et al* (eds), *Getting and Spending*, ch. 3. Cf. M. Jacob, Chapter Eleven.

of Liberal and Labour supporters in the following decade. In the Royal Commission on Food Prices in 1925, for example, Chiozza Money, a prominent Free Trader before the war, proposed combining an imperial purchasing scheme with domestic controls: the loaf would partly come from expensive domestic wheat and partly from cheaper foreign and imperial wheat.[87] Cheapness could be compromised for the sake of stable prices and secure supplies, a shift in thinking that prompted many in Labour to design new regulatory mechanisms, from purchasing agreements and import boards to the international pooling of resources.[88] Economic cycles joined trusts and profiteers as evidence of the dangers of unregulated trade. In a series of publications on the consumer point of view in 1929, for example, Christopher Addison, a Liberal turned Labour minister, argued that consumers and producers alike suffered from economic cycles. British consumers, he stressed, continued to pay £500–700 million a year more for their food because of profiteers. Only the state had the power to 'prevent the housewife being exploited in Bread prices' and basic foods by standardizing supplies, stabilizing prices, and marketing commodities effectively.[89] Developments in political thought reinforced the view that consumer interests were no longer the responsibility of social movements alone. Consumers, Harold Laski argued in 1928, had done little to curb the excessive individualism of commercial culture that threatened the survival of Western Civilization. What improvements there had been, as in the case of wartime food controls, were the consequences of state action. Consumer choices could no longer be left to the individual. '[S]ince the quality of his citizenship largely depends upon what there is for him to consume, ignorance of his wants means, in a high degree, the absence of a civic context to this aspect of his life.' It was upon the state to protect consumers and make their 'demand articulate and organised'.[90]

The co-operative movement came to accept in the 1930s and 1940s that consumer interests were best protected in collaboration with the state. It remained suspicious about policies that threatened the movement's autonomy, but there was growing pragmatism about the balance between forms of consumption best handled by social agencies and those justifying municipal or central state controls. By 1946, WCG speakers acknowledged that in the preceding hundred years the state had superseded the co-operatives as the main defender of the consumer's interests in food. Instead of fighting state controls it urged a division of labour between those spheres such as entertainment and fashion – spheres that co-operatives had traditionally ignored or condemned – where 'voluntary action and freedom of

---

87. *Why Your Food Costs More*, p. 65.

88. Trentmann, 'Erosion of free trade', ch. 4.

89. C. Addison, *The Nation and Its Food* (1929), included in P. Redfern (ed.), *Self and Society: Second Twelve Essays, Social and Economic Problems from the hitherto neglected point of view of the consumer* (London, 1930).

90. H.J. Laski, *The Recovery of Citizenship* (1928), included in Redfern (ed.), *Self and Society: First Twelve Essays* (London, 1930), essay no. 4, quote at pp. 7, 10.

choice are essential for the fullest satisfaction of consumers' needs' – and those where 'the commodity is of a standard character, or the service in universal and uniform demand' and national control consequently more advantageous.[91] In contrast to the split after the First World War, the movement fully supported controls, rationing and nationalisation after the Second.

This shift was part of a broader turn in political and economic thinking that made the control of trade and consumer demand, and the successful planning of production and investment mutually dependent. Already during the world depression (1929–32), co-operative campaigns to 'Buy British' and boost domestic agricultural production recognized that the interests of consumers rested not with cheapness and free imports but with economic stabilization and increased employment. The National Government's introduction of tariffs and marketing boards were opposed less as a violation of freedom of trade than as inefficient and socially unjust instruments of regulation. To the WCG in the 1930s, the problem with marketing boards was that milk surplus was pooled and sold at a subsidized price to manufacturers, rather than to poor consumers. Women co-operators supported marketing, but on a community basis with greater consumer representation.[92]

Support for trade controls was bolstered by public campaigns on the standard of living by Labour women and the WCG in the mid-1930s. The WCG now explicitly linked 'Pure Food and Price Control' and called on the state 'to legislate for a system of price control which will safeguard the consumer so that those who have little to spend on food may obtain the utmost possible value'.[93] The WCG alone collected 700,000 signatures from housewives in protest against high prices in their 'Cost of Living Campaign' in 1938.[94] The campaign challenged the official yardstick of the cost of living as blind to changing nutritional needs. Growing evidence of malnutrition reinforced a critique of the inequities of the application of economic criteria (price, purchasing power) to questions of public health and welfare (nutrition). Labour women found in 1936 that 37 per cent of households did not buy any fresh milk. John Boyd Orr's much cited investigation revealed that half the nation suffered from malnutrition, in spite of improved purchasing power.[95] As Labour women's *Report on Socialism and the Standard of Living*

91. WCG, 'Consumer Co-operation in the Socialist State', Notes for District Speakers (1946), p. 4.

92. WCG, *53rd Annual Report* (1935–6), p. 25; for the responsibility of the state to provide free milk, see *54 Annual Report* (1936–7), p. 11.

93. WCG, *55th Annual Report* (1937–8), p. 21.

94. Between 1933 and 1938 the price of a quart of milk increased from 5¾*d*. to 6¾*d*., the price of a 4lb loaf of bread from 7½*d*. to 9½*d*.

95. This number was based on the assumption that an expenditure of at least 10*s*. was necessary to ensure a satisfactory diet for a person each week; only half the population was able to spend that much and, according to Orr, 4½ million people could spend no more than 4*s*. See the use of his 1936 study by Labour women in *Report of the 19th National Conference of Labour Women* (1938), pp. 82 f.

stressed in 1938, when the housewife 'finds it impossible . . . to buy enough of all the high-grade foods essential of good nutrition, she is not impressed on being told that according to the official index figures she can buy more with £1 than she could buy in 1930 and that she has more £'s to spend than she had in 1930'. What housewives wanted were policies that ensured good nutrition at stable prices over time. This required state control of supplies and marketing, import boards and long-term purchasing agreements but at the same time had to be a policy of 'fair living for producers' to prevent sudden falls in prices 'where it does not pay [the farmer] to handle the crop and it is allowed to rot, while on the other hand the housewife does not benefit by cheap retail prices'.[96]

The dissociation of consumer interests from free trade and cheapness and its new association with trade regulation and fair prices became the cornerstone of Labour's 'fair shares' policy after the Second World War. Clearly, rationing and food subsidies were not supported by all consumers alike. Working-class house-wives tended to be more sceptical than men and middle-class consumers of the virtues of controls, and carried the main burdens of rationing, queuing, and high prices in post-war Britain. Women were evenly divided about bread rationing in 1948, for example, and many sympathized with the middle-class Housewives' League in its campaign to replace controls with greater 'choice'.[97] It is less clear how to weigh and interpret such divided responses by consumers from a comp-arative, long-term perspective. Perhaps it is not so surprising that a growing number of consumers reported their discontent with rationing after a total war. What is more striking is the relatively high level of continuing popular support for food control in Britain in the late 1940s and the absence of any serious challenge to the regime on the scale of European protests after the First World War, especially in Germany,[98] but also when compared to consumer pressure in Britain discussed earlier.

---

96. *Ibid.*, p. 79.

97. See now I. Zweiniger-Bargielowska, *Austerity in Britain* (Oxford: Oxford University Press, 2000); I am grateful to the author for letting me see the manuscript prior to publication. Her analysis of opinion polls, for example, reveals that following the introduction of bread rationing, one-third supported the policy while 41 per cent opposed it, with women being evenly divided and unskilled workers favouring it (p. 84). While she shows that support for rationing diminished in the late 1940s and early 1950s, it is nonetheless remarkable that as late as March 1953, a Gallup poll found 43 per cent opposed to policies bringing rationing to an end and restoring the price mechanism, with 47 per cent in favour (p. 87). See also her 'Rationing, austerity and the Conservative Party recovery after 1945', *Historical Journal*, 37 (1994), pp. 173–97; 'Bread rationing in Britain, July 1946–July 1948', *Twentieth Century British History*, 4 (1993), pp. 57–85; 'Explaining the gender gap: the Conservative Party and the women's vote, 1945–64', in Francis and Zweiniger-Bargielowska (eds), *The Conservatives and British Society, 1880–1990*. See also J. Hinton, 'Militant housewives: the British Housewives' League and the Attlee government,' *History Workshop*, 38 (1994), pp. 129–56.

98. M.H. Geyer, 'Teuerungsprotest, Konsumentenpolitik und soziale Gerechtigkeit während der Inflation', *Archiv für Sozialgeschichte*, 30 (1990), pp. 181–215; Davis, 'Food scarcity'.

It therefore deserves special emphasis that the main organizations of working-class consumers had come fully around to a programme of economic planning, trade regulation, and food control by the middle of the century.[99] Even if world food prices fell, the Co-operative party stressed in 1948, food subsidies needed to stay, not only as part of a 'national nutritional policy' but because they were an instrument 'to stabilise both production and consumption and [could] be used to stimulate either or both according to the requirements of national planning'.[100] Co-operative discussion groups were taught that

[t]he amount which we shall have to spend as consumers will depend on whether there is a policy of full employment and expanding income. The Government which we as citizens and consumers can control, can, by a spending policy, by redistributive taxation . . . ensure full employment . . . Our first interest as consumers is to see that some such policy is carried out.[101]

In the *Standard of Life* in 1951, the Co-operative Party stressed that it was not prepared to 'throw away full employment and the welfare state merely to achieve cheapness'.[102] Inevitably, this left its mark on the way consumers and their interests were represented in relation to the state and rest of economy. The Co-operative party explained Labour's policy simply as an application of 'good housekeeping' practised by 'the good housewife [who] shares out the food fairly', looks after the health of her children and invests in their future, keeps her house clean and cultivates her garden, all without forgetting about the need to balance her payments.[103] The circumspect housekeeper had replaced the image of the female shopper so dominant in Edwardian representations of the consumer comparing prices in the windows of Free Trade and Tariff Reform shops. Consumer interests had become a part of national economic management.

From a long-term perspective, the late 1940s and early 1950s marked the popular crest of social-democratic consumer politics. The WCG urged the Attlee government 'not to capitulate to the agitation to reduce or abolish food subsidies or remove price controls', indeed, to extend controls to wholesale prices.[104] The co-operative movement as a whole praised Labour for combining policies of subsidized low

99. In fact, Labour's share of the vote increased during the rationing period, from 47.8 per cent in 1945 to 48.8 per cent in 1951.

100. *Report of the National Committee of the Co-operative Party to the Annual Conference*, April 1948, p. 10. See also the earlier *Road to Prosperity* (1944).

101. G.D.N. Worswick, *The Consumer – His Place in Society*, Co-operative Discussion Group Outlines, no. 2 (January 1946), p. 11; these outlines were distributed through the education committee of the London Co-operative Society.

102. *The Standard of Life* (1951).

103. E. Oram, *Labour's Good Housekeeping* (London, 1950).

104. WCG, *66th Annual Report* (1948–9), p. 34.

and stable prices for consumers with those of nationalization and agricultural stabilization to achieve greater self-sufficiency.[105] As was pointed out again and again in the 1951 election, Labour's increase in food subsidies to £465 million a year made a contribution of 3*s*. 6*d*. to every citizen's weekly rations. The 1946 policy of free milk for schoolchildren, provisions to mothers at reduced prices, and 300,000 free meals for children were popular planks in the campaign for food and price controls. In fact, even the milk scarcity in 1948 was turned into an evidence of social democratic achievement, because it partly resulted from increased demand and consumption of milk; in 1946–7, 183 million gallons of milk were sold at reduced prices and 45 millions for free, compared to the sale of a mere 28 million gallons on the eve of the Second World War.[106] Milk policy symbolized the social-democratic meaning of consumer freedom in contrast to an out-dated individualist liberalism favoured by Conservatives and benefiting rich women who desired mink coats and free fuel to sail to Monte Carlo.[107]

When the Conservative government rolled back food subsidies and price controls, the WCG and Labour women began a public agitation for their rein-stitution. Their 'Cost of Living Campaign' in 1953–5 attacked Butler's budget cuts as a war on the housewives in which class-biased 'rationing by the purse' replaced the democratic food subsidies which had 'protected the consumer from the effects of the sacred laws of supply and demand'.[108] Pointing to the increase in the price of milk (by 3*d*. a quart) and butter and meat in the first four years under Conservative rule (1951–5), the Labour party campaigned in 1955 with images of children facing a terrifying future and a direct appeal to 'mum': 'what sort of crazy freedom is it where the shops are well-stocked but the larders are empty because people can't afford to buy?' Only Labour could 'protect the people from the viciousness of uncontrolled rising prices'.[109] Housewives and mothers needed protection against monopolists, middlemen, and gamblers. Labour promised a 'return to a system of guaranteed prices and markets and ensure real consumer choice'.[110]

---

105. The Co-operative Party continued to support the principles of the 1947 agriculture policy into the 1970s: see *Agriculture, Food and the Consumer* (1970). By that time, the United Kingdom produced over half of its total food requirements, or two-thirds of the food that could be grown in temperate climates.

106. H. Campbell, *Farmgate to Consumer* (1948), a Co-operative Party pamphlet. The Milk Act of 1934 provided £1m and contributed to an increase in the consumption of milk in schools, although half of the school population continued to receive no milk under the scheme.

107. E.g., *The Thinking Voter*, 1951 election special.

108. See *ibid.*, 72nd and 73rd *Annual Reports* (1954–6); Report of the National Committee of the Co-operative Party, 1953 and 1954. Labour women insisted in 1954 that the next election would be fought and won on the issue of high food prices and pressed for the immediate introduction of Cripps' policies of pegging prices, *Report of the 31st National Conference of Labour Women* (1954), pp. 31 f.

109. *Forward to Victory!* (1955).

110. *What Will the Harvest Be?* (1956).

Understanding the transvaluation of consumer politics would be incomplete without emphasizing the interplay between domestic and international consumer politics, and in particular the role played by discussions of the international food problem in the 1940s. Consumers' changing understanding of domestic political economy spilled over into their view of international relations and vice versa. It was the dialogue between discussions of domestic nutrition and global famine on the one hand, and between distributional justice and trade regulation on the other, that transformed the historical memory of the 'hungry 1840s' of Edwardian consumer politics into a discourse of global hunger which is still with us today.

Just as the campaign for pure, abundant milk during and after the First World War had highlighted the growing power of trusts, so it provided popular consumer politics with a new sense of awareness about the problematic nature of distribution (rather than just supply) in an unregulated food trade. Consumers began to talk about 'waste' and protest against the flow of milk into chocolate or cheese, or against farmers feeding it to pigs or even throwing it away rather than lowering the price to consumers[111] – a discussion that received added fuel from the destruction of foodstuffs during the world depression of 1929–32 and Conservative marketing boards in the 1930s. Significantly, the social-democratic historical memory that helped put Labour into power in 1945 was not only that of the unemployed Jarrow Marchers but also of the underfed consumer who suffered at the hands of wasteful producers and profiteers. *So Ill Remembered*, a co-operative pamphlet of 1947, for example, followed an account of the National Farmers' Union's advice in 1922 to keep milk off the market with the story of the sudden death of a 14-month-old child from malnutrition. Celebrating the superiority of planning over unregulated trade, it recalled how the 1920s (a period known to economic historians for falling prices and increased consumption) had meant 'Starvation in the midst of plenty'.[112]

Attacks on an unregulated food trade for allowing mass undernourishment while food was being 'ploughed back into the land or thrown into the sea'[113] were a stepping stone to the critique of global capitalism where millions starved in one country while producers burned wheat and maize in another. Fair prices to consumers and a fair return for producers were as interdependent globally as domestically. After the Second World War, the WCG campaigned for international measures to promote stable prices to prevent gluts and depressions, as well as joint policies of agricultural and industrial development.[114] More recently,

---

111. E.g., the protest by the Midland section of the WCG to the local food office cit. in *Co-operative News*, 13 December 1919, p. 13. See also the debate in the House of Commons on 10 November 1919.

112. *So Ill Remembered* (1947), p. 9: the pamphlet also cited Boyd Orr's studies of the 1930s.

113. WCG, 1936, pp. 28 f.

114. WCG, *Feeding the World*.

international food policies have been criticized by Amartya Sen and others for approaching famines in terms of 'food availability decline' rather than as crises in distribution and entitlement.[115] To be sure, consumer groups were not entirely free from this fallacy. After the war, the WCG argued that the first task of 'Feeding the World' was to increase food supply not only to satisfy hunger but to raise the global standard of living.[116] At the same time, the domestic discussion of waste, profiteering, and cycles provided the background knowledge for new internationalist arguments that identified unregulated distribution as responsible for situations where supplies were plentiful but failed to reach hungry consumers. After the Second World War, the domestic debate about the rights of consumers as citizens expanded into a movement for global human rights and family rights of mothers. British consumer groups, like the WCG, called for a world food council, pooling of global resources, and international measures for raising purchasing power and public health. The dissociation of organized consumers from Free Trade was complete. Whereas Free Trade had been premised on a non-interventionist, unilateral approach in which unregulated trade best promoted the pacific and material interests of consumers across societies, the social-democratic vision of consumption and citizenship ultimately also applied its domestic notions of entitlement and distributional justice to the global level, demanding international economic regulation and co-ordination.

British Consumer Politics in Comparative Perspective

Placed in comparative perspective, the reconfiguration of British consumer politics reveals several interesting features. Ironically, organized consumer politics in Britain from the late nineteenth to the mid-twentieth centuries was stronger than elsewhere but failed to provide consumers with the protection that other societies produced. It is therefore imperative to distinguish further between consumer *politics* and consumer *policies*. Having well-developed consumer movements does not automatically translate into an effective legal and institutional infrastructure

---

115. A. Sen, *Poverty and Famines* (Oxford: Clarendon, 1981); A. Sen and J. Drèze, *Hunger and Public Action* (Oxford: Clarendon, 1989).

116. 'To-day in this country no one need be hungry. Our food may be dull, but it is adequate . . . There are many countries in the world where food is far from sufficient to satisfy hunger, and if the peace of the world is to be preserved, the first need is for every nation to have enough food, and the second is to so increase food supplies that we and all other people shall have not merely enough to satisfy hunger or to keep us in health, but plenty so that the standard of life may be raised for the whole world.' WCG, *Feeding the World*, notes for speakers 1948. For the growing interest in the world food problem, see also the extensive discussion of human rights, the food agriculture organization, and mutual aid, e.g. notes for speakers 1949-51, 1955, and the Co-operative Party's *World Trade in Raw Materials* (1955).

protecting consumer choice and standards. The consumer politics of Free Trade secured slightly cheaper imports but the trade-off was a weak state infrastructure for more direct forms of consumer protection. Anti-adulteration legislation was more permissive and less punitive in Britain than in France or Germany. And the case of milk reform is a good example how improved patterns of consumption can be the result of a variety of state, societal, and economic initiatives. In spite of particularly organized consumer pressure, grading and pasteurization arrived relatively late in Britain, compared either to the USA, where a combination of health reformers and municipal activists had been successful already before the First World War, or to the Ruhr area in Germany, where the main pressure for improvements in hygiene and production came from within the milk trade, assisted by an increasingly extensive and punitive set of state controls.[117]

The irony of a uniquely strong organized consumer movement but lagging consumer protection in Britain was a consequence of the ways in which organized consumers understood themselves in relation to state and economy. In the early twentieth century, suspicion of state intervention reflected an optimistic view of the role of consumers in the creation of a vibrant and increasingly autonomous civil society which would reform the abuses of the economic system. The popular defence of Free Trade suggests that at certain times consumer politics could be hegemonic and supportive of modern capitalist policies and that we should be wary of equating them with 'traditional' norms or protest movements.[118]

It is tempting to invoke different 'national' types of consumer politics, but as this chapter has shown, consumer politics can go through metamorphoses in which consumers change their identity, understanding of consumption in relation to state and economy, and political objectives. The shift from the politics of the cheap loaf to that of clean milk did not incorporate consumers into a corporatist system of policy-making, as in Germany after the Second World War.[119] Nonetheless, the new vision of consumption and citizenship emerging in Britain in the decades after the First World War meant that consumers became more open to accept state regulation and co-operation with producers. Far from being natural or given, 'consumption' changed its meaning in relation to other social, economic, and political functions. From a comparative perspective, British consumer politics became less unique and began to show some similarities with very different cultures. In Japan, the rise of consumer politics in the middle of the twentieth

---

117. Controls in Germany began as early as the 1870s but became more extensive and efficient with the imperial order of 13 July 1923. Moreover, more and more members of the dairy industry in the Rhineland and Westfalia began to join their own controlling associations in the 1920s: see H. Reif and R. Pomp, 'Milchproduktion und Milchvermarktung im Ruhrgebiet, 1870–1930', *Jahrbuch für Wirtschaftsgeschichte*, 1 (1996), pp. 77–107. See also Vial, 'Milk supply'.

118. Thompson, 'Moral economy', pp. 76–136.

119. See Trumbull in Chapter Thirteen.

century was marked by a multi-layered notion of identities where consumption was balanced by concerns with employment, life-style, and health. Japanese housewives envisioned themselves primarily as *seikatsusha* (those in charge of life-style) rather than as 'consumers'. The term *shōhi* (consumption) was suspect because it connoted self-seeking individualism and waste.[120] In the social-democratic consumer politics of Britain, too, organized consumers moved away from a more adversarial understanding of social groups, where consumers represented the people and national interest vis-à-vis the sectional interests of producers, towards a more organic vision, in which consumption became part of a larger balance of activities, and where immediate consumer demands might have to be subordinated to other collective interests, such as health, employment or production.

The transition from the politics of bread to the politics of milk, then, did not merely amount to a switch of commodities but to a very different meaning and place of consumption in the political system. Arguably, it was the first stage in the fragmentation of consumer politics. Whereas consumer politics in the first half of the twentieth century were 'thick' and concentrated around very particular commodities (necessaries), they became increasingly 'thin' and diluted thereafter, so much so that 'consumption' and 'consumer choice' is applied to everything, from health and education to transport and media. Consumer politics has fragmented into a plethora of groups, ideas, and causes, ranging from the social-democratic movements charted here to neo-liberal campaigners of 'choice', from consumer safety advocates to the new social movements of the 1960s and 1970s and believers in 'quasi-markets'. Unlike Free Trade earlier, the consumer politics of milk and public health never established a general hegemony of discourse or policies. Policies for more clean milk never translated into a long-term institutional reconfiguration of the British state shaping consumer legislation in the age of affluence. From the perspective of policy, an institutional vacuum remained which was readily invaded by producers in the late 1950s.[121] From a perspective of political culture, however, the shift from bread to milk helped create the values and predispositions of new consumer movements that, as the recent campaigns against world hunger and food engineering show, continue to be important today.

---

120. P. Maclachlan, 'The Struggle for an Independent Consumer Society: Consumer Activism and the State's Response in Postwar Japan', paper presented to the conference on 'Global Perspectives on Civil Society in Japan', Harvard University and the East-West Center, Honolulu, 12–16 January 2000; S.K. Vogel, 'When interests are not preferences: the cautionary tale of Japanese consumers', *Comparative Politics*, Jan. 1999, pp. 187–207; S. Garon, 'Luxury is the enemy: mobilizing savings and popularizing thrift in wartime Japan; *Journal of Japanese Studies*, 26 (2000), pp. 41–78.

121. As in the Molony committee: see Hilton in Chapter Twelve.

Acknowledgements

Different versions of this chapter were presented at the 'Material Politics' conference (Cambridge), a Faculty Workshop of the Davis Center (Princeton), and the modern British History Seminar at the Institute of Historical Research (London): many thanks to conveners, audiences and colleagues for stimulating discussions. For further comments I should like to thank Belinda Davis, Victoria de Grazia, Heinz-Gerhard Haupt, Sue Marchand, Elizabeth Ruddick, James Vernon, and Ina Zweiniger-Bargielowska. I also gratefully acknowledge support from the Princeton University Committee on Research and from the British Academy which awarded me a visiting professorship. The chapter is dedicated to my mother, for having had the good fortune of growing up the daughter of a miller and farmer with enough milk and bread in an age of scarcity and for having had the good sense of retaining a healthy, critical attitude as an urban consumer in better times.

8

Enticement and Deprivation: The Regulation of Consumption in Pre-War Nazi Germany

Hartmut Berghoff

Consumption in Nazi Germany has been an enigma to many observers. When in 1946-48 American economists analysed Hitler's preparations for war, they were stunned by the relatively limited degree of economic mobilization on the eve of the Second World War. One of the reasons given by the research team was 'the unwillingness of the Germans to surrender a part of their prosperity level of consumption' and their 'government's disinclination to ask for civilian sacrifices'. Germany wanted to have 'both more "butter" and more "guns" at the same time. '. . . a sizeable increase in armament expenditure could have been achieved only at the expense of some decline in civilian consumption. It would have required at least a sharp curtailment of . . . civilian goods production. It appears that the German government was unwilling to ask for such sacrifices.' [1]

Since then many historians have either ignored this study or put forward very different views. They often described Nazi Germany as a state run by fanatics plundering the population in the interest of rearmament. The glittering facade of political rallies and propaganda stunts apparently hid a depressing life of deprivation and oppression.[2] Complaints about shortages, queuing, rising prices and falling quality standards are seen as features of Nazi Germany from the very beginning. Everyday life in the dictatorship seemed to be full of frustration and deprivation. Frei explains the lower standard of living compared to that in Britain, France and the US by the priority given to arms production and the corresponding lack of consumer goods. 'The regime catered for the needs of war and kept its people on

---

1. B.H. Klein, *Germany's Preparations for War* (Cambridge, Mass.: Harvard University Press, 1959), pp. 79–81.

2. I. Kershaw, *Hitler 1889–1936* (Stuttgart: Deutsche Verlagsanstalt, 1998), p. 727.

a short lead.'[3] Hachtmann stresses that poverty and hardship dominated working-class life in the 'Third Reich'.[4]

A macroeconomic analysis does not produce a clearer picture.[5] Not only is it fraught with all kinds of as yet unsolved statistical problems, neither does it reveal any spectacular overall changes. Apparently, real per capita consumption in Nazi Germany remained close to depression levels, a fact which many contemporary observers failed to notice. Germany's fast and impressive return to full employment and the skillfulness of Goebbels' propaganda machinery muddied the water.

This chapter tries to resolve the contradiction between what looked to some like an absence of 'civilian sacrifices' and to others like a dictatorship deliberately exploiting and impoverishing its citizens. How did Hitler's Germany bridge the gulf between these two conflicting but apparently contemporaneous tendencies? How did the Nazi regime regulate and change consumption. What were the methods, dimensions and rationales of the government's interventions? In this regard advertising is of particular interest. Traditionally an intermediary between producers and consumers, it additionally became a mouthpiece of Nazi material politics, when it was placed under strict supervision as early as 1933.[6] State-controlled advertising was by no means the only instrument for influencing mass consumption, but it was one of prime importance and reveals many characteristic traits of Nazi consumer politics. Along with state intervention, the actual patterns of consumption will be examined. Finally, this chapter asks how far the 'Third Reich' was successful in implementing its own concept of consumption and to what degree popular patterns of consumption proved resistant to political regulation. We have to consider two distinct phases in the period leading up to the war, when new constraints on consumption were imposed.

The Quest for Economic Recovery and for a German Pattern of Consumption, 1933–35

Hitler took office when the Great Depression was still in full swing. Dole queues reached frightening dimensions, and 34 per cent of the workforce was unemployed.

3. N. Frei, *Der Führerstaat: Nationalsozialistische Herrschaft 1933 bis 1945* (Munich: Deutscher Taschenbuchverlag, 1987), p. 94. L. Herbst claims that even in 1933–36 'everything grew stunted which did not serve rearmament at least indirectly', in *idem*, 'Die nationalsozialistische Wirtschaftspolitik im internationalen Vergleich', in W. Benz *et al.* (eds), *Der Nationalsozialismus: Studien zur Ideologie und Herrschaft* (Frankfurt: Fischer, 1993), p. 157.

4. R. Hachtmann, *Industriearbeit im 'Dritten Reich': Untersuchungen zu den Lohn- und Arbeitsbedingungen in Deutschland 1933–1945* (Göttingen: Vandenhoeck and Ruprecht, 1989).

5. H. Berghoff, 'A question of guns and butter: the politics of consumption in the "Third Reich", 1933–1942', unpublished.

6. H. Berghoff, 'Von der "Reklame" zur Verbrauchslenkung: Werbung im nationalsozialistischen Deutschland', in *idem* (ed.), *Konsumpolitik: Die Regulierung des privaten Verbrauchs im 20. Jahrhundert* (Göttingen: Vandenhoeck and Ruprecht, 1999), pp. 77–112.

In order to put Germany back to work and to tighten its political grip on the country, the Nazi administration relied on job-creation schemes and massive rearmament. In addition it played a psychological card and tried to create what present-day political commentators call the 'feel-good factor'. With every trick available to propagandistic stage machinery, the regime conveyed the message that it would beat the crisis within four years and that a bright future lay ahead. People were told to consume more, especially goods of German origin, so as to stimulate economic growth and to create jobs. The publicly owned saving banks, which catered for the average wage- and salary-earner, appealed to their customers in 1933/34: 'Savings create jobs – hoarding money is sabotaging national recovery.' Saving and spending became a patriotic duty.[7]

In order to increase consumption, the regime granted direct subsidies for household goods. The famous marriage loans helped young couples set up their homes. The scheme initially required the wife to give up her job and included a strong pronatalist drive because the amount to be paid back decreased according to the number of children. The birth of four children guaranteed a full remission of the debt. The consumer-goods sector received a major boost from a total of 300 million RM paid out by the end of 1935, and loans as high as 1000 RM or up to ten times the monthly income of an unskilled industrial worker.[8]

At the same time the consumption of foreign products was discouraged to increase German employment and to alleviate the notoriously strained balance of trade. Figure 8.1 shows the importance of curtailing of all but the most essential imports for a regime running out of gold and foreign exchange. In the interest of rapid rearmament, the 'Third Reich' recklessly sucked in more resources than it could afford. Imports were too high and exports too small. Being almost constantly threatened by a run-down of currency reserves, foreign trade was strictly regulated from 1934 onwards. Although a marked increase in German self-sufficiency occurred, the government did not reach autarchy, which it had continuously and vigorously propagated.[9] The continued disregard of Germany's limited resource base remained the fundamental problem of the Nazi economy. Consumption politics

7. Quoted in P. Borscheid, 'Sparsamkeit und Sicherheit: Werbung für Banken, Sparkassen und Versicherungen', in *idem* and C. Wischermann (eds), *Bilderwelt des Alltags* (Stuttgart: Steiner, 1995), p. 318. The regime regarded savings banks as the ideal financial institution because they were not profit-oriented and were easily controlled. Moreover they were neither 'Jewish' nor 'international' or part of the dreaded 'anonymous finance capital', according to C. Kopper, *Zwischen Marktwirtschaft und Dirigismus: Bankenpolitik im 'Dritten Reich' 1933 bis 1939* (Bonn: Bouvier, 1994), p. 21.

8. M. Schneider, *Unterm Hakenkreuz: Arbeiter und Arbeiterbewegung 1933–1939* (Bonn: Dietz Nachfahren, 1999), pp. 260–1.

9. With many countries, bilateral barter agreements were concluded. Others kept insisting on payment in convertible currency. See R.J. Overy, *The Nazi Economic Recovery 1932–1938* (Cambridge: Cambridge University Press, 1996), p. 26 and R. Erbe, *Die nationalsozialistische Wirtschaftspolitik 1933–1939 im Lichte der modernen Theorie* (Zürich: Polygraphischer Verlag, 1958), pp. 69–81.

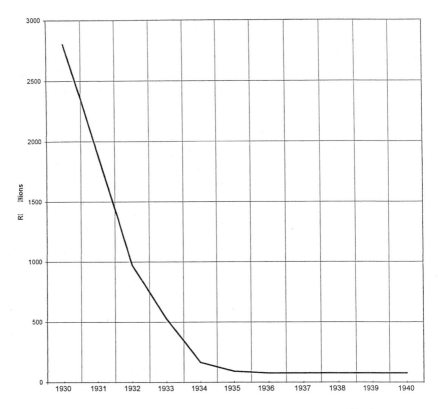

Figure 8.1   The Reichsbank's Gold and Foreign Exchange Reserves, 1930–40

Source: W. Fischer, *Deutsche Wirtschaftspolitik 1918–1945*, 3rd edn, (Opladen: Leske, 1968), p. 104.

tried to make ends meet that were simply too short from the beginning. One of the main aims was to replace imported goods by domestic ones, either by using surrogates such as barley malt for real coffee or by shifting from one product category (such as tropical fruits) to another (such as German apples). Housewives were told by the National Socialist Women's Bureau to prefer apples, potatoes, fish, sugar and rye bread and to avoid imported tropical fruits, white bread, meat and animal fat. The consumption of domestic substitutes such as the dairy product quark instead of butter, wild fruits in place of tropical imports, or spun rayon rather than cotton was advocated as a patriotic duty.[10]

10. See N. Reagin, 'Comparing apples and oranges: housewives and the politics of consumption in interwar Germany', in S. Strasser *et al.* (eds), *Getting and Spending: European and American Consumer Societies in the Twentieth Century* (Cambridge: Cambridge University Press, 1998), pp. 241–61, where she stresses that similar campaigns had already been launched by housewives' organizations during the Weimar Republic.

At the same time the regime cautiously took the first steps to keep prices in check. However, the Office for the Supervision of Prices did not have a strong position within the administrative chaos of the 'Third Reich', and was consequently unable to restrain inflationary pressure building up with economic recovery. Rising purchasing power and a scarcity of some goods combined to drive up prices from the end of 1934.[11] This and the recurring shortage of certain essential products such as butter and fat caused considerable anger among consumers. In September 1934 the Cologne Gestapo recorded widespread dissatisfaction among workers, which was 'due to a continuous deterioration of working and living conditions and never-ending price rises for food and articles of daily use'.[12] It has to be remembered that wage control was much more efficient than price control, and high unemployment had pushed down many incomes.[13]

Apart from economic and political necessities, ideology played a major role in the formation of consumer politics. National Socialism implied the idea of ideologically 'sound' – that is, truly German – patterns of consumption. It wanted to dissociate itself from what was called 'liberalistic capitalism', 'poisonous Jewish materialism' or 'degraded western culture'. If these concepts were extremely vague to say the least, the alternatives of 'German consumption' were utterly insubstantial and a source of constant confusion, if not grotesquerie. Attempts to establish a 'German fashion' to make demand independent of international (especially French) influences came to nothing. Manufacturers did not know how to bestow 'German qualities' on their products, and Nazi Germany did not develop a distinctive design of its own. Empty slogans were hard to deal with by practical men. Surrogates of inferior quality often had the adjective 'German' attached to them, so exposing the state's measures to ridicule.

The regime officially declared war on smoking because of the dangers to national health. In particular, female participation in this 'vice' was sharply criticized. Women were to give birth to a maximum number of healthy babies and to live up to the role of a hard-working mother. The president of the German Medical Association proclaimed uncompromisingly: 'German women don't smoke!' In real life, though, more and more women took up smoking. Despite massive anti-smoking campaigns, the consumption of cigarettes almost doubled between 1932 and 1940. The tobacco industry regularly ignored the regime's instructions and depicted smoking women in their advertisements (Figure 8.2). Their hedonism and elegance sharply contradicted the official concept of femininity. Apparently, industry's image of women as attractive consumers was more popular than the picture of the German mother with blonde pigtails and country dirndls. Other vices

11. A. Barkai, *Das Wirtschaftssystem des Nationalsozialismus: Ideologie, Theorie, Politik 1933– 1945* (Frankfurt: Fischer, 1988), pp. 178–9.
12. F.L. Carsten, *The German Workers and the Nazis* (Aldershot: Scolar, 1995), p. 43.
13. Hachtmann, *Industriearbeit*, pp. 92–111.

Figure 8.2   Cigarette advertisement by the brand 'R 6', 1937

Source: Westphal, Werbung, p. 56.

also flourished despite government health warnings. Brandy consumption per adult rose by 40 per cent between 1930 and 1937. At the same time, wine intake rose from 6.5 to 8.9 litres per annum. Beer consumption, however, declined from 104 to a deplorable 83 litres because of restrictions on hop growing.[14]

The use of Nazi symbols in advertisements and the design of consumer goods proliferated in the spring of 1933. Lamps and aprons ornamented with swastikas, or commercials claiming 'That's what the *Führer* wants', threatened the party's reputation. Therefore official symbols were banned from being used for commercial purposes. From the 1920s onwards, National Socialism tried to commodify politics by designing their 'product' very much along the lines of commercial advertising and by treating their symbols with the same care that manufacturers apply to their

14. One poster claimed that 2 million Volkswagen cars were smoked away each year. See R.N. Proctor, *The Nazi War on Cancer* (Princeton: Princeton University Press, 1999); *Statistisches Handbuch von Deutschland, 1928–1944* (Munich, 1949), pp. 332, 489; R. Grunberger, *A Social History of the Third Reich* (London: Weidenfeld & Nicolson, 1971), pp. 208–9; Berghoff, 'Reklame', p. 97.

trademarks. Hitler considered advertisements for soap exemplary for political propaganda. Goebbels has been accurately characterized as a 'trade mark technologist'(*Markentechniker*).[15]

Hence, the regime told advertisers to convey ideologically sound messages. The use of 'German' motifs was encouraged: that is, scenes of medieval artists or contemporary 'blood and soil' painters, people in folk costumes and bucolic scenes with blue-eyed, blonde 'Aryans', muscular heroes and marching masses. Foreign words, even if they were common product names, should no longer figure in advertisements. In general, consumer protection was taken more seriously, and sensational, manipulative or deceptive advertisements were banned. Collective advertising (*Gemeinschaftswerbung*) by trades rather than by individual businesses should overcome capitalistic competition and 'anarchic' market fluctuations, and should benefit rational planning and an 'organic economic order'. These instructions were observed to some degree, but advertisers above all had their commercial success in mind. Instead of following awkward instructions they relied on international trends or stuck to traditional methods. As we have seen, many advertisers refused to depict women as mothers and housewives but rather opted for more alluring images dictated by cosmopolitan fashion. The history of advertising in Nazi Germany is a history of conflict between official regulation and the inherent dynamics of consumerism. Very often consumers' desires and commercial self-interest weighed more strongly than ideology and military needs.

The limits of consumption politics in Nazi Germany can also be seen in the failure to eradicate large-scale retailers, as the NSDAP's programme had promised to shopkeepers who were over-represented among the party's voters. Although membership and turnover of consumer co-operatives, which had been closely associated with the labour movement, dwindled fast, retailing structures were not turned upside down after 1933. In the interest of stability and efficient mass provision, department stores did not have to go out of business. The creation of new department stores and the expansion of existing premises, however, was prohibited, and price rebates restricted to a maximum of 3 per cent.[16] In effect, the regime tried to steer a middle course between the interests of consumers and those of shopkeepers or, to put it more generally, between ideology and practical needs. The 'Third Reich' on the one hand needed more consumption to win political loyalty and to secure economic recovery. On the other, it had to manage and suppress demand to make it compatible with rearmament.

15. *Die Reklame* 1933, p. 300; Berghoff, 'Reklame', p. 81.

16. D. Schoenbaum, *Hitler's Social Revolution: Class and Status in Nazi Germany 1933–1939* (New York: Weidenfeld & Nicolson, 1966), pp. 136–41; H. Berghoff, 'Did Hitler create a new German society? Continuities and changes in German social history before and after 1933', in P. Panayi (ed.), *Weimar and Nazi Germany: Continuities and Discontinuities* (London: Longman, 2000), pp. 74–104.

Hartmut Berghoff

Containing Consumers' Desires in an Overheating Economy Heading for War, 1935–39

Germany's remarkable economic recovery turned into acute crisis in 1935/36, when industry was running out of raw materials and consumers faced severe shortages of essential goods. The bad harvest of 1934 reduced domestic food supplies even further and made an increase in food imports necessary, which in turn reduced currency reserves and imports of raw materials. Rising prices and shortages of essentials led to manifestations of public dissatisfaction. The regime basically had to chose between slowing down rearmament or restricting private consumption with brute force. Neither solution was feasible. On the one hand, Hitler categorically refused to postpone his military aggression. On the other, with the traumatic experience of November 1918 in mind, he dreaded consumers' resistance. Therefore, even in the critical situation of 1936–39 the regime increased food imports by 64 per cent.[17]

The regime opted for a third way with the Four Year Plan of 1936. It tightened up economic controls and increased the production of surrogates based on domestic resources. Unproven and excessively expensive technologies were chosen as long as they reduced Germany's dependence on imports. Simultaneously, Hitler hastened territorial expansion – for the time being without waging war. To broaden his domestic resource base he incorporated the Saar, Austria, the Sudetenland, Bohemia and Moravia into his empire. In 1936, too, the dictator decided to start military aggression sooner than originally planned in order to burden the defeated countries with the cost of his ruinous rearmament programme at the earliest possible moment.[18]

Ironically, the problem for the politics of consumption was self-made. The rearmament boom and the reduction in unemployment had pushed up purchasing power, although wages remained relatively low. The share of wages in the national income continuously declined from 1932. Not until 1937 did real wages reach pre-depression levels (1928), whereas employers' real income increased faster and more substantially. The abolition of collective bargaining by the wage decrees of 1933 had shifted the balance on the labour market in favour of the employers again.[19]

---

17. In current prices. See D. Petzina *et al.*, *Sozialgeschichtliches Arbeitsbuch III: Materialien zur Statistik des Deutschen Reiches 1914–1945* (Munich: Beck, 1978), p. 76.

18. H.-E. Volkmann, 'Die NS-Wirtschaft in Vorbereitung des Krieges', in W. Deist *et al.*, *Ursachen und Voraussetzungen des Zweiten Weltkrieges* (Frankfurt: Fischer, 1989), pp. 314–44.

19. L. Herbst, *Das nationalsozialistische Deutschland: 1933–1945* (Frankfurt: Suhrkamp, 1996), p. 238; Petzina, *Arbeitsbuch*, pp. 89–94, 106; M. Spoerer, *Von Scheingewinnen zum Rüstungsboom: Die Eigenkapitalrendite der deutschen Industrieaktiengesellschaften 1925–41* (Stuttgart: Steiner, 1995).

In spite of their relative losses, employees did benefit from economic recovery. Full employment by 1937/38 meant more overtime and more incomes per family. Of course, they would have been much higher in an economy with collective bargaining, but even Hitler did not succeed in abolishing the law of supply and demand. Employers who were facing increased recruitment problems reacted to the regime's virtual freezing of basic wages by paying higher bonuses. The overall amount of wages paid out soared from 27.4 billion RM in 1932 to 50.1 in 1940. The regime had to find a compromise between the economic logic of the Four Year Plan and the need to secure consumers' political loyalty. This meant suppressing overall consumption and, at the same time, making noticeable concessions and – even more importantly – impressive as well as credible promises. Without developing anything like a consistent strategy but rather clinging to improvisation, the regime allowed increases of consumption in some areas – especially those with a symbolic significance – and vowed higher standards of living in the near future. This attempt to square the circle created ambivalence and a virtual reality of imagined consumption, which was propagated but rarely delivered. The regime cunningly offered mouth-watering examples of mass consumption and promised more satisfaction later on. In order to reach this stage by placing Europe under German rule, consumers were asked to put up with 'temporary' restrictions.

The constant juxtaposition of enticement and deprivation generated three different kinds of consumption, reflecting the Janus-faced reality of the 'Third Reich'. First, the regime allowed *increased consumption* and considerable progress towards Western consumerism in a number of sectors. Second, there was *suppressed consumption* because rearmament required reductions in the imports of consumer goods or the reallocation of scarce raw materials from consumer- to production-goods industries. Thus, shortages of an ever-growing number of consumer items became a general feature of daily life under the Four Year Plan. Third, the regime created *virtual consumption* by opening up new horizons and promising unprecedented advances into modernity. To make this propaganda effective it concentrated on prestigious consumer goods with high levels of symbolic meaning, such as cars and holidays.

The radio is the classic example of mass consumption making considerable progress. In 1932 only 4 million radio listeners were registered. Their number rose to 9 million by 1938 and 16 million by 1943. By 1940 more than two-thirds of all households had a wireless. The regime actively supported the construction and sale of cheap standardized sets (*Volksempfänger*) in order to reach every single German. The state-run stations initially broadcast a high proportion of political programmes but soon learnt that it was more effective to dispense propaganda in small doses. Therefore, entertainment accounted for about 70 per cent of programme time in the late 1930s. Popular music, sometimes selected by listeners, was the main feature of Nazi broadcasting. Diversion rather than education or indoctrination was the radio's task, which essentially made it look very modern. However, in some aspects – the absence of commercial stations and the total ban on radio advertising in 1936 – German broadcasting had distinctly anti-modern characteristics.[20]

Although movies were already very popular in Weimar Germany, attendance nevertheless quadrupled between 1933 and 1942. The regime managed to offer an attractive range of films. Most of them eschewed direct political propaganda and confined themselves to light entertainment and subtle doses of ideology. Until 1940 Hollywood played a prominent role in filling German cinemas. Katherine Hepburn, Greta Garbo, Gary Cooper, Joan Crawford and even émigrée Marlene Dietrich were among the most popular movie stars in Nazi Germany. US productions often scored the highest attendance figures, although the state-owned UfA-concern imitated the American model with some success.

American films required dollars, and their content was not always ideologically safe. Why did Goebbels not ban them? The Propaganda Ministry grudgingly realized that Hollywood's productions were more popular than their own and that a ban would cause considerable unrest. Manipulating or indoctrinating cinemagoers into refusing to watch foreign movies seemed out of the question. American music, which was partly popularized by the movies, was a different story altogether. Time and again, the regime stated that jazz and swing undermined patriotism and that especially Afro-American musicians 'insulted the German race'. Radio programmes were 'cleaned', students instructed, and dance halls raided, although with minimal success. It proved to be impossible to change popular taste and especially juvenile subculture. Music, just as fashion, was a field where consumers forced the regime to make concessions and finally to give up attempts at reeducation.[21]

In another area consumerism was much more in line with official ideology. The *KdF* (*Kraft durch Freude,* i.e. 'Joy through strength') wing of the German Labour Front promoted organized mass tourism. Workers should get the impression of being able to overcome social barriers and to conquer hitherto unassailable bastions of middle-class privileges. Holidays compensated for relatively low wages and the loss of an independent labour movement. They were designed to win workers' political loyalty and to improve productivity. They also absorbed surplus purchasing

20. A. Schildt, *Moderne Zeiten: Freizeit, Massenmedien und 'Zeitgeist' in der Bundesrepublik der 50er Jahre* (Hamburg: Christians, 1995), pp. 209–13; P. Reichel, *Der schöne Schein des Dritten Reiches: Faszination und Gewalt des Faschismus* (Frankfurt: Fischer, 1993), pp. 159–70; Berghoff, 'Reklame', p. 87. Britain did not have commercial stations or adverts either.

21. P. Wicke, 'Das Ende: Populäre Musik im faschistischen Deutschland', in S. Schutte (ed.), *Ich will aber gerade vom Leben singen . . . Über populäre Musik vom ausgehenden 19. Jahrhundert bis zum Ende der Weimar Republik* (Reinbek: Rowohlt, 1987), p. 423.

power and diverted it from scarce agricultural and industrial products to self-made services. The average duration of paid holidays was extended from three to between six and twelve days per year. Financially, mass tourism became viable through a combination of subsidies and economies of scale. Travelling with *KdF* meant travelling in large groups. Consequently, prices were so low that no commercial operator could compete. The number of *KdF*-holidaymakers rose from 2.3 million in 1934 to 10.3 in 1938. Many of them went on holidays for the first time. Most destinations were within Germany. Trips to foreign countries and prestigious cruises to Scandinavia or the Mediterranean remained too expensive for most workers. The lower middle classes, however, benefited enormously from the cheapening of such attractive tours. Between 1934 and 1939 about 750,000 people, among them 100,000 workers, went on *KdF* cruises. A privilege of the upper middle classes had entered the mass market, even if only for its top layer. Psychologically, it was important that even those who could not afford cruises were able to perceive them as being within their reach. Dreams were not yet coming true, but millions dared to have them for the first time.[22] Their fulfilment seemed to be just around the corner. The head of the Labour Front, for example, proclaimed: 'In only ten years Germany will be changed beyond recognition. A nation of proletarians will have become a nation of gentlemen (*Herrenvolk*). The German worker will be better off than an English lord.'[23] The widening of consumers' horizons was an important step towards post-war patterns of mass consumption. Wishes were evoked, even if they could not yet be fulfilled. This among other reasons explains the relentless vigour with which post-war German society dedicated itself to material values and the catching up on consumption postponed before 1945.

To return to *increased consumption*, the housing sector must be considered. Between 1933 and 1939 a total of 2 million new dwellings were completed, which corresponds to 285,000 per year against the Weimar average of 200,000.[24] Some modern consumer durables spread with great speed. Radio sets have already been mentioned. Non-essentials such as cameras, clocks, watches, tents for camping and record players must be added. The sales of textiles rose by more than a quarter between 1932 and 1938, those of furniture and other household goods by about 50 per cent not least because of the marriage loans.[25] Mass-produced musical

22. H. Spode, '"Der deutsche Arbeiter reist": Massentourismus im Dritten Reich', in G. Huck (ed.), *Sozialgeschichte der Freizeit: Untersuchungen zum Wandel der Alltagskultur in Deutschland*, 2nd edn (Wuppertal: Hammer, 1982), pp. 281–306; D. Liebscher, 'Mit KdF "die Welt erschließen": Der Beitrag der KdF-Reisen zur Außenpolitik der Deutschen Arbeitsfront 1934–1939', *1999: Zeitschrift für Sozialgeschichte des 20. und 21. Jahrhunderts*, 14 (1999), pp. 42–72.

23. R.M. Smelser, 'Eine "braune Revolution"? Robert Ley, Deutsche Arbeitsfront und sozial-revolutionäre Konzepte', in W. Michalka (ed.), *Der Zweite Weltkrieg* (Munich: Pieper, 1989), p. 427.

24. Calculated from Petzina, *Arbeitsbuch*, p. 125. There were still 1.5 million households without their own home in 1938 many of the new houses were of inferior quality. See Grunberger, *Social History*, 1971), p. 229.

25. Grunberger, *Social History*, p. 215.

instruments such as the harmonica were sold in unprecedented numbers, the market leader more than quadrupling his German turnover between 1933 and 1939.[26] The technical modernization of German households was promoted in order to economize on energy and women's time. Gas or electrical stoves, washing machines, refrigerators, vacuum cleaners and electrical irons spread, although proliferation was rather slow. Nevertheless, industry sold rising numbers of refrigerators after 1937 in line with the regime's drive to reduce the wastage of food. The number of telephones per 100 inhabitants increased from 4.8 in 1930 to 6.1 in 1940. The consumption of electrical energy by private households and small businesses grew by 38 per cent between 1933 and 1940.[27]

Convenience food, a core product of mass consumer societies, was promoted because long-term conservation and storage of food was of highest interest to a country unable to feed itself but preparing for a major war. Therefore, the government lay in huge stocks of food in anticipation of an Allied blockade. In a highly mobile war millions of soldiers needed ready-to-serve meals. The application of tinning, packaging, refrigeration and deep-freezing technologies made great advances in the 1930s. The output of tins for vegetables and fruit almost doubled between 1933 and 1937. In 1935 the regime started research on cans for frozen food, and mass production began in 1938. In 1940 there were 14 major factories for frozen food, and 27 canning factories used high-speed freezing facilities to produce about 25,000 tons of frozen, tinned food. Huge cold-storage depots, some of them underground, were constructed. Trawlers, wagons and trucks had deep-freeze facilities built in. The spread of refrigerators in households rose from a very low level. Methods of food conservation by heat were also improved, and affected meat, dairy products and above all fruit and vegetables. New kinds of packaging such as cardboard stiffened by paraffin wax or varnish were developed. Besides, cellophane, waterproofed films or foils were introduced and eased automatic packaging.[28] A common feature of these technologies was that the regime promoted them not in order to advance convenience food per se but to make

---

26. H. Berghoff, *Zwischen Kleinstadt und Weltmarkt. Hohner und die Harmonika 1857–1961. Unternehmensgeschichte als Gesellschaftsgeschichte* (Paderborn: Schöningh, 1997), pp. 353–62; *idem*, 'Konsumgüterindustrie im Nationalsozialismus: Marketing im Spannungsfeld von Profit- und Regimeinteressen', *Archiv für Sozialgeschichte*, 36 (1996), pp. 293–322.

27. H. Kaelble, 'Europäische Besonderheiten des Massenkonsums 1950–1990', in H. Siegrist *et al.* (eds), *Europäische Konsumgeschichte: Zur Gesellschafts- und Kulturgeschichte des Konsums (18. bis 20. Jahrhundert)* (Frankfurt: Campus, 1997), p. 199; H. Vogt, *Die Gerätesättigung im Haushalt: Eine erweiterte Marktanalyse für elektrische und Gasgeräte* (Berlin: Vereinigte Verlagsgesellschaften, 1940), p. 12; U. Hellmann, *Künstliche Kälte: Die Geschichte der Kühlung im Haushalt* (Gießen: Anabas, 1990), pp. 108–17; *Statistisches Handbuch*, p. 337.

28. R. Berthold *et al.*, *Produktivkräfte in Deutschland, vol. 3, 1917/18 bis 1945* (Berlin: Akademie, 1988), pp. 140–1; H.D. Schäfer, *Das gespaltene Bewußtsein: Über deutsche Kultur und Lebenswirklichkeit 1933–1945* (Munich: Hanser, 1981), p. 122.

Germany immune to blockade. The technological steps taken in the interest of autarchy were, however, not reversed after 1945, when industry easily converted the war-related changes of food processing into basic technologies of the emerging West German consumer society.

Another product finding its way into German households during the Nazi era was the undisputed symbol of the Western consumerism. Coca Cola opened its first German branch in 1929 and increased the number of its German bottling factories from 5 in 1934 to 50 in 1939. The firm organized the refreshment service at the 1936 Berlin Olympic Games and other big Nazi sporting events. When a German competitor denounced Coca Cola as being Jewish, the company reacted by placing advertisements with the *Stürmer*, the most malicious antisemitic paper available in Nazi Germany.[29] Turnover of advertising agencies rose between 1934 and 1935 by 48 per cent. Hire purchase, a characteristic device of consumer societies to increase sales and speed up the realization of customers' wishes, reached an unprecedented level on the eve of war. The advance of consuming beyond present liquidity is a reliable indicator of the psychological mood of Germans in the late 1930s.[30] Expectations were rising, the future looked bright, and the best was yet to come. Workers remembered the period between 1935 and 1939 as 'good years'.[31]

Nevertheless, the Nazi regime regularly promised more than it delivered. Mass motorization is the classic example for consumption that remained largely *virtual*. The Nazi government promised to overcome the 'class-divisive character of cars' by making them available to the masses. The 'achievements of technology' would no longer remain privileges of 'the well-fed and the rich'.[32] This vision survived the regime's collapse and became a leitmotif of post-war politicians, architects and consumers.

Car ownership in 1932 was clearly lower than that in most Western countries but doubled up to 1937 under the impact of massive tax concessions, economic recovery and extensive road building.[33] As this increase was far too small to fulfil

---

29. This campaign got Coca Cola into trouble in its home country, where some critics blamed the drinks giant for financing Hitler. *Ibid.*, p. 118; U. Westphal, *Werbung im Dritten Reich* (Berlin: Transit, 1989), pp. 53–5.

30. Berghoff, 'Reklame', p. 91; Grunberger, *Social History*, pp. 223–4.

31. U. Herbert, '"Die guten und die schlechten Zeiten". Überlegungen zur diachronen Analyse lebensgeschichtlicher Interviews', in L. Niethammer (ed.), *'Die Jahre weiß man nicht, wo man die heute hinsetzen soll': Faschismuserfahrungen im Ruhrgebiet. Lebensgeschichte und Sozialkultur im Ruhrgebiet 1930 bis 1960, vol. 1*, 2nd edn (Bonn: Dietz Nachfahren, 1986), pp. 67–96.

32. Robert Ley, quoted by R. Mattausch, *Siedlungsbau und Stadtneugründungen im Deutschen Faschismus* (Frankfurt: Haag und Herchen, 1980), p. 153.

33. The number of people per car fell from 135 to 61. See H. Edelmann, *Vom Luxusgut zum Gebrauchsgegenstand: Die Geschichte der Verbreitung von Personenkraftwagen in Deutschland* (Frankfurt: Verband der Automobilindustrie, 1989), p. 165; R.J. Overy, 'Cars, roads and economic recovery in Germany 1932–38', *Economic History Review*, 28 (1975), pp. 466–73.

Hitler's vision of motorization on the scale of America's, he announced a people's car, the Volkswagen. The idea of a cheap car for everyone was revolutionary and unrealistic at the same time. Hitler himself stipulated a maximum price of 1000 RM which did not even cover production costs. German car manufacturers reacted without enthusiasm. Consequently, *KdF* built a giant factory in the countryside. Although construction began only in 1938 and virtually no cars for civilian use were assembled before 1945, the Volkswagen was heavily advertised and depicted as the car for all Germans. Happy blonde 'Aryans' would use it for outings or holidays. *KdF* launched a saving scheme in 1938 to enable people to make a deposit of 5 RM per week in order to become car owners in four years. Most unusually, the customers were asked to pay years in advance without receiving any interest. And yet, within twelve months a quarter of a million people joined the scheme. None of them, however, received a car before the end of war. As the Volkswagen saving scheme soaked up purchasing power, the regime succeeded in deceiving its citizens or – to put it in more technical terms – in using *virtual consumption* in one sector to prevent *increased consumption* in others.[34]

After 1945, the Volkswagen became the symbol of West Germany's 'economic miracle' and the world's most popular car. The Nazi regime had created demand it was unable to satisfy. It had built a plant that – although converted for military purposes – was ready for car production after 1945. The dictatorship had even developed blueprints and prototypes of a robust car which was up to the standards of the 1950s and 1960s. The Volkswagen, like no other consumer product, epitomizes the Janus face of Nazi material politics, the coincidence of enticement and deprivation. Two other people's projects were also heavily advertised but similarly failed to materialize. In 1936 the regime took first steps to establish regular television programmes. It announced the mass production of TV-sets (*Volksfernseher*), and high-flying plans to construct a cheap, standardized people's refrigerator (*Volkskühlschrank*). However, these plans came to nothing, for the war meant that these projects had to be cancelled.

Articles and advertisements in popular magazines offer many more examples of *virtual consumption*. These journals did not differ much from their counterparts in Western countries. They focused on celebrities and crime, gossip and scandal, fashion and sport. They also presented American patterns of consumption as a model, featuring picture stories of American actors doing their Christmas shopping in Hollywood or other everyday scenes of life in the US.[35] Schäfer's analysis of German pre-war society diagnosed schizophrenia.[36] On the one hand, people lived

---

34. H. Mommsen and M. Grieger, *Das Volkswagenwerk und seine Arbeiter 1933–1948* (Düsseldorf: Econ, 1996), esp. pp. 92–226.
35. Schäfer, *Bewußtsein*, pp. 130–1.
36. *Ibid*. See also Schoenbaum, *Social Revolution*, pp. 287–301.

in a country in which modern consumerism made great advances. On the other, they were confronted with an ideology abounding with anti-modernistic traits. National Socialism dwelled on agrarian romanticism and at the same time brought electricity and artificial fertilizers to the farms. Environmental protection and ascetic anti-consumerism were propagated by a party building an advanced motorway system. The Nazi regime combined both reactionary and modernist elements. In this blurred picture, promises of a new and better world of mass consumption, even if seldom kept, were a fundamental part of Hitler's double strategy of 'persuasion and terror'.[37]

Paradoxically, moves towards a modern consumer society were accompanied by *suppressed consumption*, by empty shelves and primitive ersatz products. The Four Year Plan of 1936 intensified the production of surrogates and the regulation of foreign trade. Moreover, a more effective system of price control was introduced. Under these conditions, steering demand by changing consumer habits became more important. For this purpose the Committee for National Economic Education (*Reichsausschuß für Volkswirtschaftliche Aufklärung, RVA*) was set up in 1936. Its task was to distinguish between desirable and unwanted consumption, and to co-ordinate all authorities dealing with consumption.

In order to gather information on existing demand, the Society for Research on Consumption (*Gesellschaft für Konsumforschung, GfK*) was founded in 1934/35. A network of 600 correspondents in every part of Germany compiled comprehensive surveys. The *GfK* inaugurated modern market research based on systematic polls in Germany. The privately-financed *GfK* saw its main task in providing industry with data on consumer behaviour. It even warned the regime that demand was not the result of a fully rational process and could therefore hardly be planned or managed. Leading *GfK*-researchers such as Wilhelm Vershofen emphasized the impossibility of manipulating consumers totally against their will. Reporting on the clothing industry, he claimed: 'You cannot create fashion, you can only find it.' In 1936 he even stated that the *GfK* should not be abused for the questionable purpose of redirecting demand. At the same time, he conceded that beyond doubt *GfK* research would be invaluable to those who wanted to change existing patterns of consumption.[38] In fact, the dictatorship received a data bases for designing its campaigns.

37. This is the very appropriate title of the general history of Nazi Germany by H.-U. Thamer, *Verführung und Gewalt: Deutschland 1933–1945* (Berlin: Siedler, 1994). See also R. Zitelmann, *Hitler: Selbstverständnis eines Revolutionärs* (Stuttgart: Klett-Cotta, 1990), esp. pp. 349–65; M. Prinz, 'Die soziale Funktion moderner Elemente in der Gesellschaftspolitik des National-sozialismus', in *idem* and R. Zitelmann (eds), *Nationalsozialismus und Modernisierung* (Darmstadt: Wissenschaftliche Buchgesellschaft, 1991), pp. 320–1.

38. G. Bergler, *Die Entwicklung der Verbrauchsforschung in Deutschland und die Gesellschaft für Konsumforschung bis zum Jahr 1945* (Kallmünz: Laßleben, 1959), esp. pp. 60, 113.

Women were inundated by brochures telling them to rationalize housekeeping. Mending clothes was more patriotic than buying new ones. Recycling and extensive gardening, the adaptation of menus to the 'needs of the nation', energy conservation and other forms of reduction in consumption figured high on the regime's agenda. Campaigns for German food were intensified. In 1937 the Women's Bureau organized 27,885 cookery courses with 613,000 participants. In 1938 figures rose to 85,985 and 1,8 million respectively.[39] These statistics demonstrate the effort the regime put into changing dietary habits, but also prove that only a minority of German women attended these courses. Millions of books and leaflets told them to switch from animal to vegetable foodstuffs as well as from protein and fat to carbohydrate. More labour-intensive methods of housekeeping, such as collecting wild berries and preserving garden fruits, were recommended. Buying finished products in the shops was discouraged. It is characteristic of the ambivalence of National Socialism that it propagated the return to self-provision at the same time as it dispensed modern consumer products such as radios and frozen meals.

From 1936 onwards the authorities staged a massive campaign under the motto 'Fight the waste' (*Kampf dem Verderb*) following reports that about 10 per cent of Germany's food went bad. Refrigeration, storage and preservation as well as waste utilization were key topics. Hitler Youth, Labour Front and other mass organizations were called upon for collections of anything from metal to kitchen scrap, from animal bones to corks from wine bottles. Predictably, the campaign was not very popular. The authorities steadily complained about people's lack of enthusiasm.[40]

Advertisers received instructions to abandon demand stimulation: '. . . it is forbidden to advertise for products whose proliferation is not in the real interests of the national economy'.[41] Creating extra demand for scarce or foreign products had to be stopped. Instead advertisers should popularise the regime's priorities and ersatz products. Advertisers were seen as subordinates of the Propaganda Ministry, a role they did not adopt wholeheartedly. In many cases they found the instructions impossible to put into practice or successfully ignored them. To convince consumers not to ask for the products they wanted was indeed a hard task. No political slogan and no advertisement could hide the fact that quality worsened and that in many ways consumer interests were sacrificed to rearmament. Consumers knew exactly that textiles made from cellophane did not keep them warm in winter, that Ersatz soap did not wash well, and that clothes and handkerchiefs woven with artificial silk required troublesome methods of laundry. Soft metal cutlery bent, unlike the familiar steel qualities. The regime sometimes went so far as to praise itself for cutting supplies, or wrapped up shortages in

39. J. Stephenson, *The Nazi Organization of Women* (London: Croom Helm, 1981), p. 132.
40. F. Huchting, 'Abfallwirtschaft im Dritten Reich', *Technikgeschichte*, 48 (1981), pp. 252–73.
41. *Seidels Reklame* 1935, p. 81. See also Berghoff, 'Reklame', pp. 98–9.

propagandistic gobbledegook. Intermittent deficits of lemons were announced in the following grotesque words: 'Only through the German soil are the finest vibrations transmitted to the blood . . . therefore, fare thee well, lemon, we need thee not. German rhubarb will replace thee altogether.'[42]

Fat, butter and margarine were already in short supply by 1933 and diverse forms of control and rationing were introduced in the following years. Whipped cream and cream cakes were banned in 1938. Sugar was advocated as a replacement for fat. The production of jam trebled between 1933 and 1937. Nevertheless, the regime's 'battle against the notorious buttered bread' was eventually lost.[43] The Germans would not go without their traditional spread. Their diet was modest by British or American standards. Anglo-Saxons ate more meat, fruit, sugar, eggs and white bread than the Germans who consumed more potatoes, cabbage and margarine. 'Even so, it was the palate and not the health . . . that suffered.'[44] In 1934/35 decrees were issued on the compulsory addition of synthetic fibres to textiles. The production of pure cotton or woollen textiles stopped. The quality of many goods deteriorated significantly, much to the dissatisfaction of consumers.

All in all, the dictatorship's hopes for changing consumption habits in line with war needs and turning Germans into political consumers did not materialize. In most cases enforced modifications of their shopping lists were strongly resented. Most of all, people remained unwilling to develop a 'political stomach'. Even tropical fruits did not vanish from German tables despite their luxury status and the dramatic shortage of foreign currency. Consumption of imported tropical fruits fell from 10 to 7 kilograms per head between 1930 and 1938. Considering the regime's effort in making German alternatives palatable to its citizens, this was not a very impressive result.[45] In 1936, advertising people were told that the 'ideal of consumer politics is the 'tractable customer'.[46] This concept never really worked, however, as consumers neither voluntarily conformed to the priorities of the state nor proved to be puppets on the strings of a totalitarian regime. Wherever possible the regime reacted swiftly when consumer complaints were mounting. Austerity measures were postponed even if they were economically necessary. In 1935/36 economic advisers recommended the rationing of bread, flour and fat. Instead, the regime increased food imports and intensified rearmament at the same time.

Popular dissatisfaction frequently originated not in absolute but in relative deprivation. Consumption of many items whose shortage was bitterly complained about grew or at least remained static. In spite of the scarcity of foreign currency, imports of cotton and woollen yarn, silk, coffee, tea, tobacco, wine and even butter

42. Quoted in Grunberger, *Social History*, p. 207.
43. F. Blaich, *Wirtschaft und Rüstung im Dritten Reich* (Düsseldorf: Schwann, 1987), pp. 30–3.
44. Grunberger, *Social History*, p. 209.
45. *Statistisches Handbuch*, p. 489.
46. *Seidels Reklame* 1935, p. 25.

rose in the late 1930s.[47] Still, without rearmament consumption of these commodities would have grown much faster. Nevertheless, complaints originated most of all from the frustration of rising expectations backed by surplus purchasing power, not from shrinking levels of consumption. Thus, the regime blamed its citizens for being unreasonable and narrow-minded. The ideological principles and military aims of the 'Third Reich' made lamentations about coffee or butter look like signs of pettiness. In 1938 white rolls were temporarily unavailable because the regime favoured the more nutritious dark ones. However, popular dissatisfaction caused the administration to give in. At the 1938 NSDAP annual convention the topic was addressed, and Göring announced that wheaten rolls would be on sale again. The applause Göring received provoked biting invectives from ideological hard-liners. Grumbling consumers were accused of 'pretending to be starving without their regular supply of . . . whipped cream'.[48] Goebbels was disgusted when shoppers – after years of rising coffee imports – complained about minor shortages of coffee. He called them 'coffee addicts' and 'old biddies' charging them with selfishness and irresponsibility: 'In times when coffee is scarce a decent person simply drinks less or stops drinking it altogether.'[49]

The recurrent over-sensitivity with which German consumers reacted to supply problems obviously belied Hitler's image of a heroic race. This is why the regime partly resorted to the suppression of consumption by authoritarian means. Some surplus spending power was absorbed by an increase in the tax burden. The state's overall fiscal revenue rose from 6 to 17.7 billion RM between 1933 and 1938, faster than the National Income. Revenue from income and property tax more than quadrupled. Industrial workers were only confronted with modest tax rises but contributions to the Labour Front and other mass organizations meant a sizeable reduction of net wages. There was little chance of evading the regime's growing appetite for money, as contributions and so-called 'voluntary donations' were automatically deducted from wages. For an average worker tax, insurance and other deductions increased from 12.9 per cent in 1932 to 17.1 per cent in 1938. Moreover, the prices of consumer goods were allowed to rise faster than wages, a fact hidden by official statistics. Shortages often meant that people had to buy more expensive goods. Quality deterioration did not lead to lower prices, so that in effect hidden price rises occurred. Scarce goods moved to grey and black markets where they were sold at higher prices.[50]

47. *Statistisches Handbuch*, p. 501; *Statistisches Jahrbuch für das Deutsche Reich* 59 (1941/42), pp. 447 and *Internationale Übersichten*, pp. 187–96.

48. *Schwarzes Korps*, 22 September 1938, quoted in R. Grunberger, *Das Zwölfjährige Reich: Der Deutsche Alltag unter Hitler* (Vienna: Molden, 1972), p. 222.

49. *Völkischer Beobachter*, 11 March 1939, quoted in Grunberger, *Social History*, p. 208.

50. Erbe, *Wirtschaftspolitik*, pp. 28–37; W.A. Boelcke, *Die Kosten von Hitlers Krieg: Kriegsfinanzierung und finanzielles Kriegserbe in Deutschland 1933–1948* (Paderborn: Schöningh, 1985), p. 51; Hachtmann, *Industriearbeit*, pp. 154–60.

Finally, the regime stepped up saving campaigns to reduce and bottle up consumption in the future. Deposits with German banks doubled between 1932 and 1939. Saving was not only propagated as a national duty but also as a means of securing more consumption. This element of enticement explains the regime's success in convincing people to postpone purchases and to entrust their money to banks instead. The Nazi government profited in two ways. First, immediate demand for consumer goods was restricted to the benefit of the already overburdened resource base. Second, people's savings could easily be tapped to finance rearmament. Instead of making people subscribe to war loans straightaway, the 'Third Reich' encouraged them to put their money into savings accounts and forced the banks to buy Treasury bills or to take up long-term loans of the government. Savers became indirect creditors of the Reich without knowing it. Therefore, in contrast to circumstances during the First World War, no public anxieties were aroused. One of the main reasons for political stability was the fact that people did not realize that their assets were gradually expropriated. Price and wage controls

Figure 8.3   Savings Bank Advertisment 'Erst Sparen – Dann Kaufen, 1939

Source: Deutscher Sparkassenverlag, *Wer den Pfennig nicht ehrt: Plakate werben für das Sparen* (Stuttgart: Sparkassenverlag 1992), p. 67.

prevented inflationary pressure caused by the Reich's ruthless expansion of the money supply from becoming visible as yet.[51] Higher levels of consumption seemed to be possible in the near future, and the regime did everything to foster this illusion. The currency reform of 1948 finally wiped out most of the deposits, and savers learnt that the regime's *virtual consumption* turned out to be a fraudulent deception.

In 1938 advertisements used the motto 'Savings make buying easy' or 'Money saved – dreams fulfilled'. In one poster the savings bank appeared as a castle to convey the idea that deposits were safe for ever. From the bank led a road to a sports car, a sailing boat, a motorcycle, a modern kitchen, a sewing machine, a radio and a garden table. In 1939 a similar poster gave the following order: 'Saving comes before buying.' Golden rays radiated from a money-box pointing to a circle of consumer goods, among them a luxury living room with radio and a suburban house. The regime knew that appealing to people's material desires was more effective than political arguments. Thus it used promises of boundless consumption in the future to make people finance an unrealistic war effort. In other words, savers were systematically deceived by a regime recklessly playing with their dreams. Nothing illustrates better the perverse interaction of enticement and deprivation which was so characteristic of National Socialism.

51. Boelcke, *Kosten*; P. Thomes, 'Sparen und Sparsamkeit im Nationalsozialismus – Gedanken zur Pervertierung einer Institution', *Zeitschrift für bayerische Sparkassengeschichte*, 10 (1996), pp. 63–81.

9

Negotiating Consumption in a Dictatorship: Consumption Politics in the GDR in the 1950s and 1960s

Philipp Heldmann

'Social scientists', Charles Maier recently remarked, 'find it difficult to accept that coercive regimes may rest on general acceptance and sometimes enthusiasm.'[1] In the case of East Germany, consumption politics may help to understand this phenomenon.[2] Much recent writing on consumption in the German Democratic Republic (GDR) meticulously tries to keep politics out.[3] Research on government, to the contrary, often neglects consumption. This is particularly true of works driven by the recent re-emergence of totalitarianism theory[4] which tends to overlook the population, merely regarding it as the object of manipulation by a vile and more or less omnipotent regime. Even scholars who do focus on the links between the

1. C.S. Maier, *Dissolution: The Crisis of Communism and the End of East Germany* (Princeton: Princeton University Press, 1997), p. 51. Many thanks to Hartmut Berghoff, Mark Landsman, Hans-Peter Ullmann and Claire Venghiattis who commented on various versions of this chapter. The usual disclaimer applies. I am grateful to the Studienstiftung des deutschen Volkes for generously supporting my PhD project, which deals with consumption politics in the 1960s.

2. Cf. K. Jarausch, 'Realer Sozialismus als Fürsorgediktatur. Zur begrifflichen Einordnung der DDR', *Aus Politik und Zeitgeschichte, Beilage zu der Wochenzeitung Das Parlament* B 20/98, pp. 33–46, esp. p. 41.

3. Cf. Neue Gesellschaft für Bildende Kunst (ed.), *Wunderwirtschaft. DDR-Konsumkultur in den 60er Jahren* (Köln et al.: Böhlau, 1996) and I. Merkel, *Utopie und Bedürfnis. Die Geschichte der Konsumkultur in der DDR* (Köln et al.: Böhlau, 1999).

4. For a discussion primarily in the context of GDR history, cf. R. Jessen, 'DDR-Geschichte und Totalitarismustheorie', *Berliner Debatte Initial*, no. 4/5 (1995), pp. 17–24; for a discussion of the concept's decline and its shortcomings in the context of Soviet history cf. M. Hildermeier, 'Interpretationen des Stalinismus', *Historische Zeitschrift* 264 (1997), pp. 655–74. For a recent attempt to revive totalitarianism theory not just politically but also intellectually, cf. C. Boyer, 'Die Sozial- und Konsumpolitik der DDR in den sechziger Jahren in theoretischer Perspektive', in C. Boyer and P. Skyba (eds), *Repression und Wohlstandsversprechen: Zur Stabilisierung von Parteiherrschaft in der DDR und der CSSR*, Berichte und Studien Nr. 20 (Dresden: The Hannah-Arendt-Institut für Totalitarismusforschung, 1999), pp. 37–48. Unsurprisingly, Boyer restricts his research here to the development of various concepts and does not discuss their (at best marginal) influence on the policies that were actually implemented.

population and the regime usually pay only scant attention to consumption.[5] In contrast, I shall argue that consumption politics permit a close look at how the regime worked and how it built ties to the population.

Other contributors to this volume demonstrate how consumers as citizens have gained substantial influence in very different political systems. Lizabeth Cohen in Chapter Ten shows how consumer consciousness was a mobilizing force for consumer citizens in the USA and how it shaped the political economy of a capitalist democracy. Authoritarian regimes, in contrast, provide their leaders with far more control over the economy; and this means politicians will be more easily held responsible for problems regarding consumption. Accordingly, one might expect a strong impact of consumer consciousness on the political economy of these states, too. Hartmut Berghoff in Chapter Eight demonstrates that this holds true for the 'Third Reich'. Consumption was an important focal point of anti-state grumbling and thus set limits to Hitler's power. These conflicts re-emerged in the 1950s and 1960s, when the majority of East Germans were experiencing their second dictatorship in succession.

The GDR was a dictatorship erected by the Soviet Union on only part of the pre-Second World War German state and which lacked popular legitimacy.[6] There was, from the beginning, another German state at its Western border, freer, larger and wealthier. To some extent, the existence of the West German state made ruling in the GDR also easier: those who were in principle opposed to communism could and frequently did leave the GDR. Even after the wall was built to stop the mass flight, the regime expelled many of its opponents to the West. This may be one reason why, compared with the rulers of the Soviet Union or Romania, the East German dictatorship needed to apply relatively little brute force. Still, the GDR developed very efficient repressive organs. The regime remained highly concerned about even non-political unrest, fearing this might trigger off political debates about the legitimacy of the GDR and the efficiency of its economy.

West Germany may have helped to stabilize the GDR in one regard; in another, it confronted the East German regime with an unattainably high standard. Germans in both the East and the West increasingly compared both states according to the levels of consumption each offered to its respective citizens. To some extent, this comparison was even justified from a communist perspective: as a centrally planned economy was supposedly more efficient than a capitalist market economy, the former should have also been able to provide for a higher level of consumption than the latter.

5. Cf. M. Fulbrook, *Anatomy of a Dictatorship: Inside the GDR, 1949–1989* (Oxford: Oxford University Press, 1995); R. Bessel and R. Jessen (eds), *Die Grenzen der Diktatur: Staat und Gesellschaft in der DDR* (Göttingen: Vandenhoeck & Ruprecht, 1996); T. Lindenberger (ed.), *Herrschaft und Eigen-Sinn in der Diktatur: Studien zur Gesellschaftsgeschichte der DDR* (Köln et al.: Böhlau, 1999).

6. Cf. Fulbrook, *Anatomy, passim*, e.g. p. 285.

Consumption was of great relevance to the population, while it hardly figured in the ruling party's ideology. Accordingly, the regime was far more prone to compromise on this subject than on issues such as freedom of the press or the educational system. Obstacles to higher levels of consumption arose more often from economic than from ideological constraints. Economic growth and high levels of consumption were seen as irreconcilable in the short term. Growth seemed to require high investment, a tight money supply, and priority for capital- and producer-goods industry with regard to investments and raw materials. To increase consumption in the short term, it was thought necessary to decrease investments, raise incomes and give priority to the consumer goods industry. Only in the long run would growth be a precondition for consumption.

This brief outline shows the importance of practical problems of consumption to the GDR regime. Exploring this phenomenon, I propose to interpret consumption politics as a series of negotiations. Negotiations will be examined on various levels: between the population and the party leaders; between the population and the regime on a local level; and within the state and party apparatus. The term 'negotiations' is used in a wide sense. It covers not just bargaining, but also reformulating compromises and arrangements and adapting them to changing circumstances – a process that requires consensus. It does not imply equal negotiating partners. Consumption politics as defined here encompasses the regulation of income, supply and prices, which are considered in turn in the next three sections.

Income

Of those gainfully employed, the majority worked in the manufacturing industry. Hence wages and premiums in this sector of the economy were the most important single factor determining the population's income. The regime's initial optimistic hopes to keep these payments under tight control were effectively quashed on 17 June 1953.

The tensions leading to this had been building up at latest since the foundation of the GDR in 1949. War damages, reparations and the inherent flaws of the centrally planned economy had led to a less than impressive economic performance, with a correspondingly low standard of living.[7] The second party conference of the Socialist Unity Party (SED) in July 1952 produced a further turn for the worse. The party intensified its focus on heavy industry and tried to overcome the private

---

7. Cf. *Ibid.*, pp. 177–87; D. Staritz, *Geschichte der DDR: Erweiterte Neuausgabe* (Frankfurt am Main: Suhrkamp, 1996), pp. 127–36. For the economic background, see C. Buchheim, 'Wirtschaftliche Hintergründe des Arbeiteraufstandes vom 17. Juni 1953 in der DDR', *Vierteljahreshefte für Zeitgeschichte* 38 (1990), pp. 415–33.

ownership of means of production through collectivization and expropriation. Other costly policies required tax and price increases. All this raised the number of refugees fleeing to the West, sent the production of foodstuffs and industrial consumer goods into a tailspin and caused widespread popular unrest in the first half of 1953.

To enhance productivity, the regime had earlier begun to discard notions of equality and had reintroduced financial incentives for workers. As a result, wages grew faster than predicted. Together with shortages in consumer goods, this led to a growing monetary overhang which threatened to build up inflationary pressure. To counter this problem and to raise productivity, the regime sought to raise work norms – thereby effectively cutting premiums for the overfulfilment of plans. In May 1953, a 10 per cent rise in work norms was announced, due to come into effect by the end of June. Work norms determined how much people had to work in a given time-span. Workers who overfulfilled these norms were eligible for financial incentives. A rise in work norms, intended not least to raise productivity, diminished the leeway for overfulfilment and hence frequently led to lower incomes. This meant economic stabilization at the expense of workers' income, thereby adding to a growing stock of social grievances.

Reports about the developments in the GDR caused the Kremlin leaders to intervene. The East German politburo had to admit publicly that it had made 'a series of mistakes'[8] and promulgated a 'New Course', a programme to raise the standard of living and to increase the rule of law – that is, to reduce the arbitrary use of power at least to some extent. One item that was surprisingly not addressed was work norms – probably because the politburo did not know about the extent of unrest on the shop floor. The open admission of mistakes and omission of the question of the work norms combined to trigger off a revolt. Even loyal communists found it hard to understand such an abrupt policy change, and workers were infuriated. The revolt was started by Berlin construction workers but spread all over the republic, eventually encompassing the entire society. Soon economic protests turned into quests for more general political change and even for the communists' resignation. The SED managed to remain in power only with the help of Soviet tanks. As a result of the revolt, the rise of the work norms had to be reversed, wages were increased and prices reduced. In addition, thousands of people who had been involved in the uprising were arrested. Unsurprisingly, this disaster led to furious discussions in the politburo, with most members demanding that the party leader Walter Ulbricht resign. His political survival was solely due to the policy change of the USSR.

---

8. The communiqué is reprinted in A. Herbst, G-R. Stephan and J. Winkler (eds), *Die SED: Geschichte-Organisation-Politik. Ein Handbuch* (Berlin: Dietz, 1997), pp. 603–5.

The bitter lesson for the population was that the regime could hardly be overthrown as long as the Kremlin was determined not to let that happen. For the regime, the event had been truly traumatic: a fierce demonstration of how fragile its power was, how dependent it was on Soviet force and how little support it commanded from the population. Repressive organs alone were not sufficient to remain in power in the long run. The communists had to seek some kind of consensus with at least part of the population. To be more specific, the politburo learned to fear discontent about the standard of living for, as had been the case in 1953, it could unexpectedly turn into a full-blown revolt. The crucial importance of these developments for relations between the population and the regime in the GDR is captured in their description as the 'inner foundation of the state'.[9]

In the following years, the SED leaders hardly dared to venture on further experiments with the wage system. Rather than reforming the system as a whole, piecemeal changes were made. The wage system became more complex and less susceptible to central control. The power to determine wages thus shifted increasingly from the politburo to the shop floor, resulting in fewer and fewer obstacles to rising incomes. As labour was in short supply, the companies often competed for workers and soft budget constraints meant these companies could not fail. Their main concern was not to be efficient but to fulfil the production plan, which emphasized gross production and neglected cost. An investigation ordered by the state planning commission described the situation as follows: 'Among the workers and employees dominates a very wide-spread "consumer viewpoint". This finds expression in extraordinarily strong pressure from below for higher earnings. Many managers avoid this pressure by yielding to it.'[10] Even if managers did not cede at once, workers commanded substantial leverage. Mary Fulbrook and Peter Hübner have pointed to the persistence of strikes in the history of the GDR.[11] Dissatisfaction with wages or work norms were common causes for strikes. These strikes were normally confined to a single factory. They were effective not because they were costly for the employers but because they could also cause trouble for local functionaries if reported to the upper echelons. Wages thus mostly grew faster than planned, albeit not at the same pace in all industries. This arrangement –

9. I.-S. Kowalczuk, A. Mitter and S. Wolle (eds), *Der Tag X 17. Juni 1953: Die 'Innere Staatsgründung' der DDR als Ergebnis der Krise 1952/54* (Berlin: Links, 1995).

10. Abt. Finanzen, Arbeitsökonomie und Preise [der Staatlichen Plankommission], 9 August 1966, Zusammenfassende Einschätzung aus den Berichten der Genossen Dozenten der Humboldt-Universität, die im Auftrage der Abteilung Finanzen, Arbeitsökonomie und Preise der Staatlichen Plankommission Untersuchungen über die Lohnabweichungen in 7 Betrieben von 3 VVB der Verarbeitungsindustrie durchführten, in Bundesarchiv Berlin (BA) DE-1 VA 47742 (federal archives, Berlin, papers of the state planning commission).

11. Cf. Fulbrook, *Anatomy*, p. 155; P. Hübner, *Konsens, Konflikt und Kompromiß: Soziale Arbeiterinteressen und Sozialpolitik in der SBZ/DDR 1945–1970* (Berlin: Akademie, 1995), pp. 178–210.

political acquiescence in exchange for increasing wages – lasted more or less up to the end of the East German state; there were hardly any serious attempts to terminate this settlement.

The most notable exception from this rule occurred in 1961/62. In the late 1950s, growing political pressure on the population and deteriorating supplies of consumer goods led to a drastic rise in the number of refugees. The Communists hoped that by building the Berlin wall to stop this mass exodus, the population would be forced to acquiesce. Wages were frozen or even cut, norms and prices were raised.[12] This did not help to solve the country's economic problems, and the crisis that had augmented the emigration beforehand persevered. In 1963, the SED launched a reform programme that included improved incentives, but the following year, wages grew faster than planned again. In the long run, the economy's need for labour combined with the party's need for acquiescence successfully undermined any attempts at regulating wages more effectively and cancelling the 1953 arrangement.

The income of some other groups such as craftsmen and the few remaining entrepreneurs was linked to their performance. Farmers in co-operatives were paid according to their co-operative's output, an incentive introduced after the crisis following the forced collectivization in 1959–60. Together with the wages and premiums of industrial workers, this implied substantial imponderables in planning the population's income. Frequently, income grew faster than expected. The regime often tried to slow down this development to ease inflationary pressure. This regularly occurred at the expense of groups who commanded little negotiating power. Women, for instance, generally had lower wages and often fewer holidays than men. Families with children and particularly pensioners are other cases in point: plans to improve their meagre benefits were repeatedly delayed or cancelled.

Supply

Before turning to the planning process and the implementation of the plans, I shall briefly outline some peculiarities of the regulatory system for the consumer goods industry. In the 1950s and 1960s, the property rights structure of this sector differed from that of other industries in the GDR insofar as it permitted relatively little central control. In the textile and furniture industries, for instance, centrally planned state-owned companies were a minority. Small companies dominated: many of

---

12. Cf. SPK, Hauptabteilung Perspektivplanung, Sektor Grundfragen des Lebensstandards, 23 November 1962, Information über die Entwicklung der Kaufkraft und deren Realisierung bis zum 31. Oktober 1962, in BA DE–1 VA 38417 and letter Eckhardt to Mewis, 19 November 1962, Konzeption über die Grundrichtung der Entwicklung des Lebensstandards bis 1970, with enclosure Grundrichtung und Probleme der Entwicklung des Lebensstandards bis 1970, in *ibid.*

them were private or semi-private, and the state-owned firms were frequently locally planned. Agriculture, however, was subject to ruthless collectivization in two waves, namely 1952–53 (interrupted because of the unrest) and then again from 1959 to 1960. For the communists, the aim of abolishing private ownership of the means of production was not negotiable. The schedule, however, was hardly strict. The regime first focused on large companies and on the investment-goods industries as, from a Stalinist viewpoint, the consumer-goods industries seemed decidedly less important.

All industries, however, regardless of their alleged relevance, were subject to both long-term and short-term planning. Long-term plans normally covered a period from five to seven years. They were less precise than the plans for single years and contained a declaration of the regime's economic aims rather than the precise means to attain these aims. Following political changes, these plans were sometimes altered. After 17 June 1953, for instance, the regime started to increase wages as well as the production and import of consumer goods to pacify the population. Less than two years later, these consumerist policies were held responsible for the growing monetary overhang and the increasing strain on the East German balance of payments. The ensuing policy change was embodied in the Second Five Year Plan 1956–60 which was supposed to promote economic growth (especially in the machine-building industry) at the expense of consumption. This plan was drafted in 1955 and 1956, but passed only in 1958, when it was all but obsolete. For at that time, the regime decided to tackle mass emigration, one of its most pressing problems.[13] Every year, hundreds of thousands fled to the West. The steadily rising standard of living in West Germany contributed substantially to this mass exodus. Family connections and friendships linking both German states provided a steady flow of information. Moreover, West German radio (later also television) programmes and commercials could be received almost everywhere in the GDR and painted a vivid picture of abundance.

Encouraged by a seeming political and economic stabilization, the SED proclaimed a new ideological offensive at the fifth party convention in June 1958. They wanted to resume, though treading more carefully, the policies that had brought about such disastrous results when taken up for the last time in 1952. The second key issue of the convention, the 'economic main task', remains somewhat mysterious: the East German economy was to prove the superiority of socialism by raising per capita consumption of foodstuffs and consumer goods above West German levels. A few weeks later, Ulbricht vowed to reach this goal by 1961. The importance of consumption was thus publicly acknowledged, together with the significance of West Germany as the bench-mark. Per capita consumption became

13. Cf. M. Lemke, *Die Berlin-Krise 1958 bis 1963: Interessen und Handlungsspielräume der SED im Ost-West-Konflikt* (Berlin: Akademie, 1995).

the professed touchstone of socialism. The intention was no doubt to cut down emigration, but what makes this bold promise so incongruous is that Ulbricht must have known it would be completely unrealizable. He knew how feeble the East German economy still was and how much productivity still lagged behind West German standards. The belief in the ideology must have carried him away. It remains uncertain whether consumption was supposed to make up for the hardships of the ideological offensive or whether both should together shape an ever more attractive socialist state.

The ideological offensive only gathered pace in the following year. Pressure on a range of social groups was increasing, and forced agricultural collectivization was resumed. Predictably, farmers and members of other pressurized groups fled in droves yet again, and agricultural production dropped sharply. Soon, it became obvious how unrealistic Ulbricht's promise had been. The number of refugees soared from 144,000 in 1959 to almost 200,000 in 1960 and did not stop there. Within the first two weeks of August 1961 alone, over 47,000 people left the GDR resulting in a total loss of population of 15 per cent since the East German state was founded in 1949. Most of these refugees were young and skilled, and the economic and political damage of this exodus can hardly be exaggerated. The most important among the manifold reasons for emigration was the West's higher standard of living, or, in other words, the hardships of everyday life in the GDR, though political motives and increasingly the fear of a close-down of the border played an important role as well. Promising higher standards of consumption to stop people from leaving the country was obviously no longer viable, and so increasing concerns both in Moscow and in East Berlin led to the decision to stop this mass exodus with brute force. In the night of 12 August 1961, the SED erected the Berlin wall – or, as they cynically called it, the 'anti-fascist protective ramparts'. The balance of power suddenly appeared to have shifted markedly. Concessions to the population seemed no longer necessary. Wages were frozen or even cut, norms and prices were raised. The main goal now was to raise investments to make up for the previous years. This shows quite clearly how the threat of emigration had forced the regime to grant levels of consumption that were higher than the regime considered economically wise.[14]

Long-term planning now emphasized the need for higher investments. The seven-year plan of 1959, still in the mode of pre-Wall consumerism, was abandoned and a new plan was drafted. As usual, this new plan had to be co-ordinated with the USSR. The head of the East German state planning commission reported the Kremlin's view to the politburo on his return from Moscow. There were no longer

---

14. Cf. for example, Ulbricht's remarks during the party convention in 1963: *Protokoll der Verhandlungen des VI. Parteitages der SED*, vol. 1 (Berlin: Dietz, 1963), pp. 69–70.

reproaches against a wasteful 'consumer ideology'[15] as in the past; on the contrary, the Soviets had doubts about the planned cutbacks in consumer-goods supply. But such an abrupt policy change away from consumerism, which moreover coincided with the consequences of forced agricultural collectivization, was not easily implemented. The regime did manage to reduce consumption but, significantly, it failed to put the resulting spare resources to use for higher investments. The economy had come to a crisis before the building of the wall; but in 1962, it reached rock-bottom. The need for reform was obvious even to the regime.

In 1963, the SED seemed indeed to be set for a new departure. Seemingly liberal reforms in economic, youth and cultural policy got under way.[16] The economic reforms focused on decentralization and stressed indirect control through financial levers. The new economic policy and the new long-term plan of 1963 still pursued the aim of raising investment at the expense of consumption, albeit at a slower pace than before. This new plan for the years up to 1970, now called 'the Perspective Plan', was reformulated and developed in the following years. Besides difficulties arising from the inherent flaws within the reforms, it left the consumption planners with the frustrating role of listing shortages and distributing what they recognized as being too little. As one member of the relevant group in the state planning commission put it in early 1965: 'One gets the impression that only the leftovers are earmarked for the standard of living.'[17]

The balance of power had perceptibly shifted after the erection of the Berlin wall, since people could no longer flee to the West. However, this shift was limited, as the memory of 17 June 1953 remained vivid and the regime still needed to provide incentives for workers. This implied not just rising wages, but also supplying consumer goods which covered, at least to some extent, a growing demand. Long-term planning followed this line throughout the 1960s.

Thus the SED party convention of 1967 introduced a new focus on technological innovation in a few producer- and investment-goods industries, mostly in the chemical industry and in machine-building. These selected industries were to accelerate growth in the entire economy and were to be modernized with first-rate machines and raw materials, stretching the GDR import capacity and raising its

15. 1 June 1962, Niederschrift des mündlichen Berichtes, den Genosse Mewis am 22.5.1962 in der Sitzung des Politbüros über den Stand der Verhandlungen in Moskau gegeben hat, in BA DE-1 VA 38417.

16. For the economic reforms, cf. A. Steiner, *Die DDR-Wirtschaftsreform der sechziger Jahre: Konflikt zwischen Effizienz- und Machtkalkül* (Berlin: Akademie, 1999); for the reforms in youth and cultural politics, cf. M. Kaiser, *Machtwechsel von Ulbricht zu Honecker: Funktionsmechanismen der SED-Diktatur in Konfliktsituationen 1962 bis 1970* (Berlin: Akademie, 1997), pp. 133–231.

17. Horst Werner was the head of a department in the people's economic council (the government body in charge of the manufacturing industry), responsible for the production of consumer goods [Sektorenleiter im Volkswirtschaftsrat]. This quote is from Übersicht über Fragestellungen, persönliche Meinungen usw. zum Programm Lebensstandard, in BA DE–1 VA 43570.

foreign debt. This implied further cuts in consumption's share of GDP, and a reduction in investment and raw materials for the consumer-goods industry. To attain the required levels of investment and still maintain a growing standard of living, the planners had to assume productivity growth rates that were more than optimistic. The ambitious plans of the late 1960s failed unambiguously – the only target which was easily met was an increase in foreign indebtedness. This contributed to Ulbricht's fall in spring 1971, together with his efforts at gaining more room for manoeuvring vis-à-vis the USSR and the attempted rapprochement with West Germany (both policies were unpopular with hard-liners in the politburo). Supply problems since 1969 and the ensuing unrest in the population did not help Ulbricht either.

His successor, Erich Honecker, started out with a keen sense for power but with little understanding of economic policy.[18] Only the former changed over time. By 1971, the planning bureaucracy's waning influence over the economy, supply problems and the increasing monetary overhang had led to a consensus in the politburo that radical changes in economic policy were needed. Without prior consultation with the state planning commission, Honecker drafted an economic programme in which he asserted that the main goal must now be to raise the population's standard of living. The specifics of this plan were not calculated until after the next party convention, where Honecker's two-fold agenda was confirmed: the dissolution of the economic reforms of the 1960s and an emphasis on a higher standard of living. While these two policies might have appeared contradictory to economists, since the former was bound to cut growth in the long run and the second actually required higher growth, from Honecker's perspective they made perfect sense as both were geared towards more control. Recentralization of the economy was to provide the planning bureaucracy with more authority, and more consumption was to increase the population's loyalty. 'You can never rule against the workers!' was how he put it. The shift of power after the construction of the wall proved only temporary. Consumption had made its way to the top of the political agenda.

If long-term plans were a means to formulate rather than to implement strategies in economic policy, there is much less doubt about the importance of the yearly plans. They focussed on production, investment and exports. Planning consumption was difficult even in the post-war years up to the late 1950s, when many goods were still rationed. When the last rationing measures were lifted in May 1958, post-war hardships had mostly been overcome. But people were now free to

---

18. For consumption politics under Honecker, cf. P. Skyba, 'Die Sozialpolitik der Ära Honecker aus institutionentheoretischer Perspektive', in Boyer and Skyba (eds), *Repression*, pp. 49–62, and his unpublished paper: P. Skyba, 'Sozialpolitik und SED-Herrschaft in der DDR der Ära Honecker'. Vortrag im Institut für Zeitgeschichte, Außenstelle Berlin am 14. Juli 1999. Many thanks to Peter Skyba for letting me have this paper.

purchase whatever was offered. Planning what and how much the population would buy proved extremely difficult. The central tool for planning consumption developed in the early 1960s was the balance of the population's income and expenditures or BEAB (*Bilanz der Geldeinnahmen und –ausgaben der Bevölkerung*). The BEAB consisted of huge tables that estimated all the different components of income and expenditures. Based on the plan's other data, the BEAB themselves served only as an internal tool and were never approved. Many of the data from the BEAB were discussed and agreed with other institutions such as the ministry of finance, the state bank and the ministry of trade and provisioning. On this basis, the latter drafted a provisioning or supply plan, trying to raise as high as possible the funds available for consumption. Its reason was that growing stocks caused trade officials much less trouble than shortages. But the ministries for the different manufacturing industries and for agriculture drafted their supply plans, too. They tried to keep their obligations as low as possible. For the ministries tried to obtain targets they could easily overfulfil, even though they focused on exports which had a higher priority. However, the link between the industry ministries' production plans and the ministry of trade and provisioning's supply plan was only indirect, as each used a different planning scheme.

The supply plans were repeatedly amended during their implementation, frequently without these changes being sanctioned. In most years, this procedure was necessary because the population's income rose faster than planned, leading to shortages or higher savings. Normally, higher earnings provided the ministry of trade and provisioning with the leverage to obtain a rise in supply, a procedure which can be described as a negotiating process within the regime, or within the state and party apparatus. Frustrated trade officials who had too little to sell also exerted pressure. In the winter of 1967, for instance, most of the textile wholesale trade in the GDR refused to buy any men's clothes at all for the next season.[19] They claimed that what the industry had to offer was too little and of unacceptably bad quality. With this, the wholesale trade forced additional fabric imports and a delay of exports of clothes. Besides these internal negotiations, the population could and frequently did write letters of complaint. Yet besides exceptional crises, when their sheer number gave these letters more influence, they drew attention merely to very specific cases of shortage. A loyal citizen would get his leather jacket or a county an extra allotment of cube sugar, but this required no fundamental changes of the overall economic plan.

Informal and inconspicuous changes to the plan helped to cope with minor problems. But the major disasters that were a recurrent feature of consumption politics in the GDR required other strategies. Two approaches are discernible: one

19. Cf. P. Heldmann, 'Konsumpolitik in der DDR: Jugendmode in den sechziger Jahren', in H. Berghoff (ed.), *Konsumpolitik. Die Regulierung des privaten Verbrauchs im 20. Jahrhundert* (Göttingen: Vandenhoeck & Ruprecht, 1999), pp. 135–59, this incident on p. 140.

was to plan in more detail, the other was to include further regulatory institutions in the process of working the plan out and implementing it. During the supply crisis following the forced agricultural collectivization after 1959, quarterly supply plans were introduced which complemented the yearly plans. A decade later, after Ulbricht's fall, quarterly plans had long since been abandoned; instead, yearly plans were specified to contain far more items. In both crises, leading politicians had to pay more attention than usual to supply problems. These topics now featured regularly on the agenda of the central committee's secretariat and of the council of ministers (i.e. the government). Sometimes, ad hoc committees were appointed to deal with the problems. In the end, the party leaders had only limited control and could not quite implement the intended growth policies, as growing incomes gave substantial leverage to demands for more consumer goods.

Prices

Nobody knows how to set prices in a centrally planned economy. This is not exactly a new insight, but it may help to understand the awkwardness of the SED in this area. Prices in market economies ideally reflect scarcity – that is, the relation of supply and demand. They are both a means to allocate everything in the market, from raw materials and machines to consumer goods, and an important source of information as high prices indicate where money can be made, and what can successfully be produced and sold. Prices in socialism, by contrast, are supposed to reflect cost. The information contained in market prices seems to be hard, if not impossible, to substitute in planned economies, which constitutes a major problem in those systems. Allocation is the task of the plan, not of the market (and hence prices). Economically, prices are therefore supposedly far less important in planned economies than in market economies. Politically, though, they often remain a key issue.

In the GDR, the regime promised its population that stable prices were a feature of the planned economy. Inflation as a capitalist vice was declared conquered. This policy of low and stable prices for consumer goods featured prominently in propaganda. It focused on three sorts of goods. First and most important were basic mass-consumption goods. This notion was not very clearly defined but included rents and many foodstuffs such as bread, for instance. Second, certain goods were kept cheap for reasons of social policy. Most important here were products for children, especially clothes, as the regime constantly sought to raise the birth rate. Third, prices for books, records and tickets for concerts or the theatre were kept low for reasons of cultural policy – that is, for educational purposes.

Based by and large on a 1944 price stop, prices for new goods were set in relation to existing prices. At first this worked reasonably well for a restricted number of standardized goods, where little change occurred. During the 1950s, however, the price of some raw materials and especially of labour rose. The production of certain goods at the set prices grew more and more difficult and then turned into a loss-making enterprise. The consumer-goods industry, though, was one of the few areas of the economy where the private sector still played a major role and where efficiency remained an immediate concern. Consequently, many of the goods in question such as household articles went out of production, and eventually subsidies were necessary to maintain output. But subsidies entailed firm controls, which made the production of subsidized goods less than appealing for state and privately owned companies alike. Children's clothes were a prominent case in point where recurrent shortages caused equally recurrent complaints. [20]

In addition, the policy of low and stable prices raised expectations that were not always easily met. Popular reaction to price increases could indeed get rather uncomfortable for the SED. For example, in the late 1950s, haberdashery started to disappear from shops because the set margins were so low that selling these articles was no longer profitable. In early 1961, before the building of the Berlin wall, the politburo ordered the government to correct this situation by raising the margins and consequently the prices.[21] The government only discussed this a few days after the erection of the wall. Despite some doubts because of the newly tense situation, price increases were put in place. Popular reaction soon proved these reservations well-founded. Both the sales assistants and the customers were infuriated at the price increases, and more inflation was expected to come. Suspicion arose that this was merely a device to raise money for rearmament – a common topic in the propaganda about a presumed nexus between inflation and militarism in West Germany.[22] Luxury items might be sold at a premium price, others argued, but not haberdashery.[23] Reports about discontent kept coming in from the localities, so that by mid-October the SED retreated, and some of the price increases were reversed.[24] Higher margins were now to be guaranteed through subsidies, though

---

20. Cf. ZK-Abteilung Planung und Finanzen, 27 May 1968, Bemerkungen zu den Vorschlägen des Genossen Halbritter über die Lösung von Problemen der Entwicklung der Einzel-handelsverkaufspreise für Erzeugnisse des Kinderbedarfs, in Stiftung Archiv der Parteien und Massenorganisationen im Bundesarchiv (SAPMO BA) DY30 IVA2/2.021/677 (papers of the SED, office of Günter Mittag).

21. Cf. letter ZK-Abteilung Handel, Versorgung und Außenhandel to Edith Baumann, 29 September 1961, Betr.: Neuregelung der Handelsspanne für Kurzwaren, in: SAPMO BADY30 IV2/6.10/130 (papers of the SED, the central committee's department of trade, provisioning and foreign trade).

22. Cf. telex from the newspaper *Freie Presse*, Zwickau, to the ZK-Abteilung Agitation und Propaganda, 12 October 1961, in *ibid.*

23. Cf. letter from Baender [director of East Berlin's main department store] to SED Kreisleitung Berlin Mitte, 13 November 1961, Betr.: Preisänderungen bei Kurzwaren, in *ibid.*

24. Cf. ZK-Abteilung Handel, Versorgung und Außenhandel to ZK-Abteilung Parteiorgane, ZK-Abteilung Agitation und Propaganda and ZK-Abteilung Planung und Finanzen, 18 October 1961, Betr.: Information über die Preise für Kurzwaren, in *ibid.*

discussions were not to end immediately. Price protests were not uncommon, but this particular case was exacerbated by the generally tense mood after the erection of the Berlin wall. By and large, low prices for basic mass consumption goods were part of a consensus between the party leaders and the population. Developments such as rising prices for raw materials and changing product ranges made frequent modifications necessary. But these adaptations were only possible as long as the population – if tacitly – consented: these prices had to be negotiated.

Prices for many goods were quite stable and low, often well below cost. These prices were financed by high taxes on other consumer goods which were consequently expensive. Here, clothing is a prime example. It remained notoriously difficult to set prices for clothes, which could never be subject to the same rules of standardization that were enforced on necessities such as bread or sugar. The production range was of considerable breadth and changed twice a year. No other group of products caused so much work in the finance administration. Attempts to standardize textile prices failed not least because privately owned companies insisted they would have to stop production if this were implemented. These small capitalist companies were extremely important, as they were almost everywhere in the consumer-goods industry, and the regime was consequently never able entirely to remove them from the economy.[25] Prices were calculated according to guidelines that varied from factory to factory and often dated from the Third Reich. Adding up these cost-oriented producer prices, taxes or (as with children's clothes) subsidies and the trade margins yielded consumer prices. The tax rate varied significantly. Generally speaking, luxury items were supposed to be heavily taxed, but this category changed over time. Synthetic fibres, for instance, were initially deemed a luxury and accordingly heavily taxed, but during the 1960s, these fibres and especially mixtures of synthetics with wool, cotton or rayon became increasingly common. The taxation on these goods was not altered, causing consumer prices to rise considerably. This is only one, albeit important, example of how inflation made its way into the planned economy. Data on inflation in the GDR is rather scarce. Annual rates of 1 to 1.5 per cent in the 1960s are a conservative estimate.[26] Inflation probably increased during this decade, and this may at least in part be due to the new economic policy after 1967 with its higher investments and the ensuing pressure on the national budget. Party leaders had

25. Cf. Staatliche Plankommission, Abt. Koordinierung der Finanzen und Preise, 16 December 1958, Stellungnahme zum Beschluß über den Maßnahmeplan zur Lösung von Grundsatzproblemen auf dem Preisgebiet, in SAPMO BA DY30 IV2/6.08/70 (papers of the SED, the central committee's department of planning and finance).

26. The rise of the consumer-goods supply was occasionally broken down into a rise due to higher quantities and a rise due to higher prices. I have set these figures in relation to annual turnover as reported in the statistical yearbooks. Cf. Ministerium für Handel und Versorgung, Bereich Preise, Zur Entwicklung des EVP-Niveaus (Durchschnittspreise), 23 November 1970, in SAPMO BA DY30 IVA2/6.10/157, and *Statistisches Jahrbuch der DDR 1978*, p. 218.

little control over this tax system. High prices were pushed through by the finance administration, as these functionaries tried to balance the state budget and prevent the monetary overhang from spiralling out of control. By and large, the price system was a complex arrangement that reconciled at least to some extent the seemingly incompatible interests of the population, the party leaders, and other groups within the state and party apparatus.

Many goods were scarce and a number of prices were kept below cost. Even prices that included high taxes were often below market clearing prices, as the continuous shortages in good clothes indicated. Under these conditions, one might expect a flourishing black market where everything was available, albeit at very high prices. And for the first years, there is no question about the existence of a quite classic black market.[27] In West Germany, the currency reform of 1948 had been accompanied by economic liberalization.[28] Many prices were no longer regulated and reflected scarcity. Therefore the black market soon ceased to exist. In East Germany, on the contrary, price regulations and rationing remained in power after the currency reform of 1948. This did not prevent shortages, but left the population with money they could not spend. Unsurprisingly, the black market continued to thrive. It only received a serious blow when the SED decided to take over the black market, just as it took over the rest of the economy. Indeed, a state-run black market existed throughout almost the entire history of the GDR.

It started out with the founding of the Trade Organization or HO (*Handels-organisation*) in 1948.[29] These shops were also called 'free shops', because ration cards were not required for making purchases. Besides goods that were normally rationed, they also offered a range of products that were available only on the black market. The prices in the HO were in the beginning roughly ten to fifteen times higher than the set prices in ordinary shops, but still a little bit lower than prices on the unofficial black market. That is, prices were set at roughly the market rate but without the risk premium.[30] The SED pursued a number of goals in setting up the HO. By introducing an attractive state-owned group of shops, they wanted to start taking over trade from private shop-owners. The SED also aimed at raising productivity: attractive goods were to build up an incentive for workers to work more, earn more and consequently be able to shop at the HO. Finally, the SED tried to soak up the growing monetary overhang. Setting up new shops with high prices made it possible to maintain stable prices in regular shops and to pretend to

27. Cf. J. Roesler, 'The black market in post-war Berlin and the methods used to counteract it', *German History,* 7 (1989), pp. 92–107.

28. For the development in West Germany cf. H. Schröter, 'Konsumpolitik und "Soziale Marktwirtschaft". Die Koexistenz liberalisierter und regulierter Verbrauchsgütermärkte in der Bundesrepublik der 1950er Jahre', in Berghoff (ed.), *Konsumpolitik,* pp. 113–33.

29. Many thanks to Mark Landsman for letting me have a draft of the second chapter of his PhD thesis on consumption policy in the GDR in the 1950s, which deals with the beginnings of the HO.

30. Cf. Roesler, 'Black market', table on p. 95.

keep the promise of overcoming inflation. Popular reaction was mixed. Some enjoyed the new shopping opportunity, while others thought it unfair and even called it a state-run black market.

A black market is normally defined as 'trading in violation of publicly imposed regulations, such as rationing laws, laws against certain goods, and official rates of exchange among currencies',[31] or as 'illicit trade in goods'.[32] The latter definition implies that the black market breaks moral and legal rules alike. The HO qualifies on both areas. Popular moral reservations have already been mentioned. As for legal rules, rationing laws and price restrictions were still in power. The HO enjoyed a special status, so to speak, as a lawbreaker arbitrarily authorized by the regime. In the course of the 1950s, however, rationing was gradually lifted in the entire economy as scarcity in many areas was overcome. Consequently, the HO prices (approximately reflecting scarcity) decreased. When the last rationing measures were lifted in early 1958, the HO lost its special status and continued as a normal retailer.

Two years later, when Ulbricht's grand promise to reach West German standards in levels of consumption had obviously failed, the politburo decided to launch a new luxury retailer. In summer 1961, the first *Exquisit* stores opened.[33] They sold fashionable clothes and shoes at extremely high prices. From the beginning, there were doubts in the SED whether these shops were reconcilable with the socialist way of life. The aim was, once again, to reduce the monetary overhang and raise money, the former to stabilize the currency, the latter to balance the budget. Clothes were an easy means to achieve this as good clothes were still very scarce. Five years later, Exquisit was complemented by *Delikat*, a new chain of luxury food shops.[34] To avoid 'political difficulties', the shops' product range was only gradually broadened to encompass the delicatessen that their name promised. Both shops offered scarce high quality goods, often imported products. Prices were set following special rules, with effective incentives for producers and particularly high taxes.[35] This was a clear violation of pricing laws, but provided for a very real demand.

31. *Encyclopaedia Britannica*, 15th edn (1985), vol. 2, p. 256.

32. G. Bannock, R.E. Baxter and E. Davis, *The Penguin Dictionary of Economics* (Harmondsworth: Penguin, 1992), p. 44. Neither the *New Palgrave* nor its German equivalent, the *Handwörterbuch der Wirtschaftswissenschaften*, has entries for the black market.

33. Most dictionaries, handbooks, etc. claim that the first shops opened only in 1962. This is wrong. See Ministerium für Handel und Versorgung, Entwurf. Entwicklung der Exquisit-Verkaufsstellen, September 1962, in SAPMO BA DY30 IV2/6.10/130, and letter from ZK-Abteilung Handel, Versorgung und Außenhandel to Günter Mittag, 28 September 1962, Betr.: Exquisit-Verkaufsstellen, in SAPMO BA DY30 IVA2/2.021/720.

34. Cf. Ministerium für Handel und Versorgung, 13 April 1966, Bisheriger Stand und weiterer Ablauf der Einrichtung von Feinkostgeschäften in der DDR, in *ibid*.

35. Cf. ZK-Abteilung Planung und Finanzen, 7 July 1971, Information über die bestehenden Regelungen zur Stimulierung von Exquisit-Erzeugnissen, in SAPMO BA DY30 IVA2/6.08/5.

The monetary overhang still increased towards the end of the 1960s, and even more so in the 1970s. High prices were less and less an obstacle for buyers.[36] A proper black market trader could be expected not to offer his goods for such a soft currency anymore. Indeed, the black market for prime consumer goods switched to a hard currency, namely the West German mark. The latest version of the state-run black market were the Intershops, which had existed since 1962. Initially, they were meant to raise hard currency by providing Western-quality goods for Western tourists.[37] In the early 1970s, many East Germans possessed hard currency which they had received from family or friends, or else which they had traded against East German marks from tourists on the unofficial black market. At the same time, the government sorely lacked hard currency – a result not least of the consumer-goods imports that were necessary to fulfil Honecker's programme. Expanding the Intershops and opening them for East Germans in 1974 channelled the population's Western mark straight into the government's coffers.

The finance functionaries promoted this black market just as they pushed through high taxes. They had to cushion the consequences of the planned economy in general and of the price regulation negotiated between the population and the regime in particular. Thus all of these shops, from HO, Exquisit and Delikat to the Intershops, were economic necessities but hardly in tune with the egalitarian aims that the GDR allegedly pursued. The regime was by no means insensitive to this contradiction. The population, too, made it clear that they were well aware of the 'corrosive social effects'[38] of this system. One petition put it like this: 'We cannot contradict the calculation that capitalist society is a two-thirds society. But how do we manage our thirds? One-third Intershop, one-third Delikat and Exquisit, one-third consumer goods that no one will buy.'[39]

Conclusion

What was the outcome of all these negotiations? The long-term result was the rise of consumption to the top of the political agenda in the Honecker years. The short-term result was less clear-cut: the regime did generally manage to depress consumption's share of national income for a considerable time, although neither at the pace nor to the extent they had hoped for. This was no straightforward

36. For example, ZK-Abteilung Leicht-, Lebensmittel- und Bezirksgeleitete Industrie, 22 October 1971, Information über einige Meinungen und Stimmungen zum gegenwärtigen Angebot von Konsumgütern in der Hauptstadt der DDR, p. 2, in SAPMO BA DY30 IVA2/2.021/714.

37. Cf. J.R. Zatlin, 'Consuming ideology: socialist consumerism and the Intershops, 1970–1989', in P. Hübner and K. Tenfelde, (eds), *Arbeiter in der SBZ-DDR* (Essen: Klartext, 1999), pp. 555–72.

38. *Ibid.*, p. 567.

39. This quote after Zatlin, *ibid.*, p. 571.

development, but rather a zigzagging between the pushing through of growth-oriented policies and the granting of concessions to the population. Growth in absolute levels of consumption was achieved through pressure for higher wages which raised demand and then again pressure to meet this demand and keep prices more or less stable.

Three notions guided the regime's policies and popular expectations alike: first, the Western, especially West German model, obvious in Ulbricht's 1958 promise; second, egalitarian ideas discernible in the discomfort with the luxury shops of the state-run black market; and third, the importance of a minimum standard of living which was reflected in cheap prices for basic mass-consumption goods. These three notions are not consistent with each other. A coherent socialist model of consumption did not exist outside academia.[40] There was not even a specialized institution that could have co-ordinated consumption policies. Instead, improvisation predominated throughout the 1950s and 1960s.

Today, the lack of coherence and co-ordination obvious in East German consumption politics may surprise supporters of totalitarianism theory; in the 1950s and 1960s, they provided the leeway that was necessary to deal with diverging interests or, in other words, they made negotiations easier and may thus have helped the regime to attain the 'general acceptance' that Charles Maier referred to, though without much accompanying enthusiasm.

---

40. Cf. P.G. Poutrus, 'Lebensmittelkonsum, Versorgungskrisen und die Entscheidung für den "Goldbroiler"', *Archiv für Sozialgeschichte*, 39 (1999), pp. 391–421.

10

Citizens and Consumers in the United States in the Century of Mass Consumption

Lizabeth Cohen

Just past the end of the twentieth century, we can take stock of what changed most in the hundred years since the previous 'fin de siècle', and find it tempting to point to *things*: automobiles and air-conditioning, television and computers, fast food and shopping malls. Not only are these different from the kinds of thing that Americans lived with a century earlier, but they are better distributed among today's Americans than were their nineteenth-century equivalents. 'Mass' consumption of the abundant fruits of mass production marked America in the twentieth century more obviously than almost anything else. As critics and scholars seek to take measure of this new 'world of things' that transformed American life, moreover, they expand their sight lines to include the multiple contexts surrounding objects of consumption – their production, distribution, acquisition, and use. We learn, for example, how new desires fed by new mass venues for popularizing consumer fantasies – such as advertising, popular magazines and motion pictures – have made mass consumption as influential over the American psyche as the American salary.

What we are just beginning to understand, however, is that mass consumption deeply shaped the most central dimensions of life in the twentieth century, and the American political economy and political culture. Although people's identities as 'citizens' and 'consumers' are often presented as opposites, the former implying an embrace of the larger public interest in the political sphere and the latter concerned with indulging individual wants in the economic sphere, it is becoming clear that no such simple distinction held true over the course of that century. Rather than isolated ideal types, citizen and consumer were ever-shifting categories that sometimes overlapped, other times were in tension, but always reflected the permeability of the political and economic arenas in twentieth-century America. In this chapter I shall attempt to sketch out an emerging map of the way American citizens and consumers together redrew the boundaries of public life during that period in US history.

I shall focus on three watershed periods when, I argue, the connection between citizen and consumer became restructured and hence the place of consumers in American political culture reconceived. Those three eras include the Progressive Era of the late nineteenth and early twentieth century, the New Deal from the early 1930s through the Second World War, and the post-Second World War period. Although these eras are standard chapters in any history of the twentieth century, rarely if ever are they considered as stages in the evolution of a consumerist vision of citizenship and the state.[1]

The consumer burst on the American political landscape as a social category with the rise of Progressivism, and from the 1890s to 1920 most of the ways that consumers would later figure into mainstream political discourse got at least an airing. Progressivism established the centrality of consumers to civic life, even if it failed to secure them a permanent place in public policy. Most crucial was the emergence of a century-long tension between two conceptions – what I call *citizen consumers* and *customer consumers* – the former being consumers who take on the political responsibility we usually associate with citizens to consider the general good of the nation through their consumption, and the latter being consumers who seek primarily to maximize their personal economic interests in the marketplace.

The rise of *citizen consumers* as a new category of the American citizenry can be seen everywhere in the Progressive movement. As David Thelan has demonstrated, turn-of-the-century Wisconsin Progressives identified consumers as an ideal, broad-based constituency for political reform, as all men and women suffered unfairly from high prices, defective products, and unresponsive politicians. Progressive political reformers campaigned for more direct democracy and specific remedies to protect consumers and taxpayers from exploitation, such as municipal and consumer ownership of utilities and fairer tax policies.[2] Kathryn Kish Sklar and others have introduced us to the social reformist National Consumers' League and its state chapters, which organized women consumers to orient their purchasing power toward 'ethical consumption' both to protect themselves as consumers from injurious goods and to lobby for protective labour legislation, child labour laws, and improvements in retail and factory work environments.[3] Lawrence Glickman

1. The analysis in this chapter is drawn from my book in progress, *A Consumers' Republic: The Politics of Mass Consumption in Postwar America* (New York: Alfred A. Knopf, forthcoming).
2. D.P. Thelan, *The New Citizenship: Origins of Progressivism in Wisconsin, 1885–1900* (Columbia: University of Missouri Press, 1972). Richard Hofstadter also made a powerful case for the importance of consumer consciousness in Progressivism: see *The Age of Reform: From Bryan to FDR* (New York: Vintage Books, 1955), pp. 170–3.
3. K. Kish Sklar, 'The Consumers' White Label Campaign of the National Consumers' League, 1898–1918', in S. Strasser, C. McGovern and M. Judt (eds), *Getting and Spending: European and American Consumer Societies in the Twentieth Century* (Washington, D.C.: German Historical Institute, and New York: Cambridge University Press, 1998); K. Kish Sklar, 'Two political cultures

has traced a shift among American workers in their conception of full citizenship from a view emerging out of the artisanal age that rejected wage labour as slavery depriving workers of their freedom as citizens, to a new perspective accompanying the rise of industrial work that championed 'a living wage' adequate to provide an American standard of living for working-class consumers. A fair shake at consumption – through the eight-hour day, government-regulated minimum wages, and union labels – now seemed to promise workers full rights as citizens.[4] And Michael Sandel has elucidated one powerful thrust in the drive for anti-trust legislation, most identified with reformer Louis Brandeis, as an attack on monopoly in order to preserve an America where consumers were best served by small, local, independent, self-governing businesses dedicated to a republican civic ideal.[5] The other effort evident in the Progressive Era but not fully developed until the 1920s when mass consumption really took off aimed at maximizing the market-oriented interests of *customer consumers*. Sandel identifies this other thrust in Progressive Era anti-trust legislating as 'consumerist', as it sought to regulate monopoly out of a commitment not to republican civic ideals but to concerns for cheaper and more efficient production and distribution to benefit consumers.

During the prosperity of the 1920s *customer consumers* took an even more central stage, as hardly anyone worried any more about protecting consumers from producers. Rather, a Republican-dominated Washington felt that the consumers' and manufacturers' joint interests were best served by allowing business to pursue unfettered technological innovations and economic efficiencies; the free market would do the rest to deliver the best quality goods at the cheapest price to *customer consumers*.

The second phase in the evolution of a consumerist political culture emerged over the long reign of the New Deal from the early 1930s through the Second World War, as *citizen consumers* became increasingly viewed as the embodiment of the public interest. In a more sustained way than in the Progressive Era, policy-makers and the general public grew to consider consumers as a self-conscious, identifiable interest group on a par with labour and business whose well-being required attention for American capitalism and democracy to work. Roosevelt forecast in his presidential campaign of 1932 that 'I believe we are at the threshold of a fundamental change in our popular economic thought, that in the future we

---

in the Progressive era: the National Consumers' League and the American Association for Labor Legislation', in L.K. Kerber, A. Kessler-Harris and K. Kish Sklar (eds), *U.S. History as Women's History* (Chapel Hill: University of North Carolina Press, 1995).

4. L.B. Glickman, *A Living Wage: American Workers and the Making of Consumer Society* (Ithaca: Cornell University Press, 1997).

5. M. J. Sandel, *Democracy's Discontent: America in Seach of a Public Philosophy* (Cambridge, Mass.: The Belknap Press of Harvard University Press, 1996).

are going to think less about the producer and more about the consumer'.[6] By the end of his presidency, Roosevelt would preside over a recalibrating of the balance between consumer and producer interests thought necessary to keep a democratic society and capitalist economy viable, through two basic strategies. The first, a political one, involved the empowerment of *citizen consumers* in the institutional infrastructure of the New Deal. The second strategy, an economic one, turned consumers' aggregate purchasing power into a vehicle for pulling the nation out of grave depression.

The incorporation of *citizen consumers* as a voice of the public interest into New Deal agencies began with the National Industrial Recovery Act (NRA), the keystone of the first New Deal's programme for economic recovery, whose basic premise was that codes of fair competition setting minimum prices and wages and maximum working hours would strengthen the buying public. In recognition of consumers' key role in recovery, the NRA administrative structure called for consumers to be represented along with labour and business on NRA code authorities, as well as through a Consumer Advisory Board and, later, a specially appointed consumer representative. Although members of the Consumer Advisory Board often expressed frustration with the business orientation of the code authorities and NRA administrators, they succeeded in 'making consumers' wants known' in the corridors of power. As the sociologist Robert Lynd, who served on the Board, noted, 'It was no secret around Washington as the NRA episode wore on that the consumer representatives . . . embodied this "public interest" in their proposals day in and day out far more nearly than did either of the far bigger and better supported advisory boards representing industry and labor'.[7] Other New Deal agencies also acknowledged consumers as a distinct constituency: the Agricultural Adjustment Administration, the Tennessee Valley Authority, the Rural Electrification Administration, the Federal Housing Administration, the Home Owners' Loan Corporation, the Federal Deposit Insurance Corporation, and the

---

6. Quoted in P. Campbell, *Consumer Representation in the New Deal* (New York: Columbia University Press, 1940), p. 17. For fuller discussion of a consumerist political culture during the New Deal, see my 'The New Deal state and the making of citizen consumers', in Strasser et al. (eds), *Getting and Spending*.

7. R.S. Lynd, 'Forward', in Campbell, *Consumer Representation*, p. 11. On the NRA and specifically the CAB, see Campbell, *Consumer Representation*, pp. 27–88; P. Campbell, *Bringing the Consumer Point of View Into Government* (Greeley, CO: Council on Consumer Information, 1958), pp. 14–17; H. Sorenson, *The Consumer Movement: What It Is and What It Means* (New York: Harper and Brothers, 1941), pp. 14–20; 'The consumer movement', *Business Week* (22 April 1939), p. 45; D.M. Keezer, 'The consumer under the National Recovery Administration', *Annals of the American Academy of Political and Social Science*, 172 (March 1934), pp. 88–97; P.H. Douglas, 'The role of the consumer in the New Deal', *Annals of the Academy of Political and Social Science*, 172 (March 1934), pp. 98–106.

Securities and Exchange Commission.[8] Roosevelt justified his new attention to consumers as 'a new principle in government' that consumers have the right 'to have their interests represented in the formulation of government policy . . . Never before had the particular problems of consumers been so thoroughly and unequivocally accepted as the direct responsibility of government. The willingness to fulfill that responsibility was, in essence, an extension and amplification of the meaning and content of democratic government.'[9] Attentiveness to the consumer also led Congress in the late 1930s to pass the first substantial food and drug regulatory legislation since the Progressive Era.[10]

The second way that consumers came to figure more centrally in the New Deal resulted from the growing conviction that consumers held the present and future health of the American capitalist economy in their hands. As government policymakers increasingly embraced Keynesian economic theory, particularly after the nosedive brought on by the 'Roosevelt depression of 1937–38', government spending to expand consumer demand became the prevailing strategy for hauling the United States out of depression toward renewed economic growth. With the Keynesian revolution, mass consumers through their spending became responsible for high productivity and full employment, whereas a decade earlier that role had belonged to producers. Keynesian attention to consumption, moreover, was expected to breed greater political democracy and economic egalitarianism. As capitalism revived, it promised to bolster democracy as an alternative to communism and fascism. And because dynamic consumer demand was thought to

8. On attention to consumers in New Deal agencies, see Campbell, *Consumer Representation*, pp. 194–261; Campbell, *Bringing the Consumer Point of View*, pp. 17–18; E. Angevine and C.F. Ware, *Effective Consumer Participation in Federal Decision Making* (Washington, DC: National Consumers' League, 1981), pp. 7–9, Erma Angevine Papers, Rutgers Special Collections (Rutgers), Box 6, Folder E-4; R.N. Mayer, *The Consumer Movement: Guardians of the Markeplace* (Boston: Twayne Publishers, 1989), pp. 23–4; P.C. Kelley, *Consumer Economics* (Homewood, Ill.: R.D. Irwin, Inc., 1953), p. 145; W.C. Waite and R. Cassady, Jr., *The Consumer and the Economic Order* (New York: McGraw-Hill, 1949), pp. 124–5.

9. *The Public Papers and Addresses of Franklin D. Roosevelt With a Special Introduction and Explanatory Notes by President Roosevelt*, 3, 'The Advance of Recovery and Reform, 1934' (New York: Random House, 1938), p. 57; G.C. Means, 'The consumer and the New Deal', *The Annals of the American Academy of Political and Social Science*, 173 (May 1934), p. 7.

10. Mayer, *Consumer Movement*, pp. 24–5; Sorenson, *Consumer Movement*, pp. 12–14; M.V. Nadel, *The Politics of Consumer Protection* (Indianapolis: Bobbs-Merrill, 1971), pp. 16–18; 'Business reports to executives on the consumer movement', *Business Week*, 22 April 1939, pp. 44–5; and from the Ruth Lamb Atkinson Papers (Atkinson), Vassar College Special Collections (Vassar): 'The FDA Museum', Box 1, File 1; unidentified speech critiquing Federal Food, Drug, and Cosmetic Act, 1938, Box 1, File 5; U.S. Dept. Of Agriculture, Food and Drug Administration, 'Digest of the New Federal Food, Drug, and Cosmetic Act, June 27, 1938', Box 1, File 5.

depend on a wide distribution of purchasing power, capitalist prosperity for the nation promised greater economic equality for all its *citizen consumers*.[11]

As policy-makers and economists in Washington were paying more attention to consumers, consumers also were asserting themselves as *citizen consumers* cognizant that their own well-being and the nation's were inseparably intertwined. Most dramatically, the New Deal's sudden attention to consumers as the voice of the public interest offered otherwise underrepresented groups – in particular women and African Americans – the opportunity to make new claims on those wielding public and private power in American society.

With the exception of the consumer co-operative and product-testing wings, women made up much of the consumer movement's leadership and rank and file during the 1930s and 1940s. Through existing and newly created organizations that energized tens of thousands of women, they lobbied New Deal agencies and Congress demanding that the federal government provide greater consumer representation and stronger legal protections against corporate abuse. Most visibly, they orchestrated impressive boycotts and other buyers' actions to protest unfair prices and other forms of market exploitation to retailers, distributors, manu-facturers, and government policy-makers, particularly through massive meat boycotts in 1935.[12] Through all these avenues female *citizen consumers* established themselves as the new protectors of the public interest. An early chronicler of the consumer movement claimed, 'Not since the demand for suffrage have women been drawn so closely together on a common issue'.[13] Women's consumer actions in the 1930s went far beyond prices and were co-ordinated on a city-wide and even national level, crossing narrow sub-communities of ethnicity, race, and class. Whether picketing outside their local butcher shops or lobbying Congress for stricter regulation of cosmetics, women had anointed themselves defenders of a safer and more equitable marketplace for the good of the nation.

---

11. A. Brinkley, *End of Reform: New Deal Liberalism in Recession and War* (New York: Alfred A. Knopf, 1995), pp. 65–85, 116–17, 231–35; A. Sweezy, 'The Keynesian revolution and its pioneers: the Keynesians and government policy, 1933–1939', *American Economic Review*, 62 (1972), pp. 116–24; G. Soule, 'This recovery: what brought it? And will it last?' *Harpers*, 174 (March 1937), pp. 337–45; J.K. Galbraith, *The Affluent Society* (Cambridge, Mass.: The Riverside Press, Houghton Mifflin, 1958), pp. 16–18, 96–7; S. Fraser, *Labor Will Rule: Sidney Hillman and the Rise of American Labor* (New York: Free Press, 1991); D. Bell, *The End of Ideology* (Cambridge, Mass.: Harvard University Press, 1988), pp. 75–80.

12. The best secondary work on the housewives' protest is by A. Orleck, 'We are that mythical thing called the public: militant housewives during the Great Depression', *Feminist Studies*, 19 (1993), pp. 147–72 and *Common Sense and a Little Fire: Women and Working-Class Politics in the United States, 1900–1965* (Chapel Hill: University of North Carolina Press, 1995), pp. 215–49. For primary sources, see clippings from the Consumers' Research Papers (CR), Rutgers, Box 30, Consumerism, 'Consumer Boycotts and Picketing, 1931–1951'.

13. 'Business Week reports to executives on the consumer movement', *Business Week*, 22 April 1939, p. 46; Sorenson, *Consumer Movement*, pp. 195–6, also 83–4.

African Americans in the urban North also mobilized as consumers, but they did so in ways unique to their racial situation. By boycotting some merchants while favouring others, organizing co-operatives, and undertaking other kinds of consumer activism, African Americans asserted themselves in the retail marketplace on an unprecedented scale. Faced with devastating economic hardship wrought by the Great Depression, Northern blacks – most of them relative newcomers to the region's cities – had little recourse. They were already enthusiastically exercising the franchise long denied them in the South. And as they were losing jobs in the private sector in record numbers, organizing at the workplace had limited impact until they could join the CIO's larger offensive later in the decade. The Communist Party offered some immediate help against tenant evictions and relief discrimination, but full-fledged membership only appealed to a small minority of blacks. The remaining, and most promising, avenue was African American spending power, which – if properly channelled – could be a powerful club for demanding jobs and fairer treatment from white store owners and for favouring black-owned businesses and co-operatives, whose greater profits would then circulate within black communities. Black residents of every major Northern city and racial leaders of diverse political persuasions recognized over the course of the 1930s the benefits of politicizing African American consumers on a mass scale. From the 'Don't Shop Where You Can't Work' campaigns that mobilized black consumers against job-discriminating white store owners in a chain of cities, to broader drives against bus companies, public utilities, landlords and movie theaters, to support for alternative black-owned co-operatives, blacks looked to the 'double duty dollar' to advance the race while they purchased.[14]

Whereas women consumer activists sought to secure rights as consumers, ranging from lower prices to protective legislation, blacks primarily used consumer power to secure other rights, especially the right to be employed in their own

---

14. For a sample of the relevant sources, see L. Cohen, *Making A New Deal: Industrial Workers in Chicago, 1919–1939* (New York: Cambridge University Press, 1990), pp. 153–4; St- C. Drake and H.R. Cayton, *Black Metropolis: A Study of Negro Life in a Northern City* (orig. published New York: Harcourt, Brace and World, 1945; repr. Chicago: University of Chicago Press, 1993), pp. 84–5, 295–6, 733–4; A. Skotnes, '"Buy where you can work": boycotting for jobs in African-American Baltimore, 1933-1934', *Journal of Social History*, 27 (1994), pp. 735–61; 'Negroes must work', *New Jersey Herald News*, 20 August 1938, reprinted in C.A. Price (ed.), *Freedom Not Far Distant: A Documentary History of Afro-Americans in New Jersey* (Newark: New Jersey Historical Society, 1980), pp. 235-6; V. Johns, 'To boycott or – not to boycott? A. We must have jobs', *The Crisis*, 41 (September 1934), pp. 258, 274; M. Weiss, '"Don't buy where you can't work": an analysis of consumer action against employment discrimination in Harlem, 1934–1940', M.A. thesis, Columbia University, 1941; J. Schwartz, 'The Consolidated Tenants League of Harlem: black self-help vs. white, liberal intervention in ghetto housing, 1934–1944', *Afro-Americans in New York Life and History*, 10 (January 1986), pp. 31–51; R. Lawson with the assistance of M. Naison (eds), *The Tenant Movement in New York City, 1904–1984* (New Brunswick: Rutgers University Press, 1986), pp. 19, 94–102, 114–16, 119–20.

communities. Blacks, too, aimed less at representing some general public interest and winning the federal government's support for their demands than at improving concrete economic conditions in Northern black communities. But like consumer activists more generally, African Americans felt part of their own national effort that put the individual's purchasing power to the service of some broader social good.

The Great Depression kept in check the alternative urge of *customer consumers* to satisfy individual wants regardless of the public interest. But as war production fuelled new prosperity, consumers' desire to spend freely threatened dangerous inflation and shortages, particularly as more and more products became needed for military use. The government's remedy was to encourage savings through war bonds, to expand vastly the reach of the income tax, and to create official wartime agencies, most notably the Office of Price Administration (OPA), to insure that responsible *citizen consumers* willing to sublimate disruptive private interests to the public interest prevailed over self-indulgent *customer consumers*. And for the most part it worked. Despite corporate objections to price controls (for regulating profits), most American consumers supported them as fundamental to mobilizing fairly for war. The OPA itself developed into an expansive bureaucracy run by paid staff in Washington, regional offices and localities and supported by legions of citizen volunteers serving on municipal War Price and Rationing Boards and Consumer Interest Committees.[15] *Citizen consumers* patriotically upholding price control and rationing not only overshadowed black-market-patronizing *customer consumers* on the homefront, but within individuals the commitment to co-operate loyally with wartime restrictions usually won out over the desire to avoid them in order to indulge long pent-up consumer appetites.[16] The remarkable redistribution of income due to wartime employment and market regulation, moreover, only reinforced the sense that the war emergency was promoting the long-held ideal of greater equality in America. Between 1941 and 1944, family income rose by over 24 per cent in constant dollars, with the lowest fifth gaining three times more than the highest fifth, essentially doubling the size of the middle class. Even *Business Week* labelled the war a 'great leveler'.[17]

15. The literature on the workings of the OPA is extensive. For particularly rich material, see CR, Rutgers, Government War Preparation Files and Persia Campbell Papers (Campbell), Consumers' Union Archives (CU), Series 1, Boxes 3 and 4.

16. C.F. Ware, *The Consumer Goes to War: A Guide to Victory on the Home Front* (New York: Funk & Wagnalls, 1942), pp. 1–3, 194–5, 204–5, 235; Campbell, *Consumer Interest*, p. 634; G.H. Gallup, *The Gallup Poll: Public Opinion, 1935–1971*, Vol. 1, 1935–1948 (New York: Random House, 1972), polls for 1940–45; 'The OPA Consumer Advisory Committee, Preliminary First Draft – For Committee Members', Campbell, CU, p. 14.

17. H. Sitkoff, 'The American home front', in B.McL. Ward (ed.), *Produce and Conserve, Share and Play Square: The Grocer and the Consumer on the Home-Front Battlefield during World War II* (Portsmouth, NH: Strawbery Banke Museum, 1994), p. 45; 'The Defense standard of living', *Business Week*, 23 August 1941, p. 60.

As this tension played out from the national policy stage to the family circle, women became even more pivotal on the homefront than they had been in the 1930s when they first agitated on behalf of 'the consumer interest'. Suddenly, women's ordinary responsibilities as chief household purchasers put them in the eye of the storm of war: their recycling of metals made ammunition plentiful, their limited consumption of sugar and shoes fed and dressed the army, their adherence to price controls kept hoarding and inflation down and morale up. Even beyond their responsible behaviour as buyers, rationers and salvagers, moreover, women staffed – and in many places directed – a massive regulation of the retail marketplace that reached into every household and every retail outlet in every municipality. As new rituals for proving patriotic citizenship emerged around obeying and enforcing OPA price, rent, and rationing regulations; participating in recycling, scrap and waste fat drives; planting victory gardens and 'putting up' the home harvest; women presided over and became the embodiment of a gender-specific definition of the 'good citizen'. Women – perceived as the power behind purchasing – shaped and implemented policies that linked the viability of a nation at war to the responsible action of female *citizen consumers*. A popular slogan such as 'Lady, it's your war, win it!' was an invitation to women to assert new female political authority, not just a line on government posters. Even the *Women's Home Companion*, a magazine steeped in traditional gender roles, credited women with 'the job of Economic Director of the Homefront . . . a man-sized job'.[18]

The realm of consumption became so pivotal to the success of the war effort, in fact, that to an even greater extent than during the 1930s it provided a crucial arena in which African Americans would experience – and contest – the discrimination they met in their efforts to participate fully in American life. Although historians have generally rooted the black struggle for 'Double V[ictory]' – freedom at home as well as abroad – in the demand for equality in defence jobs and the military, many of the frustrations voiced by African Americans in wartime revolved around their exclusion from sites of consumption: restaurants, bars, hotels, movie theaters, stores, pools, buses, and other so-called 'public accommodations' (so identified because they supposedly catered to all, whether privately or publicly

---

18. 'She's the key to the wartime market puzzle', *Advertising and Selling* (April 1943), p. 73, quoted in L. Rotskoff, 'Power of the purse: the gendering of consumption during the 1940s and 50s', Paper for American Studies 787a, Yale University, 26 December 1992, p. 21, in my possession; *To Win the War: Home Front Memorabilia of World War II* (Missoula, Montana: Pictorial Histories Publishing Co. Inc, 1995), *passim* and p. 112; Ward (ed.), *Produce and Consume*, *passim*; P. Duis and S. LaFrance, *We've Got A Job To Do: Chicagoans and World War II* (Chicago: Chicago Historical Society, 1992); A. Bentley, *Eating for Victory: Food Rationing and the Politics of Domesticity* (Urbana: University of Illinois Press, 1998); M. Jacobs, 'How about some meat?', *Journal of American History*, 84 (1997), pp. 910–41.

owned).[19] As African Americans embarked on proving themselves loyal Americans on the homefront by heeding the regulations of the OPA or by journeying to new territory north and west as soldiers and defence workers, they constantly met discrimination as consumers. And in a wartime atmosphere where good consumer and good citizen increasingly were intertwined, that unfair treatment in the marketplace took on new political significance. Whereas in the 1930s asserting their rights as consumers was part of a strategy to achieve economic power, in the context of war African Americans recognized that their political equality as citizens was at stake as well. Every time that blacks were kept off the very OPA price boards that they valued as protection against white storekeepers' arbitrary pricing, or were refused service at stores, theaters, or restaurants even when wearing a military uniform and carrying Uncle Sam's green money in their pockets, they found the assumed universality of citizenship as well as the supposed freedom of the free capitalist marketplace violated.[20] As war administrators increasingly moved consumption into the civic realm, African Americans – like women – made it a new ground upon which to stake their claim to fuller political participation. Citizenship came to be defined more broadly during the Second World War to encompass new kinds of political rituals beyond traditional voting and military service, and in the process the potential for political discontent and the grounds for mobilizing against racial discrimination grew. Roy Wilkins of the NAACP articulated how much blacks' wartime rejection in the realm of consumption symbolized for them the full depth of their exclusion when he recounted that 'It is

19. The black newspaper, *Pittsburgh Courier*, launched the 'Double V' campaign in 1942, which called for 'victory over our enemies at home and victory over our enemies on the battlefields abroad'. Quoted by M. Crawford, 'Daily life on the home front: women, blacks, and the struggle for public housing', in D. Albrecht (ed.), *World War II and the American Dream* (Washington, DC: National Building Museum, 1995), p. 110.

20. The sources I have consulted to document violations of blacks' rights as consumers during the war are too voluminous to list here. A sampling includes: 'Analysis of Reports on Negro Participation in the Work of War Price and Rationing Boards', 30 April 1945, National Association of Colored People (NAACP) Papers, Library of Congress (LC), Series II, A462, 'OPA 1945'; F.H. Williams, 'Minority groups and OPA', *Public Administration Review*, 7 (1947), pp. 124–5, including note 5; 'The OPA Consumer Advisory Committee, Preliminary First Draft – for Committee Members', p. 19; 'Asks negro voice in OPA', *New York Times*, 24 August 1942; Drake and Cayton, *Black Metropolis*, p. 753; C.S. Johnson, *Patterns of Negro Segregation* (New York: Harper and Brothers, 1943); Memos to Presidents and Secretaries of NAACP Branches, From Thurgood Marshall, Special Counsel, Subject: Discrimination and Segregation in Theaters, 8 June 1944 and 31 August 1944; 'Moving Picture Theaters', NAACP, LC, Series II, B67, 'Discrimination Theaters, General, 1940–44', and 'Discrimination Theaters, General, 1945–49'; 'What would you do?' column, *New Jersey Afro-American*, 4 April 1943 and 12 June 1943; C.L.R. James, George Bretiman, Edgar Keemer and others, *Fighting Racism in World War II* (New York: Monad Press, 1980), p. 17; 'Soldiers walk out on "Porgy and Bess" co.', *New Jersey Afro-American*, 25 December 1943; Sgt. Harold [?] to NAACP, March 21, 1944, NAACP, LC, Group II, B61, 'Discrimination: Bars, Hotels, Restaurants, 1944'; Memorandum to Mr. Konvitz from Mr. Wilkins, 27 March 1944, NAACP, LC, Group II, B 63, 'Discrimination, General, 1944'.

pretty grim . . . to have a black boy in uniform get an orientation lecture in the morning on wiping out Nazi bigotry and that same evening to be told he can buy a soft drink only in the "Colored" post exchange!'[21]

The end of war and reconversion to peacetime brought the suppressed conflict between the ideals of *citizen consumer* and *customer consumer* to a head and inaugurated a third period when the relationship of consumer and citizen was reconfigured. The immediate post-war struggle over ending or extending price control became the line in the sand that each side – business and its Congressional allies on the one hand and a broad coalition of consumer activists on the other – drew as critical to achieving their respective visions of post-war America. Whereas the corporate champions of *customer consumers* pushed for the full return of free enterprise, functioning in a free market and free of government intervention, the defenders of *citizen consumers* – consumer activists, women, African Americans, organized labour, and some veterans groups – agitated for a post-war order where the state would continue to play a role in regulating the consumer marketplace through price and rent controls, and where the good citizen would continue to be defined as one who consumed responsibly with the general good in mind. By the autumn of 1946, what OPA chief Chester Bowles, fighting for his agency's survival, called 'the battle of the century' came to a close and price control was definitively defeated.[22]

In the wake of that defeat, a new vision of the post-war order began to emerge supported by a consensus of business, labour and government interests, all of whom sought a reconversion strategy that would protect the nation from feared post-war depression and deliver post-war prosperity. Despite vicious fighting over the extension of price controls in 1946, and struggles thereafter over the balance of power in industrial relations, the tautness of government regulation, and the extent of income redistribution through taxation, minimum wage and other policies, a surprisingly wide cast of characters came to settle on the same post-war script. They agreed that economic salvation lay in a vital mass-consumption-oriented economy where good customers devoted to consuming 'more, newer, and better' were in fact good citizens. Out of the wartime conflict between *citizen consumers*, who reoriented their personal consumption to serve the general good, and *customer*

21. R. Wilkins quoted in H. Garfunkel, *When Negroes March: The March on Washington Movement in the Organizational Politics for FEPC* (New York: Antheneum, 1975), p. 23.

22. Bowles's quote in 'Battle of the century', *Time*, 4 March 1946, p. 19. Other representative sources include: 'Should the OPA be continued without restrictions?' *Bulletin of America's Town Meeting of the Air*, 12, no. 2 (9 May 1946), CR, General Files, Government War Preparation, Role of the Consumer, 'OPA, 1946'; 'Price control – good or bad?' *Talk It Over* (Washington, DC: National Institute of Social Relations, 1946); I. Mosher, 'Price control must go!' and C. Bowles, 'Price control must stay?' *Liberty*, 27 October 1946, reprinted by Department of Information, Office of Price Administration, CR, General Files, Government War Preparation, Role of the Consumer, 'OPA 1945–46'.

consumers, who pursued private gain regardless of it, emerged a new post-war ideal of the *customer as citizen* who simultaneously fulfilled personal desire and civic obligation by consuming. As *Bride Magazine* told the acquisitive readers of its handbook for newlyweds, when you buy 'the dozens of things you never bought or even thought of before, . . . you are helping to build greater security for the industries of this country . . . [W]hat you buy and how you buy it is very vital to your new life – and to our whole American way of living.'[23]

Faith in a mass-consumption-driven post-war economy came to mean much more than the ready availability of goods to buy. Rather, it stood for an elaborate ideal of economic abundance and democratic political freedom, both equitably distributed, that became almost a national civil religion from the late 1940s into at least the 1970s. For convenience sake I have dubbed it the *Consumers' Republic*. For at least a quarter century, the ideal of the *Consumers' Republic* provided the blueprint for American economic, social, and political maturation, as well as for export around the globe. The *Consumers' Republic* had many appeals. It promised great prosperity through yoking employment and economic growth to high consumer demand, and it provided a ready weapon in the political struggles of the Cold War, helping the United States to justify its superiority over the Soviet Union both at home and abroad. But perhaps most attractive was the way it promoted the socially progressive end of greater economic equality without requiring politically progressive means of redistributing existing wealth. Rather, an ever-growing economy built around the interconnected dynamics of increased productivity and mass purchasing power, it was argued, would expand the overall pie without reducing the size of any of the portions. When President Truman challenged Americans in 1950 to 'achieve a far better standard of living for every industrious family' within a decade, he characteristically reassured them that 'raising the standards of our poorest families will not be at the expense of anybody else. We will all benefit by doing it, for the incomes of the rest of us will rise at the same time'.[24]

As the *Consumers' Republic* evolved in the post-war period, it brought with it new 'rules of the game' that redefined gender and racial norms. The battle over the survival of the OPA in 1946 set the stage. Pro-price-control forces – overwhelmingly drawn from women, blacks, workers, and reformers – were painted by the victorious opposition as weak, dependent, and feminine, while the proponents of ending governmental regulation of the consumer marketplace portrayed

---

23. *Bride Magazine* quote from B. Harvey, *The Fifties: A Woman's Oral History* (New York: HarperCollins Publishers, 1993), p. 110.

24. 'Address in Pendleton, Oregon', 10 May 1950, *Public Papers of the Presidents of the United States: Harry S. Truman, Containing the Public Messages, Speeches, and Statements of the Presidents, January 1 to December 31, 1950* (Washington, D.C.: United States Government Printing Office, 1951), p. 362.

themselves as strong, independent, and masculine. From there, other structures of the *Consumers' Republic* continued reshaping gender roles to delegitimate the civic authority that women had gained on the homefront in the Second World War. More took place than simply firing women from the well-paying defence jobs that they had held in wartime. In particular, two key pillars of the *Consumers' Republic*'s infrastructure – the GI Bill of Rights and fine-tuning of the mass income tax that had first emerged with the war emergency – favoured men over women, bolstering a male-directed family economy where men disproportionately had access to career training, property ownership, capital and credit, as well as control over family finances. Men thereby became the embodiment of the post-war ideal of *customers as citizens*, limiting their wives' claims.

The chief policy instrument favouring men over women was a powerful new Keynesian programme, the GI Bill, that fulfilled multiple post-war goals at once through a trio of benefits – unemployment pay while looking for a job, tuition and subsistence allowances for further education or training, and loans to purchase homes or farms or to start a business. It also aimed to avoid the economic and political disruption that had followed the First World War. And it jump-started the post-war economy by expanding purchasing power, by injecting new capital into existing institutions ranging from colleges to banks to the housing industry, and by creating higher-earning and homeowning consumers who would make secure credit risks for future buying. Despite a powerful mythology surrounding the GI Bill that celebrates its universality, in fact these tickets to upward mobility – higher education, home mortgages, and capital to found a business – were only available to those who had served in the war, which excluded all non-veterans, but particularly most women. The 2 per cent of military personnel in the Second World War who were female took less advantage of GI benefits than their male counterparts, and discovered they were inferior to men's when they did claim them. Even women who profited through their veteran husbands, sons, and fathers did not share benefits equal to those of the men in their families. So whether in veteran or non-veteran households, women in post-war America found themselves deprived of the GI Bill's backing and thereby forced into new dependencies that limited their life options.[25]

25. The Veterans Administration and Congressional inquiries have created a rich bank of documentation evaluating the workings of the GI Bill for veterans of the Second World War, the Korean War and Vietnam War. Some of the studies I consulted have been published and are available in libraries; others were shared with me by Paul Nehrenberg, Mike Wells, and Diane Hartmann in the Washington headquarters of the Department of Veterans Affairs, and Joe Thompson in the New York Regional Office, to all of whom I am grateful. The following studies, listed in chronological order, have been most useful: Special Issue on Second World War Veterans, *Annals of the American Academy of Political and Social Science* 238 (March 1945); Reports and Statistics Service, Office of Controller, Veterans Administration, 'VA Benefits to World War II Veterans, 1945–1950: A Study of Participation by World War II Veterans in the Major Veterans Administration Programs during the Five Years after

The other major federal policy that set new gender rules for the *Consumers'* *Republic* was the institutionalization of the mass income tax which had debuted during the Second World War. The demands of financing the war and restraining inflation had moved the government to broaden the taxpayer base far beyond the wealthy few who had been paying since the adoption of income tax in 1913. Whereas only 7 million Americans filed income tax returns in 1940, by 1945 more than 42 million did. In 1948, and less dramatically in 1951 and 1954, Congress passed amendments to the tax code that adapted wartime tax policies to post-war normalcy, articulating the fiscal underpinnings of the *Consumer's Republic*. Less progressive than in wartime, when the income tax contributed to the general narrowing of the income gap, revised post-war tax codes reflected the general commitment of the *Consumers'Republic* to spread affluence through a prospering economy, not through extensive redistribution of income. In terms of establishing new gender norms, the Internal Revenue Code as amended reinforced the GI Bill in favouring the traditional male-breadwinner-headed family and the male citizen within it. Congress's adoption of the income-splitting joint return in 1948 favoured traditional married couples where the wife did not work outside the home, as here the benefits from income shifting from husband to wife were greatest. Although women's participation in the labour force would gradually climb back up after its fall at the war's end, the joint income tax return offered little incentive to wives and employers to push beyond part-time and low-paying clerical and sales jobs.[26]

VJ-Day', *c.* 1950; The President's Commission on Veterans' Pensions [Bradley Commission], *A Report on Benefits in the United States*, Printed for the Use of the House Committee on Veterans Affairs, 84th Congress, 2nd Session (Washington, DC: USGPO, 1956); Educational Testing Service, *Final Report on Educational Assistance to Veterans: A Comparative Study of Three GI Bills*, Submitted to the Committee on Veterans' Affairs, US Senate, 93rd Congress, 1st Session, 20 September 1973; R. Hammond, Project Director, '1979 Survey of Veterans, Summary Report, Reports and Statistics Service', Office of the Controller, 1979; L. Harris and Associates, Inc., 'Survey of Aging Veterans: A Study of the Means, Resources, and Future Expectations of Veterans Aged 55 and Over', conducted for the Veterans Administration, December 1983; Veterans Administration, 'Historical Data on the Usage of Educational Benefits, 1944–1983', Office of Information Management and Statistics, April 1984; U.S. Bureau of the Census, '1987 National Survey of Veterans', conducted for the Department of Veterans Affairs, July 1989.

On women and the GI Bill, see J.A. Wilentz, *Women Veterans: America's Forgotten Heroines* (New York: Continuum, 1983), pp. 163–96. Useful secondary sources on the GI Bill more broadly include D.R. Ross, *Preparing for Ulysses: Politics and Veterans During World War II* (New York: Columbia University Press, 1969) and M.J. Bennett, *When Dreams Come True: The GI Bill and the Making of Modern America* (Washington: Brassey's, 1996).

26. My understanding of the Second World War and Reconversion-era income tax was particularly helped by A. Kessler-Harris, '"A principle of law but not of justice": men, women and income taxes in the United States, 1913–1948', *Southern California Review of Law and Women's Studies*, 6 (1997), pp. 331–60; C.C. Jones, 'Class tax to mass tax: the role of propaganda in the expansion of the income tax during World War II', *Buffalo Law Review*, 37 (1988/89), pp. 685–737; C.C. Jones, 'Split income and separate spheres: tax law and gender roles in the 1940s', *Law and History Review*, 6 (1988), pp. 259–310; E.J. McCaffery, *Taxing Women* (Chicago: University of Chicago Press, 1997); S.S. Surrey,

In allowing deductions for mortgage and other interest payments, the tax code further reinforced patriarchal privilege, as loans and credit were very difficult for women to secure until the 1970s.[27] As the federal government bestowed advantages on male veterans and taxpayers, it helped create the male *customer as citizen* who dominated his household as chief breadwinner, homeowner, credit borrower, and taxpayer.

African Americans' experience within the *Consumer's Republic* was complicated. On the one hand, they encountered even more insidious discrimination than women in claiming their fair share of GI benefits. Whereas most women were excluded by virtue of not being veterans, black veterans were legitimately entitled but often suffered from the way the GI Bill was structured. In choosing to channel federal dollars to veterans through existing private institutions such as colleges, banks, and building and loans, and thereby not expanding the public sector's presence, Congress reinforced rather than challenged the discrimination that black ex-GIs routinely encountered whenever they applied to colleges or vocational training programmes, and for a house mortgage or loan to start a business.[28] On the other hand, the firm connection that the *Consumers' Republic* established between citizenship and consumption gave African Americans a vehicle by which to direct pent-up frustration from wartime discrimination into concrete action. In state after state beginning in the late 1940s, blacks mounted a civil rights movement challenging discrimination and exclusion from public accommodations, many of them sites of consumption and leisure. Battles to gain access to downtown restaurants and hotels, movie theaters and swimming pools, bowling alleys and skating rinks, and to buy everything from a beer to a house wherever one wanted, led to the passage of new civil rights legislation in many northern states. Even in the South, the ten years between the war and the Montgomery Bus Boycott of

---

'Federal taxation of the family – The Revenue Act of 1948', *Harvard Law Review*, 61 (1948); L.H. Seltzer, *The Personal Exemptions in the Income Tax* (New York: National Bureau of Economic Research, 1968), pp. 120–2.

27. M.J. Gates, 'Credit discrimination against women: causes and solutions', *Vanderbilt Law Review*, 27 (1974), pp. 409–41; *Hearings Before the Subcommittee on Consumer Affairs of the Committee on Banking and Currency, House of Representatives, 93rd Congess, 2nd Session, on HR. 14908*, 20–21 June 1974, Parts 1–3.

28. A sampling of sources illuminating the racial discrimination encountered by black veterans includes: C.G. Bolte and L. Harris, *Our Negro Veterans*, Public Affairs Pamphlet No. 128 (New York: Public Affairs Committee, Inc., 1947); 'Negro unit accuses South's postmasters', *New York Times*, 1 June 1 1947; 'Negro GI's in South seen shorn of rights', *New York Times*, 2 June 1947; 'Conference on Labor and the Veteran, sponsored by the New Jersey State Industrial Council', 3–4 March 1945, Newark, NJ, Newark Public Library (NPL), 'Q' File, 'New Jersey State CIO Industrial Union Council', p. 54; material documenting complaints about exclusion from black veterans in NAACP, LC, files: 'GI Benefits, 1945–June 1946', 'Housing, NJ, General, 1949–50', 'Veterans Housing, 1945–55', 'GI Benefits, July 1946–1949'; Interview with L. Steward in S. Terkel, *The 'Good War': An Oral History of World War II* (New York: Pantheon Books, 1984), pp. 348–9.

1955 saw rumblings of protest around black exclusion from parks, theaters, and department store lunch counters, alongside more celebrated efforts at voter registration. The federal Civil Rights Act of 1964, barring discrimination in all public accommodations throughout the nation, emerged out of – rather than launching – a grassroots movement for, literally, an equal place at the table.[29]

The benefits of the early Civil Rights Movement aside, the *Consumers' Republic* – and its magic wand of mass consumption more generally – led not just to some increase in democracy and equality created by greater prosperity, but also to new kinds of stratification and inequality. A case in point is the evolution of the post-war residential landscape. The United States came out of the Second World War faced with an enormous housing crisis. The remedy was mass housing construction of single-family homes, most of them in new suburban areas, a solution intended not only to shelter Americans but also to stimulate the demand economy under-girding the *Consumers' Republic.* By turning 'home' into an expensive commodity for purchase by many more consumers than ever before and by increasing demand for related commodities such as cars, appliances and furnishings, new house construction became the bedrock of the *Consumers' Republic.* One out of every four homes standing in the United States in 1960 went up in the 1950s, and by the same year 60 per cent of Americans could claim that they owned their own homes, in contrast to only 40 per cent as recently as in 1940.[30] The democraticizing of home ownership through the mass consumption market embodied the essence of the *Consumers' Republic,* as did the public-private partnership that supported it. Private interests carried out and profited from the home-building, subsidized by the federal government's insuring of mortgages though the Veterans Administration and the Federal Housing Administration, granting mortgage interest deductions on income taxes, and constructing federal highways to link these new suburban communities to the metropolis.

But bringing housing more centrally into the mass-consumption marketplace contributed to privileging some social groups over others. Access to mortgages, credit, and tax benefits favoured men over women, whites over blacks, and the middle class over the working class. In addition, the extensive suburbanization of the metropolitan landscape that accompanied mass home-building created new inequalities as whole communities soon became stratified along class and racial lines. While home in the *Consumer's Republic* became a commodity to be traded

29. For a case study of the African American struggle for access to public accommodations in New Jersey after the Second World War, see Chapter 4 in my *A Consumers' Republic.*

30. C. Bowles, *Tomorrow Without Fear* (New York: Simon and Schuster, 1946), p. 61; Kelley, *Consumer Economics,* pp. 464–67; H. Vatter, 'The inheritance of the preceding decades'; Dept. of Commerce,'We the Americans . . . Our Homes'; and President's Committee on Urban Housing, 'A Decent Home'; all in H.G. Vatter and J.F. Walker (eds*), History of the U.S. Economy since World War II* (Armonk, NY: M.E. Sharpe, 1996), pp. 21–3, 235–7, 358–62.

up like a car rather than an emotional investment in a neighbourhood or church parish, 'property values' became the new mantra. Of course, people still chose the towns they lived in from a range of alternatives, but increasingly they selected among homogeneous suburbs occupying distinctive rungs in a clear status hierarchy of communities, with the quality of services varying between rungs much more than they previously had for people living within larger cross-class and interracial municipalities. In particular, education, widely recognized as the best ticket to success in post-war America, became captive to the inequalities of the new metropolitan landscape, given that local communities substantially provided, and paid for, their own schools through local property taxes. The wealthier the community, the more it had to spend. By putting its faith in the potential of the private mass-consumption marketplace to deliver opportunity rather than in expanding state provisions or redistributing wealth, the *Consumers' Republic* contributed to growing inequality and fragmentation. Despite an early confidence in the universal benefits of selling to the 'mass', before very long a post-war economy and society ostensibly built on 'mass consumption' created a reality of economic and social segmentation that was only reinforced by marketing and advertising which simultaneously discovered the greater profits to be made in segmenting the mass market into distinctive sub-markets based on gender, class, race, ethnicity, age, and lifestyle. Residential suburbanization, engineering a social landscape that served property values more effectively than it served people, became one of several arenas where Americans shared less and less common physical space and civic culture, contributing to the fractured and inequitable public sphere with which many at the end of the twentieth century felt they were struggling.[31]

The shift in the centre of post-war commercial and often community life from urban downtowns to suburban shopping centres that accompanied residential suburbanization, moreover, only reinforced this trend toward social fragmentation and inequality. Suburban shopping centres became another setting where *customers as citizens* found themselves segmented into sub-markets and deprived of full and equal legal rights. Space that had been public in the urban centres became legally the private property of shopping-centre owners, and hence constitutional rights once guaranteed in the town square – such as freedom of speech and assembly – were not automatically protected unless state courts upheld them, and even then the poor, the black, and the young were often marginalized.[32]

31. For a case study of the growing class and racial segmentation of suburbia after World War II set in Northern New Jersey, see Chapter 5 in my *A Consumer's Republic*.

32. A case study of the social segmentation wrought by suburban shopping centers in Northern New Jersey, a companion to my chapter on residential suburbanization, has been published as 'From town center to shopping center: the reconfiguration of community marketplaces in postwar America', *American Historical Review*, 101 (1996), pp. 1050–81. An expanded version of this material is Chapter 6, *A Consumer's Republic*.

Few would dispute the evidence that, over the last fifteen years or so of the twentieth century, inequality of income and wealth in the United States increased. Ubiquitous are the exposés lamenting the growing gulf during that time between two Americas – one whose citizens had steady jobs, fringe benefits, and homes in the suburbs, the other whose citizens moved between welfare and minimum-wage jobs, had no health insurance, and lived in inner-city neighbourhoods or deteriorating first-ring suburbs. Analysts point the finger at many factors, but often missing is the larger, longer view that acknowledges how deeply entrenched the potential for economic inequality had been in the route America chose by which to achieve post-war abundance. In expecting the private mass marketplace in what was assumed to be an ever expanding economy to solve the nation's social and economic problems, the ideal of the *Consumers' Republic* contributed to its own failures.

At the end of the twentieth century, much as at the beginning, citizen and consumer remained permeable categories in political culture. As just one example, the Clinton-Gore National Performance Review Report of 1993 aimed at 'reinventing government', listed among its top goals 'Putting Customers First'.[33] But rather than consumers representing the public interest as they did first in the Progressive Era and more systematically during the New Deal and the Second World War, the half-century reign of the *Consumers' Republic* recast the consumer as the embodiment of more narrowly defined self-interest. When the Gore Report envisioned a new-style government, it modelled it after the efficient retail business: 'Effective, entrepreneurial governments insist on customer satisfaction . . . They restructure their basic operations to meet customers' needs'. The idealized post-war *customer as citizen* was alive and well as America moved into the twenty-first century, but in a late twist, the watchdog *citizen consumers* of the 1930s and 1940s were replaced in the 1990s by self-interested government customers who brought a consumer mentality to their relations with government, judging state services much like other purchased goods, by the personal benefit they derive from them. Over the last half of the twentieth century, American confidence that an economy and culture of mass consumption could deliver democracy and equality – that it was in fact the best way to secure them – led from the *Consumers' Republic* to the consumerization of the republic, where politicians and their customer-voters would reject whatever did not pay. A century that began with *citizen consumers* inspiring the expansion of government for Progressive reform ended with consumers inspiring government's retrenchment to enhance their customer satisfaction as citizens.

33. *From Red Tape to Results: Creating a Government That Works Better and Costs Less* (Washington, DC: USGPO, 1993), p. 6.

Acknowledgements

A version of this material has appeared in H. Sitkoff (ed.), *Making Sense of the Twentieth Century: Perspectives on Modern America, 1900–2000*, copyright (c) 2000 by Oxford University Press, Inc. Used by permission of Oxford University Press, Inc.

II

The Politics of Plenty in the Twentieth-Century United States

Meg Jacobs

Not so long ago, the concept of 'consumer politics' – that is, political activism rooted in and predicated on consumer goods – suggested a contradiction in terms. Indeed, many historians have long believed that the politics of consumption was an oxymoron. A common assumption holds that the United States – born rich, free, and middle class – has avoided pitched class struggle and systemic political unrest, in no small part, because of its material abundance.[1] In 1906 the German sociologist Werner Sombart pronounced an early death for the American social-democratic project. In answer to his famous question 'Why is there no socialism in America?' Sombart pointed to the 'comfortable circumstances' and high standard of living of the American worker. In the United States, he concluded, 'All Socialist utopias have come to grief on roast beef and apple pie'.[2] At mid-century, liberal intellectuals asserted that the American worker, now richer than ever, was more interested in second-hand pink Cadillacs than in socialist, or any other, critiques of capitalism. In popular imagination, he was 'satisfied, doped by TV, essentially middle-class in outlook'.[3] Throughout the industrialized West, scholars on both the left and the right have accepted Sombart's notion that economic abundance exerts a fundamentally depoliticizing and privatizing influence. For generations, intellectuals believed that an abundance of goods, or an indulgence in materiality, dulled the political senses and deadened any activist impulses.[4]

1. See, for example, L. Hartz, *The Liberal Tradition in America: an Interpretation of American Political Thought since the Revolution* (New York: Harcourt, Brace, 1955).

2. W. Sombart, *Why is There No Socialism in the United States?* Trans. P.M. Hocking and C.T. Husbands (White Plains, NY: International Arts and Sciences Press, 1976), pp. 105–6; Sombart's views culminated in the critique offered by the Frankfurt school. See especially H. Marcuse, *One Dimensional Man: Studies in the Ideology of Advanced Industrial Society* (Boston: Beacon, 1964).

3. H. Swados, 'The myth of the happy worker', *Nation*, 19 August 1957. See also R. Davenport, *USA: The Permanent Revolution* (New York: Time-Life, 1951).

4. J.K. Galbraith, *The Affluent Society* (Boston: Houghton Mifflin, 1958); D. Bell, *The End of Ideology: On the Exhaustion of Political Ideas in the Fifties* (Glencoe, Ill.: Free Press, 1960); W.W. Rostow, *The Stages of Economic Growth* (New York: Cambridge University Press, 1960); D. Reisman, *Abundance for What?* (Glencoe, Ill.: Free Press, 1964). For a useful overview of this

But that is not true, least of all in the United States. We can begin to appreciate the politicizing nature of consumption by rejecting the idea of mass-consumer culture as inevitably triumphant and conformist. In his 1954 classic work *People of Plenty*, the historian David Potter was the first to point to abundance as the defining element of American national character. Scholars have since assumed what Potter identified as an ineluctable shift from 'a producer's culture into a consumer's culture'.[5] But the advent of a mass-consumption economy was inherently destabilizing to the old economic, producer-oriented order. New kinds of firm, new modes of production, and new distribution channels replaced old economic arrangements and networks. A proliferation of goods and a democratization of services undermined old power relations and social hierarchies. New processes of provisioning required the creation and negotiation of new rules that at once disrupted and challenged an older local economic system. Sustained opposition to and support of this new economy led to the politicization of such fundamental change.[6]

Americans became a people of plenty to be sure, but only through a contested politics of plenty. Contrary to much of the historiography, mass consumption is neither solely technologically driven nor inherently depoliticizing. In fact, the opposites of both are true. A mass-consumer society resulted from a particular political construction of capitalism predicated on economic and political redistribution. At key moments, fights over consumer issues such as the price of meat served as the touchstone of social politics and working-class mobilization.[7] A desire for more and better goods has been both cause and consequence of political reform. Not only did Americans demand their rights as consumers but, at the same time, public policy embraced and encouraged consumer activism and an expanded sense of economic citizenship. For nearly half a century, consumerism, or what we might call an ideology of mass purchasing power, was a central pillar of the liberal agenda.

---

intellectual trend, see R.H. Pells, *Liberal Mind in a Conservative Age: American Intellectuals in the 1940s and 1950s* (Middletown, Conn.: Wesleyan University Press, 1985); J. Lears, 'A matter of taste: corporate cultural hegemony in a mass-consumption society', in L. May (ed.), *Recasting America: Culture and Politics in the Age of Cold War* (Chicago: University of Chicago Press, 1989), pp. 38–57; and D. Horowitz, *Vance Packard and American Social Criticism* (Chapel Hill: University of North Carolina Press, 1994).

5. D.M. Potter, *People of Plenty: Economic Abundance and American National Character* (Chicago, 1954), p. 173.

6. Though consumption is not central to their analyses, many classic works of this period stress tensions between new and old economic orders. See for example R. Hofstadter, *The Age of Reform: from Bryan to F.D.R.* (New York: Alfred A. Knopf, 1955) and R.H. Wiebe, *The Search for Order, 1877–1920* (New York: Hill and Wang, 1967).

7. For example, see R. Rosenzweig, *Eight Hours for What We Will: Workers and Leisure in An Industrial City, 1870–1920* (New York: Cambridge University Press, 1983); B.K. Hunnicutt, *Work Without End: Abandoning Shorter Hours for the Right to Work* (Philadelphia: Temple University Press, 1988); and D. Frank, *Purchasing Power: Consumer Organizing, Gender, and the Seattle Labor Movement, 1919–1929* (New York: Cambridge University Press, 1994).

From the turn of the century through the 1960s, an alliance of labor economists, liberal businessmen, and progressive policymakers pushed for the inclusion of the working classes into the new consumer marketplace and sponsored redistributive public policies to make their participation possible. These efforts culminated with the creation of a new configuration of state power and governmental authority during the New Deal and Second World War that endorsed a high-wage, low-price political economy and mobilized consumers to that end. This mutually reinforcing relationship between state-sanctioned institutions and a consuming public formed the core of America's politics of plenty.[8]

This dynamic relationship between consumer culture and political development has gone under-appreciated, yet it is central to any coherent account of American political economy. The reason for the oversight is straightforward: consumer politics falls within disciplinary cracks. Business historians have documented the rise of a new managerial class who created the technological processes, marketing devices, and distribution systems to deliver new goods.[9] In cultural and women's studies, scholars have explored the mediation of those goods and their use by consumers in constructing identity.[10] Labour historians have seen consumption as the negation of the realm of production and found consumerism a convenient explanation for working-class failures. None of these schools, however, situates consumption within a political economic context.[11] In political history, to the extent that such scholarship investigates consumption, attention focuses exclusively on fiscal management of aggregate demand. While scholars have documented the ideas and institutional innovations of this fiscal revolution, that story remains abstract from actual consumers and ignores the political construction of specific consumer choices.[12]

8. I develop these ideas more fully in *The Politics of Purchasing Power* (Princeton: Princeton University Press, forthcoming 2001).

9. A. Chandler, *The Visible Hand: The Managerial Revolution in American Business* (New York: Belknap, 1977); J.L. Meikle, *Twentieth Century Limited: Industrial Design in America, 1925–1939* (Philadelphia: Temple University Press, 1979); R. Marchand, *Advertising the American Dream: Making Way for Modernity, 1920–1940* (Berkeley: University of California Press, 1985); R.S. Tedlow, *New and Improved: The Story of Mass Marketing in America* (New York: Basic, 1990); S. Strasser, *Satisfaction Guaranteed: The Making of the American Mass Market* (New York: Pantheon, 1990); J. Lears, *Fables of Abundance: A Cultural History of Advertising in America* (New York: Basic, 1994); P.W. Laird, *Advertising Progress: American Business and the Rise of Consumer Marketing* (Baltimore: Johns Hopkins University Press, 1998).

10. Here the list is extensive. A seminal book is M. Douglas and B. Isherwood, *The World of Goods: Toward an Anthropology of Consumption* (New York: Basic, 1979). See also K. Peiss, *Hope in a Jar: The Making of America's Beauty Culture* (New York: Henry Holt, 1998); A.J. Clarke, *Tupperware: The Promise of Plastic in 1950s America* (Washington, DC: Smithsonian Institution Press, 1999); and the collection of essays in J. Scanlon (ed.), *Gender and Consumer Culture Reader* (New York: New York University Press, 2000).

11. A recent exception is J. Parr, *Domesticating Goods: The Material, the Moral, and the Economic in Postwar Years* (Toronto: University of Toronto Press, 1999).

12. See for example H. Stein, *The Fiscal Revolution in America* (Chicago: University of Chicago Press, 1969).

This chapter is intended to provide an overview of the politics of consumption in the twentieth-century United States. It begins by exploring the multiple grass-roots political movements that arose in tandem with new consumer arrangements at the turn of the century. The next section then demonstrates how isolated protests for more purchasing power gained momentum and became linked to the reigning New Deal political ideology in the context of the twin crises of the Great Depression and the Second World War. As this chapter will argue, the development of a mass-consumer culture went hand-in-hand with the expansion of the public sphere, the rise of a labour movement, and the growth of an interventionist state. Only the political defeat of this highly mobilizing system predicated on a strong labour movement made room for Keynesian fiscalism as a less intrusive strategy of state management.

Grass-roots Activism at the Point of Consumption, 1870–1929

Americans have a long history of political activism at the point of consumption. From the colonists' tea boycotts in the American Revolution to the sit-ins at Woolworth's counters in the civil rights era, Americans have fought for political rights through the medium of the marketplace.[13] But the creation of a new consumer economy spawned the moment of greatest activism. In the first half of the twentieth century, a new political culture of consumerism served as the transition between a nineteenth-century ideal of republican producerism and a Kennedy-era moment of Keynesian liberalism. With the proliferation of consumer goods in the era of the First World War came the transformation of the American socio-economic landscape from local insular communities to national 'consumption communities'.[14] By creating new spaces for mass consumption, and in effect legitimizing public sociability, the spread of department stores and other sites of commercial provisioning expanded the public sphere, rather than simply commodifying it. The very process of 'comparison shopping' educated and empowered consumers. A new ideology of 'more for less' encouraged a sense of entitlement.

---

13. T.H. Breen, '"Baubles of Britain": the American and consumer revolutions of the eighteenth century', *Past and Present*, 119 (1988), pp. 73–104; Breen, 'The meanings of things: interpreting the consumer economy in the eighteenth century', in J. Brewer and R. Porter (eds), *Consumption and the World of Goods* (London: Routledge, 1993), pp. 249–60; D. Frank, *Buy American: The Untold Story of Economic Nationalism* (Boston: Beacon Press, 1999), pp. 3–32; R.E. Weems, Jr., *Desegregating the Dollar: African American Consumerism in the Twentieth Century* (New York: New York University Press, 1998), pp. 56–69.

14. D. Boorstin, *The Americans: The Democratic Experience* (New York, Vintage, 1973), pp. 89–164; See also T.J. Schlereth, 'Country stores, county fairs, and mail-order catalogues: consumption in rural America', in S.J. Bronner (ed.), *Consuming Visions: Accumulation and Display of Goods in America, 1880–1920* (New York: W.W. Norton, 1989), pp. 339–75.

In the decades after the Civil War, the modern female shopper was born. By 1880, goods once formerly produced in the home became purchasable commodities. Homes now depended on prepared food and ready-made clothing for the essentials of life. A managerial revolution in production and distribution fostered technological and agricultural improvements and created dramatic increases in productivity. New American firms mass-produced not only essentials but also a seemingly infinite number of new types of consumer goods. In 1870, companies spent 30 million dollars on advertising; by 1910, this amount had increased to 600 million, or 4 per cent of national income. New brands, new services, and new ads promised to improve all facets of life, even those aspects thought sacrosanct and above market influences. As early as 1874, Macy's combined religion and commerce by introducing the Christmas store windows and ushering in the holiday shopping season. In this environment, women became key economic actors and acquired a public role as shoppers. It was their job to enter into the market as family provisioners, a role secured by the tradition of family members handing over sealed pay envelopes to the female head of the house. [15]

At the centre of this transition stood the department store. These commercial institutions embodied the new consumer ethos of service and value. Leaving behind the old motto *caveat emptor*, 'satisfaction guaranteed' proclaimed the new rights of modern shoppers. Consumers could buy on credit, have new goods delivered, and return them if they changed their minds. Shoppers touched and tried on hats, gloves, and dresses without merchants' scrutiny and without obligation to buy. These modern 'palaces of consumption', with their endless variety and choice, invited all passers-by to enter for free and to browse up and down the aisles. In contrast to local stores of the earlier nineteenth century, each item now had one fixed price. And these prices were likely to be cheaper than those at neighbourhood shops. As it boldly announced in full-page newspaper ads, Macy's prided itself on

---

15. For economic growth, see the literature cited in note 9. On women as shoppers, see E. Ewen, *Immigrant Women in the Land of Dollars: Life and Culture on the Lower East Side, 1890–1925* (New York: Monthly Review Press, 1985); E.S. Abelson, *When Ladies Go A-Thieving: Middle-Class Shoplifters in the Victorian Department Store* (New York: Oxford University Press, 1989); A.R. Heinze, *Adapting to Abundance: Jewish Immigrants, Mass Consumption, and the Search for American Identity* (New York: Columbia University Press, 1990), pp. 33–48; V. Zelizer, *The Social Meaning of Money* (New York: Basic, 1994); E. Rappaport, *Shopping for Pleasure: Women in the Making of London's West End* (Princeton: Princeton University Press, 2000). On women's domestic roles, see S. Strasser, *Never Done: A History of American Housework* (New York, Pantheon, 1982); R. Schwartz Cowan, *More Work for Mother: The Ironies of Household Technology from the Open Hearth to the Microwave* (New York: Basic, 1983); G. Matthews, *'Just a Housewife': the Rise and Fall of Domesticity in America* (New York: Oxford University Press, 1987). See also W. Gamber, *The Female Economy: The Millinery and Dressmaking Trades, 1860–1930* (Urbana: University of Illinois Press, 1997). For commercialization of all aspects of life, including marriage, see K. Dubinsky, *The Second Greatest Disappointment: Honeymooning and Tourism at Niagara Falls* (New Brunswick, NJ: Rutgers University Press, 1999), pp. 168–211.

underselling its competition. In the depression of the 1890s, this New York landmark engaged in notorious price wars. In 1909, Filene's of Boston institutionalized the idea of low prices with its automatic bargain basement, an invention soon replicated across the country.[16]

Above all, department stores legitimized public loitering. The economics of high fixed costs and the need for rapid turn-over meant that stores were dependent on impulse purchasing. Their free entry policy along with their grand physical construction and accessible lay-out of merchandise encouraged shopping as a leisurely activity. Even if one could not afford to purchase, looking was free. As historian William Leach has aptly put it, department stores democratized desire. In 1904, at least 250,000 people passed through Marshall Field's daily.[17] And once inside, shoppers could take advantage of the many non-shopping activities that stores offered from afternoon tea and classical music to public libraries to public debates over women's suffrage.[18] Breaking from an older ideology of separate spheres that had confined them to private arenas, women now moved in many commercial public spaces. Unaccompanied by men, they travelled to museums, dance halls and amusement parks, though as contemporary diaries reflect, shopping remained their predominant activity.[19] Even in working-class neighbourhoods, women shopped as leisure and as housework. In 1913, on New York's Lower East Side, the fifty-seven blocks of this Jewish immigrant neighbourhood contained 112 candy and ice-cream stores, 70 saloons, 78 barbers, 93 butcher shops, and 43 bakeries.[20]

This new public marketplace had a profound impact not only on luxuries, but also on essentials, especially the provisioning of food. Increasingly Americans obtained their final food products from the marketplace. In 1890, communities had customarily designated one day a week as the baking day, but by 1925, families

16. L. Harris, *Merchant Princes* (New York: Harper and Row, 1979); R. Hendrickson, *Grand Emporiums: The Illustrated History of America's Great Department Stores* (New York: Stein and Day, 1979); S. Porter Benson, *Counter Cultures: Saleswomen, Managers, and Customers in American Department Stores, 1890–1940* (Urbana: University of Illinois Press, 1986); W. Leach, *Land of Desire: Merchants, Power, and the Rise of a New American Culture* (New York: Pantheon, 1993). The mail-order business also freed purchases from merchant scrutiny and revolutionized distribution.

17. Leach, *Land of Desire*, p. 7; Benson, *Counter Cultures*, p. 34.

18. W. Leach, 'Transformation in a culture of consumption: women and department stores, 1890–1925', *Journal of American History*, 71 (1984), pp. 319–42.

19. J.F. Kasson, *Amusing the Million: Coney Island at the Turn of the Century* (New York: Hill and Wang, 1978); K. Peiss, *Cheap Amusements: Working Women and Leisure in Turn-of-the-Century New York* (Philadelphia: Temple University Press, 1986); N. Harris, *Cultural Excursions: Marketing Appetites and Cultural Tastes in Modern America* (Chicago: University of Chicago Press, 1990); D. Nasaw, *Going Out: The Rise and Fall of Public Amusements* (New York: Basic, 1993); S.J. Ross, *Working-Class Hollywood: Silent Film and the Shaping of Class in America* (Princeton: Princeton University Press, 1998), pp. 21–2; and S. Deutsch, *Women and the City: Gender, Space, and Power in Boston, 1870–1940* (New York: Oxford University Press, 2000).

20. Ewen, *Immigrant Women*, p. 167.

depended almost exclusively on store-bought bread. As income and productivity increased, American diets expanded and improved. Meat consumption remained high while the consumption of milk and sugar products soared. Collectively, women shoppers spent much of their time and family budget buying bread, milk, and meat.[21]

These new sites of consumption could easily become transformed into places of protest. Once the wage system was near universal, the price mechanism became a sensitive political index. In 1900, the average wage-earning or clerical family spent 40 per cent of its annual income on food. That percentage remained as high as 35 per cent in 1940.[22] As women entered into the market, they were emboldened by both promises of plenty and their prerogative as housewives. The mechanical nature and fancy packaging obscured the value of many mass-produced goods, but basic necessities presented fewer difficulties. Women could judge if bread were stale and loaves smaller. Because basic non-durable items such as bread, milk, and meat required immediate purchase to prevent spoiling, they made effective targets for consumer action. And consumers now had a collective site for protest. Thus again and again, with slight fluctuations in price, necessities became politicized. From the turn of the century through the First World War, precipitous price increases led to food riots, consumer boycotts, and rent strikes. During the war, the rhetoric of profiteering and the mobilization of women in the War Department's Community Councils for National Defense further incited protests. In 1917, on the Lower East Side, thousands of women formed the Mothers' Anti-High Price League. They marched in the streets, boycotted butchers, and sent a letter to President Wilson exclaiming, 'We housewives of the City of New York, mothers and wives of workmen, desire to call your attention, Mr. President, to the fact that, in the midst of plenty, we and our families are facing starvation . . . [T]he American standard of living cannot be maintained'.[23]

21. H.J. Stratton, *Consumer Behavior* (Harvard Business School, Baker Library, 1940), p. 87; Hazel Kyrk and J.S. Davis, *American Baking Industry, 1849–1923* (Palo Alto, CA: Stanford University Press, 1925), p. 87.

22. Ewen, *Immigrant Women*, p. 152. For budget studies, see D. Horowitz, *The Morality of Spending: Attitudes Toward the Consumer Society in America, 1875–1940* (Baltimore, Johns Hopkins University Press, 1985).

23. Ewen, *Immigrant Women*, pp. 176–83; P. Hyman, 'Immigrant women and consumer protest: the New York City Kosher meat boycott of 1902', *American Jewish History*, 70 (1980), pp. 91–105; R. Lawson, 'The rent strike in New York City, 1904–1980: the evolution of a social movement', *Journal of Urban History*, 10 (1984), pp. 235–58; S.L. Piott, *The Anti-Monopoly Persuasion: Popular Resistance to the Rise of Big Business in the Midwest* (Westport, Conn.: Greenwood Press, 1985); D. Frank, 'Housewives, socialists, and the politics of food: the 1917 New York cost-of-living protests', *Feminist Studies*, 11 (1985), pp. 255–85; J.J. Weissman, 'The landlord as Czar: pre-World War I tenant activity', in R. Lawson (ed.), *The Tenant Movement in New York City, 1904–1984* (New Brunswick, N.J.: Rutgers University Press, 1986): 39–50; M.J. Friedman, 'American consumer boycotts in response to rising food prices: housewives' protests at the grassroots level', *Journal of Consumer Policy*, 18 (1995), pp. 55–72; and A. Orelick, *Common Sense and a Little Fire: Women*

The promise of plenty mobilized multiple grass-roots movements, not least in the organized labour movement. While housewives fought for more in the market basket, workers focused their attention on the pay envelope. Lawrence Glickman, the historian of labour, has shown that as wage labour increased in the late nineteenth century, workers based their demands more on their needs as consumers than on their value as producers. Though workers were no longer self-employed, high wages could provide a comfortable life-style that signalled economic freedom. Thus by the 1870s, American Federation of Labor (AFL) members came to demand what they called a 'living wage'. And these high wages were not automatically deradicalizing. The more workers had, the more they wanted. As AFL leader Samuel Gompers explained in1887, 'Continual improvement, by opening up new vistas, creates new desires and develops legitimate aspirations. It makes men more dissatisfied with unjust conditions and readier to battle for the right'. Demands based on needs could be infinite, especially when in 1898 the United Mine Workers leader John Mitchell thought that the American standard of living should include a six-room house with indoor plumbing, a separate parlour and dining room, multiple bedrooms, and a library. The idea of an American standard of living as a right led the AFL to pursue the eight-hour day and union label campaigns.[24] In 1917, the National War Labor Board employed a living wage model, thereby establishing this standard as the basis of public policy. By 1920 all major political parties adopted living wage clauses in their campaign platforms.[25]

By the 1920s, several forces converged to develop a consumer's public policy agenda. First, women had become political actors as consumers with a moral sense

---

and Working-Class Politics in the United States, 1900–1965 (Chapel Hill: University of North Carolina Press, 1995), pp. 220–5. New systems of provisioning could incite reaction as well: on the creation of Jim Crow segregation laws in new commercial spaces in the South, see A. Meier and E. Rudwick, 'The boycott movement against Jim Crow streetcars in the South, 1900–1906', *Journal of American History*, 55 (1969), pp. 756–75; Meier and Rudwick, 'Negro boycotts of Jim Crow streetcars in Tennessee', *American Quarterly*, 21 (1969), pp. 755–63; R.D.G. Kelley, '"We are not what we seem": rethinking black working-class opposition in the Jim Crow South', *Journal of American History*, 80 (1993), pp. 75–112; and G. Hale, *Making Whiteness: The Culture of Segregation in the South, 1890–1940* (New York: Pantheon, 1998), pp. 121–97; on rural resistance to chain stores and mail order catalogues, see J.J. Bean, *Beyond the Broker State: Federal Policies toward Small Business, 1936–1961* (Chapel Hill: University of North Carolina Press, 1996), pp. 1–36; and D.A. Horowitz, *Beyond Left and Right: Insurgency and the Establishment* (Urbana: University of Illinois Press, 1997), pp. 115–37.

24. L.B. Glickman, *A Living Wage: American Workers and the Making of Consumer Society* (Ithaca: Cornell University Press, 1997), pp. 64–5, 82–3; see also Glickman, 'Inventing the "American standard of living": gender, race and working-class identity, 1880–1925', *Labor History*, 34 (1993), pp. 221–35.

25. L. Fink, *Progressive Intellectuals and the Dilemmas of Democratic Commitment* (Cambridge, Mass.: Harvard University Press, 1997), pp. 214–41.

of their rights in the marketplace.[26] At times, their activities represented no more than a grievance as with individual acts of stealing or vandalism, or collective action to obtain price relief. But increasingly their protests were linked to a larger critique of the political system and capitalism. That was particularly true as a woman's effort to do her motherly duties of raising children and keeping a clean and healthy home increasingly became public affairs. In the 1870s and 1880s, new female grass-roots voluntary associations such as the National Consumers League, the Women's Christian Temperance Union, and hundreds of other mothers' societies and clubs relied upon their moral authority as mothers and housewives to demand new regulations of the market. The Consumers League sought to improve the conditions under which working-class women produced and sold consumer goods by transforming the purchasing function of middle-class consumers into a moral force. With grass-roots support and a reliance on social science expertise, the League lobbied successfully for the passage of protective legislation for female workers.[27] This movement toward what was called municipal housekeeping signalled the extension of the women's sphere into a generalized reform impulse and a demand for a social wage.[28]

Second, the organized labour movement questioned the natural law of wages. Though they experienced organizational setbacks in the 1920s, they articulated the idea of mass purchasing power as the key to economic health. Third, liberal economists and labour experts elaborated on that idea and came to reject the classical view that competitive markets provided for maximum efficiency and protection of the consumer. In the 1920s, reformers discovered the multiple evils

26. For the idea of a moral economy, see E.P. Thompson, 'The moral economy of the English crowd in the eighteenth century', *Past and Present*, 50 (1971), pp. 76–136.

27. On the National Consumers' League, see A. Rosenberg Wolfe, 'Women, consumerism, and the National Consumers' League', *Labor History*, 16 (1975), pp. 378–92; K.K. Sklar, 'Two political cultures in the Progressive era: the National Consumers' League and the American Association for Labor Legislation', in L. Kerber, A. Kessler-Harris and Sklar (eds), *U.S. History as Women's History: New Feminist Essays* (Chapel Hill: University of North Carolina Press, 1995), pp. 36–62; Sklar, 'The Consumer's White Label Campaign of the National Consumers' League, 1898–1918', in S. Strasser, C. McGovern and M. Judt (eds), *Getting and Spending: European and American Consumer Societies in the Twentieth Century* (Washington, DC: German Historical Institute, 1998), pp. 17–35; and L.R.Y. Storrs, *Civilizing Capitalism: The National Consumers' League, Women's Activism, and Labor Standards in the New Deal Era* (Chapel Hill: University of North Carolina Press, 2000). On women's clubs, see M. Kazin, *The Populist Persuasion: An American History* (New York: Basic, 1995), pp. 79–106.

28. For the involvement of women in politics see P. Baker, 'The domestication of politics: women and American political society, 1780–1920', *American Historical Review*, 89 (1984), pp. 620–47; G. Matthews, *The Rise of Public Woman: Women's Power and Women's Place in the United States, 1630–1970* (New York: Oxford University Press, 1992), pp. 147–71; T. Skocpol, *Protecting Soldiers and Mothers: The Political Origins of Social Policy in the United States* (Cambridge: Belknap Press, 1992); and Sklar, 'The historical foundations of women's power in the creation of the American welfare state, 1830–1930', in S. Koven and S. Michel (eds), *Mothers of a New World: Maternalistic Politics and the Origins of Welfare States* (New York: Routledge, 1993).

of nominal wages, monopoly prices, waste in distribution, and consumer power-lessness. Essentially, they argued that the monopolistic structure of the economy allowed a small number of firms to impose high prices, low wages, and stylized consumer goods subject to planned obsolescence. Collectively, these three reform impulses added up to a sweeping condemnation of corporate control of the economy that only government action could offset. As the sociologist Robert Lynd put it, 'In a democratic culture in which the consumer occupies a position of such relative disadvantage in relation to business, one turns finally to the role of the government as a surrogate'.[29]

Mobilizing the Consuming Public in the New Deal and World War II, 1930–1945

The Great Depression solidified the idea of 'underconsumption' as the country's major political and economic problem. Amid the crisis of the 1930s, a consensus began to emerge within New Deal circles that income inequality and the resulting underconsumption of consumer goods had stalled the economy.[30] Convinced that underconsumption posed serious economic, social, and ultimately political threats, a group of left-liberal New Dealers saw this crisis as an opportunity to reform what they regarded as structural impediments in the economy, specifically low wages and high prices. This consumption-driven model relied not only on Keynesian pump-priming but also, and more centrally, on redistributive public policies aimed at increasing labour's wages and lowering prices to create a consuming public. In this model, a consuming public referred to a broad alliance between middle-class consumers and working Americans to fight for higher standards of living.[31] These reformers staffed the consumer divisions in the National Recovery Administration (NRA) and the Agricultural Adjustment Agency, two

29. S. Chase, *The Tragedy of Waste* (New York: Macmillan, 1925); Chase and F.J. Schlink, *Your Money's Worth: A Study in the Waste of the Consumer's Dollar* (New York, Macmillan, 1927); P.H. Douglas, *Real Wages in the United States, 1890–1926* (Boston: Houghton Mifflin, 1930); A. Berle and G.C. Means, *The Modern Corporation and Private Property* (New York: Macmillan, 1932); A. Kallet and Schlink, *100,000,000 Guinea Pigs: Dangers in Every Day Foods, Drugs, and Cosmetics* (New York, Vanguard, 1933); R.S. Lynd, 'The people as consumers', in United States, President's Research Committee on Social Trends, *Recent Social Trends in the United States* (New York: McGraw Hill, 1933), pp. 857–911; and Lynd, 'Democracy's third estate," *Political Science Quarterly*, 51 (1936), pp. 481–513.

30. On the prevalence of underconsumptionist ideas, see A. Brinkley, *The End of Reform: New Deal Liberalism in Depression and War* (New York: Alfred A. Knopf, 1995), pp. 67–72. See also S. Fraser, *Labor Will Rule: Sidney Hillman and the Rise of American Labor* (New York, Free Press, 1991); and T. Rosenof, *New Deal Economists and Their Legacies, 1933–1939* (Chapel Hill: University of North Carolina Press, 1997), pp. 28–43.

31. P.H. Douglas, *The Coming of a New Party* (New York: McGraw Hill, 1932), pp. 23, 78.

central New Deal agencies.[32] Those agencies then mobilized this consuming public at work and in the marketplace around issues of purchasing power and, in effect, transformed underconsumption from an abstract theory into the basis of political activism.[33]

The NRA's Consumer Advisory Board (CAB) articulated a far-reaching vision of a consumers' interest as a critique of a producer-dominated political economy. To bring about recovery, the NRA encouraged an increase in production, wages, and collective bargaining. President Roosevelt explained, 'The aim of this whole effort is to restore our rich domestic market by raising its vast consuming capacity'. He warned businessmen against 'taking profiteering advantage of the consuming public'. The CAB had as its mission the protection of 'the interests of the consuming public', an imaginary community of all Americans that transcended race, class, and gender. The consumers' interest and the public interest had become one. The CAB sought to further the consumers' interest by opposing price-fixing, lobbying for grade labelling, and organizing county councils as local agencies to monitor prices.[34]

Once again, women took to the streets, this time with government support and encouragement. As mothers and housewives, they protested against high costs of living that they believed resulted from wages declining more rapidly than prices.[35] The potency of consumer activism drew its strength from a reciprocal relationship

32. For an overview of the New Deal, see E.W. Hawley, *The New Deal and the Problem of Monopoly: A Study of Economic Ambivalence* (Princeton: Princeton University Press, 1966); A.J. Badger, *The New Deal: The Depression Years, 1933-1940* (New York: Hill and Wang, 1989); and J. Schwarz, *The New Dealers: Power Politics in the Age of Roosevelt* (New York: Alfred A. Knopf, 1993). See also P. Campbell, *Consumer Representation in the New Deal* (New York: Columbia University Press, 1940).

33. I develop this argument at length in Jacobs, '"Democracy's third estate": New Deal politics and the construction of a "consuming public"', *International Labor and Working-Class History*, 55 (1999), pp. 27–51.

34. Bulletin No. 2, 'Activities of the Consumers' Advisory Board of the N.R.A. and the Consumers Counsel of the A.A.A.', Folder: C.A.B. Reports and Speeches (General), Box 2 (Feb–Nov., 1935), Office Files of Emily Newell Blair, Records of the Consumer Advisory Board, Records of the National Recovery Administration, Entry 363 (PI-44), RG 9 (National Archives, Washington, DC); and Jacobs, 'Democracy's third estate', pp. 36–40.

35. M. Naison, *Communists in Harlem During the Great Depression* (New York: Grove, 1983), pp. 149–50; Naison, 'From eviction resistance to rent control: tenant activism in the Great Depression', in Lawson (ed.), *The Tenant Movement in New York City*, pp. 94–133; E. Faue, *Community of Suffering and Struggle: Women, Men, and the Labor Movement in Minneapolis, 1915–1945* (Chapel Hill: University of North Carolina Press, 1991); Orelick, *Common Sense*, pp. 229–40; Orelick, '"We are that mystical thing called the public": militant housewives during the Great Depression', *Feminist Studies*, 19 (1993), pp. 147–72; D. Clark Hine, 'The Housewives League of Detroit: black women and economic nationalism', in N.A. Hewitt and S. Lebsock (eds), *Visible Women: New Essays on American Activism* (Urbana: University of Illinois Press, 1993); B.S. Wenger, *New York Jews and the Great Depression: Uncertain Promise* (New Haven, Conn.: Yale University Press, 1996), pp. 103–35; and C. Greenberg, *Or Does It Explode? Black Harlem in the Great Depression* (New York: Oxford University Press, 1997).

between consumers and the state. Because NRA supporters had adopted a purchasing-power rationale, consumers themselves came to expect justice, or at least price relief, in the marketplace. The announcement of plans to establish county councils aroused much local sentiment. In March 1934, Tillie Kaplan of the Bronx informed the CAB that the housewives of her neighbourhood were launching 'a severe strike movement . . . against the price of bread'. They insisted that local bakers reduce the price from ten to six cents a pound. Kaplan then hoped to link these 'strike meetings' to the establishment of a New York county council. These bread strikes hearkened back to earlier battles over just prices. Now, however, these consumers had the power of the state supporting their struggles over moral economy.[36]

In the 1930s, Americans developed a new relationship with the federal government over the issue of food prices. Previously shoppers had demonstrated their sense of agency and entitlement through strategies such as comparison shopping, substituting cheaper brands, returning purchases, and bargain hunting. On occasion, women had engaged in protests. But these were isolated events aimed at immediate price relief. Under the New Deal consumers developed an ideological notion of what constituted a 'fair price' and they came to regard the government as the proper authority to assess the legitimacy of the mark-up on bread and other food items. Thus when bakers raised their prices above what the public deemed fair, consumers across the country sent thousands of bread wrappers to their new allies in Washington to demonstrate price increases. 'We are glad to see you are after the profiteers', explained a woman who signed her name 'A Consumer'. A distraught citizen from York, Pennsylvania, who sent in a newspaper clipping announcing the end to the nickel loaf, inquired, 'Is it justifiable or is it profiteering?' An Ohio woman demanded, 'Is this a fair increase? . . . It appears that improved machinery and mass production have made things worse for the consumer.' In this two-way relationship signifying a new potent political culture, government officials fed consumers product and pricing information which they then used as ammunition in their local activism.[37]

The drive of New Dealers to cultivate an aroused and informed consuming public soon reaped a response exceeding their expectations. Emboldened by the rhetoric of government officials, the Detroit Committee Against the High Cost of Living led housewives and working women in a well-publicized meat strike in August 1935. Under the leadership of radical activist Mary Zuk, the Committee demanded government intervention against the 'profiteers' and called for an immediate 20 per cent cut in the price of meat. Zuk threatened to 'mobilize half the women of

---

36. For bread strikes, see Jacobs, '"Democracy's third estate"', p. 41. I base this discussion of consumer activism in the 1930s on extensive research in the NRA records.

37. *Ibid.*, p. 42. These bread wrappers are preserved in the Records of the Agricultural Adjustment Administration, RG 145 (National Archives, College Park, MD).

Chicago' in a march on the Union Stockyards. Within weeks, housewives led meat boycotts in New York, Chicago, Miami, St. Louis, Kansas City, Indianapolis, Denver, Boston, Los Angeles, and San Francisco. After the closing of thousands of butcher shops, the price of meat decreased by several cents.[38]

At the same time that New Deal programmes mobilized consumers at the market, left-liberal reforms also mobilized consumers at work. Labour-liberals understood the organization of workers under the National Labor Relations Act (1935) as a key institutional remedy to underconsumption by giving workers the right to organize and engage in collective bargaining for higher wages.[39] Their argument asserted that unequal bargaining power led to the maldistribution of income which choked channels of commerce. That purchasing-power argument helped to legitimize the growth of the New Deal state with collective bargaining and politicized consumption at its centre, winning support from both the working and middle classes. In the context of severe depression, the purchasing power of the consumer became synonymous with wage increases. This marriage was also at the heart of a demand-based economic policy that rendered the consumption function of all citizens vital to economic health.

The conflation of consumer expectations and a consumer-oriented state structure reached its apogee when total war made all aspects of consumption and production a subject of public policy. Designed to check inflation through a system of price controls and rationing, the Office of Price Administration (OPA) served as the central arena for the politics of purchasing power at mid-century. With a staff numbering over one quarter of a million, OPA was indeed an enormous bureaucracy. This agency had as its mission the protection of consumers' pocketbooks. By 1944, OPA affected over 3 million business establishments and issued regulations controlling 8 million prices, stabilizing rents in 14 million dwellings occupied by 45 million tenants, and rationing food to more than 30 million shoppers. From gathering ration tokens and stamps to checking price lists to saving extra fat for recycling, consumers felt the government's presence at each step in the consumption cycle. OPA regulations reached into the kitchen and closet of every home, influencing eating habits and fashion. Not only did OPA achieve noteworthy success in checking inflation, but this powerful agency inspired citizens to think of themselves as politicized consumers. Wartime propaganda simultaneously transformed non-consuming and sacrifice into a patriotic act of solidarity while encouraging expectations about a prosperous post-war life.[40]

38. *Ibid.*, p. 43. See also Orelick, *Common Sense*, pp. 237–8.

39. C. Tomlins, *The State and the Unions: Labor Relations, Law, and the Organized Labor Movement in America, 1880–1960* (New York: Cambridge University Press, 1985), pp. 99–101.

40. The discussion of OPA draws on my article, '"How about some meat?" The Office of Price Administration, consumption politics, and state-building from the bottom-up, 1941–1946', *Journal of American History*, 84 (1997), pp. 910–41. I reconstruct the history of OPA from the Records of the Office of Price Administration, RG 188 (National Archives, College Park, MD).

Central to its effectiveness, OPA undertook the organization of a broad, cross-class coalition of consumers as shock troops in enforcing price regulations at the grass roots from the downtown department store to the local butcher shop. Sombart's formulation was exactly wrong; the politics of roast beef caused the public to critique capitalism at its core. In the 1940s, at a time when the American working-class movement had achieved its greatest organizational power, the price of meat became the touchstone of social politics and served as a central mobilizing impulse. By appealing to and relying on thousands of middle- and working-class shoppers to police prices, OPA validated citizens' understanding of themselves as consumers and gave them a sense of entitlement to ever-expanding living standards. These volunteer price inspectors worked with 'Little OPAs', the 5,525 local War and Price Rationing Boards. A legacy of the NRA county councils, these organizations were all-pervasive. In March 1944 alone, 41,000 volunteers checked prices at 430,000 food stores. By 1945, at least 7 per cent of all women shoppers, roughly 2.1 million, claimed to have reported a price violation.

The politicizing of the family provisioner and the resulting possibility of an organized consumer interest backed by the state proved a highly potent combination. OPA's Consumer Advisory Board initiated the distribution of price ceiling charts directly to individual consumers. As the war progressed, OPA propaganda grew increasingly militant, culminating with its image of a snarling housewife, gritting her teeth, fist clenched, proclaiming, 'I'm out to lick Runaway Prices'. The claim to being a housewife conferred new legitimacy and new authority.[41] With grass-roots consumers as government agents, price controls extended state supervision to private market transactions. And OPA was popular. Nearly one year after the end of the war, three-quarters of the public supported a continuation of controls. In addition to serving immediate needs, OPA represented a political culture premised on broad popular participation and consumer rights.

Immediately following the war, this consuming public remained powerful. There were countless strikes on the shop floors and in the storefronts. And these protests were linked by a broader purchasing-power ideology. Throughout the New Deal and Second World War, labour leaders, liberal economists, and progressive policy-makers had maintained that mass purchasing power provided the key to economic growth. For two decades, the emerging industrial labour movement had argued with much success that it best represented the nation's general welfare. Indeed, in their post-war strike against General Motors, the United Autoworkers used as their slogan 'Purchasing Power for Prosperity' and demanded that GM pay higher wages

---

41. On propaganda aimed at women, see also A. Bentley, *Eating for Victory: Food Rationing and the Politics of Domesticity* (Urbana: University of Illinois Press, 1998).

without increasing prices. The public supported the demands of these striking workers.[42]

The Defeat of the Purchasing Power Ideology, 1946–1964

Business managers who had lived through the 1930s and 1940s, who feared this politicized worker-consumer alliance, faced the post-war years with trepidation. Again and again in the post-war period businessmen and their Republican representatives felt it necessary to defeat labour and circumscribe their arena of activity.[43] If it was a liberal agenda to politicize purchasing power, then the conservative project intended to depoliticize consumption, or at least offer an alternative view that disconnected labour's demands for more from the welfare of middle-class consumers.

In 1946, OPA's very strength led to a forceful countermobilization. Business representatives from the local grocer to the National Association of Manufacturers (NAM) abhorred OPA's insistence on subjecting private pricing decisions to public scrutiny. They especially despised controls when combined with the War Labor Board's authority to regulate wages and hours. But they hated OPA more than the WLB. At the end of the war, those industries with narrow profit margins such as textiles, dry goods, groceries, and meat led the charge to eliminate OPA. They argued that controls would lead to extreme shortages and possibly a famine. In the summer of 1946, congressmen who represented these industries, especially the meat packers, severely weakened OPA's authority. In a direct challenge, one Republican representative of cattle interests declared, 'If my family needs meat I am going to get it wherever I can'. Meat producers then advanced the battle from Congress to the local butcher shop and into household kitchens by withholding their meat from market.[44]

Amid this 'famine', consumers rapidly abandoned OPA as ineffectual. This sudden shift brought to the fore inherent instabilities of the purchasing power

---

42. W. Reuther, 'GM versus the rest of us', *New Republic*, 14 January 1946, p. 42; N. Lichtenstein, *The Most Dangerous Man in Detroit: Walter Reuther and the Fate of American Labor* (New York: Basic, 1995), pp. 231–4. Gallop polls report that in the middle of the 113-day long strike, 60 per cent of the public supported the UAW's demands for higher wages. As late as May 1946, 68 per cent favored the retention of price controls. See H. Rockoff, *Drastic Measures: A History of Wage and Price Controls in the United States*, (New York: Cambridge University Press, 1984), pp. 101–2.

43. On anti-union campaigns, see H.J. Harris, *The Right to Manage: Industrial Relations Policies of American Business in the 1940s* (Madison: University of Wisconsin Press, 1982); E.A. Fones-Wolfe, *Selling Free Enterprise: The Business Assault on Labor and Liberalism, 1945–60* (Urbana: University of Illinois Press, 1994); and D. Plotke, *Building a Democratic Political Order: Reshaping American Liberalism in the 1930s and 1940s* (New York: Cambridge University Press, 1996).

44. Jacobs, '"How about some meat",' p. 933.

program that had existed all along: that it rested on a precarious cross-class consensus and was subject to short-term consumer gratification. The public had supported OPA when it had succeeded in controlling inflation and distributing goods equitably. Indeed, early in the summer of 1946, hundreds of thousands of consumers had rallied to support a renewal of a strong OPA. But now fed-up with OPA's inability to face down its enemies and force meat from the hoof to the table, the public's support turned to anger and apathy. As one enraged mother put it, 'I am just one of the many thousands of harassed housewives trying to feed a family and keep them healthy during these days of "no Meat".'[45] Unable to deliver the goods, OPA alienated the consumers whose expectations it had raised and on whose support it depended, while its labour allies worried first about securing wage increases regardless of the overall stabilization programme. NAM capitalized on the tensions between producer and consumer interests and played to the fears of a consuming public. As soon as the war had ended, NAM led a direct attack on OPA blaming price controls for the scarcity of consumer goods. They ran ads that asked 'Would You Like Some Butter or a Roast of Beef?'[46] The result was the political defeat of OPA in the November 1946 elections, appropriately dubbed the 'beefsteak' elections.

Throughout the early post-war decades, conservative forces continued to pit labour and consumer interests at odds. Their animus was not confined to OPA, but rather aimed at the whole mobilized consuming public that the New Deal had created. The inflation of the post-war period helped the conservative position. To these conservatives, the dramatic inflation immediately following the war symbolized labour's power. From this point on, conservatives explained inflation as the product of the 'wage-price spiral' forced on the nation by what was then labelled 'monopoly unionism'. The disruptive set of strikes unions waged in this inflationary era strengthened the conservatives' argument. In nation-wide newspaper advertisements, NAM blamed 'labor monopoly' and industry-wide bargaining for 'rais[ing] the prices of things you need'. A full-page ad declared, 'The price of MONOPOLY comes out of your pocket'. Another insisted, 'Industry-wide bargaining is no bargain for you'.[47] By conflating inflation, or the spectre of inflation, with labour's power and vice versa, conservatives sought to undermine their opponents' strength and challenge both the New Deal political economy and its consumption-driven model of economic growth. In 1947, conservatives used the fear of the high cost of living to win support for the Taft-Hartley Act that restricted the expansive powers labour had won in the New Deal.

45. *Ibid.*, pp. 939–40.
46. *Ibid.*, p. 935.
47. All ads found in the Records of the National Association of Manufactures, Pamphlets Collection (Hagley Museum, Wilmington, Delaware).

The alliance between consumers and organized labour had held firm in the Depression and remained intact during the war. It had served as the basis of challenging corporate America and put into place a powerful engine of economic mobility, the national collective-bargaining regime. But as economic and political circumstances changed, this alliance fractured. The stronger the unions became, the greater the tension between organized workers and the unorganized middle classes. Mild levels of inflation in the post-war era served as the issue upon which this alliance split apart. Though insignificant by post-1970s standards, the low levels of inflation of the 1950s did generate insecurity and discontent. *Business Week* referred to inflation as 'the permanent dilemma' and explained 'a prosperous country can have its own brand of discontentment . . . The complaint isn't that things are bad, but that the price of keeping them good is so high'. And anti-New Deal politicians throughout the decade capitalized on fears of escalating costs and mounting debt. Corporations, particularly those in competitive markets, succeeded in using inflation to delegitimize both organized labour and the regulatory state.[48] Through repeated political battles in the post-war decades, this conservative alliance transformed the issue of purchasing power into one handled best by macroeconomic policy as embodied in the Tax Cut of 1964. Gradually a post-war liberalism predicated on taxing private citizens to pay for public entitlements replaced the notion of a consuming public in which converting the masses into politicized consumers had been the prescription for economic growth.

Above all, the American politics of plenty suggests that the quest for high standards of living that Sombart thought so depoliticizing proved powerfully mobilizing. The ultimate defeat of a consuming public and the resulting privatizing of consumption in the post-war decades obscured its radical potential to conservative economists and New Left scholars alike. But in the context of depression and war, a consumer politics had laid the basis for an interventionist New Deal state. Early twentieth-century consumerism celebrated both the freedom of the marketplace and the growth of the state to assure participation in that market. By reconnecting different levels of political activity from familial consumption to marketplace relations to Congressional policy-making, the history of consumption politics illuminates the evolving relationship among labour, capital, the market, and the state.

---

48. 'Inflation: the permanent dilemma', *Business Week*, 24 May 1952, pp. 32–3. I expand these ideas more fully in Jacobs, 'The American middle classes and the fear of inflation in the 1950s', in O. Zunz (ed.), *Postwar Social Contracts Under Stress* (New York: Russell Sage Press, forthcoming 2001).

12

Consumer Politics in Post-war Britain

Matthew Hilton

In July 1999, the British Labour Government published its new consumer manifesto, *Modern Markets: Confident Consumers*. In the foreword, Stephen Byers, Secretary of State for Trade and Industry, announced that the 'White Paper puts consumers centre stage. It recognises for the first time that confident, demanding consumers are good for business. They promote innovation and stimulate better value and in return get better products at lower prices'.[1] In the rhetorical alliance between consumers and industry, the Government redefined citizenship to place 'consumers at the heart of policy-making'. The document pledged to reformulate competition policy to improve choice and value-for-money, to modernize consumer law, to ease the means by which consumers can seek redress and to enable the consumer voice to be heard in Government.

In its assumptions about the definition of the needs of consumers, *Modern Markets: Confident Consumers* parallels the 'customer as citizen' commercial ideology which Lizabeth Cohen argues characterizes the US *Consumer's Republic*.[2] Consumerism is acknowledged as a central tenet of citizenship in the modern state yet it is a consumerism of shopping (*customer consumer*), rather than of an informed, socially-aware, political activism (*citizen consumer*) which she suggests dominated the consumer politics of the New Deal era. This is a model which might equally be applied to twentieth-century British history, since the White Paper can be seen as a culmination of several decades of modern consumer-protection legislation which began with the final report of the Molony Committee on Consumer Protection in 1962. This led directly to the creation of the Consumer Council in 1963 and the Trades Descriptions Act of 1968 which, in turn, were followed by a flurry of legislation in the 1970s that included the 1973 Fair Trading Act, the 1974 Consumer Credit Act, the 1977 Restrictive Trade Practices Act and the 1978 Consumer Safety Act.[3] However, all of these later measures, which were

---

1. Department of Trade and Industry, *Modern Markets: Confident Consumers. The Government's Consumer White Paper*, Cm. 4410 (London: The Stationery Office, 1999), p. 1.

2. See Chapter Ten.

3. G. Borrie, *The Development of Consumer Law and Policy: Bold Spirits and Timorous Souls* (London: Stevens & Sons, 1984); G. Smith, *The Consumer Interest* (London: John Martin, 1982).

supported by further legislation in the 1980s and 1990s, might be said to have been the logical extensions of an agenda of consumerism first set out by the Molony Committee which sought to help the consumer make a 'wise and informed choice'.[4]

Choice, value-for-money, redress, information and education form the language of a dominant type of consumer politics which protects the consumer from within the market place, rather than offering a critique of or challenge to it. It is certainly not the only consumer politics which has existed in post-war Britain. For instance, the state has encouraged the collective consumption of various services provided by the BBC and the nationalized industries, the Design Council has considered factors other than price in the manufacture of commercial commodities, and successive governments have continued to restrict the sale (or 'corral' the market as Gary Cross puts it) of products judged to fall outside the remit of the free market, such as tobacco, alcohol and other psychoactive substances.[5] Furthermore, the specific sites of material politics have remained important and consumers have chosen to boycott various goods for a variety of moral and political reasons, while some have organized more general consumer political bodies based on ethical or environmental principles.[6] But the consumer politics put forward by the Molony Committee has come to dominate successive governments' understanding of the issue as well as providing the framework for many of the institutions of customer-consumer citizenship.

The Molony Committee was appointed to review the existing legislation on consumer protection and to examine other means for the 'protection of the consuming public'.[7] Concern had been expressed in Parliament and elsewhere that the rapid expansion of the economy was leaving the consumer defenceless against powerful commercial forces which had rendered much of the existing legislation outdated. Methods of consumer protection set out in the 1875 Sale of Foods and Drugs Act, the 1893 Sale of Goods Act, the Weights and Measures Acts (1878–1936), the Merchandise Marks Acts (1887–1953), the 1938 Hire Purchase Act and the various precedents established through the common law

---

4. *Final Report of the Committee on Consumer Protection*, Cmnd. 1781 (London: HMSO, 1962), p. 16.

5. P.J. Maguire and J.M. Woodham (eds), *Design and Cultural Politics in Post-war Britain: The Britain Can Make It Exhibition of 1946* (London: Leicester University Press, 1997); M. Hilton, *Smoking in British Popular Culture, 1800–2000* (Manchester: Manchester University Press, 2000); G. Cross, see Chapter Fourteen.

6. D.A. Aaker and G.S. Day (eds), *Consumerism: Search for the Consumer Interest*, 3rd edn (Basingstoke: Macmillan, 1978); Y. Gabriel and T. Lang, *The Unmanageable Consumer: Contemporary Consumption and its Fragmentation* (London: Sage, 1995); *The Ethical Consumer Guide to Everyday Shopping* (Manchester: ECRA Publishing, 1993).

7. *Final Report*, p. 1.

were felt to have become a confusing entanglement of central and local admin-istrative procedures.[8] The complexity of modern commerce bewildered the consumer, making him or her 'vulnerable to exploitation and deception': 'Even if no advantage is taken of his [*sic*] ignorance, his ill-informed approach to the shopping problems arising in an era of plenty and prosperity is likely, it is said, to lead him into purchases unsuited to his needs.'[9] In its response to these problems, the Committee made 214 recommendations, all of which were of an extremely practical nature to do with issues such as the desirability of informative labelling, voluntary standards on production quality and the need for stricter legislation concerning guarantees, trade descriptions and hire purchase contracts. Care was taken to avoid as far as possible any statement of general consumer 'rights', though the Committee did propose the creation of an independent Consumers' Council, funded by the government, to co-ordinate, oversee and inform itself of the nature of consumer problems and to represent the consumer at all levels of state activity.[10]

What is perhaps most significant about the Molony Committee is that it placed the 'consumer', rather than the more general 'public', at the centre of political debate.[11] This is more than a question of semantics, since references to 'consumer issues' were still trivialized and treated with mirth in Parliament as late as 1959 and some MPs continued to filibuster rather than seriously debate consumer topics.[12] Nevertheless, the productivist bias of the members of the Committee meant that the aim was merely to 'fortify' the existing system of consumer protection without 'significantly altering' it.[13] They offered no radical reinterpretation of the consumer, synonymously interchanging the term with that of 'shopper' which they defined as an essentially economic agent: 'one who purchases (or hire purchases) goods for private use or consumption'.[14] Instead they heaped praise on British

8. J. Burnett, *Plenty and Want: A Social History of Diet in England from 1815 to the Present* (London: Nelson, 1966); J. Phillips and M. French, 'Adulteration and food law, 1899–1939', *Twentieth-Century British History*, 9 (1998), pp. 350–69; *Final Report*, pp. 8–15; Borrie, *Development of Consumer Law*, pp. 7–9; Smith, *Consumer Interest*, pp. 131–3, 210–14; C.D. Harbury, *Efficiency and the Consumer* (London: Fabian Society, 1958), pp. 6–7; L. Tivey, 'Quasi-government for consumers', in A. Barker (ed.), *Quangos in Britain: Government and the Networks of Public Policy Making* (Basingstoke: Macmillan, 1982), pp. 144–7.

9. *Final Report*, p. 16; Public Record Office, Kew (hereafter PRO) BT 258/879, Committee on Consumer Protection, *Committee Papers*: 'CCP5: Alleged inadequacies in present arrangements for consumer protection and guidance'.

10. *Final Report*, pp. 299–315.

11. In competition policy immediately prior to the Molony Committee, little explicit reference was made to the consumer. See, for example, *Monopolies and Restrictive Practices Commission, Collective Discrimination: A Report on Exclusive Dealing, Collective Boycotts, Aggregated Rebates and Other Discriminatory Practices*, Cmd., 9504 (London: HMSO, 1955).

12. The MP, Frederick Willey, claimed that 'It has become conventional to make an amusing speech on this subject', *House of Commons Debates* (hereafter *H. C. Deb.*), 602, 20 March 1959, cols. 837, 868.

13. *Final Report*, p. 269.

14. *Ibid.*, p. 1.

industry, criticizing only a 'small minority' of manufacturers or 'irresponsible importers' who too readily accepted inferior foreign goods.[15]

But was this model of consumer politics the only one available to the members of the Committee? Chapters Three and Seven on British material politics, certainly suggest that other definitions of consumerism and citizenship existed. Working-class radicals formulated politics of consumption based on well-established notions of the rights and social duties of the consumer as well as the obligations of the state to meet a clear set of wants and needs. This chapter will first consider, therefore, the other versions of consumerism articulated both immediately before and during the establishment of the Molony Committee in 1959. Secondly, it will explore the actual workings of the Committee to show how potential alternatives were deliberately excluded while a long succession of producers were invited to speak for the consumer. However, a third section will also show that a new consumer activism had emerged in the 1950s based on affluence rather than scarcity, and older consumer groups such as the Co-operative Movement had to reformulate their consumer politics to cope with abundance as well as with necessity. Although the Molony committee was initially sceptical of bodies such as the Consumers' Association, there actually emerged a shared discourse and ideology of consumerism which facilitated a closer relationship between governments and the new consumer groups from the 1960s onwards. This forms the substance of a final section in which I argue that consumer citizenship in modern Britain was a consequence of liberal and voluntarist traditions of state development, rather than the corporatism of West Germany or the grass-roots activism of France identified in Chapter Thirteen. Throughout, it will emerge that the social *duties* attached to earlier forms of consumer citizenship have become increasingly absent in this officially-sanctioned consumerism, while an incremental series of practical *rights* of consumer citizenship have been conceded so that a particular type of 'confident consumer' has emerged in the 'modern market'.

Noel Thompson in Chapter Three and Frank Trentmann in Chapter Seven both demonstrate the centrality of consumption to traditions of radical political economy. By the end of the nineteenth century, the writings of John Ruskin and William Morris inspired a duty-bound, socially-aware consumer citizenship that penetrated especially the writings of the economist J.A. Hobson.[16] The Co-operative

15. *Interim Report of the Committee on Consumer Protection*, Cmnd. 1011 (London: HMSO, 1960), p. 5.

16. J. Ruskin, *Unto This Last: Four Essays on the First Principles of Political Economy* (1862), in *The Works of Ruskin*, Vol. 17 (London: Smith, Elder & Co., 1872); W. Morris, *How We Live and How We Might Live* (1885), and *Useful Work and Useless Toil* (1884), in A. Briggs (ed.), *William Morris: Selected Writings and Designs* (1962; Harmondsworth: Penguin, 1977), pp. 117–35, 158–78. See also N. Thompson, *The Market and its Critics: Socialist Political Economy in the Nineteenth Century* (London: Routledge, 1988), chapters 9 and 10; N. Thompson, 'Hobson and the Fabians: two roads to socialism in the 1920s', *History of Political Economy*, 26 (1994), pp. 203–20.

Movement in particular was argued to provide the means for a collective control of consumption based on sound moral and political principles, yet which also enabled all co-operators to express their individuality, as they knew all efforts of an aesthetic or spiritual nature that they put into their ordinary consumption patterns would be catered for by a co-operative store that they themselves owned.[17] Moral and economic questions were thus inseparable in ideas about consumption as the Co-operative Movement advocated both the need for individual responsibility and the collective distribution of commercial goods. While some writers continued to emphasize the more Victorian self-help virtues of personal responsibility in consumption,[18] and particularly in temperance as a means of controlling industry, others were more firmly located within the Co-operative Movement. Beatrice Webb wrote in her diary how she had been inspired by the 'prophet' J.W.T. Mitchell, who had realized the 'real meaning' of co-operation which was to serve consumers as an end in itself rather than as a means to achieve the goal of worker control and ownership of production.[19] The Webbs began to explore the history of the moral economy, using such examples to work out a theory of consumption in which eventually a 'democracy of co-operative consumers' would complement a similar 'democracy of producers' created by the trade union movement.[20] Such ideas opened up the potential of the co-operative societies and located consumption as the theoretical means of creating a new state and society.

Frank Trentmann's essay makes clear the extent to which these ideas were articulated into a practical political programme by members of the First World War Consumers' Council. A politics of consumer citizenship was formulated based on an understanding of the social duties of consumers and the obligation of the state to respect their rights in regard to the basic necessities of life. Although the Consumers' Council failed to become a permanent body championing the ordinary consumer's cause against the 'profiteering' capitalists and 'organised forces of the trading community',[21] a number of writers in the inter-war period continued

---

17. P. Gurney, *Co-operative Culture and the Politics of Consumption in England, c. 1870–1930* (Manchester: Manchester University Press, 1996).

18. H. Withers, *Poverty and Waste* (London: Smith, Elder & Co., 1914); R.S. Moffat, *The Economy of Consumption: an Omitted Chapter in Political Economy* (London: Kegan Paul, 1878); E.J. Urwick, *Luxury and Waste of Life* (London: J. M. Dent, 1908); W. Hoyle, *Our National Resources; and How They are Wasted. An Omitted Chapter in Political Economy* (Manchester: John Heywood, 1871).

19. B. Webb, *The Discovery of the Consumer* (London: Ernest Benn, 1928), pp. 11–16.

20. S. Webb and B. Webb, 'The Assize of Bread', *Economic Journal*, 14 (1904), pp. 196–218; S. Webb and B. Webb, *The Consumers' Co-operative Movement* (London: Longman, Green & Co., 1921).

21. Consumers' Council archive, Marion Phillips papers, Manchester Labour History Archive (hereafter CC) CP 316/1: The Consumers' Council, *Statement of their Resignation from the Ministry of Food*, p. 1; R.A. Bayliss, 'The Consumers' Council, 1918–1921', *Journal of Consumer Studies and Home Economics*, 3 (1979), pp. 37–45; R.A. Bayliss, 'The Consumers' Council Bills, 1929–1939', *Journal of Consumer Studies and Home Economics*, 4 (1980), pp. 115–23.

the call for a consumer politics. Percy Redfern in particular was clear about the potential of a united consumer movement:

> We – the mass of common men and women in all countries – also compose the world's market. To sell to us is the ultimate aim of the world's business. Hence it is ourselves as consumers who stand in central relation to all the economics of the world, like a king in his kingdom. As producers we go each unto a particular factory, farm or mine, but as consumers we are set by nature thus to give leadership, aim and purpose to the whole economic world. That we are not kings, but serfs in the mass, is due to our failure to think and act together as consumers and so realise our true position and power.[22]

For Redfern, 'A social philosophy, a human ideal and a new economic method are all to be found in consumers' service. It is the consumer who stands at the gates of a new social order.'[23] He hoped to mobilize a 'consumer consciousness' to eradicate poverty and to instil a 'religious sense of the meaning of life' so that consumers would take care to ensure fair systems of production all around the world.[24] The means by which this was to be achieved was through co-operation, though a more centralized, efficient, innovative and varied type of co-operation than that which existed in Britain in the 1920s.

Redfern's writings, however, were much more than an attempt to revitalize the Co-operative Movement, and the collection of 24 essays he commissioned for his *Self and Society* series in 1928 and 1929 demonstrate the wider implications envisioned for consumption.[25] According to writers such as Harold Laski and Philip Snowden, consumption was the key to modern citizenship, and they urged fellow co-operators to strive for a theory or social philosophy of the state in order to ease the 'co-operative commonwealth' into the institutions of the modern nation.[26] Other essays turned, as with the Webbs, to medieval examples to suggest ways in which trade unions and consumer interests might be reconciled,[27] and Leonard Woolf suggested that co-operation's internationalism would bring about and necessitate world peace, a theory of consumption which he articulated further in his other works.[28] A variety of writers saw the organization of consumers as a means of

---

22. P. Redfern, *The Consumer's Place in Society* (Manchester: Co-operative Union, 1920), p. 12.

23. *Ibid.*, pp. 16–17.

24. *Ibid.*, p. 56.

25. P. Redfern (ed.), *Self and Society*, 2 vols (London: Ernest Benn, 1930).

26. H. Laski, *The Recovery of Citizenship* (London: Ernest Benn, 1928); P. Snowden, *The Faith of a Democrat* (London: Ernest Benn, 1928).

27. W.M. Citrine, *Labour and the Community* (London: Ernest Benn, 1928); M. Bondfield, *The Meaning of Trade* (London: Ernest Benn, 1928); A.E. Levett, *The Consumer in History* (London: Ernest Benn, 1929).

28. L. Woolf, *The Way of Peace* (London: Ernest Benn, 1928). See also his *Socialism and Co-operation* (London: National Labour Press, 1921).

fostering a more religious outlook, assisting women's emancipation, and creating a more discriminatory attitude towards the arts,[29] while a number of economists saw this new focus on consumption as a solution to the productivist bias of classical economics.[30] Here, the series of pamphlets complemented a number of other, admittedly relatively unknown, early twentieth-century consumer advocates whose politics was firmly based on a class-based critique of capitalism, who called not on workers but on consumers to overthrow the existing structures of state and society.[31]

These ideas persisted throughout and beyond the Second World War. In 1947, the Co-operative Party still urged that 'the State should be controlled in the interests of the consumer', basing this advocacy of the 'sovereignty of the consumer' on 'the Socialist ground that consumer control is *the only true classless* control'.[32] The Fabians, too, wished to rectify the economic system that left the consumer 'at the mercy of the producer', placing their faith in the power of state intervention to promote a new awareness and respect for consumer problems.[33] In Parliament, the Labour MP Elaine Burton championed the consumer cause throughout the 1950s, her 1955 pamphlet demonstrating her detailed knowledge of consumer problems as she urged state intervention to rectify any abuses of the market.[34] Burton also looked back fondly to the security of the wartime Utility Schemes which maintained a minimum level of standards in manufacture, subjected the items to price control and exempted them from purchase tax, 'in order to keep down the price of essentials and hold the cost of living in check'.[35]

These notions of consumer citizenship were, however, born of necessity rather than of abundance. Rising living standards in the 1950s gave rise to a new set of consumer problems to which the Co-operative Movement's 'consumer commonwealth' appeared less relevant. The collectivist tendencies of consumer politics did not provide the answers for a new group of consumers concerned not with shortage and adulteration (which the welfare state had in many cases solved), but with proliferation and plenty. Newly affluent consumers now appeared more

29. H. Johnson, *Religion Interferes* (London: Ernest Benn, 1928); E. Sharp, *Daily Bread* (London: Ernest Benn, 1928); I. Brown, *Art and Everyman* (London: Ernest Benn, 1929).

30. G.W. Daniels, *Capital, Labour and the Consumer* (London: Ernest Benn, 1929). See also E. O'Duffy, *Consumer Credit* (London: The Prosperity League, 1934).

31. T. Billington Greig, *The Consumer in Revolt* (London: Stephen Swift, 1912); F. Henderson, *Capitalism and the Consumer* (London: George Allen & Unwin, 1936).

32. H. Campbell, *Wanting and Working* (London: Co-operative Party, 1947).

33. L. Freedman and G. Hemingway, *Nationalisation and the Consumer* (London: Fabian Publications, 1950).

34. *H. C. Deb.*, 602, 20 March 1959, col. 858; E. Burton, *The Battle of the Consumer* (London: Labour Party, 1954).

35. *Final Report*, p. 76; Burton, *Battle of the Consumer*, p. 10.

concerned with the problems of making an expert judgement on the ever-expanding range of consumer goods available. The difficulties facing the housewife were said to be those of coping with the changes that had taken place in retailing methods, the introduction of high-pressure sales techniques and manipulative advertising, and the escalating number of new plastic, electronic and highly technical goods which made it impossible for supposedly traditional forms of consumer knowledge and discrimination to apply.[36] In short, the pace of economic change was said to have outstripped the consumer's ability to stay informed of such developments. She, and increasingly he, needed advice in determining personal and individual preferences in order to avoid returning home with a product unsuited to her or his needs. John Hilton's radio broadcasts during the war (*John Hilton Talking*) were followed up by his regular 'Advice Bureau' in the *News of the World* which aimed to increase the 'liaison between the citizen and state'.[37] After the war more specific consumer-advice columns appeared in other national newspapers, the most famous being in the *Guardian*, written by Elizabeth Gundrey who went on to publish several books on practical consumer-choice problems.[38]

The growing consumer awareness was maintained by the publication of Robert Millar's *The Affluent Sheep* in 1963, but by then the tone of modern consumer activism had been set by the incorporation of the Consumers' Association (CA) in 1957 as a non-profit-making private company. Inspired by the lead of the American Consumers Union, Michael Young brought together a broad range of professional people from across the political spectrum who included Lord Beveridge, Sir Julian Huxley, Anthony Crosland, the wives of Hugh Gaitskell, Jo Grimond and Roy Jenkins, and the Conservative MP, P.C. Goodhart, with Caspar Brook as Director and Eirlys Roberts as Editor. The organization concerned itself principally with the comparative testing of commercial products, the results being published in its monthly member's magazine, *Which?*, from October 1957. At the end of its first year, the CA had 85,000 members and 165,000 by 1960, demonstrating a popular demand for independent judgements of freely available products. In 1961 the CA gave its support to the establishment of local consumer groups, 49 of which affiliated to form the Federation of Consumer Groups in 1963. (There were over

---

36. Association of Scientific Workers, *Spotlight on Shopping: Consumer Research* (London: Association of Scientific Workers, 1951); D. Lazell, *Consumers and the Community: A Study Guide on the Application of the Rochdale Principles to Modern Consumer Problems* (Loughborough: Co-operative Union, 1961); R. Millar, *The Affluent Sheep: A Profile of the British Consumer* (London: Longmans, 1963); *Final Report*, p. 129.

37. E. Nixon, *John Hilton: The Story of His Life* (London: George Allen & Unwin, 1946), p. 305.

38. E. Gundrey, *Your Money's Worth: A Handbook for Consumers* (Harmondsworth: Penguin, 1962); *At Your Service: A Consumer's Guide to the Service Trades and Professions* (Harmondsworth: Penguin, 1964); *A Foot in the Door: An Exposé of High Pressure Sales Methods* (London: Frederick Muller, 1965).

80 one year later.)[39] Also in this year, the independent non-profit making Research Institute for Consumer Affairs was established to inform and guide the public about the value-for-money of various goods and services.[40] Although the CA would provide many ideas for consumer protection by successive governments, the principal motivation of its almost entirely middle-class membership was to secure value-for-money rather than to offer any critique of the fundamentals of free-market capitalism. Its emphasis on the rights of individual consumers to be able to choose from a range of fairly priced quality products made it a substantially different organization from those which had earlier stressed the social duties of citizen-consumers to advocate the state-sponsored or collectivist provision of staple commodities.

These organizations of private consumers complemented the activities of several special interest groups such as the Automobile Association and the earlier Electrical Association for Women and the Women's Gas Federation, as well as the work of private organizations such as the Good Housekeeping Institute which awarded its own seals of approval to specific commodities. In addition, since the 1940s there had emerged a number of public and independent bodies which existed as part of the state apparatus. The nationalized industries had their central and regional consumer councils and the Citizens' Advice Bureaux, the Medical Research Council and the Council for Industrial Design were all concerned with consumer issues.[41] Most directly related to consumer protection, however, were the Women's Advisory Committee (WAC) set up in 1951 and representing 22 women's organizations which later fed into the Consumer Advisory Council (CAC) set up in 1955. These two bodies existed as part of the British Standards Institute (BSI), advising the parent body on the applications of standards to domestic goods. The BSI standards dealt mainly with issues of safety, but from 1957 the CAC began to publish its own quarterly *Shopper's Guide*, edited by Elizabeth Gundrey. As with *Which?*, *Shopper's Guide* engaged in comparative testing and was available to CAC Associates upon subscription. There were 50,000 Associates by 1959 who also had available to them other services of the CAC, such as information sheets on specific goods, negotiations with retailers and manufacturers in the light of customer

---

39. PRO BT 258/882,: 'CCP81: Submission by Consumers' Association Ltd.'; Smith, *Consumer Interest*, pp. 284–7; L. Tivey, 'The politics of the consumer', in R. Kimber and J.J. Richardson, *Pressure Groups in Britain: A Reader* (London: Dent, 1974), pp. 198–200; Consumers' Association, *Thirty Years of Which? 1957–1987* (London: Consumers' Association, 1987); Consumer Council, *Information for Consumer Education* (London: Consumer Council, 1965).

40. L. Syson, *Fair Trading* (London: Research Institute for Consumer Affairs, 1964).

41. Tivey, 'Politics of the consumer', p. 201; Harbury, *Efficiency*, pp. 22–3; PRO BT 258/879, Committee on Consumer Protection, *Committee Papers:* 'CCP14: Submission by the Good Housekeeping Institute'.

complaints, the publicizing of BSI standards and an advisory service which was dealing with 1,500 letters a week in 1958.[42]

By the end of the 1950s there were, then, several private and public bodies purporting to speak for the consumer. It would seem natural, therefore, that a committee examining the whole issue of consumer protection would have included some representatives of the CAC, the Co-operative Movement or the CA as its members. The Board of Trade, however, had other ideas as to who was best qualified to understand the consumer interest. The initial membership of the committee stood in stark contrast to the working-class representatives of the Labour movement that had constituted the First World War Consumer Council. The chair, J.T. Molony, was a barrister and, of the eleven others, two were solicitors (B. Kenyon and D.I. Wilson) with some experience of previous protection legislation and five were businessmen, including a member of the Retail Trading Standards Association (J. Ramage) and Lord Geddes, former director of the Shell Group as well as of several other companies. There seemed an implicit assumption that in the free market businessmen were immediately qualified to represent the consumer, no matter how little direct experience they had of such work. However, to temper such interests, four women were also appointed: two 'housewives' with no obvious experience of consumer work (Mrs L. Beauchamp and Mrs B. Diamond); a former solicitor who, after marriage, gave up practice to work for various women's committees (Mrs D.R. Stone); and Miss A.L. Richmond, a veteran trades unionist who tripled up as the working-class and Scottish representative.[43]

Complaints were immediately aired in Parliament from the Labour and Co-operative consumer lobby of Elaine Burton, Norman Dodds, Herbert Morrison, George Darling and A.E. Oram. They repeatedly asked, in indignant tones, why the Co-operative Movement, with its thirteen million members, was not represented on the Committee, and why there was so little experience of working-class consumer problems among the members appointed when it would have been so easy to mobilize the voice of the working-class housewife.[44] The Conservative Patricia McLaughlin, usually a consumer advocate, came to the government's defence on this point with the interesting assumption of homogeneity when she argued that the two housewives already on the committee would be 'perfectly capable to put the housewife's case satisfactorily'.[45] The fears of the government

---

42. PRO, BT 258/879, Committee on Consumer Protection, *Committee Papers*: 'CCP4: Letter from Chairman of the CAC of the BSI'; 'CCP 12: Submission by WAC'; 'CCP 13: Submission by CAC'; Harbury, *Efficiency*, pp. 14–16.

43. BT 258/879, 'CCP 6: Terms of reference and minutes of appointment'; *H. C. Deb.*, 610, 27 July 1959, col. 74.

44. *H. C. Deb.*, 608, 9 July 1959, col. 1560; 609, 16 July 1959, cols 571–2, *43*; 610, 27 July 1959, col. 65.

45. *H. C. Deb.*, 610, 27 July 1959, col. 48.

critics were seemingly confirmed once the Committee began to meet, as the voices of Diamond and Beauchamp hardly appear in the minutes, dominated as they were by the more experienced Molony and Geddes. The one woman who was capable of making and certainly *did* make her presence felt, Richmond, unfortunately had to retire in May 1960 because of ill health, having only attended nine meetings.[46] She was replaced by another woman with a firm belief in the benefits of consumer protection, Mrs I.O. Stewart, but the latter was by no means as vociferous and the dominant male members of the committee were happy to impose their voice on the consumer interest despite the underlying assumption which often surfaced that consumption lay in the realm of the woman's expertise.

Beyond issues of class and gender, MPs were also concerned about what they perceived as the limited terms of reference of the Molony Committee, which did not include the investigation of the provision of services as well as of goods. Molony himself, though, was happy with the limitations imposed on his Committee, commenting that the member's lack of knowledge of the subject matter of the enquiry helped foster a more 'detached' analysis and that it was important to consider only what was 'practically possible' rather than what was 'theoretically desirable in the interests of the consumer'.[47] His language of 'common-sense', 'balanced judgement' and 'fair treatment' to industry precluded any of the radicalism that had marked 1920s consumerism and limited the 'first objective' of the Committee to, in the words of the secretary, 'ensure that the consumer gets goods which satisfy his requirements'.[48] This was a consumer protection agenda of value-for-money, choice and competition, not of the transformation of the means of distribution. With such an initial agenda it is unsurprising that the Committee's findings were careful not to offer any challenge to the existing economic system: 'our findings in respect of particular trades demonstrated all too clearly that there is no single axiomatic approach'.[49]

The actual workings and procedures of the Committee seemed designed to confirm the member's prior assumptions. Evidence was taken from a total of 277 sources, 27 of which were from individuals, 56 from local and central government bodies and 13 from newspapers. There were 39 written and oral representations received from professional organizations and special-interest groups, which included some consumer bodies such as the CA and the Co-operative Union, but the bulk of the evidence was taken from 33 companies and 109 trade associations or bodies representing trading interests.[50] This productivist bias was hardly

46. PRO BT 258/878, Minutes of Meetings of Committee on Consumer Protection: *Meeting 16, 2 May 1960, minute 16:78.*
47. *Ibid., Meeting 1, 31 July, 1959, minute 1:5.*
48. PRO BT 258/880, 'CCP4: Draft programme of work'.
49. *Final Report*, p. 91.
50. *Ibid.*, Appendix B, pp. 317–21.

surprising given the close relations Helen Mercer has shown to have existed between industry and government throughout the post-war development of competition policy and the consequent scepticism with which existing consumer bodies were regarded.[51] The Committee was more than willing to pick out the faults of the CAC (that its Associates were largely middle-class) and the BSI (that it was insufficiently independent of business), yet they would skirt over the oral evidence these organizations could provide on what they knew to be the usual consumer complaints or their definition of the 'consumer interest'.[52]

But where this bias showed itself most prominently was in the attitude towards the CA, an organization that actually did not differ substantially from the Committee in its philosophy of market-based consumerism. Despite the solid reputation already attached to *Which?* for its objective independence, the Molony Committee continued to highlight the opportunities for corruption which existed in its comparative testing procedures. They expressed qualms about the oligarchic nature of the CA's self-perpetuating constitution and the motives of its members. They found it incredible to believe that the organizers of the CA had not formed the company for personal gain, provoking a deeply critical attitude to any evidence the CA presented and an almost enthusiastic willingness to listen to criticisms from other quarters.[53] Whereas business interests were asked to state their position on the issue of consumer protection, when Michael Young and Caspar Brook gave evidence to the committee in an interview, the onus was placed upon them to prove that the CA was not corrupt, was independent and that its business was conducted solely in the interests of the consumer. Their appearance before the committee took the form of a trial in which they were expected to defend themselves against what turned out to be a spurious charge that the CA's testing methods had unfairly treated two particular firms.[54] Even when Young and Brook had eased the minds of the Committee, Winifred Fordham, a former Director of CA who had resigned over the company's policy of independence from all manufacturing interests, was summoned to fuel further the suspicions of the Committee that there must necessarily be something dubious about an organization which did not appear to offer any direct financial rewards to its members.[55] As a further reflection of the committee's attitude to the CA, it constantly bemoaned the lack of evidence directly from the consumer, but it dismissed out-of-hand a survey conducted

51. H. Mercer, *Constructing a Competitive Order: the Hidden History of British Anti-Trust Policy* (Cambridge: Cambridge University Press, 1995).

52. PRO BT 258/878, *Meeting 4, 16 November 1959, minute 4:17; Meeting 5, 7 December 1959, minute 5:22; Meeting 6, 21 December 1959, minute 6:25; Meeting 7, 4 January 1960, minute 7:29.*

53. *Final Report*, p. 122; BT 258/878, *Meeting 3, 2 November 1959, minute 3:9;* BT 258/878, *Meeting 15, 11 April 1960, minute 15:77; Meeting 18, 30 May 1960, minute 18:101;* BT 258/883, 'CCP 114: Submissions by S. N. Bridges & Co. Ltd. and Wolf Electrical Tools Ltd.'

54. BT 258/878, *Meeting 25, 5 December 1960, minute 25:146.*

55. BT 258/878, *Meeting 33, 10 April 1961, minute 33:205.*

through *Which?* on the grounds that the CA's members were largely middle-class.[56] Given that the Committee itself was content to have no working-class representatives on its panel and that any summary of consumer views might have been better than the 'voiceless' position the *Final Report* suggested it had to deal with, the rejection of the CA's evidence appears a little high-handed.

This treatment of the organized consumer must also be contrasted with the evidence provided by businesses and trading interests. Despite the complaints which would later be made in Parliament about the predominance of manufacturers' views being represented in the evidence provided,[57] the Committee had no problems inviting companies to give oral evidence one after another. The messages that voluntary measures were better than compulsion, that competition was the best form of consumer protection, that consumers themselves were often largely to blame in issues of safety and that there was too much unnecessary 'grumbling' on the part of consumers were all actually treated with the necessary criticisms by the members of the Committee, but the constant repetition of the same messages served to eclipse any views of consumers themselves.[58] The questioning that trade representatives were subjected to was also less rigorous than that given to the CA. For instance, R. Diplock of the Retail Trading Standards Association (RTSA), a voluntary body created by the retail trade to prosecute some of the worst offences of retailers, was hardly expected to receive an aggressive examination from Ramage, a Committee member who was also on the Council of the RTSA.[59] Likewise, Attwood, President of his own market research company, was unlikely to take a belligerent stance against the many representatives of the advertising industry called in for questioning. Indeed, there existed a certain clubbishness between the Committee and industry, the secretary's notes to written depositions often mentioning characteristics which he deemed relevant: Diplock, in particular, was said to be a 'cheerful and forceful character (once, I believe, a rugger player of some distinction)'.[60] And there was too a frequent appeal to a national identity in that 'real' British traders would never engage in practices for which consumer protection was necessary. The 'national tradition', it was alleged, was one of voluntarism, not compulsion or 'professionalism'.[61]

---

56. BT 258/878, *Meeting 3, 2 November 1959, minute 3:9;* BT 258/880, 'CCP 20: CA Questionnaire'.

57. *H. C. Deb.,* 678, 20 May 1963, col. 136.

58. BT 258/878, *Meeting 14, 4 April 1960, minute 14:66; Meeting 20, 4 July, 1960, minute 20:116; Meeting.*

59. BT 258/879, 'CCP 9: Proposed submission by the Retail Trading Standards Association'; BT 258/878, *Meeting 27, 9 January 1961, minute 27:167.*

60. BT 258/879, 'CCP 9: Proposed submission by the Retail Trading Standards Association', note by Mitchelmore [Secretary].

61. BT 258/878, *Meeting 31, 6 March 1961, minute 31:191.*

Again, the significance of these examples becomes more apparent in contrast to the treatment of possible alternative viewpoints. A Co-operative pamphlet, published especially for the Molony Committee and submitted as evidence, was merely noted in the minutes.[62] No further discussion was deemed necessary and no representatives were called in to provide oral evidence, a somewhat surprising decision given that many thought this by now traditional representative of the consumer ought to have had a special seat on the committee from the beginning. Similar treatment was given to a Political and Economic Planning Pamphlet and to the detailed plans for consumer protection laid out by the Trades Unions Congress.[63] Elaine Burton's submission, containing as it did many statements of complaint from actual consumers, was dismissed as 'loose thinking and loose language' which 'made no positive contribution'. The Committee agreed 'that it contained no valid evidence or worthwhile suggestion which had not already been advanced from other quarters'. Yet Burton's submission did at least contain the direct opinions of consumers, something which the Committee claimed to be after, but here regarding their views as 'the unthinking acceptance, by an ill-informed and uncritical section of the community, of equally ill-informed statements'.[64] The Committee also received 1,000 letters from members of the public as evidence, a sample which it claimed was too small and which appears to have been consequently overlooked.[65]

The Committee thus disregarded any sources of evidence which might have clashed directly with the interests of business. But this productivist bias was not necessarily entirely due to the permeation of manufacturing concerns within government. The analysis has so far assumed that alternative politics of consumption were available to the Molony Committee but, during this period of affluence, this was not necessarily the case. While the consumer politics born of poverty and necessity highlighted in Thompson's and Trentmann's chapters gave rise to new understandings of the organization of society and economy, as well as the relationship between citizens and the state, organizations of the political Left appeared less imaginative in their formulation of consumer politics born of prosperity. Indeed, the long-held ascetic disdain of 'wants' held to be 'unproductive' or not 'real' explains the Left's difficulties with more affluent consumption (if not with the social consumption of necessities). Thus, when various political groups began to

---

62. BT 258/882, 'CCP 9: Co-operative Union, Memorandum for Submission to the Molony Committee on Consumer Protection'.

63. BT 258/878, *Meeting 18, 30 May 1960, minute 18:100*; BT 258/880, 'CCP 28: Submission by TUC'; BT 258/884, 'CCP 136: PEP Pamphlet, Consumer Protection and Enlightenment'.

64. BT 258/878, *Meeting 17, 16 May 1960, minute 17:90*; BT 258/882, 'CCP 84: Submission by Miss Elaine Burton'.

65. BT 258/878, *Meeting 45, 20 November 1961, minute 45:271*.

offer their own suggestions in the debates engendered by the establishment of the Molony Committee, the actual measures proposed – by bodies as diverse as the Co-operative and Conservative Parties – were often quite similar. Robert Millar, the Fabians, the Association of Scientific Workers, the Conservatives and various women's groups were all broadly in favour of the greater use of labelling, the promotion of standards, the extension of comparative testing and the dissemination of its results, the restriction of misleading statements and the creation of an independent body to represent, educate and inform itself of the consumer interest.[66]

Where these organizations began to disagree, however, was over the extent of state involvement. The right-wing Bow Group, of course, ruled that compulsion should only be used when all voluntary methods of control had been shown to fail, a sentiment shared by many other consumer groups.[67] Because the politics of consumption did not match on to the typical polarities of post-war politics, the consumer's cause was led by the Co-operative Party and the CA, rather than by the Labour Party. Here, a more interventionist administration was not assumed and many of the consumer groups failed or never even attempted to formulate a clear relationship between the rights and duties of the citizen-consumer and the obligations of the state. As Margaret Digby admitted, and as historians have picked up on, the Co-operative Movement never settled the issue of its relationship to the state and that this limited the practical role of its day-to-day running and policy formation.[68] Elsewhere, while consumers enjoyed the benefits of an expanding economy, liberal notions of the individual and his or her freedom within the market unhindered by a centralized bureaucracy prevailed. Whereas the creation of the welfare state and the post-war consensus in British politics had articulated a positive role for government in relation to the citizenship of workers, the precise relationship between the individual consumer, consumption and the state was by no means as clear.

Robert Millar perhaps best highlighted the dilemma when he asked the question, 'How far should the State go?'[69] He thought that because everybody is a consumer it was difficult for the state to act on the consumer's behalf since the consumer

---

66. Millar, *Affluent Sheep*, p. 199; Harbury, *Efficiency*, pp. 1–3; Association of Scientific Workers, *Spotlight on Shopping*, pp. 24–7; M. Baynes, *Advertising on Trial: The Case for the Consumer* (London: Bow Group, 1956), p. 2; P. Goodhart, M. Bemrose, J. Douglas, I. MacArthur, P. McLaughlin, J. B. Wood, *Choice: A Report on Consumer Protection* (London: Conservative Political Centre, 1961); P. Goodhart, *A Nation of Consumers* (London: Conservative Political Centre, 1965); BT 258/882, 'CCP 90: Submission by National Federation of Women's Institutes'; 'CCP 91: Submission of the National Council of Women of Great Britain'; 'CCP 92: Submission by the Women's Group on Public Welfare'; 'CCP 93: Submission by the Women's Co-operative Guild'.

67. Baynes, *Advertising*, p. 47.

68. M. Digby, *The World Co-operative Movement* (London: Hutchinson, 1949), p. 155; Gurney, *Co-operative Culture*.

69. Millar, *Affluent Sheep*, p. 177.

was not a distinct interest group, such as trade unionists. He admitted that the crux of the problem was that there was 'no clearly-expressed consumer philosophy with the backing of a powerful, all-class, all-party action group'.[70] However, he failed to produce an answer to his question and he retreated into a politics of pragmatism: 'Doctrinaire political attitudes soon lose their importance when shirt collars come out of the washing machine smaller than they went in.'[71] Instead, he asked another question, not of what *ideas* were going to lead the consumer movement, but *who*: 'Who will be the shepherds?' was his rather elitist final chapter title, explicitly labelling the ignorant, apathetic, careless and irresponsible mass of consumers as a herd of sheep.[72]

But by ignoring the state, Millar concentrated solely on the consumer and he produced a philosophy of consumption which borrows heavily from classical liberal economic assumptions about the rationality of the individual consumer. If the free market was criticized for failing to protect the consumer, the answer of Millar and other commentators and movements was to promote the super-consumer: 'efficient', 'rational', 'scientific', 'objective', 'informed', 'discriminating' and motivated purely by a desire to obtain value-for-money. 'Two nations' of consumer would then emerge, according to Millar, with the educated shoppers of the CA leaving behind the 'fickle', 'ignorant', 'deluded' and 'illogical'.[73] This dichotomy was shared across the political spectrum. The Fabian Harbury spoke of the need for consumers to overcome their 'embarrassing' 'ignorance', 'inability', 'short-sightedness' and 'wasteful', 'irrational' expenditure that one ought to expect of an 'Amazonian boy' were he to find himself in London. He argued that consumers needed to overcome the dictates of fashion, religion, national identity and custom to reach the 'enlightenment' of 'rational' 'efficiency'.[74] Conservatives aimed to make the consumer 'think' and just about all groups agreed on the need for the education of the individual consumer to arm him or her against the barrage of information, true and misleading, which came from the producers.[75] The CA embraced this style of consumerism most completely so that one recent comment-ator has claimed that '*Which?* repudiates the irrationalist anti-Enlightenment thrust of postmodernism'.[76] All design is reduced to function and all purchases are decided by a cost-benefit analysis that leaves no room for questions of aesthetics, style or impulse-buying. *Which?* therefore offers a theory of consumption far removed from the Morrisian traditions of the Left in the early twentieth century.

70. *Ibid.*, p. 178.
71. *Ibid.*, p. 184.
72. *Ibid.*, pp. 192–6.
73. *Ibid.*, p. 196.
74. Harbury, *Efficiency*, pp. 2–5.
75. Baynes, *Advertising*, p. 18.
76. A. Aldridge, 'The construction of rational consumption in *Which?* Magazine: the more blobs the better', *Sociology*, 28 (1994), pp. 899–912.

Such language has important implications for the relationship between the state and the consumer and the nature of modern citizenship. In one sense, the dichotomies employed by the modern consumer movement are direct descendants of those of Mill ('productive' versus 'unproductive'), Ruskin ('wealth' versus 'illth'), the temperance movement ('use' versus 'abuse') and a whole host of radical and liberal political polarities: useful versus wasteful; necessity versus luxury; collective versus private. The difference is that the dichotomies of rational and irrational, efficient and inefficient, informed and ignorant are those which locate consumption, rhetorically at least, as a purely economic (or at least a less explicitly moral) act: the consumer as shopper. The modern consumer movement, following the lead of the US consumer organization started in the 1930s, constructed itself as existing beyond morality and politics, though Lizabeth Cohen in Chapter Ten reminds us that this in itself is a highly political act as consumers were encouraged to enter into a nation-building exercise as they literally purchased the American dream. The implications in the British context are perhaps slightly less clear, but a movement which claimed not to have a moral or political project (despite Michael Young's brief advocacy of a 'third force'[77]), removes also the opportunity for a critique of the existing social and economic system. Whereas the consumer citizens of Thompson in Chapter Three and Trentmann in Chapter Seven demanded social responses to their politics of poverty, the consumer politics of prosperity was largely satisfied with the existing social and economic structure. Despite the initial mistrust of the CA by the Molony Committee, therefore, few ideological differences existed between the private consumers and productivist officials of the central state. Both shared a broad support for a free market and the differences which did emerge between the two groups were more to do with practical considerations. For instance, immediately after the final report of the Molony Committee was published, disagreements arose in Parliament about the types of individual that ought to be allowed on the new Consumers' Council and about the practical problems which would emerge thereafter on different matters of consumer protection and representation.[78] But the shared discursive framework of private consumer activists and various state institutions enabled much further collaboration to take place. Indeed, the links of personnel and administration between the state and the CA enterprise would become extremely close over the next two decades, the distinction between private and public blurring to such an extent that the director of the CA would be able to proclaim in 1980 that his organization had contributed to more legislation in the twentieth century than any other pressure group.[79]

---

77. Tivey, 'Quasi-government for consumers', p. 138.
78. *H. C. Deb.*, 674, 26 March 1963, col. 138; 676, 23 April 1963, col. 9; 677, 15 May 1963, col. 173; 678, 20 May 1963, cols 33–160.
79. Smith, *Consumer Interest*, p. 288.

Whereas such an analysis suggests close similarities with the American context and the emergence of the 'customer as citizen' outlined by Lizabeth Cohen, there are important differences to bring out as the state has subsequently responded to growing consumer awareness. Gunnar Trumbull in Chapter Thirteen makes a clear distinction between the consumer politics of affluence in France and in Germany. In France, modern consumerism emerged from a grass-roots, highly politicized activism which acted as a watchdog on industry. Its confrontational 'consumer-citizen's' movement stands in contrast to the corporatist model adopted in Germany in which consumers were given an official voice in government, encouraging a more moderate consumer politics, though with much less grass-roots activism. Neither of these models is directly applicable to the relationship between the British consumer and the state, its history fitting neither a pluralist nor a corporatist analysis.[80] The Consumers' Council of 1963 was not the recognition of a self-organized body, nor was it the establishment of an adversarial politics of incorporated interests. At this time, Britain's consumerism lacked the radical attack on producer interests that would soon be symbolized by Ralph Nader's almost moral crusade of mobilized consumer-citizens in the USA.[81]

Instead, what one can discern is the piecemeal addition to the state apparatus according to the liberal and voluntarist traditions of British social policy.[82] While these might have given way to a more centralized or corporatist state bureaucracy in the sphere of production, liberal notions about the consuming individual restrained the intervention of the state in the sphere of consumption. As was seen above, producer interests certainly played a leading role in the nature of consumer protectionism, but they received no ideological challenge because consumers of the new consumerism calculated their own interests according to similar systems of knowledge. In a sense, they had accepted or internalized the notion of the rational consuming individual. Any additional measure of consumer protection introduced by the government, therefore, took place as a recognition of the rights of consumers as articulated incrementally by both private and public official consumer representatives. The Molony Committee and the subsequent machinery of consumer protectionism were not the consequences of a 'third force' in British politics with its framework of ideological principles concerning the social rights and duties of consumers and citizens in relation to government. The Molony Committee, as a landmark in state involvement in consumer affairs, owed little to the new consumer movement, but the new consumer movement did share much in common with the

---

80. However, Len Tivey has argued that, by the 1970s, the National Consumer Council could be 'regarded as an attempt to insert an item of state corporatism into the pluralist structure': Tivey, 'Quasi-government', p. 150.

81. Smith, *Consumer Interest*, pp. 300–1.

82. M. J. Daunton, 'Payment and participation: welfare and state-formation in Britain 1900–1951', *Past and Present*, 150 (1996), pp. 169–216.

ideological assumptions of the *Final Report*. Gone were the earlier radical collectivist political critiques of the consumer society, but in their place was a campaigning organization far more likely to have a practical influence on government policy, according to its reformist, individualist, rational economic agenda.

13

Strategies of Consumer-Group Mobilization: France and Germany in the 1970s

Gunnar Trumbull

Introduction

Consumer groups underwent a period of rapid expansion from 1970 to the early 1980s in both France and Germany. While governments in the two countries passed legislation and created regulatory bodies to increase consumer confidence, consumer groups pursued initiatives for promoting the consumer interest in government and with business. Yet the conception of consumer interests and identity espoused by these groups differed in ways that depended on the context of their interaction with industry. In France, consumer groups took on the status of a watch-dog to industry, looking out for transgressions, mobilizing against high prices and dangerous products, and filing frequent lawsuits. In Germany, relations between consumer groups and producers were more amicable. German consumer groups consulted with industry, participated on technical committees, helped to enforce competition and cartel regulations, and disseminated technical product information to consumers.

French and German consumer groups also interacted in distinctive ways with their governments. In France, the consumer movement took on a political valence. Each of the major labour unions created its own consumer group, as did some political parties. These groups were given policy access in the form of a new Ministry of Consumption, so that consumerism quickly became a new arena for political struggle. In Germany, by contrast, consumer groups avoided politically polarized issues and party affiliations. Their contribution to policy debates occurred within the economics and agriculture ministries. Their policy input was normally technical rather than political in substance. Thus, while French consumer groups took on the manners of a political and social movement, German consumer groups comported themselves as technical specialists with only an advisory role in government policy.

Differences in French and German consumer-group interaction with business and with government led them to espouse different views of the consumer interest and different policy solutions to consumer grievances. In Germany, the consumer was perceived largely as an economic actor functioning on a par with producers and distributors. Consumer protection in this conception focused on the goal of ensuring proper market competition. Hence consumer grievances were understood in terms of market failure. German consumer policies accordingly focused on providing consumers with high-quality information and on enforcing the institutions of quality production in German industry. This approach to consumer protection is similar to what Matthew Hilton has described as the 'consumer as shopper' model in Britain, and to what Lizabeth Cohen has described as the 'customer consumer' model in the United States after the Second World War, except that the German state took an active role in disseminating accurate product information.

In France, by contrast, the consumer was seen as a political actor and understood as a consumer-citizen. Consumer protection in this conception focused on the goal of creating and enforcing new political rights for consumers. French consumer groups favoured policies that worked to insulate consumers from the uncertainties of modern products and from risks inherent to the free marketplace. This approach is similar to patterns of consumer protection that have evolved in the United States since the 1960s.

Consumer groups in France and Germany elaborated different sets of goals, benchmarks, and priorities in response to the distinctive forms of administration, law, and industry they confronted in the two countries. The French conception of the consumer interest was primarily *ends-based*, focused on creating fundamental legal and political protections for consumers. The German conception of the consumer interest was primarily *means-based*, focused on creating a fair domestic marketplace in which consumers could operate. But the priorities for consumer protection elaborated by domestic consumer groups did not necessarily reflect pre-existing consumer goals. They emerged instead from the organizational strategies of consumer groups operating in very different institutional environments.[1]

French and German Consumer Groups

Differences in the organization of consumer groups in France and Germany emerged most strikingly from their record of individual membership. French consumer groups in the early 1980s estimated that they had a total of 2 million

---

1. H.M. Sapolsky, 'The politics of product controversies', in H. Sapolsky (ed.), *Consuming Fears: The Politics of Product Risk* (New York: Basic Books, 1987), p. 183.

members; German consumer groups estimated as many as 8 million members.[2] But these figures contrast strikingly with a 1978 survey of individual consumers in France and Germany that asked whether respondents were members of organizations that '. . . have no links with manufacturers or traders and whose specific aim is to inform and defend the consumer'. Responses showed that almost no German consumers identified themselves as current members of consumer groups, defined in this way, compared with 3 per cent of French consumers. Only 8 per cent of Germans reported that they would be willing to become members of such a group, compared to 27 per cent in France. Yet the survey also found that 55 per cent of Germans had heard of this kind of consumer organization, compared to only 44 per cent of French respondents.[3] The different participation levels therefore arose not from different levels of consumer awareness, nor from a stunted consumerist agenda in Germany. They reflected instead entirely different strategies of consumer organization that had been adopted in the two countries. Whereas France's consumer associations genuinely constituted a popular movement, Germany's consumer associations cultivated little grass-roots support.

Indeed fundamental differences emerge at all levels of the French and German consumer movements. For analytic purposes, consumer groups in France and Germany can usefully be divided into three kinds: peak-level consumer associations, nationwide consumer associations, and their regional and local affiliates. Important differences appear between French and German consumer groups in each of these categories.

Germany's peak-level consumer association, the Council of Consumer Groups (Arbeitsgemeinschaft der Verbraucherverbände, or AgV) represents all other consumer groups in national debates. Germany's AgV thus embodies the principle of corporatism applied to consumer interests. France's central consumer association, the National Consumption Institute (Institut national de la consommation, or INC), acts independently of other consumer groups, serving as a technical resource on consumer questions for the government, for business, and for consumers and other consumer groups. Thus France's INC functions primarily as a technical resource and provides no co-ordination or representation of other consumer groups.

Nationwide consumer associations also differ importantly in France and Germany. In Germany, these groups are functionally distinct. Specific consumer-protection goals such as consumer education, product testing, and legal defence

2. 'Un hypersyndicat?' *Le Nouveau Journal*, 28 September 1979; H. Piepenbrock, 'Die Legitim-ation der Verbraucherverbände zur Wahrnehmung von Verbraucherinteressen', in H. Piepenbrock and C. Schroeder (eds), *Verbraucherpolitik Kontrovers* (Koln: Deutscher Instituts-Verlag, 1987), p. 102.

3. G.H. Gallup, *The International Gallup Polls: Public Opinion 1978* (Wilmington, Delaware: Scholarly Resources Inc., 1979), p. 365.

are each taken up by a single nationwide association that specializes in that area. In France, by contrast, nationwide consumer groups tend to offer a combination of services to consumers, competing directly with one another for consumer recognition, membership, and public influence. Because they often provide overlapping services, France's national-level consumer groups have commonly been criticized for their conflict and lack of co-ordination.

Perhaps the most striking difference between the French and German consumer movements, however, arises in consumer groups organized at the regional and local levels. In France, these groups have worked to mobilize consumers in order to pursue policy initiatives. Consumers who joined these groups participated regularly in price surveys (relevés de prix), consumer boycotts, and protests against specific retailers and producers. In Germany, by contrast, regional and local consumer groups (Verbraucherverbände and Verbraucherstellen) focused their efforts almost exclusively on providing consumers with accurate technical information through a network of consumer advisory centres. What was the reason for these different approaches?

Technical Specialization in Germany

The primary reason for Germany's low level of membership in consumer groups is that these groups have actively discouraged it. Germany's peak-level consumer association, AgV, has less than 100 individual members. These are people who, as described in §4 paragraph 1 of the by-laws of the AgV, are particularly suited to furthering the goals of the organization. These members also satisfy a legal accreditation requirement necessary for the AgV to bring legal suits in cases of misleading advertising or unfair sales contract. By law, accredited consumer organizations must have at least 60 individual members. (French law, by comparison, requires that consumer groups have at least 10,000 members in order to receive a similar legal accreditation!) Why did the AgV discourage further membership?

One explanation is the corporatist status of the AgV. As a peak-level organization with corporatist deliberative rights, the AgV has a dual goal of coordinating the interests of its member consumer organizations and of representing the general consumer interest to the government. Admitting individual members could therefore be seen to undermine the corporatist formula of group representation. Yet even consumer groups at the regional and local levels do not have an extensive tradition of individual membership, and these groups are not bound by corporatist goals. Of the eleven state-level consumer centres (Verbraucherzentralen) in West Germany, only five have permitted individual membership in their by-laws, and even these have done so only in limited numbers. In Hessen, for example, the Verbraucherzentrale permits six individual members. States such as Berlin and

Hamburg, which do allow unlimited individual membership in their consumer centres, have generally experienced only low levels of participation.[4]

A second explanation for low memberships is the high level of funding that German consumer groups receive from *Land* and federal sources. Supported by the state, these groups have little organizational need to attract paying members. German consumer groups have consistently received almost four times as much government funding as have French consumer groups. Moreover, the role of government support has been perceived differently in the two countries. Whereas government funding to consumer organizations in Germany is seen as a legitimate remuneration for consumer groups that have taken on duties that would otherwise have to be performed by the state, government funding in France is viewed by many as a compensated *weakness (faiblesse compensée)* that keeps consumer groups from achieving their full potential.[5]

But state funding alone cannot explain low consumer membership. While government funding to German consumer groups is indeed higher than in France, there is also a strong variation in funding levels among Germany's individual federal states. Much of government spending on consumer associations comes from *Land*

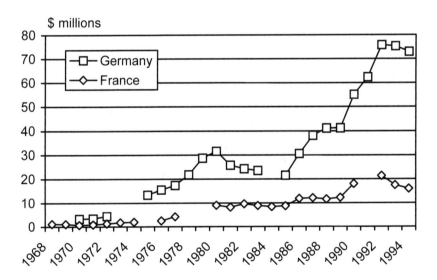

Figure 13.1   Government support to consumer organizations in France and Germany (in millions of US dollars), 1970–1990 (compiled by the author, data incomplete).

4. *Ibid.*

5. A. Carnelutti, 'Consommation et société', *Revue française d'administration publique,* 56 (October–December 1990), p. 584.

governments, with different *Länder* placing more or less emphasis on consumer protection. Bavaria in 1980 spent only 0.19 DM per person on consumer groups, compared to 1.28 DM per person in Bremen.[6] Hence while some federal states far outspent France on consumer groups, others also spent far less per capita. Yet there is no sign that consumer groups in the less generous states attempted to pursue more extensive grass-roots organizational strategies.

The most important reason for a low level of consumer participation in Germany was the view among consumer representatives that individual consumer activism would hurt the general consumer interest. A common criticism raised against Germany's low-membership strategy argued that the interests represented by groups without members were unlikely to reflect the real concerns of working-class consumers. These critics lambasted German consumer groups for a lack of creativity in the strategies they employed for defending the interests of consumers.[7] Consumer groups, they argued, followed a conformist agenda that risked to diverge from actual consumer interests. Yet among German consumer advocates, this lack of representation was commonly understood to be desirable. Because individual participants in consumer activism were likely to be of a higher socio-economic level, policy-makers argued, it was feared that they would skew the representation of consumers in that direction.[8] Consumer groups themselves argued that admitting individual members into Germany's consumer organizations would unduly bias their representation towards the interests of the middle class.[9] The consumer centre of Northrhein Westfallen, for example, wrote in 1985 that, 'in the context of socially oriented consumer work, we must consider the problems and information needs of specific minorities that are possibly not represented, or even opposed, by the majority or average citizen'.[10]

Instead of pursuing a grass-roots mobilization, German consumer groups cultivated a technically sophisticated staff and leadership that would enable them to advise consumers wisely on product choice and to consult on technical committees with industry. These staff members, often with technical training, had neither an interest in nor a facility for grass-roots mobilization. Consumer groups

6. J. Bornecke, *Handbuch der Verbraucherinstitutionen* (Bonn: Verlag Information für die Wirtschaft, 1982)..

7. R. Rock, B. Biervert and W.F. Fischer-Winkelmann, 'A critique of some fundamental theoretical and practical tenets of present consumer policy', *Zeitschrift für Verbraucherpolitik* 4/2 (1980), p. 98.

8. C. Czerwonka and G. Shöppe, 'Verbraucherpolitische Konzeptionen und Programme in der Bundesrepublik Deutschland', *Zeitschrift für Verbraucherpolitik* 1/3 (1977), pp. 286–7

9. C. Czerwonka, G. Schoppe and S. Weckbach, *Der aktive Konsument: Kommunikation und Kooperation* (Göttingen: Verlag Otto Schwarz, 1976), p. 193.

10. 'Im Bereich sozialorientierter Verbraucherarbeit müssen Probleme und Informationsbefürfnisse spezifischer Minderheiten berücksichtigt werden, die möglicherweise von der Mehrheit, also auch vom Bevölkerungsdurchschnitt, nicht empfunden oder sogar konträr beurteilt werden', in *Die Verbraucherberatung in Nordrhein-Westfalen aus Sicht der Bevölkerung 1984/5* (Bielefeld, 1985), p. 1.

at the national level were functionally specialized and tended to hire and train employees in their particular area of specialization. Thus Germany's product testing association, *Stiftung Warentest*, hires employees with technical training suited to organizing and analyzing the results of product testing. Consumer groups at the local and regional level (Verbraucherzentralen) also focus their activities primarily on providing accurate product information to consumers. The core of this activity is a system of consumer information offices (Verbraucherstellen) that provide product advice free of charge to the general public. Consumers interested in buying a camera, for example, can call or visit a consumer centre to discuss possible options, specifications of particular brands and models, and considerations that they should take into account when purchasing. The results of comparative product tests are still distributed for free to visiting consumers. These advisory centres proved very popular. Between 1973 and 1974 alone, the number of consumer visits to these centres grew by 30 per cent from 540,000 to 700,000.[11] By 1995, total instances of consumer advice by the Verbraucherstellen across Germany – including visits, phone conversations and correspondence – exceeded 4 million per year.[12] Information centers in Nord-Rhein Westfallen alone were contacted by consumers 860,000 times.[13]

The advice offered by these centres has been viewed favourably both by consumers and by producers. In a 1984 evaluation of consumer centres conducted for the Verbraucherzentrale in Hamburg: 35 per cent of visitors reported that they were fully satisfied ('voll und ganz zufrieden') with the advice they had received; 66 per cent reported that they were at least partly satisfied ('teileweise zufrieden'). For 29 per cent of respondents, this was their first visit to a Verbraucherzentrale. The largest portion sought information about small and large household equipment (45.6 per cent), with another sizeable group interested in phonographs and televisions (23 per cent). Only 3.7 per cent were interested in information about services. Over 90 per cent said they would go back to the consumer centre for future purchases. Only 3.7 per cent said they would not return.[14]

Producers also favoured consumer advice centres, precisely because they helped to educate consumers about new products. Albrecht Schultz, former member of the board of directors at Braun, explains that brand-name manufacturers had a strong interest in consumer advising because accurate information helped keep

11. Kommission für wirtschaftlichen und sozialen Wandel, *Wirtschaftlicher und sozialer Wandel in der Bundesrepublik Deutschland: Gutachten der Kommission* (Göttingen: Verlag Otto Schwartz & Co., 1977), p. 417.

12. Calculated by author from annual reports of consumer centres.

13. Verbraucherzentrale NRW, *Das Jahr '95* (1996), p. 5.

14. L. Maier, 'Zur Wirksamkeit der Produktberatung in Verbraucherzentralen: Ergebnisse einer Umfrage', in V. Lübke and I. Schoenheit (eds), *Die Qualität von Beratungen für Verbraucher* (Frankfurt: Campus Verlag, 1985), p. 189.

consumers from being disappointed, thereby encouraging repeat purchases.[15] Moreover, content analysis of advice given at consumer advisory centres shows that price was rarely if ever discussed, and that advisors working at the centres also rarely mentioned where products could be bought cheaply.[16] Hence advice from the centres informed consumers about quality without emphasizing the need to shop for lower prices.

Popular Mobilization in France

Unlike in Germany, consumer groups in France were the focus of a high level of popular interest and membership. Surveys confirm that individual consumers have long shown enthusiasm for French consumer associations. A 1971 survey conducted by the National Consumption Institute (INC) found that 20 per cent of French over 15 years old said they were 'ready to belong' to a consumer organization.[17] Another poll three years later found that 75 per cent of the population felt that the government should support consumer organizations and give them input into government policy making.[18] This high level of popular support persisted at least to the end of the twentieth century. A 1996 survey found that 74 per cent of all French paid attention to the recommendations of consumer organizations.[19]

French consumer groups experienced an enormous growth beginning in the early 1970s. With this growth came a fragmentation of organizations and interests that remained an enduring feature of the French consumer movement. There were at the time thirteen major national consumer associations in France. In general, these groups emerged from four different sources. Family groups that arose during the Vichy occupation under the Pétainist mantra of 'travail, famille, patrie' evolved in the 1970s towards consumer concerns. Trade unions in the 1970s began to form their own consumer associations as they realized that consumerist politics could in many instances reinforce class politics. The French co-operative movement also took on the consumer interest, publishing for a short time the results of comparative product tests in their publication *Labo-Coop*. Finally, a small group of organizations, including the Federal Union of Consumers (UFC), emerged in the late 1960s with a broad constituency and an exclusive focus on the consumer interest. Most of these groups published their own consumer protection magazines, and the total circulation of these publications grew to over two million by 1980.

15. A. Schultz, 'Das Interesse der Industrie an adäquater Beratung des Verbrauchers durch Handel und Verbraucherberatungsstellen', in Lubke and Schoenheit (eds), *Die Qualität*.

16. U. Beier, 'Schwachstellen einer mit vergleichenden Warentestberichten arbeitenden Produktberatung: Eine Übersicht über empirische Untersucheungsergebnisse', in Lübke and Schoenheit (eds), *Die Qualität*, p. 189.

17. 'Prêts à adherer'. D. Pons, *Consomme et tais-toi* (Paris: Epi, 1972), p. 97.

18. G. Cas, *La Défense du Consommateur* (Paris: Presses Universitaires de France, 1975), p. 82.

19. B. Epinay, 'Le lobby consommateurs veut monter au filet: ses moyens le contraignent en fond de court', *Les Echos*, 3 October 1996.

Table 13.1   Growth in local consumer unions affiliated with the UFC

	1974[a]	1976[b]	1978[c]	1980[d]
local unions	28	80	117	170
union membership	5,000	20,000	32,000	50,000

a. J.-M. Biais, 'L'Etat se dépense pour les consommateurs', *La Vie Française*, 30 January 1978.
b. 'C'est Schweppes!' *Rouge*, 1 December 1976.
c. C. Boris, 'Les consommateurs entrent en politique', *Politique Hebdo*, 5 February 1978.
d. J. Doyère, 'Les associations de consommateurs', *Le Monde Dimanche*, 16 November 1980.

Beginning in 1968, France also experienced a rapid growth in local consumer unions affiliated with these national associations and oriented towards grass-roots mobilization. The UFC, for example, which had acted primarily as an information centre during the 1960s, started taking on affiliated local unions beginning in 1971.[20] Over the course of the decade the number of these local unions grew to 170. The number of union militants grew to 50,000 (see Table 13.1).[21] This level of mobilization allowed the UFC and other consumer groups with similar grass-roots support to undertake public efforts unimaginable in the German context. In 1979, for example, 110 of the local UFC affiliates surveyed 27,735 stores in order to assess compliance with price-labelling laws.[22] This sort of mobilization was a central component of French consumer-group activities. But activism often came at the cost of technical expertise. Jean-Claude Jacquet, a consumer representative to France's National Council on Consumption, acknowledged the need for greater technical competency among France's consumer representatives, but warned that this competency must 'be grounded in a dense associational life, at the risk of failing to translate the real hopes and needs of consumers'.[23]

Competition among French consumer groups for broader popular legitimacy took the form of grass-roots mobilization focused on political and economic protest actions. Over time, the consumer interest in France came to be identified with these activities. The resulting organization of French consumer groups, grounded in a competition over the provision of consumer services and with a strong emphasis on consumer mobilization, has helped to cultivate a distinctive national identity for the consumer as politically active and economically threatened.

20. M. Wieviorka, *L'Etat, le Patronat, et les Consommateurs: Etude des mouvements de consommateurs* (Paris: Presses Universitaires de France, 1977), pp. 71–3.
21. J. Doyère, 'Les associations de consommateurs', *Le Monde Dimanche*, 16 November 1980.
22. 'Une enquête de l'Union fédérale des consommateurs', *Le Monde*, 12 Dec 1979.
23. 's'appuyer sur une vie associative intense, sous peine de ne plus pouvoir traduire les aspirations et besoins réels des consommateurs'. 'Le financement des organisations de consommateurs', *Inc Hebdo*, 583 (26 February 1988), p. 5.

Gunnar Trumbull

Consumer Groups in Institutional Context

Consumer groups emerging in France and Germany had different organizational priorities that emphasized different kinds of consumer interest. From their strategies of organization emerged distinctive conceptions of the consumer identity in the two countries. In Germany, the consumer came to be seen as an economic actor working on an equal status with producers and distributors. In France, the consumer came to be perceived as a consumer citizen with political rights to protection from market risks. But why did French and German consumer groups pursue different organizational goals?

The answer lies in the distinctive political, legal, and economic setting in which these groups grew and matured. Consumer groups in each country adopted organizational strategies that permitted them to pursue consumer protection most effectively given the pre-existing institutional setting into which they emerged. In the political sphere, Germany's tradition of corporatist interest representation legitimated consumer group access to negotiations and policy forums. Because they did not have to fight for political access, these groups had few motivations to mobilize consumers at the grass-roots level. In France, by contrast, consumer groups saw mobilization as their best option for political expression. Hence groups with more members enjoyed more political power.

The organizational priorities set within the political sphere were reinforced by nationally distinctive legal and industrial contexts. In the legal sphere, German consumer groups were permitted to act collectively only in narrowly-defined areas of competency. Restrictions on collective law suits (Verbandklage) discouraged broad-based legal activism by Germany's consumer groups. French consumer groups, by contrast, could bring suits in all areas of consumer interest. Thus, even though French courts generally sided in favour of industry, French consumer groups were able to publicize their goals by pursuing legal cases against industry on a wide range of consumer issues.

Finally, the way in which industry was organized in the two countries also shaped the priorities of consumer groups. In Germany, where industry associations were powerful and production standards were created and policed by industry itself, consumer groups strove for a technical competency that would permit them to interact effectively with existing standard-setting bodies. In France, by contrast, where industry was bound by few associational ties, consumer groups were forced to interact with companies on an individual basis. This kind of one-on-one interaction required that consumer groups mobilize large constituencies both in order to exert pressure on companies and in order to gain the manpower necessary to negotiate with companies individually.

Consumer Groups in the Political Arena

French consumer groups saw politics as a route to organizational expansion. Political parties mobilized around consumer issues. The government worked to incorporate consumer interests into policy formation. Soon the political spectrum came to be represented in miniature within the consumer movement itself. In contrast, Germany's consumer groups shied away from politicizing the consumer interest. Because both the peak consumer group (AgV) and the regional consumer associations (Verbraucherzentralen) had effective organizational monopolies on consumer-interest representation, they appear to have feared that a move towards a more radical politics of consumption would undermine their status. One consequence is that French consumer groups were willing to engage heavily in politics, while German consumer groups have avoided an explicitly political consumerist agenda.

The French government undertook a number of institutional changes designed to integrate consumer interests into government policy-making. The first such move was the creation of the National Consumption Council (Conseil national de la consommation, or CNC) on 19 December 1960, at the instigation of Jean Fontanet.[24] It was created to pursue three goals: to create a meeting place for consumers and a place for them to intervene directly in the government, to contribute to the growing cohesion of consumer groups, and to bring together ministers whose work bore on consumption. Composed of 14 Ministerial members and 14 consumer representatives, it met every six weeks.[25] The fact that the newly created CNC incorporated family groups (UNAF, UFCS, CNAPF) is generally thought to have made it more difficult for consumer groups to consolidate and become professional, contributing to the later fragmentation of the French consumer movement.[26]

Beginning in 1976 with the creation of the Secretariat of State for Consumption under the Ministry of Economics, consumer interests have generally been represented within the French government. The first Consumption Secretariat, led by Christiane Scrivener, focused on employing government regulatory powers to provide better information to consumers. 'On the general economic plan, consumers cannot play a decisive role in assuring that production is better adapted to their real needs unless they are better informed and are better able to express themselves. Their information will eventually condition the orientation of our

---

24. J. Dubois, *Les Structures administratives de la consommation* (Doctoral Thesis. Paris: Université Paris II, 1984), p. 216.

25. M. Garrigou, *L'Assaut des consommateurs pour changer les rapports producteurs–vendeurs– consommateurs* (Paris: Aubier-Montaigne, 1981), pp. 32–3.

26. Dubois, *Structures administratives*, p. 274.

economy.'[27] Scrivener's proposals reflected traditional étatist solutions to new consumer problems. Consumers with grievances against businesses could submit these to the government-sponsored 'postal box 5000', which helped to resolve conflicts. A newly created Committee on Abusive Clauses studied consumer contracts in order to eliminate contract clauses that worked to the disadvantage of consumers. And on 28 February 1977 the government created an inter-ministerial group to co-ordinate consumer politics.[28]

In 1978 the Secretariat was abolished, but the new Minister of Economics and Finance René Monory, who commonly referred to himself informally as a minister of consumption, avowed a strong interest in consumer issues. Monory argued that inflation might be held down if the 2 million members of consumer organizations joined under one umbrella organization.[29] In 1979, he encouraged the formerly neutral National Consumption Institute (INC) to develop 'a consumer counter-force to counterbalance the technical skills and advertising of producers'.[30] This move was adamantly opposed by the largest employers' association, the CNPF, on the grounds that the INC should not combine the roles of information provision and market control. Monory also dramatically expanded government funding to consumer organizations.

Despite their fragmentation, French consumer groups did manage to act together in order to intervene in government policy-making. As early as the late 1960s consumer groups participated in the Consumption Committee of the Sixth French Plan.[31] On 8 May 1972, eleven of France's national consumer associations created the Coordination Committee for Consumer Organizations (Comité de coordination des organizations de consommateurs, or CCOC). The group was not long-lived, but they did push for consumer protection legislation – permitting a 7-day grace period for door-to-door sales, and allowing advertisements to include company names – that was eventually enacted.[32] On 29 April 1975 the same eleven consumer groups published a comprehensive proposal for a new package of consumer

27. 'Sur le plan de l'économie générale, les consommateurs ne pourront jouer un rôle décisif pour que l'outil de production soit mieux adapté à leurs besoins réels que s'ils sont mieux informés et s'ils peuvent mieux s'exprimer. Leur information conditionne à terme l'orientation même de notre économie.' C. Scrivener, 'Le droit des consommateurs à l'information', *Allocutions ministérielles*, Secrétariat d'Etat à la Consommation (11 October 1976), p. 2.

28. M.-E. Bordes and S. George, *Politique de la Consommation dans la Communauté Européenne* (Memoire, Université de Droit, d'Économie et de Sciences Sociales de Paris, 1982), p. 45.

29. 'Un hypersyndicat?' *Le Nouveau Journal*, 28 September 1979.

30. 'un contre-pouvoir consommateur [pour] contrebalancer la technicité des producteurs et l'action de la publicité.' G. Prévost, 'Consommation: "l'agressivité" de l'INC préoccupe de plus en plus le CNPF', *Les Echos*, 28 May 1979.

31. C. Romec, 'Organisations de consommateurs', *Reforme*, 15 December 1975.

32. 'Onze associations nationales créent un conseil de coordination des organisations de consommateurs', *Le Monde*, 16 May 1972.

legislation.[33] In a 30-page charter, they called for the abolition of the National Consumption Institute (INC) and the creation in its place of a technical organization dominated by consumer representatives and oriented towards serving consumer associations. They also proposed the creation of a High Council on Innovation and Safety (Conseil supérieur de l'innovation et de la sécurité) where consumers, professionals and government officials could meet on an equal footing in order to give consumer input into product materials and production, to detect so-called 'false innovations', and to avoid the waste that resulted from them. A special tax on industry would finance commissions to promote consumer education and competition policy.[34] These initiatives were not in the end successful, but the effort did introduce consumer groups to high politics, and they would continue to speak out in the political arena.

A common denominator of German consumerism, on the other hand, was that consumer groups themselves were not a strong force pushing for new consumer protections.[35] Moves for reform came instead from a combination of business interests, political parties, government bodies, and experts in the field. First the SPD, then the CDU, created working groups on consumer politics within their parties. The SPD group was led by Anke Riedel-Martiny, the CDU group by Walter Picard.[36] New initiatives sometimes created unusual alliances. The centrist Free Democratic Party, for example, allied with the German Confederation of Labour (DGB) to call for the creation of a consumer academy.[37] Germany's peak industry association, the Bund Deutscher Industrie (BDI), called for the government to support better consumer information through improved consumer education and more consumer advisory centres.[38] Indeed the peak consumer group, AgV, had been so passive in its support of new consumer policies that the CDU, pushing for office in 1981, criticized it as an organization 'whose services are so little demanded in the free market that it must be supported almost exclusively through state support'.

The AgV appears to have feared that any move into politics would undermine its own authority. Whereas the AgV prior to 1969 had called for consumers to be represented by their own consumer ministry, they changed their position in the 1970s to favour an AgV advisory role within existing ministries.[39] In 1973 the

---

33. Garrigou, *L'Assaut des Consommateurs*, p. 238.

34. 'Onze organisations d'usagers proposent une charte nationale', *Le Monde*, 30 April 1975.

35. H. Schatz, 'Consumer interests in the process of political decision-making: a study of some consumer policy decisions in the Federal Republic of Germany', *Journal of Consumer Policy*, 6 (1983), p. 388.

36. W.H. Glöckner, 'Aktion "Gelber Punkt" – Ins Rote verfälscht', *Vorwärts*, 18 October 1973.

37. Czerwonka and Shöppe, 'Verbraucherpolitische Konzeptionen', p. 286.

38. Bund Deutscher Industrie, *Jahresbericht* 1973/4 (Köln, 1974), p. 45.

39. K. Wieken, *Die Organisation der Verbraucherinteressen im internationalen Vergleich* (Göttingen: Verlag Otto Schwartz & Co., 1976), p. 27.

Federal Cartel Office (Bundeskartellamt, or BKA) called for competition and consumer policy to be merged into a single national office modelled on the US Federal Trade Commission. While this would have increased political scrutiny of consumer issues, the AgV opposed the project, both for fear that they would lose their own status and because they genuinely doubted the utility of the new office in furthering consumer interests.[40] Instead, individual ministries began creating committees to consider consumer issues. The Economics Ministry created a Consumer Advisory Council (Verbraucherbeirat) in 1972. This Consumer Council included 6 members of consumer associations, 3 government representatives, 3 academics, 3 union representatives, and 1 member of the press.[41] The Ministry of Food, Land, and Forest created its own Consumer Committee (Verbraucheraus-schuß) in 1975.[42] But the committees remained strictly advisory, and were never capable of exerting political pressure for consumer protection.

Consumer Groups in National Legal Context

The legal framework in France and Germany set the rules by which consumer groups interacted with industry. Most importantly, the law defined how consumer groups could represent collective consumer interests. In neither country was the law particularly friendly to the consumer. But whereas German law worked to contain and structure the kinds of opposition that consumer groups could raise against industry, French law became the arena in which consumer groups proved their autonomy and mettle.

France and Germany both permitted legal action by consumer groups against transgressions by industry, but the nature of the legal action differed in the two countries. Even at the end of the twentieth century neither country allowed broad class-action suits as employed in the United States. Each instead granted limited rights to consumer groups to protect consumers. In Germany, collective suits (Verbraucherverbandklagen) were limited to two areas of law in which consumer-group legal actions have been explicitly permitted. The 1965 amendment to the Law on Unfair Competition (Gesetz über unlauteren Wettbewerb, UWG) established a high threshold for misleading advertising and empowered consumer groups to help enforce that standard. Approximately 1,000 UWG cases were brought by consumer groups between 1965 and 1977, and 516 were brought in 1979 alone.[43]

40. E. Guenther, 'Verbraucherpolitik, Ziele, Mittel und Traeger', *Marktwirtschaft*, 2 (1973), p. 4.
41. 'Zwei DGB-Vertreter im Verbraucherbeirat', *Informations Dienst* (Düsseldorf: Bundes-pressestelle des Deutschen Gewerkschaftsbundes, 11 August 1982), pp. 1–2.
42. K. Focke (Bundesminister für Jugend, Familie und Gesundheit), 'Verbraucherpolitik in der Marktwirtschaft', *Bulletin des Presse- und Informationsamtes der Bundesregierung*, 65 (30 May 1973), p. 645.
43. European Consumer Law Group, *Reports and Opinions – September 1977–March 1984* (Louvain-la-Neuve, Belgium: Cabay, 1984), pp. 278–9.

The 1976 law on standard terms of sale (Gesetz über Allgemeingeschäftsbeding-ungen, AGB) granted consumer groups the right to file suits against companies employing illegal sales terms. A smaller but important number of AGB cases are brought by consumer groups each year.

These laws, while relying on consumer groups to enforce certain consumer policies, did little to extend the legal activism of consumer groups in general. First, the collective legal suit was not extended to other kinds of legal action. Hence consumer groups could not weigh in on liability suits, warranty disputes, or other kinds of collective consumer grievances. This restriction was unusual from a legal perspective in the German context because Germany, unlike France, has a long tradition of recognizing group legal suits (Verbandklage), at least as that has applied to labour and producer associations. Moreover, consumer-group legal actions were restricted to blocking illegal activity, but did not, except under extraordinary circumstances, extend to compensating consumers for losses.[44] Neither of these provisions worked to generate legal dynamism within the consumer movement.

It is interesting to note that until 1980, consumer advisory centres also faced a statutory limitation on the kinds of legal advice that they could give to individual consumers. While they were allowed to broach matters bearing on contract law, Germany's Law on Legal Consultation (Rechtsberatungsgesetz) did not permit them to give free advice on tort law. Because products liability in Germany falls primarily under tort law, advisory centres could often not discuss legal recourse for product damage. Even those consumer associations entrusted with pursuing legal action against companies that contravened consumer laws, such as the Consumer Protection Union (Verbraucherschutzverein, VSV), were not allowed to give legal advice to individual consumers, since such free legal advice was prohibited.[45] A 1980 change in the statutory lawyer fee scale (Rechtsanwalts-gebührenordnung, BGB I, 1507) made possible a more liberal treatment of consumer advisory centres under the Rechtsberatungsgesetz.[46]

In France, the 1973 loi Royer granted consumer groups broad rights to represent consumer interests in the courts. These rights were quickly curtailed by restrictions on the kinds of damages that they could claim. Unlike class-action suits pursued on behalf of consumers in the United States, French consumer groups were not permitted to act on behalf of specific consumer interests. Instead, they were permitted to recover only for damages to the general interests of consumer organizations. In practice, consumer groups often pursued their own cases alongside

---

44. Individuals received compensation only if it could be shown that they would not have purchased the product if the company had acted lawfully – a burden of proof that was in practice rarely met.

45. A. Schoreit, 'Zur Rechtsberatung des Verbrauchers in der Bundesrepublik Deutschland', *Journal of Consumer Policy*, 1/2 (1977), p. 118.

46. N. Reich, 'Rechtsberatung im Verbraucherschutz', *Zeitschrift für Rechtspolitik*, 3 (1981), pp. 53–4.

individual consumer cases in order to offer legal and technical support. One consequence of this limitation is that French consumer groups were unable to rely on large damage payments and legal fees to defray the costs of their legal actions, as US consumer groups commonly do. Of the 1,300 lawsuits brought by consumer associations from 1973 to 1982, 87 per cent resulted in awards of less than 5,000 francs.[47] Moreover, consumer groups wishing to pursue legal suits had to be accredited by the government. Accreditation required proof that a consumer group had at least 10,000 members and that consumer protection was its primary function. This threshold gave strong incentives to attract individual members. By 1979, 12 national and 62 regional consumer groups had been accredited to pursue civil actions. Yet even given this high level of accreditation, and the 450 cases filed in that year, the total damages for all cases combined amounted to only 440,000 francs.[48]

Consumer-group litigation remains a staple of French consumer association activity. In a 1989 survey of French consumers, 76 per cent reported that consumer associations were either very or fairly accessible for help with consumer litigation, whereas only 29 per cent felt that the government administration was equally capable. And whereas only 2 per cent of respondents reported that they personally would rely on the government for support with a consumer grievance, 17 per cent reported that they would use consumer associations.[49]

In December 1985 the National Consumption Council (CNC) considered the creation of a true class-action suit ('action de groupe'). The move was proposed by the new State Secretariat for Consumption, Henri Emmanuelli. Industry representatives on the CNC opposed the move, citing the experience of other countries, notably the United States, that employ class-action suits. 'Can we support a project that will be only a lure and source of disillusion for the consumer and that will entail grave economic consequences for French enterprises?'[50] After the elections of 1986, the new Minister of Consumer Affairs, Jean Arthuis, expressed support for class-action suits, but on the condition that it be imposed at the European level.[51] Given the probable preferences of other European countries, especially Germany, this eventuality appears unlikely.

---

47. A. Morin, 'L'Action d'intérêt collectif exercée par les organisations de consommateurs avant et après la loi du 5 janvier 1988', in T. Bourgoignie (ed.), *Group Actions and Consumer Protection* (Brussels: Story Scientia, 1992), p. 65.

48. European Consumer Law Group, *Reports and Opinions*, pp. 272–3.

49. 'Les Français et les organisations de consommateurs', *Inc Hebdo*, 633 (7 April 1989), pp. 9–13.

50. 'Peut-on en effet soutenir un projet qui ne sera pour le consommateur qu'un leurre et une source de désillusion et qui va entraîner de graves conséquences économiques pour les entreprises françaises?' 'Action de groupe', *Consommateurs Actualités*, 494 (31 January 1986), p. 18.

51. A. Chambraud, P. Foucher and A. Morin, 'The importance of community law for French consumer protection legislation', *Journal of Consumer Policy*, 17 (1994), p. 29.

Outside of the courtroom, consumer groups in both countries have resorted to boycotts to protest against dangerous or highly-priced goods. French boycotts have been greeted with strong popular acclaim, and often with support from French trade unions. But if France's experience with product boycotts has been extensive, it has not always been successful. In 1978, for example, the UFC called for a boycott of the Shell company in response to the wreck of the Amoco-Cadiz oil tanker. The courts found in Shell's favour, but fines were eventually suppressed by the appeals courts.[52] Consumer groups were also commonly more focused on confrontation than on technical analysis. On 16 June 1975, for example, the Villejuif Association populaire de familles (APF) distributed brochures to a hospital, based on a report from the Ministry of Health, warning that Schweppes added the chemical E330 to their beverages. Schweppes sued the group on the grounds that E330 was simply the designator for citric acid.[53]

German product boycotts were less common than their French counterparts, but they typically achieved a greater level of success, especially in cases of dangerous products or excessive prices. In 1971 a boycott of real estate agents for the excessive fees they charged (Vorab-Maklergebühren), in which consumers stood before real estate offices and handed out leaflets to potential customers, resulted in a law one year later making such fees illegal. The first large-scale consumer boycott, which occurred in September 1973 in protest against the high price of meat, was supported by trade unions and was relatively successful.[54] A 1980 boycott against estrogen in veal, in which France also participated, was the first in which environmental and consumer protection groups worked together. As a result, the companies Nestlé and Lacroix took their veal products off the market.[55] In 1982, the Consumer Centre of Stuttgart launched a boycott of Aral and BP because of their high oil prices, and managed to have the prices reduced.[56]

Unlike French courts, the German legal system has been more permissive with boycotts that do not have explicitly competitive goals. This difference in the courts' stances toward consumer boycott has resulted in part from the perceived technical competency of these groups. In Germany, where consumer centres cultivated a high level of familiarity with product markets, boycotts they launched were typically well-informed and targeted at flagrant transgressions. In France, where consumer groups had little technical expertise, courts sided systematically with

52. 'La cour d'appel confirme l'interdiction du boycottage des produits Shell', *Le Monde*, 15 June 1978.

53. 'C'est Schweppes!' *Rouge*, 1 December 1976.

54. W.H. Glöckner, 'Verbraucherpolitik im Aufwind', *Die Neue Gesellschaft*, 5 (May 1974), p. 424.

55. 'Autofahrer gegen ölkonzerne – Boykott letzte Waffe der Konsumenten', *Frankfurter Rundschau*, 24 July 1982.

56. W. Renschke, 'Der Boykott – sein Möglichkeiten und sein Grenzen', *Verbraucher & Markt '82* (Bonn: 4 November 1982).

business in boycott cases, although higher courts typically reduced fines to a token 1 franc on appeal.[57] These court conflicts, which became increasingly common between French consumer groups and industry, grew into a symbol of autonomy for these groups, advertising that they had not been co-opted and were at the leading edge of the consumer struggle.

Consumer Group Interaction with Producers

Not all interaction between consumer groups and producers was conflictual. In tandem with the legal actions taken by consumer groups, the 1970s also saw the rise of extensive collaborations between producers and consumers. French and German consumer groups worked together with industry to elaborate standards for product sales and design that would be mutually acceptable. Yet, again, the nature of this collaboration was different in the two countries. In France, consumer groups negotiated directly with industrial sectors, and later with individual producers. In Germany, by contrast, consumer groups supported technical representatives to sit on product-design committees in which consumer goods were discussed. The legitimacy of Germany's consumer representatives derived from their technical knowledge and ability to interact with industry experts. The legitimacy of French consumer groups derived precisely from their wide popular support and broad membership.

In 1975, France's largest employer association, the CNPF, created a new Committee on Industry, Commerce, and Consumption (CICC) to co-ordinate business interaction with consumers groups. Paul Simonet, the head of the new committee, declared that they were '. . . very open to all forms of dialogue, especially in the domain of information'.[58] They felt that consumer groups should be encouraged and developed, although they argued against funding them through a tax on advertising, as some consumer advocates had proposed.[59] Simonet felt that consumerism was '. . . a profound and lasting movement that corresponds to the evolution of life in society, and with which we [business] should establish an open and constructive dialogue'.[60] This opinion appears to have been shared by many of France's companies as well. A 1977 survey of producers found that 24 per cent had already held at least one dialogue with a consumer association. Consumer groups, for their part, were more than willing to join in such discussions.

---

57. R.-X. Lanteri, 'Prix: que peuvent faire les consommateurs?' *L'Express*, 20 September 1976.

58. '. . . nous sommes très ouverts a toute forme de concertation, plus particulièrement dans le domaine de l'information . . .'; 'Opinions sur la fonction consommation et la libre entreprise', *Humanisme et Entreprise*, 102 (April 1977), p. 16.

59. A. Roux, (President CNPF), 'La réforme de l'entreprise', *CNPF Patronat* (February 1976), p. 29.

60. G. Lavergne, 'Eux, les clients', *CNPF Patronat*, 429 (November 1981), p. 22.

The same survey found that 81 per cent of consumer associations wished for a consultative role with industry.[61]

Early efforts at dialogue were aimed primarily at standardizing sales practices in particular sectors. In 1974, for example, the president of the National Council on Consumption (CNC), Francis Pécresse, called for the formation of a trial forum for negotiations between consumers and retailers. This led to the creation in 1975 in Toulouse of a trial Committee for Recourse and Information on Sales and Consumption (Comité de recours et d'information commerce consommation, or CRICC). Consumers were represented by the consumer groups FFF and the UFCS. The more radical UFC refused to sit down in any context with professionals. On 24 March 1976, the first meeting took place with the new Secretariat for Consumption, in the person of Christiane Scrivener, attending. This was the first strictly equal meeting of consumers and producers in France, and resulted in agreements about the sales of furniture and dry cleaning.[62] In another instance, in 1975, consumers groups and the food industry created the Communal Organization of Consumers, Workers and Farmers (Organisation commune des consommateurs, travailleurs, agriculteurs, or OCCTA) to set labelling standards for food products.[63] And in 1976, the French standard-setting body AFNOR created experimental standard X 50.002 based on negotiations between consumers and producers about after-sales service for kitchen products.[64] All of these agreements, and there was a very large number of them, were strictly voluntary for producers.

Consumer negotiations with industry were not always amicable. In 1975, for example, at a meeting convened by AFNOR on the subject of 'The Quality Challenge' ('Le Defi de la qualité'), the union consumer group OR-GE-CO suggested applying the notion of consumer-producer dialogue in order to improve product quality. The CNPF greeted the idea with hostility.[65] While they welcomed consumer input in selling products to consumers, they opposed any direct consumer participation in product design. They also opposed any government intervention in their negotiations with consumers for fear that the negotiations might spread to questions of design and production.[66] Consumer groups, for their part, soon became frustrated that the negotiated agreements were not being employed by industry. As early as 1976, during the negotiations of the Consumption Group of

61. 'Le Consumerisme', *Libre Service Actualités*, 632 (30 June 1977), pp. 134–6.

62. Garrigou, *L'Assaut des Consommateurs*, p. 162.

63. M. Lecroel, 'Force Ouvrière et les Consommateurs', in R. Mauriaux (ed.), *Force Ouvrière, les consommateurs et l'écologie* (Paris: FNSP-CEVIPOF, 1994), pp. 17–18. OCCTA was dissolved in 1990.

64. S. Caroit, *Les Relations entre les associations de consommateurs et les centrales syndicales* (Paris: Sorbonne, dissertation, 1994), p. 30.

65. M. Dumez, 'Le Défi de la Qualité', *Information Consommation OR-GE-CO* 7 (April 1975), pp. 1–2.

66. Lavergne, 'Eux, les clients', p. 23.

the 7th French Plan, the business contingent complained of a 'certain climate of hostility and tartness that . . . impregnated the meetings of the Commission and of the working groups'.[67] Finally, in an open letter published on 11 January 1980, 11 major national consumer associations renounced participation in all collective agreements with business until some form of enforcement mechanism could be established.

The new Socialist Government in France saw consumer organizations as an indirect means of regulating business practice, and proposed breaking the impasse by making the outcome of negotiations between business associations and consumer groups binding on all businesses affected by the decision. The CNPF strongly opposed this corporatist solution, and the government was eventually forced to back down. In its place they pursued two new strategies. The first was to transform the National Consumption Committee (CNC), formerly a forum for consumer groups to express their interests to the government, into a tripartite negotiating table at which not only consumer groups and the government but also professional groups would be present. It was called, somewhat confusingly, the National Consumption Council (Conseil national de la consommation, or CNC). Decisions arrived at in this new forum would not be binding, but the presence of the government went a long way to alleviate the frustrations expressed by consumer groups.[68]

The second strategy was to permit consumer groups to negotiate binding contracts, so-called 'quality contracts', with individual companies for a limited time-frame. Unlike earlier agreements between consumer and professional groups, these quality contracts were company-specific and legally enforceable. Producer participation was strictly voluntary, but those companies that did sign agreements could advertise this as an advantage of their products. Not all consumer groups participated in the programme. The UFC, for example, felt that quality contracts did little to improve product quality, and because they were only negotiated with French firms, the UFC felt that they would hurt French consumers in the long run by excluding foreign products.[69] Labour-oriented consumer groups such as INDECOSA-CGT, by contrast, favoured quality contracts as an additional forum for negotiating with employers. Indeed quality contracts were often initiated through discussions with local labour unions, which called on the government to push nationalized industries into quality contracting.[70]

67. 'sensibles à un certain climat d'hostilité et d'aigreur qui a, dans l'ensemble . . . imprégné les réunions de la Commission et de ses groupes de travails', Commisariat Général du Plan, *Rapport du comité Consommation: Préparation du 7e plan* (Paris: Documentation Française, 1976), p. 69.

68. D. Ferrier, *La Protection des Consommateurs* (Paris: Dalloz, 1996), pp. 80–1.

69. 'Contrats de qualité: 3 questions – 3 réponses', *Informations Indecosa-CGT* 29 (January 1983), p. 4.

70. 'Contrats qualité – Des questions sérieuses', *Informations Indecosa-CGT* 14 (March 1986), p. 2.

Unlike French consumer groups, which negotiated with industry outside of any formal setting and without their agreements being generally binding, German consumer groups contributed to producer decisions from within industry associations that set product standards. The most prominent case of this was the introduction in 1975 of a consumer council to German industry's main standard-setting body, Deutscher Industrie Normung (DIN). Consumer representatives, with political backing from the Economics Ministry, were admitted to those technical standard-setting committees that dealt directly with consumer-product safety. Over 200 consumer representatives thus gained access to over 10 per cent of all DIN technical-standard-writing bodies. These safety standards were in turn made mandatory on all producers by a 1980 amendment to the Equipment Safety Law (Gerätsicherheitsgesetz, or GSG). For consumer groups, the effect was to channel their efforts into the training of technically sophisticated representatives who could contribute directly to industry standard-setting.

Consumer Organization and the Divergence of Consumer Interests

Claus Offe and Philippe Schmitter have observed that corporatist institutions of interest representation such as those found in Germany may fail to grant adequate access to new kinds of interest that arise in society because these new interests go underrepresented at important bargaining tables.[71] The case of consumer-interest representation in Germany suggests that this criticism, at least for emerging consumer interests, is not accurate. In fact, consumer groups were able to gain access to a variety of important bargaining tables in Germany. The institutions of corporatist-interest representation actually legitimated the integration of consumer interests into industry decision-making on a par with other economic interests. The legitimacy of consumer input was not contested by industry, and a variety of forums were established in which consumer interests could be expressed. German consumer representatives were even admitted, beginning in 1973, to the 'Concerted Action' negotiations at which wage and money-supply levels were set in Germany.[72]

It was not the lack of policy access, but rather the fact of automatic access to policy forums, that had a decisive impact on the kinds of consumer interests that were emphasized in Germany. Consumer groups tailored their organizational strategies towards issues and competencies that suited the bargaining tables to

71. P.C. Schmitter, 'Interest mediation and regime governability in contemporary Western Europe and North America', in S. Berger (ed.), *Organizing Interests in Western Europe: Pluralism, Corporatism, and the Transformation of Politics* (New York: Cambridge University Press, 1981), pp. 285–327.

72. H. Gieskes, 'Gesucht wird der mündige, nicht der vevormundete Verbraucher', *Die Welt*, 25 October 1978.

which they were granted access. These groups felt no strong need to organize individual consumers because the principle of corporatism already legitimated their access to important policy forums.

In France, by contrast, where consumer groups focused their efforts on political action and member mobilization, consumer interaction with industry became radicalized. French producers complained that the 'strong and imperative language' employed by consumer groups reflected a tendency to exaggerate problems in a way that undermined the integrity of the consumer movement as a whole.[73] But this kind of exaggeration was precisely the goal of French groups, which were forced to cultivate interest among consumers in order to pursue the consumer interest.

Thus the national distinctiveness of consumer regulatory regimes may have its origins not merely in underlying cultural proclivities but also in the organizational form of those groups that came to represent consumers. In a 1997 survey of consumers across Europe, for example, *Eurobaromètre* found that French consumers were far more concerned about product safety across a broad range of product types than were their German counterparts. On average, over half of all French consumers expressed concern about the safety of consumer products, compared with only 21 per cent of all German consumers.[74] Some of this difference may reflect actual variation in the safety level of products in the two countries. But risk-perception is also highly subjective, and it seems likely that the different ways in which consumer interests were represented in the two countries may have contributed significantly to the way in which consumers perceive risk. The activism and contentiousness of French consumer groups may have promoted a scepticism among French consumers in relation to producers. By contrast, the constructive engagement of German consumer groups with industry may have generated an atmosphere of greater trust. While these arguments remain hypothetical, they do suggest ways in which the organizational form of consumer groups may influence the way in which consumers in different countries perceive their interests.

---

73. A. Poirée, *Les Discours consuméristes et leur perception par les Français* (Paris: I.C.C.-C.N.P.F., 1984), pp. 45–6.
74. *Eurobaromètre* (1997), pp. 9–22.

Corralling Consumer Culture: Shifting Rationales for American State Intervention in Free Markets

Gary Cross

The consumer as citizen has been central to the two centuries of consumer politics discussed in this book, but it has been a hard sell in free-market societies. The consumer citizen implied that consumption was more than the clearing of markets or fulfilling subjective needs through goods; it challenged economic orthodoxy and dominance of producer interests over politics. The corporatist models of the early twentieth century have increasingly given way to a laissez-faire orthodoxy that champions consumer choice, but also gives priority to personal wealth over democratic access to and protection in markets. When modern politicians began to understand their constituencies as consumers in the 1980s, they stressed not shared interests but meeting individual needs for goods and services. It never has been easy to conceive of consumers as citizens. This is because citizenship implies common interests that consumers outside of special circumstances (for example, monopoly exploitation and shortage crises) seldom possessed. More important still, consumer citizenship suggests a dysfunctional market – that buyers have distinct rights over producers and need protection from the informational or financial advantage of the latter – and that government has an obligation to enable consumers with 'purchasing power'. More subtly still perhaps, the consumer citizen suggested alternatives to private spending – goods and services acquired in the public interest or, even more threatening to capitalist orthodoxy, limits on consumption altogether.

The twentieth century brought affluence, and with it the spread of consumer markets and culture into every corner of life. Doubtless, most Americans embraced these new opportunities, finding in consumer goods not only comfort, convenience, and pleasure, but also new ways of creating personal identity and communicating meanings in an increasingly impersonal and mobile society. This expansion of the range of personal consumption, however, also made it more difficult to justify any constraint on markets. As in other forms of consumption politics, options for effective action in corralling particular kinds of spending narrowed in the twentieth century, although without ever vanishing. By exploring the rationales and movements for corralling consumption in twentieth-century America, we reveal still another set of potentials and paradoxes in the history of consumption politics.

All forms of consumer politics and especially movements for constraining commodity markets have faced substantial difficulties in American history. American legal and intellectual culture left few strictures on market rights: under most conditions, legal intervention was allowable only when business organized restraint of trade or when it exploited a consumer incapable of making a rational choice. To be sure, because informal social and cultural constraints have been so weak in this highly mobile and diverse nation, Americans were obliged to rely on law rather than mere social pressure to regulate alcohol, gambling, shop hours, and business zoning. A prohibitionary legal culture (often dressed in the language of religion and morality) complemented an exceptionally open market. Nevertheless, in a culture which so highly honoured economic growth and freedom to buy and sell goods, only under special conditions could consumption be corralled and, at that, controls had to be adapted to the prevailing individualism. Regulation of the consumer market could be justified only to preserve the sanctity of the private home, eliminate individual 'temptations' inherent in a free market and affluent society, and maximize individual choice and knowledge of consumer markets through regulation of commerce. None of these discourses of consumption restraint fared well in the twentieth century. By its end, one unassailable appeal to corral consumption remained – safeguarding the private rights of parents and the 'innocence' of the young.[1]

Americans had long attempted to separate the home from the market. Indeed, the key to the success of an impersonal economic efficiency in the nineteenth century was to take trade and production from the home, which in turn freed time and space for intimate family life.[2] A striking example of this principle from the early twentieth century was the effort to control early radio advertising. Because messages were transmitted over public radio frequencies, it was legally permissible to regulate broadcasting.[3] Because Americans lacked a consensus about national

---

1. Background sources include: J. Appleby, *Capitalism and a New Social Order, The Republican Vision of the 1790s* (New York: New York University Press, 1984); J.E. Crowley, *This Sheba Self: The Conceptualization of Economic Life in Eighteenth Century America* (Baltimore: Johns Hopkins University Press, 1974); M. Merrill, 'Putting capitalism in its place', *William and Mary Quarterly* , 52 (1995), pp. 315–26; D. Shi, *The Simple Life: Plain Living and High Thinking in American Culture* (New York: Oxford University Press, 1985), pp. 50–214.

2. R. Fishman, *Bourgeois Utopias: The Rise and Fall of Suburbia* (New York: Basic Books, 1987), pp. 3–17 and 155–81 especially.

3. S. Smulyan, *Selling Radio: The Commercialization of American Broadcasting, 1920–1934* (Washington: Smithsonian Institution Press, 1994), ch. 1, pp. 41, 44, 65–6; G. Archer, *Big Business and Radio* (New York: American Historical Company, 1939), p. 31.

cultural ideals, they failed to adopt the high-minded, public-service mission of the early British Broadcasting Corporation that depended financially on licence fees. Instead, in a context of laissez-faire insurgency, an advertising-driven system of two networks emerged by 1927 (NBC and CBS). Nevertheless, American broadcasters were not free to turn radio into an audio billboard in the home. Virtually everyone recognized that radio transmission disturbed the quiet and harmony of the home; and ads threatened the well-established division between public commerce and private intimacy. Even the advertisers' journal, *Printers' Ink* admitted in 1923, that 'the family circle is not a public place, and advertising has no business intruding there unless it is invited'.[4] Through the 1930s, the networks financed 'sustained programmes' advertising-free which featured classical music from such as the NBC Symphony, children's educational programmes, and even the news.[5]

This did not last for long.[6] The networks and manufacturers learned that radio ads were extraordinarily good at selling national name-brand goods. The Depression undermined high-minded constraint as advertisers pressed for more freedom to peddle commodities and services to cash-strapped Americans. Sustained programming was gradually reduced and relegated to the off-peak listening hours. College education stations closed and the Communications Act of 1934 ignored the pleas for special treatment, thus reinforcing the commercialization of radio. Programmers found that Americans would accept the commercial din in exchange for celebrity radio. According to CBS's William Paley, commercial radio was 'a new force for the distribution of goods as well as in the dissemination of ideas'.[7] Americans were unable to preserve the home as a refuge from commerce. In the nineteenth century, home catalogues and magazine and newspaper advertising had prepared the way for electronic selling. And, in the twentieth century, despite the

4. *Printers' Ink* (February 22, 1923), p. 157; R. Marchand, *Advertising the American Dream* (Berkeley: University of California Press, 1988), p. 89; F. Arnold *Broadcast Advertising: The Fourth Dimension* (New York: Wiley and Sons, 1931), p. 42; E. Barnouw, *A Tower in Babel: A History of Broadcasting in the United States*, II (New York: Oxford University Press, 1966), p. 177; O. Pease, *The Responsibilities of American Advertising* (New Haven: Yale University Press, 1958), p. 34.

5. J.F. MacDonald, *Don't Touch That Dial: Radio Programming in American Life, 1920-1960* (Chicago: Nelson-Hall, 1979); P. Lazarsfeld and F. Stanton (eds) *Radio Research 1941* (New York: Deul, Sloan and Pierce, 1979), pp. 110–39, 189; D. Czitrom, *Media and The American Mind: From Morse to McLuhan* (Chapel Hill: University of North Carolina Press, 1982), pp. 102–12.

6. Smulyan, *Selling Radio*, pp. 61, 71; Marchand, *Advertising the American Dream*, pp. 109–10; Barnouw, *Tower*, p. 237.

7. 'An appraisal of radio advertising today', *Fortune* (September 1932), p. 3 ; A. Marquis, *Hopes and Ashes* (New York: Free Press, 1986), pp. 25–40; E.E. Grumbine McNally, *Reaching Juvenile Markets* (New York: McGraw Hill, 1938), pp. 69–117; C. McGovern, 'Sold American: inventing the consumer, 1890–1940', PhD dissertation, Department of History, Harvard University, 1993, pp. 46, 334–43; Barnouw, *Tower*, pp.109–10, 238; Smulyan, *Selling Radio*, pp. 126–32; W. Paley, *Radio as a Cultural Force* (New York: CBS, 1934), pp. 104–5, p. 1 for quotation.

popular middle-class ideology of 'simplicity', the American home was anything but a sanctuary from consumption.[8]

Rather more effective than social arguments for constraining consumption were those based on challenging unequal or manipulated trade. The unequal exchange between the aggressive seller of a potentially addictive product such as alcohol or gambling and the 'vulnerable' buyer particularly excited concern throughout modern American history. While temperance movements were hardly unique to the U.S. (paralleling as it did similar efforts in Britain), still the American effort to prohibit all forms of drinking was exceptional (in contrast, for example, to the British focus on voluntary abstinence and restricting public drinking hours and licensing). In the American context, the drink and gambling transaction was a particularly powerful problem. Since the early nineteenth century, Americans recognized that their particular combination of freedom and prosperity allowed 'vice' to flourish: professional gamblers and 'Medicine Show' charlatans had ample opportunity to prey on the unprotected who had coins in their pockets. As 'civilization' moved west, so did repression of gambling and other vices. These efforts went beyond eliminating disorder or creating the discipline necessary for honest business and hard-working labour. Vice reform also meant saving 'sinners' from the temptations of affluence in a society where social bonds were weak. As early as the 1820s, temperance advocates understood the potentially addictive character of alcohol. Like the devil, drink took control of those persons lacking self-control and unprotected by family, community or their surrogates, the temperance society. In contrast to Europe, in the rather unique conditions of American frontier society, where individuals often lacked the social and psychological support of friends and family, the 'temptation' of drink and gambling was particularly strong. More stable social conditions produced a dramatic decline in alcohol use, dropping from 7 gallons of alcohol per capita in 1830 to 2.5 gallons in 1910. Yet, the Anti-Saloon League and others won alcohol restrictions in about half of the states by 1913. A clear majority accepted prohibition in the 18th amendment of 1919.[9]

Prohibition was a challenge to the free market and thus a radical measure in capitalist America. While commonly understood today as a peevish attempt by rural conservatives and industrialists to impose their values upon the free-spirited or immigrant workforce, the prohibition movement was also an attempt to address

8. D. Horowitz, *The Morality of Spending: Attitudes Toward the Consumer Society in America, 1875–1940* (Baltimore: The Johns Hopkins University Press, 1985), ch. 6; J. Scanlon, *Inarticulate Longings: The Ladies' Home Journal, Gender and the Promises of Consumer Culture* (New York: Routledge, 1995), ch. 4; T.J. Lears, *Fables of Abundance* (New York, Basic Books, 1994), ch. 6.

9. M.E. Lender and J. Martin, *Drinking in America: A History* (New York: Free Press, 1987), pp. 95, 119, 129,. 137; J.C. Burnham, 'New perspectives on the prohibition "experiment" of the 1920s', in E. Monkkonen (ed.), *Prostitution, Drugs, Gambling and Organized Crime* (New York: K.G. Saur, 1992), pp. 97–114.

a common problem of affluence – eliminating a highly appealing, but potentially self-destructive, product from the market.[10]

Perhaps inevitably, the sizeable minority in 1919 who rejected and evaded prohibition gradually turned into a strong majority. Within a decade, repeal won support of leading industrialists such as the Du Ponts and powerful Democrats such as John Raskob. The well-funded Association Against the Prohibition Amendment argued that Prohibition was a failure and a threat to free enterprise and personal freedom – a very potent combination of appeals. Following Roosevelt's inauguration in 1933, repeal won the support of almost 73 per cent of state convention delegates. Prohibitionists were easily isolated as kill-joys and even un-American with their denial of personal choice and responsibility in drinking.[11] Appeals for restraint were a vital check in a society that seemed to have so few self-limitations.

Gambling also became a target of those seeking to monitor the compulsive consumer. In modern America, it was a particular threat because it mocked the work and production ethic; this in turn justified American materialism. Local bannings drove gambling to the margins of the nation (ultimately to the western desert). Eastern states abandoned state lotteries in the 1830s and nearly all regions had ended them by the Civil War. In 1894, New York state forbade off-track betting on horse races and, in 1911, even closed down the tracks. Again, the object was to protect gamblers from themselves.[12] Attacks on potentially addictive consumption was more legalistic and uncompromising in the U.S. than elsewhere. Probably this was the consequence of relatively weak social and cultural constraints on individual behaviour. But, by the same token, efforts to form a moral consensus around legal constraints were also doomed to failure.

In the 1930s, restrictions were also lifted on gambling just as they were for alcohol. Legalization of charitable gambling (e.g. bingo) began in Massachusetts in 1931 while other states legalized pari-mutuel betting in 1933. Las Vegas became a legal

10. E. Behr, *Prohibition: Thirteen Years that Changed America* (New York: Arcade, 1996), p. 26; D. Kyvig, 'Sober thoughts: myth and realities of national prohibition after fifty years', in D. Kyvig (ed.), *Law, Alcohol, and Order* (Westport, Conn.: Greenwood Press, 1985), pp. 3–20. Other assessments include R. Hofstadter, *The Age of Reform: From Bryan to FDR* (New York: Knopf, 1955), p. 292; A. Sinclair, *Prohibition: The Era of Excess* (New York: Atlantic Monthly Press, 1962); J. Rumbarger, *Profits, Power, and Prohibition* (Albany, N.Y.: SUNY Press, 1988); P. Stearns, *The Battleground of Desire: The Struggle for Self-Control in Modern America* (New York: New York University Press, 1999), ch. 9.

11. Lender and Martin, *Drinking in America*, pp. 152–5; Burnham, 'New perspectives', pp. 97–114; K. Meier, *The Politics of Sin: Drugs, Alcohol, and Public Policy* (Amonk, NY: M.E. Sharpe, 1994), ch. 5; Kyvig, 'Sober thoughts', pp. 3–20.

12. R. Brenner, *Gambling and Speculation* (New York: Cambridge University Press, 1990), pp. 82, 88; R. Munting, *An Economic and Social History of Gambling in Britain and the USA* (Manchester: Manchester University Press, 1996), pp. 6–54.

Mecca for the gambler in 1931. Popular opinion remained cautious, however. Repeated attempts at reviving state lotteries failed in the 1930s, despite an incentive to find an alternative to taxes for scarce public revenues. Keeping gambling outside the everyday marketplace limited its temptation and impact on the worlds of work and family.[13] That standard, however, finally broke down in the late 1970s. After decades of isolating legal gambling to the distant deserts of Nevada, New Jersey allowed casino gambling in Atlantic City in 1978. Within a decade, the dike was broken when Indian reservations (free from state laws governing gambling) opened gaming centres. By 1994, casinos were operating in 23 states, many near population centres. Promoters argued that gaming would revitalize sick local economies' revenue that otherwise would be siphoned off by other states, and that communities would remain at home. Instead of government restraining it, public authorities joined the business. Soon after New Hampshire revived its state lottery in 1964, others followed. Far from being a watchdog, governments encouraged gambling through massive ad campaigns for their own lotteries.[14]

In the twentieth century, arguments for protecting the individual from obsessive consumption declined while assumptions of individual responsibility and personal choice increased. Combating addiction was always problematic. Distinguishing need from obsession or legitimate marketing from 'pushing' dependency faced all members of the affluent society. Moreover, the line defining unacceptable consumption shifted to the margins where it was criminalized and severely punished. In the 1980s, during a time when experimentation with illegal drugs actually declined, especially among the white middle class, efforts to control use increased. In part, because drug-use could be identified as a minority and urban problem, repression could become an alternative to a more positive economic and social policy toward inner cities and disadvantaged minorities. By 1986, the Reagan administration won legislation permitting the military to gather intelligence on the drug trade and dramatically increasing penalties for users and dealers. Partially as a result, the rate of incarceration more than doubled in the U.S. between 1985 and 1995. The call for constraint all too easily slipped into attacks on the character and culture of minorities – 'wet' immigrants or city folk at the beginning of the century, crack cocaine-crazed blacks at the end. When prohibitionists identified minorities with addictive behaviour, they obscured from themselves the obsessive character of their own consumption desires.[15]

13. H. Marx (ed.), *Gambling in America* (New York: H.W. Wilson, 1952), p. 156; J. McMillen, 'Understanding gambling', in J. McMillen, *Gambling Cultures: Studies in History and interpretation* (New York: Routledge, 1996), ch. 2.

14. R. Goodman, *The Luck Business* (New York: Free Press, 1995), pp. xi, 3' 10, 16, 19, 123, 131, 132 and R. McGowan, *State Lotteries and Legalized Gambling* (Praeger: Westport, Conn., 1994), pp. 15–16, 84.

15. P. Jenkins, *Synthetic Panics: The Symbolic Politics of Designer Drugs* (New York: New York University Press, 1999), ch. 5 and L. Tiger, *The Pursuit of Pleasure* (New York: Little Brown, 1992), pp. 110–12.

A third effort to constrain consumption involved the attempt to protect the 'uninformed' buyer. A major theme of early twentieth-century Progressivism was the growing inequality between the consumer and producer. Industrial corporations controlled markets, leading to price-gouging and misinformed consumers. The failure of the anti-trust movement showed just how difficult it was to define and protect the consumers' interests. It was no easy task to determine what was a 'safe' product or to set the boundaries of hyperbole in advertising. Businesses viewed as a threat to economic freedom almost any attempt to regulate advertising or the contents of foods, drugs, and other products. The Pure Food and Drug Act of 1906 did little more than require disclosure of narcotics and alcohol content in patent medicines and prohibit manufacturers from claiming ingredients not present. The Federal Trade Commission, assigned in 1914 the modest role of policing deceptive commercial practices, had become in the 1920s more an umpire between competing business than a defender of consumers' interests. Despite legislation, proposed in 1933, that would have given the consumer-oriented Food and Drug Administration authority over false advertising, the Wheeler-Lea Act of 1938 bestowed the generally pro-business FTC control over deceptive advertising.[16]

Given the difficulties of the legislative route, advocates of consumer protection were obliged to emphasize consumer education. Stuart Chase and F.J. Schlink, both well-known opponents of deceptive advertising, founded Consumer's Research (CR), a product-testing and information service in 1929. By offering the individual detailed and plain information about the quality and features of practical goods, CR tried to counteract commercial propaganda. CR's object was to make free enterprise work better by creating a better informed and more powerful consumer community. By raising shoppers from the ranks of the patronized and manipulated mass, spending could become a genuinely rational act.[17]

Despite serious efforts through the 1930s, no effective consumer-rights group emerged to challenge manufacturers. Theoretically, in an age when everyone was a consumer, these issues should have dominated politics. But consumers were also producers and had to have jobs with good wages to be serious spenders. While

16. F. Fox, *Madison Avenue Goes to War* (Provo, Utah: Brigham Young University Press, 1975), ch. 2; R. Marchand, *Creating the Corporate Soul: The Rise of Public Relations and Corporate Imagery in American Big Business* (Berkeley: University of California Press, 1998), pp. 301–11; R. Mayer, *The Consumer Movement: Guardians of the Marketplace* (Boston: Twyane, 1989), pp. 24–5; H.J. Kenner, *The Fight for Truth in Advertising* (New York: Round Table Press, 1936), p. 27; H. Sorenson, *Consumer Movement: What It Is and What It Means* (New York: Harper and Brothers, 1941), pp. 12–14.

17. R. Babson and C.N. Stone, *Consumer Protection: How it Can be Secured* (New York: Harper and Brothers, 1938), ch. 12; S. Chase, *The Tragedy of Waste* (New York: Macmillan, 1925); S. Chase and F. Schlink, *Your Money's Worth* (New York: Macmillan, 1927); A. Kallet and F. Schlink's *100,000,000 Guinea Pigs: Dangers in Everyday Foods, Drugs, and Cosmetics* (New York: Vanguard, 1933); F. Schlink, *Eat, Drink, and Be Wary* (New York: Grosset & Dunlap, 1935); McGovern, 'Sold American', ch. 5 and ch. 6, especially pp. 201–11, 246–81, 272, 289, and 307.

they bought many and diverse things, consumers usually produced only one thing. Thus, they had a strong, more focused interest in defending their producer status than their many consumer roles. Occasionally, as Lizabeth Cohen notes in Chapter Ten, neighbourhood shoppers joined to stop price-gouging by alien shopkeepers. Moreover, morally inspired middle-class women coalesced to use their purchasing power to improve working conditions of women workers in sweated trades. In the 1930s, popular books attacking deceptive marketing and dangerous or worthless products put advertisers and some producers on the defensive. Nevertheless, it was quite easy for business to bounce back.

Advertisers assumed the language of statesmanship when they claimed to 'serve' consumer citizens who as shoppers voted with their purchases. In the 1930s, ad people insisted that they were the guardians of choice all-too-often threatened by government. They redefined freedom to mean not civil liberty or the right to work but the freedom to find identity in the choice of goods to buy.[18] GM's 'The American Way' ad campaign showed American commitment to progress through industry and consumer goods, and promoted corporate freedom to develop new and exciting products.[19] By the end of the 1930s, the consumer-rights movement was divided, harassed by anticommunist baiting, and largely reduced to product-testing services (such as offered by *Consumer Report*). This narrowing of the scope of consumer rights to the right to be informed about the pricing and attributes of goods has tended to reinforce the individualism and materialism of American consumption society.[20] To be sure, the Second World War produced still one more effort at regulating consumption in the public interest with the Office of Price Administration. Although designed to control hoarding of vital materials and resources for the war effort, it also strove to limit inflation and price-gouging the consumer.[21] After 1945, however, consumers did not become a political force capable of defending their rational and utilitarian needs against the power of the corporation and advertising. Instead, they were assigned a role that was more expedient to business. As Meg Jacobs in Chapter Eleven and Lizabeth Cohen in Chapter Ten note, the movement for consumer rights was transformed into the right to consume in an economy that with little public intervention promised increased purchasing power.

18. McGovern, 'Sold American', pp. 75–7, 101–03, 107.

19. 'American Way' ad by G.M., *Saturday Evening Post* (7 November 1936), pp. 34–5; R. Durstine, 'Advertising', in H. Stearns, *America Now, An Inquiry into Civilization in the United States* (New York: Scribner's Sons, 1938), pp. 167, 172, 176, 181.

20. 'AFA Meeting', *Printers' Ink*, 29 (June 1939), p. 67; 'Guinea Pigs, Left March', *Forum* (October 1939), pp. 153–4. See also McGovern, 'Selling Americans', pp. 371–2.

21. C. Ware, *The Consumer Goes to War* (New York: Funk & Wagnalls, 1941), pp 194–235.

The consumer-rights movement was resurrected in the late 1950s as part of a broader movement against the growing power of big corporations. Senator Estes Kefauver was the first to propose a Department of the Consumer in the cabinet, convinced that the market alone could not protect consumers' interests. A group of liberal politicians saw a better-educated and more affluent citizenry demanding safer and higher-quality products. They noted also that consumers were frustrated by their difficulty in determining true credit costs or making knowledgeable comparisons between similar products.[22] Consumer exploitation had replaced labour exploitation as the central problem of modern society and consumers needed friends in government.[23]

At its core, this critique attacked the sort of manipulative advertising that intended to deceive the uninformed consumer. Vance Packard's *Hidden Persuaders* revived the idea popularized by F.J. Schlink and Stuart Chase in the 1920s that business tricked consumers into buying goods they really did not need. Packard exposed a new trend in advertising called motivational research. This technique used depth psychology to sell goods by associating them with status and by preying on feelings of personal inadequacy. Packard's book became a best-seller.[24] Scandals in 1958 over TV quiz shows, during which sponsors fed answers to popular contestants to raise ratings, added to a growing discontent with hard-sell TV ads and commercial manipulation.[25] Lack of standards in packaging made comparisons of size and prices impossible. Advertising efforts to make meaningless distinctions between different brands of detergent and toothpaste only drove up prices.[26] Even the sacred cow of the 1950s consumerism, the car, was under attack for its stress on the annual model-change over utilitarian improvements and the resulting excesses of fins and chrome. That certainly was Ralph Nader's point in his *Unsafe at Any Speed: The Designed-in Dangers in the American Automobile* (1965). This young consumer advocate argued that rising car injuries resulted not from collisions per se but from lack of seatbelts, cushioning and other safety measures in American

22. L.B. Creighton, *Pretenders to the Throne: The Consumer Movement in the United States* (Lexington, Mass.: Lexington Books, 1976), p. 33; B. Murray, *Consumerism: The Eternal Triangle* (Pacific Palisades: Goodyear, 1973), pp. 16–55.

23. W. Magnuson and J. Carper, *The Dark Side of the Marketplace: The Plight of the American Consumer* (Englewood Cliffs, NJ: Prentice-Hall, 1968), pp. ix, 59.

24. V. Packard, *Hidden Persuaders* (New York: McKay, 1957), pp. 19, 25, 59, 117 and D. Horowitz, *Vance Packard and American Social Criticism* (Chapel Hill, N.C.: University of North Carolina Press, 1994), p. 133.

25. D. Vogel, *Fluctuating Fortunes: The Political Power of Business in America* (New York: Basic Books, 1988), p. 31.

26. S. Margolius, *The Innocent Consumer vs. the Exploiters* (New York: Trident, 1967), pp. 1, 6, 7, 11, 107, 113; S. Margolius, *The Responsible Consumer* (Public Affairs Pamphlet No. 453, September 1970), pp. 1, 3, 4. See also D. Caplovitz, *The Poor Pay More: Consumer Practices of Low-Income Families* (New York: Free Press, 1963); H. Black, *Buy Now, Pay Later* (New York: William Morrow, 1961), pp. 6 and 105.

cars.[27] Nader argued that corporate influence over regulatory agencies and monopolistic pricing was as important as deceptive merchandising. Consumers needed organization to redress this imbalance.[28]

Regulatory agencies, long in slumber, showed renewed life after 1960. The Federal Trade Commission (FTC) greatly stepped up its role in regulating advertising, especially after a 1974 law allowed it to regulate whole industries. The Federal Communications Commission (FCC) was equally activist, forcing the broadcasters in 1974 to accept a voluntary limit on ad time.[29] The 1960s and early 1970s produced an extraordinary array of consumer protection laws ranging from the Hazardous Substances Labeling Act of 1960, requiring warnings on dangerous household products, to the Automobile Safety Act of 1966, which compelled seat beats and other safety measures on new cars, and the Truth in Packaging Act (1966), obliging weight and content information on product labels. The Consumer Product Safety Commission of 1972 provided for a continuous review of consumer goods for risks. Growing evidence that tobacco caused cancer led the Federal Trade Commission in 1964 to impose warnings on cigarette packages and to outlaw TV and radio commercials in 1971.[30]

From one perspective, these laws were necessary to secure the confidence of buyers and borrowers in an ever more complex and impersonal market. From another standpoint, they expressed the newly found power of consumer groups. Working with reform-minded members of Congress and recently energized regulatory agencies, these groups took on some of the most powerful industries in the country. Only in 1967 had the Consumer Federation combined 147 organizations into an effective lobby.[31]

By the end of the 1970s, however, the brief ascendancy of the consumer-rights movement had ended. The advertising industry won a critical point in 1976 when the Supreme Court recognized ads could be protected speech. A coalition of farm,

27. R. Nader, *Unsafe at Any Speed: The Designed-in Dangers in the American Automobile* (New York: Grossman, 1965); see also J. Jerome, *Death of the Automobile* (New York: Norton, 1972); E. Rothschild, *Paradise Lost: The Decline of the Automobile-Industrial Age* (New York: Random House, 1973); D. Gartman, *Auto Opium: A Social History of American Automobile Design* (London: Routledge, 1994), ch. 7.

28. R. Nader, 'A citizens' guide to the American economy', in R. Nader (ed.), *The Consumer and Corporate Accountability* (New York: Harcourt, Brace Jovanovich, 1973), pp. 4–18, 51; R. Nader, 'The great American gyp', in Murray, *Consumerism*, pp. 39–51; Creighton, *Pretenders to the Throne*, ch. 5.

29. 'The great medicine show', *Time* (22 October 1956), pp. 87–8; 'New crackdown on commercials', *Business Week* (19 December 1959), pp. 72–3; 'A code of ethics for advertising', *Saturday Review* (9 June 1962), pp. 47–8.

30. Especially good on consumer rights is Vogel, *Fluctuating Fortunes*, chs 1 and 7.

31. Vogel, *Fluctuating Fortunes*, pp. 29, 39, 40, 93, 106–8. For a conservative view, see P. Weaver, 'Regulation, social policy and class conflict', *Public Interest* (Winter 1978), p. 59 and I. Kristol, *Two Cheers for Capitalism* (New York: Basic Books, 1978), pp. 27–8.

grocery, and other independent businesses defeated a proposal in 1978 for a federal consumer-protection agency. The election of Ronald Reagan in November of 1980 accelerated this trend. In 1981, Reagan appointed the conservative activist, Mark Fowler, to the Federal Communications Commission. He rejected a sixty-year-old principle that broadcasters had a duty to serve the public interest. By 1983, Fowler had abandoned FCC requirements that radio and TV stations provide public-service and news programming and limit advertising. He also eased restrictions on the number of TV stations a company could purchase and insisted that broadcasters should be treated as business people and not be expected to serve as trustees of culture.[32] The aggressive attack on manipulative ads also ended with James Miller's accession to the FTC. Like Fowler, this conservative economist felt his commission was to be a servant of efficient markets rather than a guarantor of public rights and responsibilities. He embraced a narrow definition of deceptive ads, and insisted that cost/benefit analysis be a guide to which cases should be pursued in court.[33]

Why was the power of the consumer-rights movement so brief? One answer, offered by David Vogel, is that it succeeded only when business interests had temporarily lost control of Congress. By 1976, business groups had begun to learn how to lobby a more decentralized Congress and to use Public Action Committee funds and grass-roots lobbying to regain dominance in Congress. Ironically, the best years of the consumer-rights movement in the 1970s may have been under the conservative Nixon rather than the liberal Carter administration. The key was business influence in Congress, not the party in power in either the executive or the legislative branch.[34]

The ideology of the unfettered market dominated American political discourse for most of its history. Under normal circumstances, consumers had little collective interest in any particular product, while manufacturers had a very strong incentive to organize and lobby to keep their costs down or prices up. Thus, producers easily isolated consumer activists. Given a narrow range of legal or regulatory options, FTC staff were prone to seemingly petty concerns (investigating a TV advertiser who deceived viewers by using marbles in a soup commercial to make the meat in the bowl rise and look better). By the late-1970s, free enterprisers had no difficulty in portraying regulators as tyrants and hair-splitting legalists who caused inflation. Indeed, 'big government' has never recovered from this characterization.

32. 'FCC Won't Force Child Programs', *Boston Globe* (12 February 1983), p. 35.

33. W. MacLeod and R. Rogowsky, 'Consumer protection at the FTC during the Reagan administration', in R. Meiners and B. Yandle (eds), *Regulation and the Reagan Era* (New York: Holmes & Meier, 1989), pp. 71–88; 'Deceptive ads', *Business Week*, (2 December 1985), pp. 136–7.

34. Vogel, *Fluctuating Fortunes*, ch. 8. See also T. Edsall, *The New Politics of Inequality* (New York: Norton, 1984) and T. Ferguson and J. Rogers, *Right Turn: The Decline of the Democrats and the Future of American Politics* (New York: Hill & Wang, 1986) on the resurgence of business in the 1970s.

In ways these attacks on reformers is ironic. Consumer-rights advocates were hardly the sworn enemies of the free market. Indeed, most assumed the basic principle of capitalism – the 'rational consumer' who tried to maximize personal utility. Regulation was intended to facilitate reasoned choice or minimize manipulation. The opportunity to develop a social vision of consumption or explore alternatives to the acquisition of things in the market was all too often lost.[35]

The disappointing results of these movements for constraint in consumption suggest not that Americans simply embraced completely the individualistic implications of the market. Moral panics about various forms of consumption and cultural wars about how to deal with them persisted throughout the twentieth century. The problem of setting limits remained, but the terms around which to argue for boundaries became very narrow indeed. Only in the most restricted sense could the 'home' be called a sanctuary from the market; only in the most confined way could the vulnerability or ignorance of the individual consumer be grounds for regulating the market. In this context, a fourth argument for regulating consumption became especially potent – saving the children. This is not to say that attempts to protect childhood from aggressive marketers has ever been particularly successful. Quite otherwise. Still, childhood serves as a surrogate for other arguments – the sanctity of the family and home and the vulnerable and ignorant consumer – and thus has remained practically the singular argument for restraint.

Throughout the century, much consumption-restraint rhetoric was buried in the cult of the child. By 1900, especially for white middle-class Americans, children had become 'priceless', no longer economic assets to be sent to work at an early age. So too they were to be only guardedly introduced to the world of consumption, to be protected from sex, violence, drugs, and alcohol, as well as alluring pleasures found in magazines, movies, amusement parks, and dance halls.[36] Despite the potential advantage of selling directly to children, merchandisers were very careful not to offend the sentiments of parents. Children should not be 'lured' through advertising into wanting a toy or sweet because they lacked the rational capacity of the adult. Until the 1930s, toy-makers appealed to parents, not children and, even in the 1930s, toy and candy companies did not advertise on children's radio programmes. The merchandisers' self-constraint (moral or economic) meant that legislation was unnecessary.[37]

35. Creighton, *Pretenders to the Throne* , pp. 4–5, 98–104

36. V. Zelizer, *Pricing the Priceless Child: The Changing Social Value of Children* (New York: Basic Books, 1985), pp. 3–21, 103–12.

37. D. Macleod, *The Age of the Child: Children in America, 1890–1920* (New York: Twayne Publishers, 1998), pp. 111–18; Zelizer, *Pricing the Priceless Child*, p. 13; and R. Marchand, 'Precocious consumers and junior salesmen: advertising to children in the United States to 1940', unpublished paper supplied by the author.

The twentieth-century youth, however, gradually became a major target of manufacturers of novelty, fantasy, and fun. Especially the growth of new kinds of goods designed for children and new means of disseminating them created a new concern about regulating the market's access to children. These included new sugared breakfast cereals and candy that appeared after the Second World War; the more aggressive marketing of toys (such as Barbie dolls) designed to appeal to children's play patterns and based on licensed images of children's film and TV fantasy; and the growing use of children's entertainment programming to advertise directly to the young. This is a complex process that cannot be explored here, but it did form a critical backdrop to an expanded concern about controlling consumption by the 1970s.[38]

Given traditional concerns about protecting the 'innocence' of the young, reformers in groups such as Action for Children's Television (ACT) and the FTC turned their guns on the 200 million dollars worth of ads pitched per year to children by the early 1970s. In 1971, ACT called for the elimination of kid ads altogether, claiming that children under 12 years old were incapable of making rational consumer choices and that commercials were an interference with parental rights to educate their own children.[39] In order to avoid government control, the National Association of Broadcasters recommended in 1974 (and the FCC adopted) rules limiting ads shown per hour of children's TV to 12 minutes and prohibiting 'program-length commercials' (shows featuring toys in the story lines).[40] In 1977, President Carter's appointee to the FTC chair, Michael Pertschuk, decided to attack commercials directed toward children, noting later that he had framed 'the issue as an inescapable and conservative extension of the common law's historic strictures against the commercial exploitation of minors'. By their very nature of appealing to the innocent young, these ads could be deemed 'unfair'. Pertschuk saw this as an opportunity for drawing a boundary that limited 'market speech' at a moment when consumers were concerned about both ads and their impact on children.[41]

In February 1978, the FTC agreed to open an inquiry into prohibiting children's TV advertising; its staff report argued that to ban these ads was not a violation of

38. G. Cross, *Kids' Stuff: Toys and the Changing World of American Childhood* (Cambridge, Mass.: Harvard University Press, 1997), esp. chs 4, 6, 7; S. Bruce and B. Crawford, *Cerealizing America: The Unsweetened Story of American Breakfast Cereal* (Boston: Faber & Faber, 1995), pp. 103–214.

39. 'Caveat pre-emptor', *Saturday Review*, (9 January 1971), p. 37; S. Ward, 'Kids' TV – marketers on hot seat', *Harvard Business Review* (July 1972), pp. 16–28; J. Seldin, 'The Saturday morning massacre', *Progressive* (September 1974), pp. 50–2; E. Kay, *The Act Guide to Children's Television*, revised edn (Boston: Beacon, 1979), pp. 221–2.

40. W. Moody, *Children's Television: The Economics of Exploitation* (New Haven, Conn.: Yale University Press, 1973), pp. 83–116; E. Palmer, *Children in the Cradle of Television* (Lexington, Mass.: Lexington Books, 1987), pp. 32–6.

41. M. Pertschuk, *Revolt against Regulation* (Berkeley: University of California Press, 1982) pp. 12, 69–70; 'The FTC broadens its attack on ads', *Business Week* (20 June 1977), pp. 27–8.

First Amendment (free speech) rights because the 'state has a legitimate interest in curtailing speech that interferes with the paramount parental interest in the child rearing process'.[42] This was an extraordinary attack on a growing belief of American business – that children, like adults, were markets. It was a defence of parental rights in an arena where those rights were being increasingly ignored.

This effort, too, was short-lived. Admakers attacked any interference in the 'right' of children to have information about the products they bought and enjoyed.[43] Even the *Washington Post* in 1978 mocked the FTC for their attack on kid ads, accusing the agency of becoming a 'National Nanny' by trying 'to protect children from the weaknesses of their parents'. In the Spring of 1980, Congress prohibited the FTC from banning 'unfair' ads (rather than openly deceptive ones), in effect derailing the FTC attack on the inherent 'unfairness' of ads directed toward children. Admitting defeat, the FTC dropped its initiative, a turning point in the decline of the consumer-rights movement.[44]

In the early 1980s, Reagan's FCC chair Mark Fowler suggested that public TV could take over the role of provide quality children's programming if the advertising market would not pay for it. He eliminated those rules that had governed ads on TV since the 1970s and ushered in an era of unrestrained commercialization of children's culture.[45] Deregulation allowed merchandisers to transform kids' programmes into ads. Cartoon shows such as He-Man or G.I. Joe, created by or for toy companies to promote lines of action-figure toys, became common.[46] Despite some efforts to reverse these policies after Reagan's departure in 1988, little changed.

While reformers in the 1970s failed to make childhood the wedge to restrain commercialization, innocence and its protection remained the surest arrow in the reformer's quiver at the end of the century. Continued concern about children's consumption reflected anxiety about the breakdown of boundaries in other areas

42. Federal Trade Commission, *FTC Staff Report on Television Advertising to Children* (Washington: FTC, 1978), pp. 11, 20, 243, 267. See also F.E. Barcus, *Commercial Children's Television* (Newtonville, Mass.: Action for Children's Television, 1977).

43. S. Fox, *Mirror Makers* (New York: Morrow, 1984), pp. 315–8; K. Mason, 'Revamping Saturday morning children's television', *Vital Speeches of the Day* (15 January 1979), p. 207; M. Thorn, 'Advertising', *Nation's Business* (October 1979), pp. 85–8.

44. Cross, *Kids' Stuff*, pp. 185–6; Pertschuk, *Revolt against Regulation*, pp. 69–70; D. Kunkel and D. Roberts, 'Young minds and marketplace values: issues in children's television advertising', *Journal of Social Issues*, 47 (1991), pp. 57–72; Vogel, *Fluctuating Fortunes*, p. 168.

45. 'Evangelist of the marketplace', *Time*, 1 November 1983, p. 58; D. Swann, *The Retreat of the State* (Ann Arbor: University of Michigan Press, 1988), p. 179; 'Fowler no fan of federal pre-emption on children's TV', *Broadcasting* (14 February 1983), p. 85.

46. D. Kunkel, 'From a raised eyebrow to a turned back: the FCC and children's product-related programming', *Journal of Communications*, 38 (1988), p. 91; N. Carlsson-Paige and D. Levin, 'Saturday morning pushers', *Utne Reader*, 2 January 1992, pp. 68–9.

(for example, the spread of TV home and Internet shopping).[47] The focus on children reflected the relative absence of alternative arguments. Protecting the young combined defence of a timeless community (family) along with correcting an unequal exchange in guarding the interests of the vulnerable and ignorant consumer.

The banner of innocence has most recently been raised in the battle against tobacco consumption. The assault by public health officials on the cigarette intensified in the late 1980s with new regulations that drove smokers from many public places. By 1993, the Environmental Protection Agency had even declared that 'passive smoking' was a serious health risk. At the same time, health and other officials became increasingly frustrated by continued success of cigarette-makers in introducing new generations to the habit. While cigarette smoking had declined sharply among adults (from 42.5 per cent in 1965 to 25.5 per cent in 1990), under-age smoking had remained relatively steady since 1980 (at about 30 per cent of high school seniors having smoked in the preceding month even though state laws prohibited the selling of tobacco products to anyone under 18 years of age). Manufacturers had been targeting teen smokers since at least 1950. By the 1980s, they had learned that smokers maintained extraordinary brand loyalty, a fact that raised the economic advantage of winning the contest for brand adherence with first-time smokers. Because up to 90 per cent of adult smokers adopted the habit when they were teenagers, the tobacco companies had an obvious interest in winning the under-aged to smoking. The Surgeon General stated the point simply in 1994: 'if adolescents can be kept tobacco-free, most will never start using tobacco'.[48]

Concern for the health of children was, of course, paramount, but the attempt to protect the young from tobacco advertising and product access was one practical way of extending regulation of tobacco-consumption in general. While Supreme Court decisions in the 1970s had broadened the rights of commercial speech (such as advertising), the Court still recognized the principle of 'deceptive' ads and the government's interest in protecting children from them. Youths under 18 years of age were, by law, not free agents in a market transaction. The tobacco companies' claim that smokers were responsible agents (because they had been alerted to the risk by the warning labels on every package) did not apply to the under-aged. Ads

---

47. I develop these points in my *An All-Consuming Century* (New York: Columbia University Press, 2000), ch. 6.

48. E. Swecker, 'Joe Camel: will "Old Joe" survive?', *William and Mary Law Review*, 249 (1995); J. McCullough, 'Lighting up the battle against the tobacco industry', *Rutgers Law Journal*, 28 (1997); Food and Drug Administration, 'Regulations restricting the sale and distribution of cigarettes and smokeless tobacco products to protect children and adolescents', *Federal Register*, 11 August 1995, pp. 41317, 41330, 41350.

that evoked emotional responses rather than communicating information (as in speech) were deceptive, especially to minors.[49]

In 1995, the Food and Drug Administration (FDA) decided to reduce tobacco access and advertising appeals to youth while, of course, claiming 'not [to] restrict the use of tobacco products by adults'. It introduced a series of proposals that would ban cigarette vending machines wherever children would have access to them; require tobacco ads in magazines with an under-aged readership of 15 per cent to be in 'black and white text only format'; outlaw tobacco billboards within 1000 feet of a playground or school; and prevent cigarette logos from publicizing sponsorship of sporting or other cultural events. The FDA claimed that nicotine addiction had become a 'pediatric disease', causing life-shortening maladies in the young. Obviously the tobacco companies objected that all this was an attack on free speech and a denial of adult access to 'information' about tobacco products. The FDA responded: Ad restrictions did not deny information, only the emotional appeals of the ads. 'Information regarding price, tar and nicotine levels, and taste, information typically important to adults who smoke, can be communicated effectively to adults thorough words alone' without comical, status, or sexual images. The objective presumably was 'restricting only those elements of advert-ising . . . that affect young people'. Obviously the appeal of the cigarette for many adults was similar to that for children – emotional and associational. Protecting children from their own 'prerational' responses was to impose 'rationality' upon adults. The 1995 report made it clear, 'Without the restrictions contained in this proposed rule designed to prevent future generations from becoming addicted to tobacco products, there cannot be reasonable assurance of the safety and effective-ness of cigarettes and smokeless tobacco products.' Within this bureaucratic prose is the none-too-subtle joke: cigarettes will be 'safe' when no one uses them![50]

A debate between those defending the health of vulnerable and uninformed children and those promoting the free-speech rights of cigarette-makers may be tough for Big Tobacco to win in the long run. Nevertheless, the industry was able to defeat a new consumption tax (designed presumably to price children out of the market for tobacco products). The Republican majority insisted that the proposal was a 'new tax burden' and still another government intrusion into personal freedom. The issue shifted from protecting kids from tobacco to cracking down

49. M. Davis, 'Developments in policy: the FDA's tobacco regulations', *Yale Law and Policy Review*, 15 (1996); C. Martin, 'Ethical advertising standards: three case studies', *Journal of Advertising*, 23 (September 1994), pp. 17–25; O.L. Reed, 'Should the first amendment protect Joe Camel?', *American Business Law Journal*, 32 (February 1995), pp. 311–20; R. Mandelbaum et al., 'Mangini v R.J. Reynolds', *American Lawyer* (March 1996), p. 120; Swecker, 'Joe Camel'.

50. FDA, 'Regulations Restricting', pp. 41314–316 and 41351 and FDA, Executive Summary, 'The Regulations Restricting the Sale and Distribution of Cigarettes and Smokeless Tobacco to Protect Children and Adolescents', 7 May 1998, website fda.gov/opacom/campgaigns/tobacco/ execrule.html

on illegal drug use and juvenile violence. An out-of-court settlement between the tobacco companies and the states in late 1998 required the industry to pay 206 billion dollars (over 25 years) for health and anti-smoking programmes in exchange for ending state suits against the companies and acceptance of many of the FDA proposals.[51] Still, the cost to tobacco was far less than the 368 billion demanded a year before, and likely would be easily absorbed.

Whatever the ultimate fate of the child-protection strategy on regulating consumption of 'marginal' goods and services, it is likely to shape the future debate about gun control, pornography, and alcohol as well as efforts to constrain commercialization on a wider front.[52] These will not be easy battles to win, not because the child-saving appeal is weak, but because business and free-market forces are so strong. The terms of restraint on consumption narrowed significantly in the twentieth century, and especially after the late 1970s. Explanations come from various directions – declining consensus around the presumptions of community and individual vulnerability; the weakening of countervailing institutions against corporate interests; and narrowing of consumer rights to a public policy that fosters market consumption rather than articulating consumer interests. The surviving rhetoric of constraint remains that of protecting children – a rhetoric that contains elements of discredited discourses, but that is still relatively unassailable – an expression of the guilty conscience and also an inevitable hypocrisy.

51. S. Nielsen, 'Though it coughs up bucks, big tobacco gets last Yuks', *Seattle Times*, (6 November 1998), p. B4; M. Murphy, 'Tobacco accord signed', *Arizona Republic*, (21 November 1998), p. A1; 'The tobacco bill', *New York Times*, (18 June 1998), p. A1.
52. See for example G. Overholser, 'Charlton Heston, meet Joe Camel', *Washington Post*, (4 May 1999), p. A23.

Index